Broadcasting in America

A Survey of Electronic Media

Brief Edition

Sydney W. Head
University of Miami

Christopher H. Sterling
The George Washington University

with contributions by
Susan Tyler Eastman
Indiana University

Lemuel B. Schofield
University of Miami

Houghton Mifflin Company   **Boston**

Dallas   Geneva, Ill.   Palo Alto   Princeton, N.J.

Cover photograph courtesy Intelsat; color manipulation in ColorStudio on Macintosh Computer at SIS, Inc.

Acknowledgments for photographs on chapter opener pages: Chapter 1—Spencer Grant/Photo Researchers; Chapter 2—Keystone/FPG International; Chapter 3—Alex Webb/Magnum; Chapter 4—Gorchev and Gorchev; Chapter 5—NASA photo; Chapter 6—AP/Wide World Photos; Chapter 7—Courtesy WGBY, Springfield, MA; Chapter 8—Courtesy PBS; Chapter 9—Courtesy Turner Broadcasting System, Inc.; Chapter 10—Courtesy Nielsen Media Research; Chapter 11—Michael Siluk/Image Works; Chapter 12—© Declan Haun; Chapter 13—Arvid Garg/Photo Researchers; Chapter 14—AP/Wide World Photos.

Printed in the U.S.A.

Library of Congress Catalog Card Number: 90-83035

ISBN: 0-395-54445-9

BCDEFGHIJ-D-987654321

Contents

CHAPTER 5

Technological Innovation and the Future of Broadcasting

CHAPTER 6

Commercial Operations   **155**

CHAPTER 7

Noncommercial Operations   193

CHAPTER 9

Programs: Network, Syndicated, Local

CHAPTER 11

Social Effects   **305**

CHAPTER 12

Regulation: Laws, Agencies, and Pressure Groups   327

CHAPTER 14

Global View   387

List of Exhibits

Preface

This brief version of *Broadcasting in America* abridges and updates the sixth edition (1990) for the benefit of instructors who would like to use the original text but find its 19 chapters too many for their needs. The reduction to 14 chapters suits classes taught on the quarter system, for example, and those that require one or more additional books of readings. The brief version drops some of the exhibits, examples, and sidebar topics, and is written more succinctly.

Coverage

This edition of *Broadcasting in America* retains the same basic structure and underlying goal of viewing the electronic mass media in a broad academic perspective. These media, both as products of contemporary social forces and as social forces in their own right, are viewed in context. They impinge on many academic areas ranging from economics to law, from history to social science. Though study of the electronic mass media can be interesting and rewarding in itself, it can also both enrich the study of other subjects and in turn be enriched by them.

Tracking a Changing Industry   The current editions of *Broadcasting in America* respond to recommendations of reviewers and instructors and to recent developments in the field. For example:

- The profound changes brought about by cable television, satellites, video-cassettes, digital signal processing, and deregulation have been more thoroughly assimilated throughout the text than was possible heretofore.
- The history chapters have been recast and streamlined to take into account the longer perspective now available on the history of the electronic mass media. This recasting has meant sacrificing some of the details of early broadcasting development to enlarge on the evolution of cable television, satellite relays, and other later developments.
- The technical chapters introduce in more depth the newer technologies such as communication satellites, digital processing, and high-definition television. (Some of this technical information has been separated from text and put into sidebar exhibits.)
- The chapter on commercial operations explores the pervasive bottom-line thinking that has resulted in such industry-shaking events as General

Electric's absorption of RCA. This chapter also includes a down-to-earth analysis of the contemporary media job market with special reference to opportunities for women and minorities.

- The program chapters show how new economic forces have affected programs, programming, and program production. They reflect the emergence of cable television as a major player with its own creative agenda and its own programming strategies.
- The chapter on audience ratings describes the pros and cons of people-meter technology, and the beginnings of cable television ratings reports.
- The first of the two chapters devoted to regulation surveys the forces outside the electronic mass media that control their day-to-day operations. The second chapter focuses on the broad First Amendment issues that arise from the tendency to treat the electronic mass media differently from the press, as well as the novel freedom-of-speech claims brought about by technological convergence. Together, these chapters explore the fall-out from the increased reliance on marketplace competition and conservative judicial thinking.
- The final chapter takes into account the changing international role of U.S. media in the face of shifting world forces. This chapter recounts how the growing reliance on market-based economies, reflected in the emergence of the European Common Market and in the *perestroika/glasnost* policies of the Soviet Union, impacts upon the media.

Further Updates in Regulation, Competition, and Technology   Events that occurred in the year between the production of the full-length and the brief editions have been incorporated. These updates include:

- Further evidence of retreat from the zealous deregulatory policy of the Reagan years, including the trend toward reregulation of cable television.
- The corresponding worldwide trend toward liberalization of media regulation, especially in the Soviet Union, East European countries, but also in the Third World.
- The emergence of telephone companies as prospective players in the electronic mass media arena.
- Settlement of some pending issues by Supreme Court decisions, such as its affirmation of the FCC's rules awarding minorities preferences in licensing.
- Progress toward high-definition television and new DBS projects.

Contributing Authors   The chapters on programs and economics are based on contributions by specialists in these fields, Susan Tyler Eastman (Indiana University) and Lemuel B. Schofield (University of Miami). Professor Eastman, senior editor and a contributor to *Broadcast/Cable Programming: Strategies and Practices* (Wadsworth, 3d ed., 1989), has taught "The BIA Course" for more than a decade. Professor Schofield, associate dean of the University of Miami School of Communication, combines extensive experience as an attorney and as a television station manager with that of teaching broadcast/cable management courses. In addition to writing the economics chapter, he generously provided economic data for the program chapters and other sections of the book.

Ancillary Support   Professor Louise Benjamin of Indiana University has prepared a new *Instructor's Resource Manual with Test Items* for the brief edition. It includes chapter analyses and summaries, review of learning objectives and key concepts, lecture and activity suggestions, and a bank of multiple-choice test items.

Acknowledgments

Sydney W. Head, the original author of *Broadcasting in America* and coauthor of the sixth edition, wrote the abridgement, with extensive advice and help from the full-length edition coauthor, Christopher H. Sterling. Contributing authors Susan T. Eastman and Lemuel B. Schofield also helped by checking the revisions and supplying update information.

The authors and contributing writers are grateful to the many people in the academic and business worlds who gave valuable expert advice and specialized assistance. We wish to acknowledge in particular the advice on legal material we received from Erwin Krasnow of Verner, Liipfert, Bernhardt & McPherson. We also benefited greatly from critiques of the first-draft manuscript by the following instructors: Don M. Flournoy, *Ohio University*; H. Bruce Fowler, *University of Arizona*; Linda T. Krug, *University of Minnesota–Duluth*. We assume responsibility for the use made of the assistance given by these and other advisors.

Sydney W. Head   *Christopher H. Sterling*
Miami, Florida   *Washington, DC*

Broadcasting in America

A Survey of Electronic Media

Introduction to Broadcasting

Broadcasting had its beginnings and matured into a virtual necessity within the life span of persons now living. The remarkable speed with which broadcasting saturated the entire world attests to its universal appeal.

Back in the 1920s, when radio broadcasting began, youngsters used to build crystal sets—inexpensive radio receivers with no batteries or other visible source of power. With intense anticipation a crystal-set builder would clamp on earphones and probe the uneven surface of a glittery, dime-size crystal with a stiff wire called a cat's whisker. The contact generated faint, scratchy sounds in the earphones.

Suddenly the cat's whisker would touch a mysteriously sensitive spot on the crystal—and the set would come alive! The crystal somehow turned invisible, inaudible radio waves into a faint electric current that reached the earphones as voice and music. The thrill of that moment was unforgettable.

As the senior author of this book can testify, that moment could awaken a lifelong interest in the miracle of wireless communication. And the interest never flagged because miracles never ceased. FM broadcasting and black-and-white television followed, and after them came color pictures. Cable television arrived, then communication satellites, optical-fiber cables, CD recordings, cellular telephones, camcorders, VCRs, and—as the commercials say—much,

EXHIBIT *1.1*   The Everywhere Medium

Modern radio broadcasting is a mobile, personal medium. The widespread use of headsets in the 1990s harks back to the earliest days of radio in the 1920s, before loudspeakers were developed.

Source: Photo from Blumebild/FPG International.

much more. Now a new chapter in the story, high-definition television, is about to open.

Why Study Broadcasting?

People today cannot directly experience the naive original excitement of hearing wireless for the first time on a crystal set. Broadcasting and related media have been around so long that people take them for granted. They have become a pervasive element of the very environment in which we live, an ever-present background.

Broadcasting Has Consequences   Pervasive though it is, why should broadcasting be taken seriously as a subject of study? Why not be a couch potato—just sitting back and enjoying programs? Most people do just that.

That so many televiewers turn into couch potatoes suggests one good reason for studying the subject: broadcasting has *effects*—consequences for both the individual and society. Indeed, its effects pervade the entire world.

Broadcasting Is Universal   That very universality also makes broadcasting worthy of study. It ranks as the most nearly universal means of public communication, conveying information (and sometimes misinformation), entertainment, education, and attempts at persuasion. Radio sets can pick up programs almost anywhere on Earth. More than 200 countries and dependencies have their own radio broadcasting stations. About 85 percent of them also have television stations. Even in remote places where people have no local access to stations, they pool their money to buy videocassettes and backyard satellite dishes—anything to gain access to programs.

universality of broadcasting

More homes boast radio and television receivers than any other modern amenity. Millions of people who lack electricity, indoor plumbing, refrigerators, telephones, and common medicines nevertheless own radios. Travelers often note with astonishment that festering slums around the world bristle with television antennas.

availability of broadcasting

Virtually everyone, everywhere, finds something of interest in broadcasting. For some, the interest remains only casual, rising to the level of listening to a rock station or watching *thirty something*. Some want to play their own part in broadcasting—as actors, writers, producers, executives. Others want to capitalize on it in their businesses or professions. Those with scholarly interests find that broadcasting offers challenges in virtually every field of study, from anthropology to zoology.

Media Influence Works Both Ways   Even people with no specialized vocational, utilitarian, or research interest in the medium have a stake in learning more about it than appears on the surface. As consumers, we buy products advertised by means of broadcasting, which in some ways is the

EXHIBIT 1.2 Popular Subject

By 1990, more than 300 colleges and universities offered coursework or majors in radio-television or allied subjects. Some 35,000 students majored in the study of electronic media.

Source: Photo courtesy Turner Broadcasting System, Inc.

most influential dispenser of advertising. And it has its impact on us in other ways, whether or not we actually watch or listen.

Some people want to make that influence flow both ways. They try to modify broadcasting to make it serve their interests more effectively. They may, for example, demand that programs portray minorities more fairly, give children better role models, or avoid sex and violence. Advocacy groups boycott objectionable programs and the advertisers who support them. They may urge stiffer regulations and campaign for the passage of more effective laws controlling broadcasters.

With such varying motives for study in mind, the authors designed this book to serve the needs of all who want a basic introduction to broadcasting in America. The book identifies the influences that shape the medium, explores how the system affects society, and analyzes the steps society takes to control that influence.

1.3 *Some Essential Terms*

The focus on the word *broadcasting* in the discussion so far does not mean the book ignores cable television and other alternative program sources. On the contrary, it fully explores these alternatives.

Sources of television and radio programs have grown so varied that no single word describes them all. The most inclusive descriptive phrase may be the term used by the U.S. government regulatory agency, the Federal Communications Commission (FCC)—*electronic mass media*. The FCC uses that rather awkward phrase to distinguish broadcasting and related media such as cable television from common carriers. These terms need further exploration, not just to split hairs over definitions but to point out how classification as one type of enterprise or the other results in legal and financial consequences.

Common Carriers vs. The Electronic Mass Media One way to find out whether a communication service qualifies as an electronic mass medium is to ask who has responsibility for its content. A telephone company is a typical example of *common carrier*. A telephone company manager has no right to say who will make calls or to edit conversations. A broadcast station manager does.

All the communication services so far mentioned need government licenses or franchises. Those who hold permits to operate electronic mass media such as broadcasting or cable television have the right to select performers and speakers and to edit what they say and do. In fact, they have the legal responsibility to do so.

In exchange for assuming this responsibility, owners of electronic mass media come under the protection of the First Amendment to the Constitution, which guarantees freedom from government interference with "speech" and "the press." Operators of common carriers, however, supply communication facilities such as a telephones and satellites without assuming any responsibility for what is normally transmitted on those facilities. Having no speaking role, in person or through staff members, they have no need to invoke constitutionally protected freedom to speak at will by telephone or satellite.

key concept: responsibility for content of broadcasting message

The fundamental differences between electronic mass media and common carriers have several other practical results, usually involving tradeoffs—each advantage tends to be offset by a disadvantage. The public can demand, as a right, equal access on equal terms to a common carrier, such as a telephone system. No one can assert such a right to use a broadcasting station (except for political candidates, who are entitled to *equal opportunities* to use broadcast and cable television facilities). It is easier to obtain a license to operate a common carrier than to obtain one to operate a broadcasting station or cable system. The government, however, usually controls the fees that common carriers charge their customers and their profit levels. The electronic mass media may charge whatever the traffic will bear and may make as much profit as they can, so long as competition prevails.

***Broadcasting* Defined** Writers and speakers often assume that *any* program or message transmitted over the air or even over cable constitutes "broadcasting." But to qualify as broadcasting, programs or messages must meet specific tests. As defined legally, **to broadcast** means

> to send out sound and pictures by means of radio waves through space for reception by the general public.

The phrases "by means of radio waves through space" and "reception by the general public" have key significance. For example, under this definition, cable television systems do not broadcast because they send programs through cable, not "through space."

Communication "by means of radio waves" includes many nonbroadcast services, such as CB radio, police calls, taxi dispatching, beepers, and mobile telephones. However, these services operate *point-to-point* (from a source to one intended recipient) or *point-to-multipoint* (from a source to more than one specific recipient). Anyone with a suitable receiver can intercept such transmissions, but they are not intended "for reception by the general public" and therefore do not count as broadcasting.

The verb *to broadcast* was adopted to distinguish the new radio communication method from the previous point-to-point orientation of radiotelegraphy and radiotelephony. "Broadcasting" expresses the idea of scattered dissemination to anonymous, undefined destinations. The term comes from the farmer's act of hand-sowing grain by *casting it broadly*. The sower lets seeds fall where they may.

When stations broadcast, they scatter "seed" (that is, radio waves carrying programs) across the land. If the radio waves happen to fall where a receiver is turned on and tuned in, they sprout into sound or pictures. This usage introduced a new meaning into the English language, causing some initial doubt as to the grammatical rules the word *broadcast* should follow, as related in Exhibit 1.3.

Hybrid Services   The broad distinctions between common carriers and electronic mass media became debatable when certain new, hybrid services emerged that have characteristics of both types of service, referred to here as *hybrids*. Cable television, for example, at first occupied a particularly ambiguous position. Most cable systems operate much like common carriers. They enjoy local monopolies and exercise no editorial control over most of their programs, which come from broadcast stations and cable-program networks. Should these factors put cable operators in the same legal basket as common carriers?

cable TV as hybrid service

Or, since cable systems carry broadcast programs and sometimes originate their own programs in the manner of broadcasters, should they be subject to the same laws as broadcast stations? The question was argued for over 30 years until Congress finally resolved it in 1984 by adopting a new law. It gave cable television its own special status as an acknowledged hybrid—neither a common carrier nor a broadcaster but a mixture of the two.

Cable operators continue to claim the same First Amendment rights as broadcasters. For example, they maintain that for a city to impose certain

EXHIBIT **1.3** Invention of "Broadcasting"

Unrecognized Heroes. The Announcer who said 'broadcasted'.

Not only the technology of broadcasting but also its language had to be invented. Prior to 1921 broadcasting was popularly known as "radio telephony" or simply "wireless." The latter term, in fact, prevailed in Britain for many years. In 1926, shortly after its founding, the BBC (British Broadcasting Corporation) began recruiting distinguished literary figures such as George Bernard Shaw and Rudyard Kipling to serve on an Advisory Committee on Spoken English. The committee met several times a year to settle the fate of "debatable words" (Briggs, 1961: 242).

The new verb "to broadcast" itself became one of the debatable words because of doubts as to whether its past tense should take the form "broadcast" or "broadcasted." The committee decided in favor of the irregular past tense, "broadcast," following the precedent of the verb "to cast." Therefore one says "Yesterday he broadcast the news," not "he broadcasted."

Notice in the 1920s British cartoon the announcer's formal dress, which the BBC then required, as indeed did NBC when it was founded.

Source: Cartoon from Asa Briggs, *The History of British Broadcasting* Vol. I, *The Birth of Broadcasting* (London: Oxford University Press, 1961), p. 243.

---

limitations on a cable system it franchises would violate the cable owner's right of free speech. This claim's legality has been challenged, but so far the courts have upheld the cable operators.

Direct-broadcast satellite (DBS) services offer another example of a hybrid. Usually satellites function as common carriers, but direct-to-home satellite transmission seems equivalent to regular broadcasting, with the station located in space instead of on the ground.

However, DBS program providers scramble their signals to prevent anyone other than paying subscribers from receiving them. This barrier to reception by the general public puts DBS services in the point-to-multipoint rather than the broadcast category. The FCC settled the question in 1987, when it defined DBS transmissions intended only for paying subscribers as *nonbroadcast* services.

signal scrambling makes services nonbroadcast

Even the telephone, the classic example of a common carrier, has become somewhat hybridized. It takes on a mass entertainment/information role when used for "dial-it" services, sometimes called *mass announcement services*. For a price, listeners can hear, and in some cases participate in, audio "programs" by dialing numbers with special prefixes. This usage strays from the telephone's traditional one-on-one private message exchange role. Pornographic dial-it services have even brought into question the common carrier's traditional hands-off policy with regard to message content.

Relays   Broadcasting depends heavily on a service that clearly falls into the common-carrier category—*relays*. Networks use relays to transmit their programs from their headquarters to their affiliated stations throughout the country. News-production teams at the site of an ongoing news event use relays to send on-the-spot coverage of the event back to station or network studios.

Relays often use radio links, but even when relaying broadcast programs "by means of radio waves through space," they function as common carriers, not broadcasters. They send private, point-to-point transmissions not intended for reception by the general public.

The terms *relay, broadcasting, common carrier,* and *electronic mass media* have been analyzed in some detail at the very outset to call attention to fundamental distinctions. These terms recur over and over again as the subject matter unfolds. Their usage in each context calls for a clear understanding of their meanings.

1.4   *This Book's Organization*

The book tackles broadcasting in America in nine stages: history, technology, broadcasting as a business (commercial station and network operations), public broadcasting, programs, program ratings, social effects, government regulation, and broadcasting in the rest of the world. The following topic-by-topic summary gives a foretaste of the subject matter and introduces some of the recurring themes and issues.

History   Chapters 2 and 3 trace the evolution of the electronic media from its 19th-century forebears, the cable and the telephone, to satellites and high-definition television. The first radio broadcasting stations began regular operations in 1920, and it took only a few years for this new communication concept to become firmly established. Television broadcasting began in earnest in 1948, following a hiatus in development imposed by World War II (1939–1945).

1920: first broadcast station launched

1948: true beginning of TV as a mass medium

As far back as the early 1940s, the Federal Communications Commission (FCC) was uneasy about the way national networks had come to dominate the radio industry. The commission began making rules to curb existing networks and to encourage competition by new networks. In keeping with the American policy of licensing each station to serve a specific local community, the commission sought to keep networks from treating affiliates as mere repeater stations for network programs.

These rules, first applied to radio networks, were later extended to television. The commission still wants to increase network television competition

EXHIBIT **1.4**   TV: User-Friendly

only 2 simple controls

TURN IT ON — SELECT STATION - that's all!
BRAND-NEW and BEAUTIFUL CONSOLE gives life-size pictures at lower cost!

Motorola TELEVISION

Early television receivers, like early radio sets, had to be painstakingly tuned in, often with several controls. Eventually came simple push-button tuning and even remote controls that now enable effortless grazing from channel to channel.

Source: Photo from the Collection of Howard Frank.

by encouraging new companies to challenge the ABC/CBS/NBC group. For example, in 1990 the commission waived certain network rules to help the new Fox Broadcasting Company establish itself as a viable fourth commercial national television network.

Partly because of the network rules, by the late 1970s independent (unaffiliated) television stations began to make inroads on the three traditional networks' commanding position as the chief programmers and moneymakers in the business.

Another threat to television network dominance came with cable television. It started around 1950, soon after mass television broadcasting itself. For some years, government regulations kept cable on a leash, subservient to broadcasting. In the late 1970s and early 1980s, court rulings and a zealous new Washington deregulation philosophy cut cable loose from these restrictions. Cable then began spectacular growth, reaching half of the television households in the country by 1987.

by 1987, cable had reached half of all U.S. homes

Although it costs a lot to install cable in each subscriber household within a cable system's coverage area, most consumers are willing to pay the price for the sake of more programs. Those who have access to cable do not mind that it abandons broadcasting's unique advantage, wirelessness. Those who have no access to cable are concerned, however. Without cable, they either depend on wireless transmission or get no programs. Direct-broadcast satellite broadcasting would restore wirelessness, bringing programs to those beyond the reach of cable. But as a subscription service, it would still cost more than traditional broadcasting.

In sum, an era of intense competition is at hand. Traditional broadcasting services, after progressing steadily since sound radio emerged in the 1920s, face profound challenges from new media and new technologies. Will unrelenting competition and irreversible technical change radically alter traditional broadcasting or even, as some predict, displace it entirely? This survey of broadcasting in America has to confront that insistent question at every turn.

Technology   The subject of Chapters 4 and 5, *technology* plays a central role, as the comments on history suggest. Radio broadcasting had close ties with the technologies from which it evolved—the telegraph, the telephone, and radio ship-to-shore communications.

Later, as technology progressed ever more rapidly, *technological convergence* began to occur. Formerly distinct communication modes—the telephone, broadcasting, cable television, motion pictures, printing, data storage and transmission, and even mail—began to overlap, growing less clearly defined. People get newscasts from dial-it telephone services; they fax letters instead of mailing them; they receive broadcasts by wire and from superstations a thousand miles away. Differences blur and new combinations emerge. In this convergence process, computers play a central role, bridging the gaps between formerly discrete modes of communication.

Convergence presents broadcasting with unforeseen challenges that will inevitably alter broadcasting's future. A basic understanding of the underlying technology is essential for evaluating these challenges.

Broadcasting as a Business   In the American system, the free-enterprise market drives mass communication. Consumers' needs and desires, as understood and interpreted by profit-oriented firms, play a decisive role. Commercial operations are the subject of Chapter 6.

To succeed, a new consumer technology requires investors willing to gamble on being able to generate mass public demand. Investors count on finding a cadre of early buyers who ignore price for the sake of being first on the bandwagon. Enough of these early buyers must be found to justify starting up mass production. When that occurs, costs come down to an affordable level for the majority.

new-technology enthusiasts help develop media products

The television receiver is a remarkable example of this process. An incredibly complex piece of sophisticated technology, extremely expensive at first, it later became affordable to the masses when sold in the millions worldwide, year after year. That same cycle may be about to repeat itself. In a few years, high-definition television (HDTV) receivers will appear on the market with a price tag of several thousand dollars apiece. If enough buyers hop on the bandwagon, the price will come down, though HDTV receivers will still cost more than the present low-definition receivers. Will the mass public want high-definition pictures enough to set the mass-production cycle in motion by paying the added price?

Mass demand eventually equipped virtually every home with one or more of the current low-definition television receivers. Consumers bought them originally just to see broadcast programs. But the universal availability of the electronic screens in homes afforded a unique opportunity for exploitation by nonbroadcast media. Two principal beneficiaries of this opportunity have been cable television and videocassette recorders.

Mass demand enables advertising to support most American broadcasting services. Even public broadcasting, though technically noncommercial, depends heavily on corporate underwriting, and the shouldering of production costs by corporations allegedly gives them influence over decisions about which public-broadcasting programs will receive funding. Thus broadcasting's dependence on advertisers, both direct and indirect, gives the advertising marketplace a key role and hence a prominent place in this book.

role of advertising

Economic factors drive broadcasting and other electronic mass media toward *centralization*. Program production and other functions become concentrated at centers where the best facilities and creative talents can be assembled and where national advertisers, agencies, and other business interests have their headquarters.

The centralizing tendency runs counter to public-service considerations that favor *localism*. However, local resources alone can generate only a limited program range—certainly not the high-quality programs needed to match the output of rival mass media. A recurrent theme of broadcasting in America is the struggle between the economic urge to centralize and the public-interest goal of maintaining localism.

key theme: centralization vs. public interest

Public Broadcasting Noncommercial operations are treated in Chapter 7. Public stations use specially designated noncommercial, educational channels. Nevertheless, both public and commercial services rely on the same mass communication technology and follow much the same basic production, program, and scheduling strategies.

The difference lies in their concepts of mission. Public broadcasting's role remains ambiguous. It lacks commercial broadcasting's clear-cut goal—that of making money. Public broadcasting serves various masters with varying goals. In the heightened competitiveness of the 1990s media environment, public broadcasting, even more than commercial, faces perplexities in defining a workable mission and finding financial support.

Programs At the heart of the matter are programs, the subject of Chapters 8 and 9. Whether profit or public-service goals dominate, the electronic mass media's success hinges on *programs as motivators*. Programs stimulate the mass purchase and use of sets, without which the system as we know it could

EXHIBIT *1.5* The Sports Program Medium

Ever since the first big-time sports event, the Dempsey-Carpentier fight, was aired in 1921, a trend toward live sports events has been a mainstay of broadcasting and cable TV.

Source: Photo courtesy of Turner Broadcasting System, Inc.

broadcasting as the most democratic of media

not exist. Broadcasting, as the most democratic of media, relies on audiences freely opting to watch or listen, solely because of programs.

By their all-inclusive nature, broadcast stations and networks ideally attract extraordinarily large audiences. If the goal is limited to small, well-defined audiences, there are cheaper and more effective ways of reaching them. Broadcasting tends to cut across demographic differences that usually divide people into separate consumer groups—age, sex, education, social status, and income. To achieve this universality exacts a price on program quality, a recurrent topic of concern in this survey.

The *continuousness* of broadcast services—essentially 24 hours a day—creates a program supply problem never before faced by an information/entertainment medium. Only by invoking a strategy here called the *parsimony principle* could broadcasters meet the demand. The principle calls for squeezing the maximum use out of program materials. Chapters 8 and 9 describe some of the parsimonious tactics used by producers, program suppliers, and program users.

Continuousness of service also means that broadcasting can provide programs in *real time*. News and sports events especially benefit from broadcasting's unique ability to cover events as they happen. Satellites enormously enhance this ability. Cable television's multichannel nature gives it the freedom to dedicate entire channels to news, public affairs, sports, and other specialized program types. Dedicated channels enable continuous real-time coverage of ongoing events for hours—even days—on end.

Program Ratings Those notoriously controversial but indispensable numbers, program ratings, are described in Chapter 10, which tells how listening/viewing is monitored and quantified. Whether electronic mass media depend on advertisers, government, foundations, or private donations, they find continuous, objective measurement of audiences vitally important.

Ratings have a controlling influence on programs, schedules, and other aspects of the electronic mass media. An elaborate and costly machinery for generating regular program ratings and other measurements has evolved to supply them. Chapter 10 describes the gathering and processing of listening/viewing data and explains how such measurements as program ratings and shares are derived.

Social Effects The previous chapter on ratings tells about set-tuning and the limited range of effects that can be deduced from tuning data. Chapter 11 considers larger social effects. Virtually every special-interest group claims that television has specific, identifiable effects. Such groups want either to prevent alleged unfavorable effects or to encourage the presumed favorable effects they hope will promote their goals.

People want to know how political advertising affects election outcomes; how reactions to television sex and violence influence children's behavior; how depictions in dramatic presentations shape our perception of minorities and other groups; how the alleged political biases of the electronic media affect audience attitudes; how the very presence of cameras influences crowd behavior. Chapter 11 discusses some of the difficulties of proving such effects, reviews the development of media research, and cites some of the landmark theories and findings.

Government Regulation Whatever the difficulties of objectively measuring the impact of electronic mass media, society assumes that such impact *does* occur and imposes controls accordingly. Chapters 12 and 13 tell about government regulation. All countries impose official regulations, but constitutional democracies put limits on government interference with the media. In the United States, the First Amendment to the Constitution gives public communication explicit protection from official interference. But not all media receive the same degree of protection. The press, broadcasting/cable, and common carriers operate under somewhat different legal regimes, and therefore each has a somewhat different First Amendment standing.

First Amendment has different impact on various media

Broadcasting uses a limited public resource—a portion of the electromagnetic spectrum. That use is licensed by the government. Programs enter the intimacy of the home, where even the youngest child hears or sees them. As the new domain of broadcasting law emerged, it reflected these special attributes, imposing an obligation to operate in *the public interest*. Cable, though similar to broadcasting in so many ways, differs as to licensing and First

Amendment status. The courts have seen a basic difference between broadcasting, which can enter every home without bidding, and cable, which enters only some homes and only upon payment of a subscription fee.

Government controls have been affected by an influential recent element in the arena of social control—*deregulation*. According to deregulatory theory, the public itself should monitor and control the electronic mass media. If, for example, parents object to programs their children watch, they should prevent children from watching, rather than expecting the government to prevent the media from disseminating the objectionable programs. If the public gets fed up with too many commercials, it should force moderation by tuning to less heavily commercialized stations.

The deregulation movement may have peaked in the 1980s. A movement toward *re-regulation* emerged in several arenas where deregulation had softened government controls. The social-control chapters critically analyze the deregulation/re-regulation movements.

EXHIBIT 1.6   News Around the World

Despite language differences, TV news looks about the same everywhere, as suggested by these examples from India and Mexico newcasts.

Sources: (Left photo) P.J. Anthony/NYT Pictures; (right photo) Sergio Dorantes/NYT Pictures.

Broadcasting Around the World Though focused on broadcasting in America, this survey cannot ignore broadcasting in other countries. Chapter 14 explores how other countries confront the problems discussed in previous chapters. This closing chapter describes some alternative ways of doing things. It also reports on criticisms directed at America's global influence. In appraising the American system and predicting its future course, it may be helpful to consult other countries' experiences.

In the End 1.5

This introduction pointed out in the beginning that people who read a survey of broadcasting in America are likely to have many different goals in mind. It would therefore be presumptuous to expect any particular outcomes from a reading of this book. Nevertheless, the authors hope that, in the end, readers come away with something to say in answer to at least the following basic questions:

- How did broadcasting come into being?
- How does broadcasting differ from nonbroadcast electronic mass media?
- How does technology limit coverage areas of stations, cable systems, and networks?
- How do economic considerations cause centralization of program production?
- How do centrally produced programs get distributed to the outlets that deliver them to the public?
- How does the continuousness attribute affect programming?
- How can credible audience ratings be obtained?
- How does the regulation of broadcasting differ from the regulation of other mass media such as the press and cable television?
- How can advocacy groups influence the behavior of stations, cable systems, and networks?
- How did deregulation affect the electronic mass media?
- How did the backlash against deregulation come about?
- How does American broadcasting influence other countries?
- How might broadcasting in America benefit from the experience of other countries?

central questions of this book

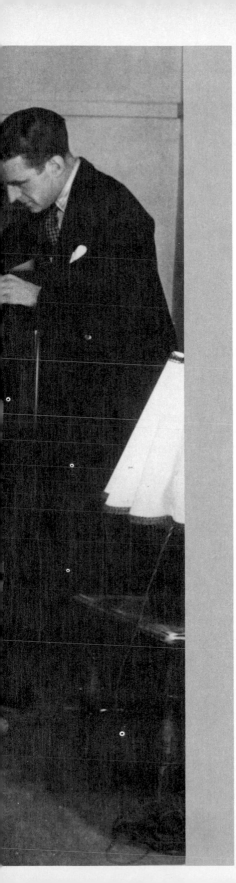

From Radio to Television

2 As guide posts in the history that follows, three key dates are worth remembering for their special significance: 1896, the year of the original Marconi radio patent; 1920, the start of regular broadcasting; and 1948, when television emerged as a mass medium. The dates of the two world wars are also significant because they punctuated phases in broadcasting development: 1914–1918, World War I, stimulated rapid evolution of wireless technology and set the stage for the

debut of radio of broadcasting; and 1939–1945, World War II, temporarily delayed the emergence of television but also contributed to it by developing the use of the ultra-high-frequency band. That development made it possible to license hundreds of spectrum-hungry television stations soon after the war ended. Before any of these events occurred, however, a groundwork had been laid that enabled broadcasting to develop with amazing speed, once technology and industry opened the door.

2.1 Precedents

Public appetite for the kinds of programs radio would bring in the 1920s had been developed decades earlier. The 19th-century popular press and the phonograph and motion-picture industries of the early 20th century cultivated the habits of mass-media consumption, making it possible for broadcasting to catch on without delay.

Urbanization   These older media grew out of fundamental social changes brought about by the Industrial Revolution (roughly 1740–1850). For centuries, the primary occupation of people living in Western countries had been agriculture. But industry increasingly drew people away from the land. By the mid-19th century, most people lived and worked in cities.

Concentrations of urban populations became the target of what we now call the **mass media**—means of communication that use technology to reach large parts of the total population simultaneously, or almost so, with news and entertainment of a kind that ordinary people find attractive, and at a price that ordinary people can afford to pay.

Penny Press   Urban concentration, rising literacy, and increased leisure time all contributed to transforming the print medium. Once an expensive amenity available primarily for the elite, it became a commonplace product for the masses. The **penny press** signaled this transformation. After 1833, the New York *Sun* led the trend toward mass-oriented, mass-produced papers. Copies sold for a penny, first in the thousands and eventually in the hundreds of thousands.

origin of mass media

Prior to that time, newspapers had small circulations and concentrated on news of commerce, party politics, and other "serious" subjects. The popular press broadened the range of subjects, exploiting news of everyday events, sensational crimes, gossip, human-interest stories, sports, and entertaining features—all presented in a breezy, colloquial style that contrasted with the flowery essay style of the past.

Popular newspapers widened their appeal by cutting across lines of class, sex, age, political party, and cherished beliefs. By the 1890s some mass-oriented newspapers had circulations of over a million.

Vaudeville   Early broadcasting inherited the entertainment role earlier fulfilled by **vaudeville**. Immensely popular in the 1880–1920 era, vaudeville featured song-and-dance teams, short plays, Irish tenors, ethnic comics, and performing animals. Well-known vaudeville acts toured the nation, filling theaters in cities large and small. At its peak, the vaudeville circuits sold more tickets than all other kinds of entertainment combined.

The Phonograph A late-19th-century invention, the **phonograph** also helped prepare the public for radio broadcasting. Owning a phonograph in a large, handsome cabinet accustomed people to investing in a piece of furniture that brought entertainment into the home. By the end of World War I, on the eve of the introduction of broadcasting, some 200 phonograph manufacturers turned out more than 2 million players each year.

the phonograph as furniture

In the 1920s, radio introduced improved electronic means of sound reproduction at a time when recordings still depended on obsolete acoustic methods. They were not fundamentally different from those first used by inventor Thomas Edison in 1878. Devastated by competition from radio broadcasting and loss of buyers because of the Great Depression, the phonograph industry came near to extinction by 1933.

In the end, though, radio proved a blessing for the recording industry. It widened the mass audience for music of all kinds and also supplied the technology for improved sound-recording quality.

radio saves phonograph industry

Motion Pictures Like the phonograph industry, the cinema had become well established by the time broadcasting began in the 1920s. Moviegoers became accustomed to serial dramas, which eventually had their counterparts in broadcasting. Thus, movies as well as vaudeville contributed to preparing the audience for broadcasting.

Movies, too, benefited from radio's electronic technology. The lack of **synchronized sound**—the precise matching of sound and action—long stymied progress toward acceptable "talkies." They finally began in earnest in 1928, with several rival sound systems competing for acceptance. One of these sound-on-film systems had been developed by RCA, the owner of the first national radio network—an example of the many links between broadcasting and motion pictures in the 1920s, long before the advent of television brought the two visual media together in an even closer relationship.

radio aids talking movies

Wire Communication 2.2

Broadcasting benefited not only from the consumption habits cultivated by these prior forms of mass communication, but also from its direct technological and industrial antecedents, the **telegraph** and the **telephone**. These pre-broadcast technologies communicate from point to point rather than to the general public, as does broadcasting.

point-to-point vs. broadcast transmission

The Telegraph The British developed **electrical telegraphy** in the 1820s as an adjunct to railroad operations. Electrical impulses sent along a wire caused deflections of a pointer in a detecting device at the receiving end. An operator "read" the message by interpreting the movements of the pointer.

S.F.B. Morse, telegraph inventor

An American inventor, Samuel F. B. Morse, conducted extensive telegraph experiments in the 1830s. The American experiments came at a time when westward expansion put a high premium on rapid means of communicating over long distances. Morse made significant improvements in the telegraph, devising a receiver that made a permanent record of the coded messages on strips of paper. He and a partner devised the **Morse code** to translate numerals and letters into the dots and dashes of telegraphic code. That same code served for early pre-broadcast radio communications.

In partnership with the federal government, Morse installed the first operational telegraph line in the United States in 1844. However, Congress feared that the federal post office would lose money if the government competed with itself by running the telegraph, so the government sold its interest in Morse's installation to private investors, retaining the right to regulate the

Western Union monopolizes telegraphy

privatization of telegraph

telegraphic service. By the end of the Civil War, a single company, Western Union, had emerged as the dominant force in electrical telegraphy.

role of PTTs in other countries

The decision to privatize the telegraph set the United States on a telecommunications path different from that of other countries. Most central governments kept their national telecommunications systems under Post and Telegraph (PTT) administrations, which also often later had some control over broadcasting. However, in recent years PTT monopolies came under increasing attack when countries began leaning toward the American policy of privately owned, competitively operated telecommunication services.

Communications over **transatlantic telegraph cables** began in 1866, enabling exchange of information between Europe and America in minutes instead of weeks or months. The submarine cable and telegraphy generally had an early and lasting association with news. Even before the electric telegraph became available, newspapers had begun to share the costs of news gathering. The French news agency, Havas, dates back to 1835, and the British Reuter Telegram Company started in 1851. Reuters, as it now is called, "followed the cable" wherever it led around the globe, establishing one of the first international **news-wire services**. An association of small New York

Associated Press news service

news agencies formed in 1856 became the Associated Press in 1882, now a major supplier of broadcast news and operator of a radio network.

The Telephone   Inventors next turned their attention to the wire transmission of speech itself, seeking a way to eliminate the tedious encoding and decoding of telegraph messages. Many investigators were struggling with this problem and were on the verge of a solution in 1876, when Alexander Graham Bell applied for the key telephone patent.

Bell organized the original Bell Telephone Company a year later, when he secured a second essential patent. But the inventor and his friends could not raise enough development capital (telephony costs a great deal, initially, to construct). Though control over the patents soon passed to others who went

on to develop the company known today as the American Telephone and origin of AT&T
Telegraph Company (AT&T), the Bell name still stands for "telephone."

Rather than spread to ungainly proportions by trying to serve the entire country directly, AT&T adopted a policy of franchising regional operating companies. These firms received the exclusive and permanent right to use the Bell patents. They in turn gave AT&T substantial holdings in their stocks. By the time the original patents ran out in 1893–1894, AT&T held controlling interests in the franchised companies.

Furthermore, AT&T had developed the long-lines network, which connected the regional telephone companies with one another. In 1914 AT&T assured its supremacy in the long-distance field by acquiring a license to use a crucial electronic invention, the Audion (described on page 25). That device made coast-to-coast telephone service possible.

With its 1881 purchase of Western Electric as its manufacturing arm, AT&T kept the whole process of manufacture, installation, and servicing within the Bell companies. Its control of long-distance voice communication by wire had an important bearing on the future progress of radio broadcasting, which depended on such wire links for network operations.

AT&T and its Bell Companies monopolize long-distance telephony

Three giant manufacturing firms also played key roles in broadcast developments—Western Electric (AT&T's manufacturing arm), General Electric (GE), and Westinghouse. They largely dictated the direction of the electrical industry and set the tone for the industry's reaction to early wireless communication, as will become clear in the next section.

Wireless Communication 2.3

Once the telephone made a wire communication of speech possible, the next logical step was **wireless telegraphy**—a means of communicating at a distance without costly physical links to every household. The quest for wireless stimulated the inventive juices of numerous scientists and tinkerers in the last quarter of the 19th century.

Hertzian Waves   Inventors in many countries claimed to have been the first to solve the problem. Most claimants had common access to critically important scientific knowledge about **electromagnetic energy** published by two physicists. In 1873, James Clerk Maxwell made a remarkable prediction. He theorized that an invisible form of radiant energy must exist—electromagnetic energy. He described it mathematically, foreseeing that it resembled light radiating out from a source in the form of waves.

Maxwell's electromagnetic energy theory

In 1888, Heinrich Hertz reported on brilliant laboratory experiments that conclusively proved the validity of Maxwell's theory. Hertz generated electromagnetic waves, transmitted them down the length of his laboratory, detected them, measured their length, and showed that they had other wavelike properties similar to those of light.

Hertz proves Maxwell right

In effect, Hertz demonstrated radio. But he sought to verify a scientific theory, not to invent a new way of communicating. It remained for other experimenters to communicate with what they called **Hertzian waves**. Later, the scientific community adopted the term *hertz* as the standard way to express wave frequency. A **hertz**, usually abbreviated **Hz**, means one wave-cycle per second. A 60-Hz wave oscillates at the frequency of 60 cycles per second.

"The Right Releasing Touch"

A tireless young experimenter, Guglielmo Marconi, is credited with inventing radio as a means of communication. He supplied "the right releasing touch," as a Supreme Court justice put it in upholding Marconi's primacy in a patent suit (US, 1942: 65). Stimulated by Hertz's paper, Marconi experimented with Hertzian wave signals in the early 1890s, first sending them across the space of an attic, then for greater distances on the grounds of his father's estate in Italy.

As soon as Marconi had convinced himself that wireless telegraphy amounted to more than a laboratory toy, he patriotically offered it to the Italian government, only to be rebuffed. Still only twenty-two, Marconi next went to London, where he received a more encouraging reception. In 1896 he registered his patent in England, and the next year he launched his own company, known as British Marconi, to manufacture wireless-telegraphy equipment and to offer wireless services to ships and shore stations. Exhibit 2.1 shows Marconi with one of the machines that displayed coded wireless messages.

British Marconi company founded

EXHIBIT 2.1   Guglielmo Marconi (1874–1937)

In a 1902 photo, the inventor examines the paper tape bearing a radiographic message in Morse code. Though radio equipment still remained crude, well-developed wire-telegraphy equipment could be readily adapted to record wireless messages. Seated is George Kemp, Marconi's most trusted engineering assistant.

Source: Photo courtesy Smithsonian Institution, Washington, DC.

To a remarkable degree Marconi combined the genius of the inventor with that of the business innovator. As inventor he persisted tirelessly, never discouraged even by hundreds of failed attempts at solving a problem. In 1909, Marconi shared the Nobel Prize in physics with Germany's Ferdinand Braun for achievements in wireless telegraphy.

As a business manager, Marconi had rare entrepreneurial talent and a flair for effective public relations. In the early years of the century, he repeatedly staged dramatic demonstrations of wireless reception to prove the usefulness of his system to skeptical officials, scientists, investors, and equipment buyers.

Among Marconi's business ventures, the U.S. branch of his company, known as American Marconi, had a decisive influence on the development of broadcasting in America. Founded in 1899, American Marconi developed a virtual monopoly on U.S. wireless communication, owning 17 land stations and 400 shipboard stations. All these facilities used a wireless extension of the telegraph principle—point-to-point communication between ships and shore stations, between ships at sea, and to a lesser extent between countries.

Marconi's American company

This limitation to radiotelegraphy continued for the first 20 years of radio services because the relatively crude Marconi equipment could modulate a transmitter's output only by turning the radio energy on and off, producing the dits and dahs of Morse code. Telephones could have been used as microphones for transmitting wireless speech, but methods had not yet been found to impress such complex information onto radio waves. Operators could *hear* Morse code, but only as a single monotonous tone.

The Vacuum Tube   The solution to this and other radio problems came with the invention of an improved **vacuum tube**, capable of sensitive, rapid, subtle variations in accordance with the changing volume and pitch of actual sounds. Lee de Forest had followed up on research leads suggested by Edison's 1883 electric lamp and a two-element tube (**diode**) patented by a Marconi researcher, Ambrose Fleming, in 1904.

Lee de Forest's vacuum tube research

De Forest's crucial improvement consisted of adding a third element to the tube, turning it into a **triode**. He positioned the new element, the **grid**, between the filament and the plate. A small voltage applied to the grid could control with great precision the flow of electrons from filament to plate. Thus a weak signal could be enormously amplified yet precisely modulated. De Forest first used the triode, or **Audion**, as one of his associates dubbed it, in 1906.

The triode vacuum tube represented a great leap forward—out of the age of mechanics into the age of electronics. **Electrons**—particles of energy smaller than atoms—could be controlled. Not only communications but virtually all science and industry has been revolutionized by this transforming power to manipulate electrons.

It took more than a dozen years to develop the Audion and the new circuits to go with it. Its first practical application improved not radio but telephony. In 1913, AT&T purchased from de Forest the right to use vacuum-tube

first long-distance telephony

repeaters (amplifiers in telephone lines), achieving the first coast-to-coast telephone service two years later.

Commercial Uses of Wireless   During its first two decades, the wireless business made its money from supplying point-to-point and point-to-multipoint services between ships, between shore and ships, and to some extent between continents. Overland wireless-telegraphy services had little appeal because telephone and telegraph lines satisfied existing needs. Manufacturers had few customers for wireless equipment. The mass market for millions of broadcast receivers and thousands of broadcast transmitters lay in the future.

Wireless offered unique advantages to maritime commerce. In fact, for some of his first public demonstrations of his system, Marconi chose international yacht races with their attendant publicity as testing grounds. Wireless

yacht races used to demonstrate radio

EXHIBIT 2.2   The *Titanic* Disaster, April 1912

Source: Photo from UPI/Bettmann Archive.

A luxury liner advertised as unsinkable, the *Titanic,* struck an iceberg and sank in the Atlantic on her maiden voyage from Britain to the United States in April 1912. One heroic Marconi radio operator stayed at his post and went down with the ship, although the second operator survived. Some 1,500 people died—among them some of the most famous names in the worlds of art, science, finance, and diplomacy—partially because each nearby vessel, unlike the *Titanic,* had but one radio operator (all that was then required), who had already turned in for the night. Only by chance did the operator on a ship some 50 miles distant hear distress calls from the *Titanic.* It steamed full speed to the disaster site, rescuing about 700 survivors.

The fact that for days radiotelegraphy maintained the world's only thread of contact with the survivors aboard the rescue liner *Carpathia* as it steamed toward New York brought the new medium of wireless to public attention as nothing else had done. Subsequent British and American inquiries revealed that a more sensible use of wireless (such as a 24-hour radio watch) could have decreased the loss of life. Because of such findings, the *Titanic* disaster influenced the worldwide adoption of stringent laws governing shipboard wireless stations. The *Titanic* tragedy also set a precedent for regarding the radio business as having a special public responsibility. This concept carried over into broadcasting legislation a quarter of a century later.

also gained invaluable publicity from its life-saving role in maritime disasters. Such an incident occurred as early as 1898. In 1909, when S.S. *Republic* foundered off New York, wireless-alerted rescue ships saved all the passengers. Each year the number of rescues increased. Exhibit 2.2 tells about the most dramatic of them all.

radio to the rescue in disasters at sea

Radio had commercial possibilities in the field of long-distance communication across oceans as an alternative to submarine telegraph cables, which were enormously costly to install. Because of technical limitations, however, transoceanic radio service did not become strongly competitive until vacuum tubes came into general use in the 1920s.

On the eve of U.S. entry into World War I, General Electric (GE) developed a new type of pre–vacuum tube radio-frequency generator to enable sending transatlantic messages reliably. The 200-kilowatt **alternator**, as it was called, put out a powerful very-low-frequency (VLF) signal at about 20 kHz. It represented a major improvement in long-distance radio communication, of significant importance in wartime.

During the 1920s, vacuum-tube transmitters displaced alternators. Tubes enabled using the short-wave (high-frequency) portion of the spectrum, which turned out to be much more efficient than the lower frequencies that had previously been used for long-distance communication. A sharp rise in transatlantic radio traffic followed.

short-waves used for long-distance radio

Military Wireless   Naturally, the major naval powers of the world took an interest in military applications of wireless from the outset. In April 1917, when direct American participation in World War I began, the U.S. Navy recognized that wireless presented a threat to national security. Enemy spy agents could (and in fact did) use radio to send information to the enemy about ship movements, for example. Therefore the navy took over all wireless stations in the country, commercial and amateur alike. It either dismantled them or ran them as part of the navy's own training and operational programs.

U.S. Navy seizes all radio facilities

The Army Signal Corps also used radio, as did the Air Service. Some 10,000 soldiers and sailors received training in wireless. After the war, they remained an informed cadre of amateur enthusiasts, laboratory technicians, and electronics manufacturing employees. They helped popularize the new medium, constituting a ready-made audience for the first regular broadcasting services when they began two years after the war ended.

ex-service personnel form first audience

In order to mobilize the total wireless resources of the country for war, the navy decreed a moratorium on patent lawsuits over radio inventions. Manufacturers agreed to participate in a **patent pool**. The pool made all U.S. radio patents available, maximizing wireless progress without risk of infringement suits—a cozy arrangement revived by rival companies voluntarily after the war.

By the end of the war, big business had developed a stake in wireless and was ready to branch out into new applications. AT&T had added wireless rights to its original purchase of telephone rights to de Forest's Audion. GE had the patents for the powerful alternator and the ability to mass-produce vacuum tubes. Westinghouse, also a producer of vacuum tubes, joined them in looking for new ways of capitalizing on wireless. But before they could move forward, they had to come to terms with another, differently motivated player—the U.S. Navy. It, too, had claims on wireless.

2.4   *Emergence of Broadcasting*

Throughout the early 1920s, eager experimenters constantly sought the key to **radiotelephony**—the essential precursor of broadcasting.

Fessenden
radiotelephone
experiments

Early Radiotelephone Experiments   In 1906, Reginald Fessenden made the first known radiotelephone transmission resembling what we would now call a broadcast. Using an ordinary telephone microphone and an alternator to generate radio energy, Fessenden made his historic transmission on Christmas Eve from Brant Rock, on the Massachusetts coast south of Boston.

Fessenden himself played a violin, sang, read from the Bible, and played a phonograph recording. Ships' operators who picked up the transmission

EXHIBIT 2.3   Lee de Forest (1873–1961)

It was, by sort of this equipment and through these two headphones that the voice of Madame Farrar was heard at Brooklyn Navy Yard in October 1907 — She being the first woman to sing over the Wireless Telephone

Frank E. Butler

The inventor in 1907 with a transmitter like the one used in his famous 1907 broadcast, along with a shipboard receiver of the type that picked up the transmission.

Source: Photos courtesy Smithsonian Institution, Washington, DC, and Culver Pictures.

by chance far out at sea could hardly believe they were hearing human voices and musical sounds. Their earphones had previously brought them only the monotonous drone of Morse code.

Lee de Forest, the prolific inventor who patented the Audion, loved classical music and saw radiotelephony as a miraculous opportunity to make it available to the masses. In 1907, hard on the heels of Fessenden, de Forest made experimental radiotelephone transmissions from a building in downtown New York City. Some of his equipment is shown in Exhibit 2.3.

De Forest radiotelephone experiments

By 1916, de Forest had set up in his Bronx home an experimental transmitter over which he played phonograph recordings and made announcements. He even aired election returns in November 1916, anticipating by four years the opening broadcast of KDKA, usually regarded as the first regular broadcasting station. With some justification, de Forest called himself in his 1950 autobiography, *Father of Radio*.

Government Monopoly: The Road Not Taken
World War I ended in November 1918, yet the navy did not relinquish control of radio facilities until early in 1920. The critical decisions made during this 18-month period profoundly affected the future of broadcasting in America.

Was radio too vital to entrust to private hands? The navy thought so, and it supported a bill in the House of Representatives late in 1918 proposing, in effect, to make radio a permanent government monopoly. Despite strong arguments from navy brass at the hearings, the bill failed to win committee approval. Thus radio took the road of private enterprise in the United States, though in many other countries governments remained in charge as radio expanded in the postwar years.

Origin of RCA
Restoration of private ownership in 1920, however, would have meant returning most commercial wireless-communication facilities in the United States to a *foreign* company, American Marconi. Disturbed at the prospect of American Marconi consolidating its U.S. monopoly by capturing the exclusive rights to the alternator, the navy strongly opposed the deal. British Marconi, the parent of the American subsidiary, found itself caught in a squeeze play. With tacit government approval, the GE board chair, Owen D. Young, negotiated the purchase of American Marconi stock by American companies—what today might be called a semi-friendly takeover.

Marconi's American company bought out by U.S. interests

GE thereupon created a new subsidiary of its own in the fall of 1919 to run American Marconi's wireless-telegraphy business—Radio Corporation of America (RCA), shortly to become the premier force in American broadcasting. Under RCA's charter, all its officers had to be Americans and 80 percent of its stock had to be in American hands.

RCA founded

Westinghouse and AT&T joined GE as investors in the new corporation. AT&T sold its interest in 1923, but RCA remained under GE and Westinghouse control until 1932, when an antitrust suit forced them to sell their stock, making RCA an independent corporation. Thus it remained for some seven

RCA becomes independent corporation

EXHIBIT **2.4** Sarnoff and Paley: Giants of Early Broadcasting

Both of the network broadcasting pioneers came from immigrant Russian families, but there the similarity ceases. Sarnoff (top) rose from the direst poverty, a self-educated and self-made man. In contrast, Paley (bottom) had every advantage of money and social position. After earning a degree from the Wharton School of Business at the University of Pennsylvania in 1922, he joined his father's prosperous cigar company.

The differences between Sarnoff and Paley extended to their personalities and special skills. Sarnoff was "an engineer turned businessman, ill at ease with the hucksterism that he had wrought, and he did not condescend to sell, but Bill Paley loved to sell. CBS was Paley and he sold it as he sold himself" (Halberstam, 1979: 27).

Sarnoff had been introduced to radio by way of hard work at the telegraph key for American Marconi, Paley by way of leisurely DX listening: "As a radio fan in Philadelphia, I often sat up all night, glued to my set, listening and marveling at the voices and music which came into my ears from distant places," he recalled (Paley, 1979:32).

Paley's introduction to the business of radio came through sponsoring of programs. After becoming advertising manager of his father's cigar company in 1925, he experimented with ads on WCAU in Philadelphia. Impressed with the results, he explored getting into the radio business and late in 1928 took over the struggling CBS network.

Both men, shown here in about 1930, were highly competitive and pitted their companies against each other for 40 years before Sarnoff's retirement in 1969.

Source: Photos: Sarnoff, courtesy RCA; Paley, courtesy CBS.

decades until, in one of corporate history's great ironies, GE bought RCA back again. The details of this historic transaction are related in Section 3.10.

If RCA became broadcasting's leading corporation, David Sarnoff became broadcasting's leading corporate executive. As a junior American Marconi executive, he moved with the company into RCA. There he helped to convert RCA from a collection of radio-telegraph firms into a major corporation presiding over numerous subsidiary companies. In 1930, Sarnoff became president of RCA; in 1947, he became board chair. In 1969, he finally retired, having played a major role in the creation of network radio, the evolution of television, and the conversion of television to color. Today these top-flight research laboratories bear his name. Exhibit 2.4 tells more about his career. — David Sarnoff as leader in broadcasting developments

Cross-Licensing Agreements RCA and its parent companies each held important radio patents, yet each found itself blocked by patents held by the — role of patents in early radio development

EXHIBIT 2.5 Conrad's 8XK and Its Successor, KDKA

Frank Conrad's transmitter (*left*) typified the improvised setups used by wireless inventors and experimenters. It contrasts with the first KDKA transmitter facilities (*right*), with which the Harding-Cox election returns were broadcast on November 2, 1920.

Source: Photos courtesy Westinghouse Broadcasting Co., Pittsburgh, PA.

others. In the 1919–1923 period, AT&T, GE, Westinghouse, RCA, and other minor players worked out a series of **cross-licensing agreements**, modeled after the navy-run patent pool of World War I. Under these agreements, each company had its own slice of the electronics manufacturing and services pie.

Within a few years, however, these carefully laid plans fell into utter confusion because of the astonishingly rapid growth of a brand-new use for radiotelephony—**broadcasting**. The immediate provocation for this development came in 1920 from Dr. Frank Conrad, an engineer with Westinghouse in Pittsburgh. Conrad operated an amateur radiotelephone station, 8XK, in his garage. Exhibit 2.5 shows his setup.

Frank Conrad's amateur broadcasts

The First Broadcasting Station

Conrad fell into the habit of transmitting recorded music, sports results, and bits of talk in response to requests from other amateurs. These informal transmissions (hardly "programs" in the formal sense) built up so much interest that newspapers began to comment on them. Similar amateur transmissions had been made by others elsewhere around the world, but Conrad's 8XK set a unique chain of events in motion.

Managers of a Pittsburgh department store, noting the growing public interest in wireless, sensed that the general public might be willing to buy receiving sets to pick up Conrad's broadcasts. They installed a demonstration receiver in the store and ran a box in their regular newspaper display advertisement of 22 September 1920: "Air Concert 'Picked Up' by Radio Here . . . Amateur Wireless Sets made by the maker of the Set which is in operation in our store, are on sale here $10.00 up."

first sale of home radios

Westinghouse executives glimpsed in this ad the possibility of a novel merchandising tie-in: they could create a demand for radio receivers by regularly transmitting programs for the general public. Accordingly, they converted a Westinghouse radiotelegraph transmitter for use in radiotelephony. It went on the air as station KDKA from an improvised studio at the Westinghouse factory in East Pittsburgh on 2 November 1920.

origins of KDKA

KDKA's opening coincided with the presidential election of 1920, enabling the maiden broadcast to take advantage of public interest in the voting results. KDKA's first program consisted of news about the Harding-Cox election returns, fed to the station by telephone from a newspaper office, interspersed with phonograph and live banjo music. After the election, KDKA began a regular daily hour-long schedule of music and talk.

radio's first election broadcast

KDKA met five criteria that qualify it as the oldest U.S. station still in operation, despite many claims based on earlier experiments, demonstrations, and temporary operations. KDKA (1) used radio waves (2) to send out uncoded signals (3) in a continuous, scheduled program service (4) intended for the general public and (5) was licensed by the government to provide such a service (Baudino and Kittross, 1977). However, no broadcasting licenses as such existed at the time; KDKA had the same kind of license as ship-to-shore radiotelegraphic stations.

was KDKA first broadcasting station?

Unhampered by competing signals, KDKA's sky wave could be picked up at great distances. Newspapers all over the country and even in Canada printed the station's program schedule. As other stations came on the air, some observed a "silent night" once a week to enable their listeners to receive weak DX (long-distance) signals from far-off stations whose transmissions would be otherwise drowned out by the local stations.

In its first year of operation, KDKA pioneered many types of programs that later became standard radio fare: orchestra music, church services, public-service announcements, political addresses, sports events, dramas, and market reports. But KDKA totally lacked one now-familiar type of broadcast material—commercial announcements. Westinghouse bore KDKA's entire expense for the sake of promoting sales of its own products. The company took it for granted that *each firm* that wanted to promote its wares over the air would have to open its own station.

no commercials in first broadcasts

Broadcasting Becomes an Industry 2.5

Westinghouse did not have the field to itself for long. Department stores, newspapers, educational institutions, churches, and electrical equipment supply dealers all found fascination in operating their own broadcasting stations.

In the spring of 1922 the new industry began gathering momentum. By May more than 200 stations had been licensed, and the upward trend continued the next year, with the number reaching 576 early in 1923.

Divergent Philosophies   RCA entered the field in 1921, purchasing WJZ, a second station built by Westinghouse to reach the New York market. WJZ assumed responsibility for producing its own programs, as had KDKA. But when AT&T put its station, WEAF, on the air in 1922, it took a different approach. The telephone company explained that it would "furnish *no programs whatsoever* over that station" (U.S. Department of Commerce, 1922: 7, italics added). AT&T thought of broadcasting as a **common carrier**—merely a variation of telephony. In a 1922 press release about WEAF, AT&T explained its theory:

WJZ, RCA's broadcast station

WEAF, AT&T's station

> Just as the [telephone] company leases its long distance wire facilities for the use of newspapers, banks, and other concerns, so it will lease its radio telephone facilities and will not provide the matter which is sent out from this station. (quoted in Banning, 1946: 68)

It soon became clear, however, that the idea of filling the schedule entirely with leased time simply would not work. Advertisers had no idea how to prepare program material capable of attracting listeners. In order to piece out its schedule, the telephone company found itself getting into show business after all—a decidedly uncomfortable role for a regulated monopoly bent on maintaining a serious and dignified public image.

Thus the Radio Group (Westinghouse, GE, and RCA) and the Telephone Group (AT&T and Western Electric), as they became known, started with

Radio Group squares off against Telephone Group

opposing theories about the way broadcasting should work. In the end, it turned out that each group was partly right.

The Telephone Group correctly foresaw that the spectrum could accommodate only a limited number of channels, nowhere near enough for each large company in the country to have its own station. Instead, each station would need to make its services available to many different advertisers. AT&T miscalculated, however, in emphasizing primarily those interested in *sending* messages instead of those interested in *receiving* them. Public good will had to be earned with listenable programs to pave the way for acceptance of advertising. In this matter, the Radio Group's strategy of providing a program service prevailed. It took about four years for these conflicting theories of broadcasting to sort themselves out.

Radio Advertising WEAF called the sale of commercial time **toll broadcasting**, an analogy with telephone long-distance toll calls. It first leased facilities for a toll broadcast on 28 August 1922, when a Long Island real-estate firm paid $50 for ten minutes of time. It spent the entire ten minutes extolling the advantages of living in Hawthorne Court, an apartment complex in the Jackson Heights section of New York. AT&T would not allow mentioning anything so crass as price.

early attempts at advertising

In 1923 the first weekly advertiser appeared on WEAF, featuring a musical group the client called "The Browning King Orchestra"—a device to ensure frequent mention of the client's name. However, the script carefully avoided mentioning the fact that Browning King sold clothing. This reluctance to advertise openly did not last long. (By 1928, under the pressure of rising operating costs and advertiser interest, direct advertising had become acceptable.)

advertising agencies become producers

Broadcasters had not yet developed commercial programming and production skills, leaving a vacuum that advertising agencies filled. They took over commercial program production, introducing program **sponsorship**. Sponsors did more than simply advertise—they also brought to the stations the shows and the talent that served as vehicles for their advertising messages. Later on, during the height of network radio's popularity, advertisers and their agencies controlled most major entertainment shows, a surrender of control that broadcasters lived to regret.

Networks AT&T based its next move on its interpretation of the cross-licensing agreements, claiming the exclusive right to connect broadcasting equipment to its telephone lines. In other words, only WEAF could set up a network. It began in 1923, with the first permanent station **interconnection**—a telephone line between WEAF and WMAF, a station in Massachusetts. By October 1924, AT&T had set up a **chain**—network—of 6 stations. In October 1924, it put together a temporary coast-to-coast chain of 22 stations to carry a speech by President Calvin Coolidge. AT&T used its long-distance telephone lines to link ("chain") together its network stations, first using ordinary lines but by 1926 setting aside special telephone wires for the exclusive use of its radio network.

AT&T uses telephone lines for first network

Denied the use of AT&T telephone interconnection for its network, the Radio Group's station turned to Western Union's telegraph lines. Telegraph wires were designed only for the simple on-off pulses of electricity that form Morse code. They do not carry radio as well as wires designed for voice. Nevertheless, in 1923 WJZ formed a wire link to a station in Washington, DC, and by 1925 had succeeded in organizing a network of 14 stations.

radio group resorts to telegraph wires to interconnect network

Cross-Licensing Revisited   The growing market for broadcasting equipment, especially radio receivers, upset the careful balance among commercial interests that the cross-licensees had devised. The agreements covered only point-to-point wireless, not broadcasting, which of course did not exist at the time the agreements were made. A federal suit alleged that the patent pool violated **antitrust laws** by aiming to control the manufacture and sale of all radio equipment. The suit added urgency to the need for change. AT&T had concluded in any event that its original concept of broadcasting as a branch of telephony had been a mistake.

Accordingly, in 1926, the signatories of the cross-licensing agreements redistributed and redefined the parties' rights to use their commonly owned patents and to engage in the various aspects of the radio business. Briefly, AT&T kept the rights to **two-way telephony** but sold WEAF and its other broadcasting assets to the Radio Group for $1 million. AT&T also agreed not to manufacture radio receivers. RCA, though originally a service company, won the right to manufacture receivers but agreed to lease all its **network relays** from AT&T.

It would be difficult to overestimate the impact this 1926 agreement had on the future of broadcasting in America. As long as the two groups of major communications companies fought about fundamental policies, broadcasting's economic future remained uncertain. The 1926 agreements removed that uncertainty.

Origin of NBC   A few months after the 1926 cross-licensing settlement, the Radio Group, under Owen Young and David Sarnoff's leadership, created a new RCA subsidiary, the National Broadcasting Company (NBC)—the first American company organized solely and specifically to operate a broadcasting network. NBC's $4^{1}/_{2}$-hour coast-to-coast inaugural broadcast reached an estimated 5 million listeners. However, not until after 1928 did coast-to-coast network operations begin on a regular basis.

NBC founded—first broadcast network

Starting with the new year in 1927, RCA divided NBC into two semi-autonomous networks, the Blue and the Red. WJZ (later to become WABC) and the old Radio Group network formed the nucleus of the Blue; WEAF (later to become WNBC) and the old Telephone Group network formed the nucleus of the Red.

NBC forms Blue and Red networks

Origin of CBS   In 1927, soon after NBC began, an independent talent-booking agency, seeking an alternative to NBC as an outlet for its performers, started a rival network. It went through rapid changes in ownership, picking up along the way the name Columbia Phonograph Broadcasting System as a result of an investment by a record company. The record company soon withdrew but left behind the right to use the Columbia name. In September 1928 William S. Paley purchased the "patchwork, money-losing little company," as he later described it.

rise of power for William S. Paley and CBS

When he took over, CBS had only 22 affiliates. Paley quickly turned the failing network around with a new affiliation contract. In his autobiography a half-century later he recalled:

> I proposed the concept of free sustaining service . . . I would guarantee not ten but twenty hours of programming per week, pay the stations $50 an hour for the commercial hours used, but with a new proviso. The network would not pay the stations for the first five hours of commercial programming time . . . [t]o allow for the possibility of more business to come, the network was to receive an option on additional time.
>
> And for the first time, we were to have exclusive rights for network broadcasting through the affiliate. That meant the local station could not use its facilities for any other broadcasting network. I added one more innovation which helped our cause: local stations would have to identify our programs with the CBS name. (Paley, 1979: 42)

origin of CBS name

Paley's canny innovations became standard practice in network contracts. He also simplified the firm's name to Columbia Broadcasting System (the corporate name later became simply CBS, Inc.) and bought a New York outlet, now WCBS, as the network flagship station. From that point on, the CBS radio network never faltered, and Paley eventually rivaled Sarnoff as the nation's leading broadcasting executive. Exhibit 2.4 compares their colorful careers.

2.6 *Government Regulation*

One final stone remained to be put in place to complete the foundation of broadcasting in America—national legislation capable of imposing order on the new medium.

1912 Radio Act   The federal government's decision to return radio to private control after World War I did not mean abandonment of government oversight. Since the beginning of telegraphy, governments throughout the world had recognized the need for both national and international regulation to ensure fair and efficient operation of telecommunication systems.

telegraphy paves way for international regulation

The first international conference specifically concerned with wireless communication took place in Berlin in 1903, only six years after Marconi's first patent. It dealt mainly with the Marconi company's refusal to exchange messages with rival maritime wireless systems. The conference agreed that humanitarian considerations had to take precedence over commercial rivalries in maritime emergencies. Three years later, at the Berlin Convention of 1906, nations agreed to equip ships with suitable wireless gear and to exchange SOS messages freely among different commercial systems.

Finally, prodded by the terrible lesson of the 1912 *Titanic* disaster (Exhibit 2.2), Congress confirmed the 1906 Berlin Convention rules by modifying a 1910 wireless act requiring radio apparatus and operators on most ships at sea. A few weeks later, the Radio Act of 1912, the first comprehensive U.S. legislation to govern *radio* (not broadcasting, which had yet to emerge) called for federal licensing of all land transmitters. Despite its unsuitability as a broadcasting law, the 1912 act remained in force until 1927—throughout broadcasting's formative years. agreement to use SOS messages

U.S. Radio Act of 1912

The 1912 law worked well enough for the point-to-point services it had been designed to regulate. Broadcasting, however, introduced demands on the spectrum never imagined in 1912. The act instructed the secretary of commerce to grant licenses to U.S. citizens "upon application therefore," leaving him no grounds on which to *reject* applications. In 1912, Congress had no reason to anticipate rejections. Presumably all who needed to operate radio stations could do so.

Herbert Hoover, the secretary of commerce in broadcasting's first years, at first tried to make all radio stations share a single channel, just as shipboard stations did. Channel sharing worked well enough for ships' messages. Unlike broadcast stations, ships could save up outbound messages and take turns at sending them on an assigned frequency (a separate full-time frequency had been set aside by international agreement exclusively for emergency SOS messages).

Unregulated growth of broadcast stations in the mid-1920s soon created intolerable interference. Exhibit 2.6 indicates how highhanded licensees could be in refusing to abide by regulations of the hapless secretary of commerce. interference caused by inadequate regulation

Secretary Hoover, an ardent believer in free enterprise, hoped that the radio business would discipline itself, without the need for government regulation. To that end, he called a series of four annual national radio conferences in Washington, DC. At the first one, in 1922, only 22 broadcasters attended, but by the fourth conference, in 1925, the number had risen to 400.

Hoover commented repeatedly on the fact that here was an industry that actually *wanted* government regulation. From year to year the conferees grew more explicit in their pleas for federal intervention.

Finally, in 1926 a federal court decision confirmed that Hoover had no legal power to enforce his rules under the 1912 act. He had brought suit against Zenith Radio Corporation's WJAZ in Chicago for operating on unauthorized frequencies at unauthorized times. The court found in favor of the station, remarking that "Administrative rulings cannot add to the terms of an act of Congress and make conduct criminal which such laws leave untouched" (F, 1926: 618).

In less than a year, 200 new stations took advantage of the government's inability to enforce licensing rules. Late in 1926, President Coolidge Congress tackles interference problem

EXHIBIT **2.6**   Church vs. State in Radio Broadcasting

An example of the bizarre regulatory problems facing the secretary of commerce was the station owned by Aimée Semple McPherson, a popular evangelist of the 1920s. She operated a pioneer broadcast station that "wandered all over the waveband" from her "temple" in Los Angeles. After delivering repeated warnings, a government inspector ordered the station closed down. Secretary Hoover thereupon received the following telegram from the evangelist:

> PLEASE ORDER YOUR MINIONS OF SATAN TO LEAVE MY STATION ALONE. YOU CANNOT EXPECT THE ALMIGHTY TO ABIDE BY YOUR WAVE-LENGTH NONSENSE. WHEN I OFFER MY PRAYERS TO HIM I MUST FIT INTO HIS WAVE RECEPTION. OPEN THIS STATION AT ONCE. (Hoover 1952: II:142)

Evangelist McPherson, after being persuaded to engage a competent engineer, was allowed to reopen her station.

Source: Photos from UPI/Bettmann Archive.

sent a message to Congress urgently recommending enactment of a proposed new act to regulate broadcasting. As he put it, "the whole service of this most important public function has drifted into such chaos as seems likely, if not remedied, to destroy its great value" (Coolidge, 1926).

1927 Radio Act   The Radio Act of 1927 that followed embodied the recommendations of Hoover's Fourth Radio Conference. By no means a government move to encroach on free enterprise, the 1927 act represented what most of the broadcasters themselves wanted. It provided for a temporary Federal Radio Commission (FRC) to bring order into broadcasting. The problems proved endless, however, and Congress eventually made the commission permanent.

The FRC defined the broadcast band, standardized channel designation by frequency instead of by wavelength, closed portable broadcast transmitters, and reduced the number of stations allowed to operate at night (because AM signals travel father at night, causing cochannel interference).

These and other FRC moves gave investors confidence that broadcasting would not be ruined by uncontrolled mavericks of the airwaves. The passage of the Radio Act of 1927 and the start of continuing FRC supervision meant that the period of stable growth could at last begin.

The Depression Years, 1929–1937   2.7

Shortly after passage of the Radio Act of 1927, the pall of the Great Depression settled on the nation. A third of all American workers lost their jobs. National productivity fell by half. None of the present-day welfare programs existed to cushion the intense suffering caused by unemployment, poverty, and hunger.

Role of Broadcasting   For the first time the number of radio stations on the air actually decreased, as indicated in Exhibit 2.7. Not only the depressed state of business but also the house cleaning done by the FRC accounted for this temporary setback.

In this time of great trial, radio entertainment came as a godsend—the one widely available distraction from the grim realities of the daily struggle to survive. Listener loyalty became almost irrational, according to broadcast historian Erik Barnouw:

> Destitute families, forced to give up on icebox or furniture or bedding, clung to the radio as to a last link of humanity. In consequence, radio, though briefly jolted by the Depression, was soon prospering from it. Motion picture business was suffering, the theater was collapsing, vaudeville was dying, but many of their major talents flocked to radio—along with audiences and sponsors. (Barnouw, 1978: 27)

Roosevelt and Presidential Radio   President Franklin D. Roosevelt, coming into office in 1933, lifted the nation's spirit with a ringing affirmation in his inaugural address: "The only thing we have to fear is fear itself." CBS and NBC broadcast the speech throughout the country. Roosevelt proved to be a master broadcaster, the first national politician to exploit the new medium to its full potential in presidential politics.

EXHIBIT **2.7**   Growth of Radio Stations, 1920–1990

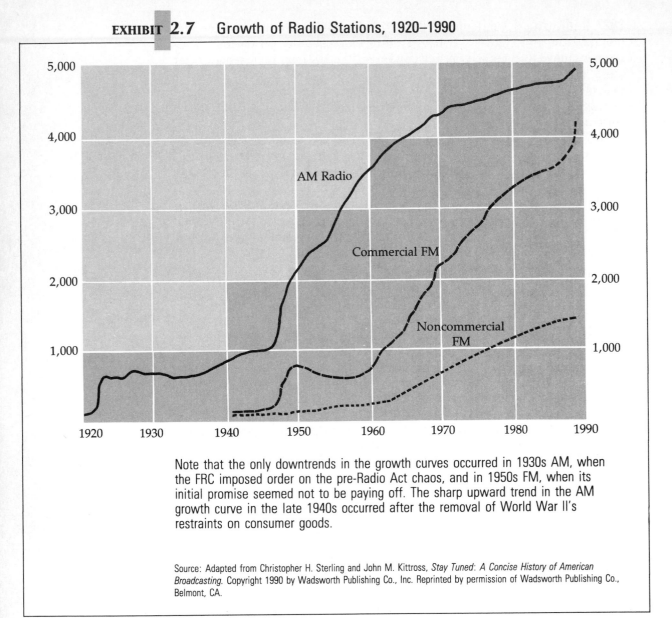

AM Radio

Commercial FM

Noncommercial
FM

Note that the only downtrends in the growth curves occurred in 1930s AM, when the FRC imposed order on the pre-Radio Act chaos, and in 1950s FM, when its initial promise seemed not to be paying off. The sharp upward trend in the AM growth curve in the late 1940s occurred after the removal of World War II's restraints on consumer goods.

Source: Adapted from Christopher H. Sterling and John M. Kittross, *Stay Tuned: A Concise History of American Broadcasting.* Copyright 1990 by Wadsworth Publishing Co., Inc. Reprinted by permission of Wadsworth Publishing Co., Belmont, CA.

Roosevelt's fireside
chats

Soon Roosevelt's distinctive, patrician accent became familiar to every listener who tuned to his *fireside chats,* the term used to suggest the informality, warmth, and directness of these presidential radio reports to the people. It was a brand-new phenomenon in American politics.

Origin of 1934 Communications Act   The Roosevelt administration made a significant impact on the evolution of communication regulation. In 1934, the president sent a message to Congress proposing to eliminate overlapping jurisdictions among several federal agencies that dealt with telegraph, telephone, and radio matters. He urged formation of a single communication authority to pull together related federal responsibilities for regulating both wire and wireless. After making its own study of the situation, Congress passed the law now in place—the Communications Act of 1934.

It created a new regulatory body, the Federal Communications Commission (FCC), one of many agencies set up in the flurry of New Deal government activity. A half-century later, Republican FCC Chair Mark Fowler would dismiss the agency he headed as "the last of the New Deal dinosaurs." He viewed the FCC as an outdated monster created in an earlier age by the rival Democratic party.

FCC: one result of the New Deal

Network Rivalries   During the Depression years, CBS began to chip away at NBC's privileged position as the first network and the subsidiary of powerful RCA, inheritor of both the Telephone and the Radio Groups' prestige and facilities. CBS's leader, William Paley, worked obsessively to lead his upstart network out of NBC's shadow. Big advertisers and star performers automatically selected NBC over CBS when given a choice. It did no good for CBS to build up successful programs: "We were at the mercy of the sponsors and the ad agencies," wrote Paley. "They could always take a successful show away from us and put it on NBC" (Paley, 1979: 174).

NBC vs. CBS

NBC remained a wholly owned RCA subsidiary. RCA itself had grown into a giant, diversified corporation with worldwide interests in communications services and manufacturing. Conscious of its history as the pioneer network, NBC tended to assume the role of a dignified elder among broadcasting organizations.

The Mutual Broadcasting System (MBS) started with a premise different from that of the older networks. In the early 1930s, only two of the major-market clear-channel radio stations remained without network affiliation—WGN–Chicago and WOR–New York. In 1934 the two formed a cooperative network organization with WXYZ–Detroit and WLW–Cincinnati. The four stations pooled some of their own local programs to form the nucleus of a network schedule. Their chief asset at the start, *The Lone Ranger,* had been introduced to the air by WXYZ in 1933.

Mutual Broadcasting System—third radio network

MBS attempts to expand into a national network were frustrated by the fact that stations totaling 98 percent of all nighttime wattage had already committed themselves to NBC or CBS. MBS complained to the FCC about this virtual monopoly of the older networks.

The word *monopoly* was a red flag to the FCC, which charged into an in-depth investigation of network practices. After three years of study, the FCC issued its **Chain Broadcasting Regulations**, so sweeping in scope that NBC and CBS declared that if implemented the new rules would devastate the network business. Basically they aimed at giving network affiliates more control over their airtime and the networks less clout in forcing affiliates to defer to their interests. They will be discussed in detail later.

The outraged networks fought the rules all the way to the Supreme Court, but in 1943 the Court finally settled the argument in favor of the FCC—a watershed ruling affirming the constitutionality of the commission's rule-making powers (US, 1943). NBC had to end its dual network operation, eventually selling the weaker Blue Network, which in 1945 became the American Broadcasting Company (ABC). Under the new regulations, MBS expanded rapidly. Radio's resulting four-network pattern endured until the late 1960s.

ABC is formed from NBC Blue

four-network radio pattern established

<table>
<tr><td>2.8</td><td>

Early Radio Programs

</td></tr>
</table>

As detailed in Section 2.1, early radio drew on familiar sources for program material, especially vaudeville acts, some of which proved readily transferable to the new medium.

Comedy The first network radio entertainment program to achieve addictive popularity was a prime-time, five-days-a-week situation comedy, *Amos 'n' Andy*. Charles Correll ("Andy") and Freeman Gosden ("Amos") came to radio from vaudeville as a typical song-and-patter team.

popularity of Amos 'n' Andy

At a Chicago station manager's suggestion, they tried their luck at a radio-comedy series. The two white performers developed a black dialect show in ghetto English, featuring the ups and downs of the "Fresh Air Taxicab Company of America, Incorpolated."

Amos 'n' Andy became the top network show in the early 1930. Traffic stopped on the main streets of towns across the country and movies halted in midreel at 7 P.M. for the nightly 15 minutes of chuckles over the antics of Amos, Andy, the Kingfish, Lightnin', Madam Queen, and a host of minor characters, most of whom the versatile Correll and Gosden played themselves.

Today the impersonation of blacks by white actors using exaggerated dialect and comedy situations based on ghetto poverty could not be seriously proposed. As early as 1931, a Pittsburgh newspaper asked the FCC to ban the series, alleging racism, but its defenders argued that most blacks seemed to enjoy the program just as much as whites. CBS dropped a television version (with black actors) in 1953 because of opposition by the National Association for the Advancement of Colored People, but the series continued in syndication until 1966.

Music Radio relied heavily on music from its very beginning. In the mid-1930s more than half of all radio programming consisted of music, three-quarters of it carried on a sustaining (non-sponsored) basis. Large stations often had their own live musical groups, and the networks even supported symphony orchestras. In its early years, CBS devoted a quarter of its entire schedule to music. NBC began regular broadcasts of the Metropolitan Opera in 1931.

Metropolitan Opera on the air

Musicians and composers welcomed these new live-performance opportunities, but many stations could afford only recordings. Putting recordings on the air might expose them in a single playing to more listeners than would hear them in live performances over the course of a year. This rapid consumption via radio alarmed musical creators and performers. The musicians' union tried keep recordings of all kinds off the air, and copyright holders demanded heavy payment for performance rights.

musicians' union opposes recorded music on air

Under the copyright law, the playing of a recording in public for profit constitutes a "performance." As such, it obligates the user (in this case the radio station) to pay the copyright holders (who may include composers of the music, lyricists, and music publishers) for performing rights.

Music copyright holders rely on music-licensing organizations to act on their behalf in monitoring performances and collecting copyright fees for the use of both live and recorded music. The first such U.S. organization, the American Society of Composers, Authors, and Publishers (ASCAP), dates back to 1914.

radio and music copyright restrictions

ASCAP, first music licensing society

As early as 1922, ASCAP began making demands for substantial payments by broadcasters for using musical works in its catalog, whether broadcast live or from records. These demands imposed an unexpectedly heavy financial burden. In 1923, station owners and managers formed the National Association of Broadcasters (NAB) to deal with ASCAP's demands on an industry-wide basis.

In 1937, when ASCAP announced yet another fee increase, the broadcasters began a boycott of ASCAP music, later creating their own cooperative music-licensing organization, Broadcast Music, Inc. (BMI). Eventually, BMI built up a comprehensive library representing more than a million musical works owned by some 55,000 publishers and writers. Competition from BMI moderated ASCAP demands, but licensing terms (**blanket licensing** covering the entire ASCAP catalog versus **per-item licensing**, for example) have been a constant source of lawsuits ever since.

broadcasters fight ASCAP with an organization of their own

Recordings The musicians were not the only ones to oppose airing recordings. The radio networks banned recorded programs. At that time *recorded* meant quality inferior to broadcast quality. Moreover, the networks regarded their unique ability to distribute live programs as a major asset.

networks ban use of recorded programs

When radio began, phonographs still used relatively primitive technology. Discs ran at 78 revolutions per minute, allowing time for only three or four minutes on a side. In 1929, broadcasters began using better-quality 16-inch ETs (electrical transcriptions). ETs revolved at 39-1/3 rpm, permitting fifteen minutes to a side. They served for radio-program syndication and for the specially recorded subscription music libraries on which stations then relied.

ET (before it meant extraterrestrial!)

ABC dropped the network recording ban in 1946 in order to lure Bing Crosby away from NBC. The laid-back crooner hated the tension and risks of real-time broadcasting, which were compounded by the need to repeat each live program in New York a second time for the West Coast to compensate for time-zone differences. Crosby himself invested in a then

Bing Crosby's interest in tape recording

little-known company, Ampex, which developed magnetic-tape recorders based on German World War II technology. As soon as broadcast-quality audio-tape recorders became available, ABC agreed to let Crosby break the network ban by recording his weekly prime-time program. Soon the other networks followed ABC's lead.

News News, no less than music, depends both on outside sources of supply and on technology. Most news comes from press associations, or wire services, so called because they first flourished with the telegraph. The newspapers calculated that they could suppress early competition from radio by denying broadcasters access to the major news agencies—at that time the Associated Press (AP), owned cooperatively by newspapers themselves; the International News Service (INS); and the United Press (UP).

NBC inaugurated regular 15-minute nightly newscasts by Lowell Thomas in 1930 on its Blue Network—a sign that radio might soon seriously compete with newspapers. Warned that news-agency services might soon be cut off, CBS began forming its own news-gathering organization. The newspaper publishers, realizing that they could not hold back the tide, proposed a way of limiting the damage in 1933. The result, known as the Biltmore Agreement, set up the Press-Radio Bureau, an agency designed to funnel just enough news to radio to satisfy the broadcasters, but not enough to satisfy the hunger of listeners, who would thus continue to purchase newspapers.

The Press-Radio Bureau never worked effectively. Only about a third of the stations subscribed to it, and several independent radio-news services sprang up to fill the gap. Broadcasters also took advantage of an escape clause in the agreement that exempted news commentaries. Many radio newscasters became instant commentators.

In 1935, the United Press agency broke the embargo on unrestricted release of news to radio, joined soon by International News Service (these two merged to form today's UPI in 1958). The Press-Radio Bureau finally expired, unmourned, in 1940 when the Associated Press began to accept radio stations as members of the association.

The press associations eventually acquired even more broadcasters than publishers as customers. They began offering services especially tailored for broadcast stations, including audio feeds ready to go directly on the air. Central to broadcasting's victory in the "radio war" was the growing strength of the national networks, which were soon to start carrying news of a real war.

2.9 *Radio in World War II, 1939–1945*

The last shackles of the Great Depression fell away only in the late 1930s, when the country began to increase production in response to the growing threat of war in Europe and the Pacific.

During world War II, which the United States joined in 1941, radio escaped direct military censorship by complying voluntarily with common-sense rules. For example, broadcasters avoided live man-on-the-street interviews and weather reports. Radio had a role to play internationally in psychological warfare, and in 1942 President Roosevelt appointed a well-known CBS radio newscaster, Elmer Davis, to head the newly created Office of War Information (OWI). The OWI mobilized an external broadcasting service that eventually became known as the Voice of America, which still broadcasts to foreign countries today.

origin of Voice of America

Radio Drama   Wartime restrictions on civilian manufacturing, imposed in 1942, cut back on station construction and receiver production. Nevertheless, during this period the number of radio stations on the air more than doubled, reaching just over a thousand by the end of 1946 (Exhibit 2.7 shows the growth curve).

Manufacturers of consumer goods devoted their capacity to military needs but continued to advertise their peacetime products to keep their names before the public. The government allowed them to write off these advertising costs as business expenses even though they had no products to sell. The tax break stimulated manufacturers to spend freely. Released from the normal competitive pressures to maximize audiences with sure-fire, mass-appeal material, some advertisers invested in high-quality dramatic programs of a type not previously heard on American radio, though such programs were not uncommon in Europe.

wartime advertising

Radio developed its own playwrights, notably Norman Corwin and Arch Oboler, who won their chief literary fame in broadcasting. CBS commissioned Corwin to celebrate the great moment of Allied victory in Europe with an hour-long radio play, "On a Note of Triumph," in 1945. This emotional program climaxed an extraordinary flowering of radio art—original writing of high merit, produced with consummate skill, and always live, for the networks still banned recordings. With the end of the war years and the artificial wartime support for culture, competitive selling resumed, and this brief, luminous period of radio creativity came to an end.

Arch Oboler and Norman Corwin, legendary radio drama writers

Wartime News   As the threat of European war loomed in the mid-1930s, NBC began developing European news operations to cover rapidly developing events. To counter NBC, Paley decided on a bold CBS stroke—a half-hour of news devoted to a Europe-wide roundup on the 1938 Nazi incursion into Austria, originating live from key points: London, Paris, Rome, Berlin, Vienna.

The networks' ban on the use of recorded material created tremendous problems of coordination and timing for the complex production. But in that historic half-hour, anchored by Robert Trout and featuring reports by William Shirer, Edward R. Murrow (who is shown in Exhibit 2.8), and others, "radio came into its own as a full-fledged news medium" (Kendrick, 1969: 158). Thereafter, on-the-spot radio reporting from Europe became a daily feature of the news.

networks continue ban on use of recordings

EXHIBIT **2.8**   Edward R. Murrow (1908–1965)

CBS news reporter Murrow is seen walking not far from the BBC's Broadcasting House in downtown London during the Second World War. He and other American reporters used a tiny studio located in a subbasement. Once, when the building took a hit during a German bombing raid, Murrow continued his live report as stretcher bearers carried dead and injured victims of the raid past the studio to the first-aid station.

First employed by CBS in 1935 as director of talks in Europe, he came to the notice of a wider public through his memorable live reports from bomb-ravaged London in 1940, and later from even more dangerous war-front vantage points. Unlike other reporters, he had a college degree in speech rather than newspaper or wire-service experience. The British appreciated his realistic and often moving word-and-sound pictures of their wartime experiences, and American listeners liked the way he radiated "truth and concern," as William Paley put it (1979: 151).

Widely admired by the time the war ended, he became the core of the postwar CBS news organization. He served briefly as vice president for news but soon resigned the administrative post to resume daily newscasting. As an on-the-air personality, he survived the transition to television better than others, going on to appear in *See It Now* and in often highly controversial documentaries. He resigned from CBS in the early 1960s to direct the U.S. Information Agency under President Kennedy.

Source: Photo from CBS News.

Later in 1938 came the Munich crisis. The Allies abandoned Czechoslovakia to Hitler, climaxing eighteen days of feverish diplomatic negotiations among the great powers. During these tense days and nights, pioneer commentator H. V. Kaltenborn achieved fame and fortune by extemporizing a remarkable string of 85 live broadcasts from New York, reporting and analyzing news of each diplomatic move in Europe as reports came in by wire and wireless.

H. V. Kaltenborn reports on European war crisis

News staffers at CBS would shake Kaltenborn awake (he slept on a cot in a studio) to hand him the latest bulletin. Going on the air immediately, Kaltenborn first read the bulletin, then ad-libbed his own lucid, informed commentary. "Even as I talked," wrote Kaltenborn, "I was under constant bombardment of fresh news dispatches, carried to my desk from the ticker room. I read and digested them as I talked" (Kaltenborn, 1938: 9).

Thanks to CBS's early start, Paley's enthusiastic support, and his good luck in assembling a superlative staff of news specialists, CBS set a high standard for broadcast journalism during the war years, establishing a tradition of excellence that lasted into the 1980s. Then corporate takeovers and cable competition (discussed in detail later) began to erode the proud standards for broadcast news initiated in those pioneer days.

At this point in radio chronology, television began a spectacular rise that was to profoundly affect radio in the near future. The radio story picks up again in Section 2.13.

Pre-1948 TV Development 2.10

Experimental television existed for decades before television actually became a mass medium. Early television produced crude pictures, interesting only as curiosities. Exhibit 2.9 shows the quality achieved in1929, still far below an acceptable level. Public acceptance awaited pictures with sufficient resolution (detail) and stability (absence of flicker) for comfortable viewing—a standard at least as good as that of the home movies then already familiar to consumers.

Mechanical vs. Electronic Scanning
Inventors sought a way to break down pictures rapidly into thousands of fragments for transmission, bit by bit, and then to reassemble them for viewing. Experimenters tried to perfect a mechanical device, a large, ungainly disc that spun rapidly in front of a light beam. Holes in the disc let light through to scan each picture-frame line by line. In the mid-1930s, mechanical scanning reached a dead end with pictures composed of up to 240 lines per frame. Satisfactory resolution for sustained viewing needed well over 400 lines, a rate that only electronic technology could achieve with the requisite precision.

No single inventor can claim a breakthrough in electronic television such as Marconi achieved with his original radio patent. Television was a corporate rather than an individual achievement. However, two inventors are remembered for solving specific parts of the puzzle—Farnsworth and Zworykin.

Philo T. Farnsworth, a self-taught American genius, devised the **image dissector**—a device for taking pictures apart electronically for bit-by-bit transmission. Though he fell out of the race early, his patents stood up in court and eventually RCA, the corporate leader in American television development, had to secure licenses from him for its own system.

Vladimir Zworykin immigrated from Russia in 1919 and worked as an engineer for Westinghouse. In 1923, he invented the **iconoscope**—the first

(margin notes)

CBS pre-eminance in broadcast journalism

mechanical TV scanning reaches dead end

Farnsworth, pioneer TV inventor

Zworykin invents TV pickup tube

EXHIBIT **2.9** First U.S. TV Star

During the early experiments with electronic television, RCA laboratories used, as a moving object to televise, a 12-inch papier mâché model of a popular cartoon character, Felix the Cat, posed on a revolving turntable under hot lights. The image at left shows how Felix looked on television in 1929 when picture definition was still only 60 lines per frame.

Source: Photos courtesy NBC.

electronic camera pickup tube suitable for studio operations (shown in Exhibit 4.9).

David Sarnoff put RCA's enormous resources behind the drive to perfect television as early as 1930. Exhibit 2.9 shows an early RCA experimental setup. Sarnoff hired Zworykin in 1930 to head a celebrated research group at the RCA laboratories in Camden, New Jersey. Entrusted with the task of producing a marketable television system, the Camden team systematically investigated all aspects of electronic television development. It tackled not only the technological problems but also the subjective problem of discovering the picture-quality standards needed to win full public acceptance.

TV Goes Public   It took the Camden researchers nearly a decade to attain 441-line resolution, which was deemed adequate for a full-dress public demonstration. Sarnoff chose the 1939 New York World's Fair, with its "World of Tomorrow" theme, as a suitably prestigious and symbolic showcase for the RCA electronic television demonstration. For the first time the general public in America had a chance to see (and to be seen in) electronically generated moving pictures.

1939 World's Fair TV demonstration

The 1939 demonstration stimulated enormous interest, but industry-wide agreement on engineering standards did not come until 1941, when the FCC decided to adopt a black-and-white standard, postponing the color issue. It accepted the National Television System Committee (NTSC) recommendations, which upped the line frequency to 525 per frame at 30 frames per second—the standards still in effect in American television today.

NTSC TV black-and-white standards adopted

Within the year, however, war against Japan and Germany halted production of civilian consumer electronics. Further development of civilian television had to be shelved for the duration. During World War II six experimental stations remained on the air—two in New York City and one each in Schenectady, Philadelphia, Chicago, and Los Angeles. They devoted their four hours of airtime a week primarily to civilian defense programs. About 10,000 receivers existed, half of them in New York City.

TV's role in World War II

The end of the war in 1945 did not, as some expected, bring an immediate upsurge in television activity, despite a backlog of 158 pending station applications. Many experts believed that all-out development should await adoption of a color system. Moreover, potential investors wondered whether the public would buy receivers that cost many times the price of radios.

Nevertheless, progress behind the scenes resumed. In 1945 the *image orthicon tube* began to come into use. It improved camera sensitivity and eliminated the need for the uncomfortably high levels of studio light that the ionoscope had required. In 1946, AT&T opened its first intercity **coaxial-cable** link, between New York and Washington, DC, enabling the start of live network interconnection. Finally, in the summer and fall of 1948, the long-anticipated television gold rush erupted.

first coaxial cable link enables first network TV

Growing Pains: Channels, Color, Networks 2.11

Thus 1948 became the critical turning point in American television history, the transition from the experimental phase to the mass-medium phase. By that year, the number of television stations on the air had increased to 48. The number of cities served by television reached 23. The audience grew in one year by an astonishing 4,000 percent. Regular network service to a few cities began. Major advertisers started experimenting with the new medium, and top-drawer programs were launched. However, television's growing pains had still not quite ended; the list of things to be done included increasing the number of channels available, adopting a color system, and establishing full-scale national networks.

1948: start of TV's golden era

The Freeze   In giving the initial go-ahead for commercial television in 1941, the FCC had made available only 13 channels (later reduced to 12) to serve the entire United States—compared with 107 AM channels and 100 FM channels. As more and more stations began to go on the air, it became obvious that the demand for stations would soon exceed the supply of channels. Moreover, miscalculation of the distance needed to separate stations assigned to the same channel resulted in serious cochannel interference.

prefreeze stations enjoy monopoly

In September 1948 the FCC abruptly froze the further processing of television-license applications pending solution of these problems. The freeze had no effect on applicants whose permits had already been approved. For the nearly four years of the freeze, 108 prefreeze stations enjoyed an enviable monopoly.

The FCC held a long-drawn-out series of hearings to settle the engineering and policy questions that had brought on the freeze. The much-anticipated decision, the basic charter of present-day American television, came on 14 April 1952 in the FCC's historic **Sixth Report and Order** (FCCR, 1952).

UHF TV channels allocated

The new rules supplemented the 12 VHF (very-high-frequency) channels with 70 new channels. In order to find room in the spectrum for this addition, the FCC had to use a block of frequencies in the UHF (ultra-high-frequency) band, numbering the channels 14 and up. The use of this much higher range of frequencies had been developed for radar detection during World War II. Exhibit 4.12 summarizes the current channel numbers and their locations in the spectrum, showing how the FCC had to use four separate bands of frequencies to get sufficient spectrum space.

channels distributed by means of allotment table

Channel-Allotment Plan   An allotment table, providing for a maximum of 2,053 stations, awarded the use of one or more channels to each of 1,291 communities (the prefreeze plan had allotted channels to only 345 cities). More than 66 percent of the allotments fell in the UHF band. The FCC reserved about 10 percent (later increased to 35 percent) of the total for noncommercial educational use, mostly in the UHF band.

Exhibit 2.10 gives an example of how the allotment table separates stations on the same channel throughout the country, spacing them to avoid cochannel interference.

The number of stations more than tripled in the first postfreeze year, as shown in Exhibit 2.11. Nevertheless, the new channel-allotment plan had serious defects. For one thing, there were still too few channels to give viewers in every market an equivalent range of choices. Some had only one channel, some two or three, and so on. Viewers in any given market needed access to at least five channels to have the option of choosing among the three networks, an independent station, and a public station.

UHF Problem   The FCC's decision to intermix VHF and UHF allotments in many localities put UHF stations in such markets at a serious disadvantage. UHF waves have an inherent propagation weakness as compared to VHF waves. The commission had tried to ensure equal coverage potentials for both

EXHIBIT **2.10**   Station Separation: Sample TV-Channel Allotment

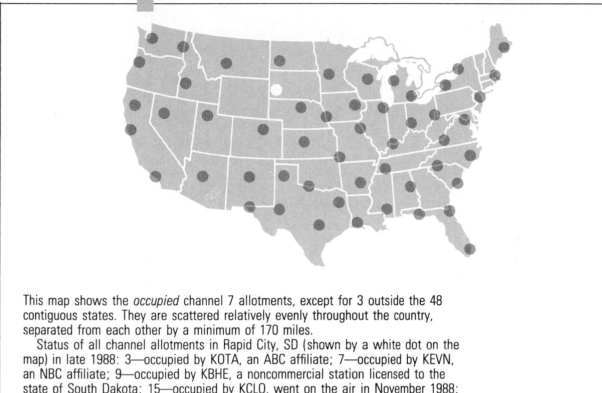

This map shows the *occupied* channel 7 allotments, except for 3 outside the 48 contiguous states. They are scattered relatively evenly throughout the country, separated from each other by a minimum of 170 miles.

Status of all channel allotments in Rapid City, SD (shown by a white dot on the map) in late 1988: 3—occupied by KOTA, an ABC affiliate; 7—occupied by KEVN, an NBC affiliate; 9—occupied by KBHE, a noncommercial station licensed to the state of South Dakota; 15—occupied by KCLO, went on the air in November 1988; 21—not on the air.

VHF and UHF stations by authorizing UHF to use higher power. Even if added power could have had the desired effect, however, years would pass before maximum-power UHF transmitters became available. And long after UHF television began, set manufacturers still built VHF-only receivers, forcing viewers in markets with UHF stations to buy difficult-to-use UHF converters.

intermixture of VHF/UHF channels puts UHF at a disadvantage

Faced with overwhelming disadvantages, UHF television began to slip backward, reaching a low point of only 75 stations in 1960. The FCC tried a variety of measures to encourage the failing UHF stations. Its most useful step came in 1962, when it persuaded Congress to amend the Communications Act so that the FCC could require manufacturers to equip all receivers with built-in UHF tuners.

all-wave TV receivers aid UHF development

By 1965, some of the FCC's efforts had taken effect. UHF began a steady, though not spectacular, growth. FCC financial reports indicate that until 1974 UHF stations as a group continued to lose money. Thereafter their average profit margin increased over each year. In mid-1990, 550 UHF and 549 VHF commercial stations were on the air.

EXHIBIT **2.11**   Growth of TV Stations, 1948–1988

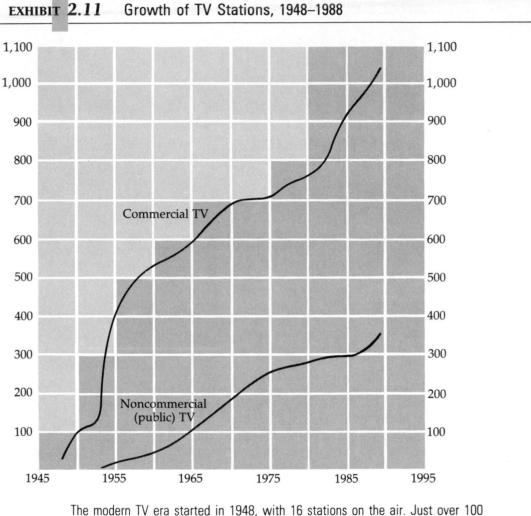

The modern TV era started in 1948, with 16 stations on the air. Just over 100 stations had been authorized when the 1948–1952 freeze imposed a temporary ceiling. After that the number shot up, reaching 400 by 1955. Growth began to slow down at that point but has never actually stopped. Noncommercial stations developed more slowly, starting with the first two in 1954.

Source: Adapted from Christopher H. Sterling and John M. Kittross, *Stay Tuned: A Concise History of American Broadcasting.* Copyright 1990 by Wadsworth Publishing Co., Inc. Reprinted by permission of Wadsworth Publishing Co., Belmont, CA.

At best, however, UHF stations can achieve only 80 to 85 percent of the coverage enjoyed by competing VHF stations. UHF proponents still hope that improved receivers and antennas—as well as carriage of UHF stations on cable television—will someday equalize coverage with VHF except in areas of rough terrain and in cities with many tall buildings.

Despite the addition of the UHF channels and efforts at improving the viability of stations that use them, the *Sixth Report and Order* saddled the television industry with long-term problems. The frustration of viewers who wanted more varied program options than the allotment table made possible led ultimately to the development of cable television and other substitutes for over-the-air reception from stations.

viewer demand for more program options encourages cable

Color TV   Another technical problem lingered after the 1948 turning point. CBS and RCA/NBC wrangled over the postponed issue of color. CBS promoted a partly mechanical system, RCA an all-electronic system. Finally, in 1953 all parties agreed to another NTSC proposal, an electronic system patterned closely on RCA's. An important argument in its favor was that it had **compatibility**—black-and-white sets already in use could pick up the newly approved color signals and display them in monochrome.

NTSC color-TV standard adopted

However, color telecasts on a large scale developed slowly. Five years after the 1953 adoption of the NTSC standards, only NBC offered programs in color. Full network color production in prime time came finally in 1966. By 1972, nearly two decades after adoption of color standards, only half of the country's homes had color television sets. Today, however, manufacturers make only color sets, except for small black-and-white portables.

TV Relays   Full-scale live-television network operations had to await completion of AT&T's coaxial-cable relay links, which joined the East and West Coasts in 1951. Until the cable reached them, affiliates had to use **kinescopes** of network shows—films of television programs photographed as they were displayed on the face of a receiver tube.

Kinescope recordings of network programs had become available in 1948, but their poor quality discouraged their use. In 1956 the Ampex Corporation demonstrated a successful videotape recorder, which saw its first practical use that fall on CBS. In a rare spirit of cooperation, competing manufacturers put aside their rivalries and opted for a compatible professional videotape standard initially. **Videotape** brought an end to the era of live production, as related in Section 2.12.

Ampex develops videotape

Ceiling on Networks   The FCC's 1952 *Sixth Report and Order* tended to limit television to three national networks. It left too few cities with four channels to allow a fourth network to compete nationally on an even footing. Even if independent commercial stations in every market combined to form a fourth network, it would be able to reach only about 85 percent of the population, whereas ABC, CBS, and NBC each can reach more than 95 percent of television homes.

Nevertheless, there have always been pressures to create a fourth national television network. MBS, the fourth radio network, lacked the money to branch into television, but from 1946 to 1955 a fourth chain did exist—Du Mont Television Network. It was founded by Allen B. Du Mont, notable for development of the cathode-ray tube, one form of which is used as the display

Du Mont as fleeting fourth TV network

tube in video monitors and receivers. Du Mont also pioneered in the man-ufacture of early television sets.

Fox makes another attempt for a fourth network

The Du Mont network survived only as long as lack of interconnection facilities kept networking in check. Once interconnection relays became gen-erally available, Du Mont could not sign up sufficient affiliates to compete with the larger, older and richer networks. (The Fox Broadcasting Company's effort at mounting a fourth network is discussed in Section 3.10.)

2.12 *Golden Age of TV Programs, 1948–1957*

If we look back with nostalgia to radio's "golden era" of the 1930s and 1940s, we may justifiably feel the same way about television's first decade as a mass medium, 1948 to1957.

Programs as Motivators In that decade, the networks put first priority on stimulating people to buy sets. Only attractive programs could do that:

> It was the only time in the history of the medium that program priorities superseded all others. If there was an abundance of original and quality drama at the time . . . it was in large part because those shows tended to appeal to a wealthier and better-educated part of the public, the part best able to afford a television set in those years when the price of receivers was high. (Brown, 1971: 154)

live TV drama in pre-videotape era

Most programs, local and network, were necessarily live—a throwback to the earliest days of radio. Videotape recording had not yet been invented. Original television plays constituted the most memorable artistic achieve-ments of television's live decade. "Talent seemed to gush right out of the cement," wrote the pioneer *New York Times* critic, Jack Gould (1973: 6).

TV vs. Hollywood Television programs could, of course, have been re-corded from the very beginning by photographing them originally on motion-picture film. Economic, technical, and industrial barriers delayed adoption of this solution. Hollywood's traditional single-camera method of production is slow and cumbersome, costing far too much for general television use; and it took time to adapt film production to the physical limitations of television, with its lower resolution, its smaller projected-picture area, and its more restricted range of contrast.

Moreover, idealists opposed the use of film, counting on television to escape the Hollywood straitjacket and to bring about a new, less trite mass-enter-tainment genre. The two points of view stood as far apart as their two centers— television in New York and film in Los Angeles. But the economics of the motion-picture and television industries drove them ever closer together. Inexorably, as the technical barriers to producing television programs on film fell and as Hollywood accepted the use of videotape, the production base for entertainment programs shifted to the West Coast.

In the 1956–1957 season, 63 percent of all network programs still came from New York, nearly all of them live. Most production on the West Coast was done on film. In 1958 NBC moved *Studio One,* for a decade the most prestigious of the New York live-television-drama series, to Hollywood. It died within months, marking the end of television's live decade.

closedown of *Studio One* ends live TV era

Hollywood's old-line feature-film producers saw television as a threat, much as newspaper publishers had feared that radio would undermine the news business. Producers and distributors refused to release their best and most recent feature films to television for a dozen years. Only pre-1948 films could be shown on television. The 1948 cutoff date signified the year in which feature-film production contracts began to contain restrictive clauses prohibiting future release to television.

only pre-1948 films first available for TV

Not until the early 1960s did Hollywood conclude that the television bane could also be a boon. Movie producers realized they need not fear that audiences would stop buying tickets at the box office just because they could see theatrical features on television. Moreover, networks were ready to pay substantial fees to show "post-48" films—product that in most cases had little or no residual value for theatrical release. In the end, feature-film producers found they could profit not only from theatrical release but also from delayed release to cable television and the VCR market as well as broadcasting.

Pat Weaver's Innovations

In terms of television's own program formats, many of the seminal program ideas of the first decade sprang from the fertile imagination of Sylvester "Pat" Weaver. He became NBC's vice president for television in 1949, leaving NBC six years later as board chair.

For example, disregarding conventional wisdom about not disturbing established viewing habits, Weaver occasionally canceled regularly scheduled shows to run one-time **spectaculars**, 90 minutes long. The other networks refused to take such risks at first, but eventually Weaver's spectaculars became common practice on all networks as **specials**.

Weaver foresaw that the single-sponsor show, the hallmark of big-time network radio, simply could not last in prime-time television. Program costs would eventually become far too high for single advertisers to afford full sponsorship. Instead, Weaver introduced **segmented sponsorship**, which enabled a number of different advertisers to share the spotlight in a single program. He also introduced the **magazine format**, which combines a number of separate features within a single, unifying program framework. The morning show *Today,* for example, survives as testimony to Weaver's lasting impact.

origin of *Today* show

Network Rivalries

Despite Weaver's success with specific NBC innovations, CBS steadily gained in the overall ratings race. In consequence, NBC let Weaver go in 1955. That same year, CBS achieved the number-one place in the ratings, a rank it would hold undisputed for 21 years.

Meanwhile, the third network, ABC, found itself in somewhat the same position that CBS had occupied in the early days of network radio. Top advertisers and performers automatically chose CBS or NBC, turning to ABC

ABC struggles to succeed in TV

only as a last resort. A government-decreed corporate breakup helped rescue ABC in 1953. When a Justice Department antitrust suit against the big Hollywood motion-picture studios forced them to sell off their expensive theater chains, one of the spun-off companies, Paramount Theaters, merged with ABC in 1953. Paramount injected much-needed funds and established a link with Hollywood that eventually paid off handsomely, helping ABC to achieve equal status with CBS and NBC.

Paramount Theaters and ABC merge

In 1954, Walt Disney, the first of the major studio leaders to make a deal with television, agreed to produce a series of programs for ABC called *Disneyland* (1954–1957), later continued on NBC under various titles until it was finally dropped in 1981. The deal gave Disney free television promotion for his California theme park (just then opening) as well as for Disney feature films. ABC acquired in turn a unique program feature that tapped the best of Hollywood's expertise. Disney went on in later years to become a primary program source for both broadcast and cable television programs.

Disney breaks the TV barrier

In search of a new and different image, ABC later began to pay special attention to audience demographics, tailoring prime-time shows to target young, urban, adult viewers. Less concerned with the older networks' traditional concern for program balance, ABC leaned heavily on action, sex, and violence in most of its prime-time programming.

2.13 *Radio's Response*

Television's takeoff year, 1948, marked both a high-water mark and the beginning of the end for full-service network radio. In that year, radio networks grossed more revenue than ever before or since, excluding profits from their owned and operated stations. For more than 15 years, the four networks had dominated radio broadcasting, but television was about to end their rule.

Four-Network Pattern By 1948, MBS, the network whose complaints against CBS and NBC had precipitated the chain broadcasting investigation, had more than 500 radio affiliates and advertised itself as "the world's largest network." However, these numbers meant little because most MBS affiliates were located outside the major urban centers and operated on low power. The entire history of the Mutual Broadcasting System has been marked by frequent changes in ownership. During a four-year period in the 1950s its ownership changed six times.

MBS fails to develop TV network

For the types of full-service network programming that prevailed in the pre-television era, four radio networks seemed the maximum the traffic would bear. The four supplied their affiliates a full schedule of varied programs, much as the major television networks do today. Now radio networks by the dozen are possible not only because there are more stations but also because each contemporary network provides only a narrow range of programs.

radio networks adapt to radio-station formats

Sponsorship of the major radio-network programs and stars hastened the decline in radio-network fortunes after 1948. As television captured the mass audience, it lured away major radio advertisers and with them went the star performers and their programs. By the early 1950s, the complacent pre-television days had ended. William Paley, who led CBS through this transition, recalled, "Although [CBS's radio] daytime schedule was more than 90 percent sponsored, our prime-time evening shows were more than 80 percent sustaining. Even our greatest stars could not stop the rush to television" (Paley, 1979: 227).

sponsorship undermines radio networks

The ultimate blow came when radio stations actually began refusing to renew network contracts—a startling change, considering that previously a network affiliation had always been regarded as a precious asset. But program commitments to the networks interfered with the freedom to put new, tailor-made, post-television radio-program formulas into effect. By the early 1960s, only a third of the radio stations had network affiliations. Networks scaled down their services to brief hourly news bulletins, short information features, a few public-affairs programs, and occasional on-the-spot sports events.

radio networks adapt to radio-station formats

Rock to the Rescue   With the loss of network dramas, variety shows, and quiz games, radio programming shrank essentially to music and news/talk, with music occupying by far the majority of the time on most stations. Providentially for radio, this programming transition coincided with the rise of a new musical culture, one that found radio an ideally hospitable medium.

Early in the 1950s, a Cleveland disc jockey, Alan Freed, gained national recognition by

> playing a strange new sound. A sound that combined elements of gospel, harmony, rhythm, blues, and country. He called it "rock and roll." And people everywhere began to listen. . . . It transcended borders and races. . . . Rock and roll sang to the teenager; it charted his habits, his hobbies, his hang-ups. (Drake-Chenault Enterprises, 1978: 1)

Radio proved to be the perfect outlet for this new form of expression. In the 1960s, rock lyrics spread the slogans of the disenchanted and the disestablished in a coded language, in defiance of the conventional, conservative standards that broadcasting leadership had previously sought to maintain.

Radio's programming answer to television came in the late 1950s—the **Top-40 format**. The name referred to the practice of rigidly limiting DJs to a prescribed playlist of current best-selling popular recordings. Top-40 specialists frequently reprogrammed bottom-ranked stations and lifted them to the top rank in their markets in a matter of months.

playlist governs radio music scheduling

Paradoxically, the spectacular success of the Top-40 formula came as much from its ruthlessness in repelling listeners as from its skillfulness in attracting them. Formula programmers relied on consistency above all else; they programmed relentlessly for their target audience, no matter how many other segments of the audience took offense. In the early days this often meant junking old programs that had been attracting audiences for years. Listeners complained, but program elements that violated the formula had to go.

A second ingredient in Top-40 success was an equally single-minded dedication to ceaseless promotion and advertising. Call letters and dial position had to be indelibly imprinted on the listener's mind, usually by endless repetition and promotional gimmicks.

FM's Rise to Dominance

Radio's renewed focus on music brought FM to the fore. In its first quarter-century, the word *broadcasting* simply meant AM radio. In 1933, Edwin Armstrong had invented a much-improved alternative method of audio transmission using **frequency modulation** (**FM**), but for almost 30 years it languished as a poor relation of the established AM system. At the close of World War II the FCC gave FM a further setback by moving it from its prewar channels to its present location at 88 to 108 MHz, in the VHF band. This 1945 move made obsolete the half-million FM receivers that had been built to work on lower frequencies.

Early interest in FM stations, mostly as minor partners in AM/FM combinations, peaked in 1948, with more than a thousand stations authorized. But in that year television's rapid climb to power began, pushing FM into the background. In 1949 alone, 212 commercial FM stations went off the air, and total authorizations continued to decline until 1958, as shown in Exhibit 2.7. In that year, FM began to recover from its decade-long slide. Its revival came not only from greater audience interest in its improved sound quality but also from the lack of spectrum space for new AM stations and from a new pro-FM FCC policy.

For example, in 1961, the FCC approved technical standards for FM stereophonic sound. In 1965–1967 it adopted the **nonduplication rule**, which required AM/FM owners, first in major markets and then in smaller markets, to start programming their FM stations independently of AM sister stations. These measures proved effective in moving FM out of the AM shadow and gave FM status as an independent service with its own format specializations. Increased listener interest galvanized manufacturers into making FM receivers more widely available. By 1974 the majority of sets had FM, and two years later so did most car radios. By the 1980s a reverse trend had set in: some radios were marketed with FM-only tuning.

Whereas the FCC had helped FM by adopting an official standard for stereophonic transmission, it hindered AM by refusing to stipulate which of several AM-stereo systems should be adopted (details of this regulatory turnabout are found in Chapter 12). As the 1990s began, the AM segment of the industry had its back to the wall, and both the FCC and AM broadcasters were scrambling for solutions. AM was blamed for abandoning music formats to FM; for neglecting to push through technical improvements that could minimize interference, improve quality, and achieve stereophonic sound; and for reacting to FM competition with copycat programming strategies.

During the 1970s and beyond, television broadcasting, too, found itself backed into a corner. The next chapter deals with the era of new competition that threatened to undermine the entire broadcasting industry in its traditional form.

Era of New Competition: 1970s and 1980s

Rival program-delivery services started gathering momentum in the late 1970s. They posed unprecedented challenges to the traditional radio and television broadcasting services that had evolved over the previous half-century. The new services responded to a seemingly insatiable public appetite for more listening and viewing choices.

business, and regulatory innovations that stimulated these developments:

- Cable television began as an extender of existing broadcasting-station coverage areas in the 1940s. By the 1960s it started to take on a life of its own, expanding its program offerings with some original programs and pay television. By the 1980s, most American viewers received their programs by cable instead of directly over the air from broadcast transmitters.
- The 1959 invention of the integrated computer chip led to a new generation of sophisticated electronic consumer products.
- In 1975, home videocassette recorders went on sale.
- In the same year, HBO announced plans to distribute its pay-cable network programs to cable systems via satellite.
- By 1979–1980, FM radio had overtaken the original broadcast medium, AM radio. AM began a steady decline. Only recently did the Federal Communications Commission and the industry take positive measures to halt AM's downward slide.
- In that same season began another decline, that of the prime-time broadcast television audience. Cable and other optional program sources steadily eroded the near-monopoly of the once invincible ABC/CBS/NBC network triumvirate.
- During the 1980s, all these trends received the blessing of the Federal Communications Commission. Formerly, the FCC had acted as broadcasting's shield against new competition. But the FCC of the 1980s adopted a policy of minimum regulation. It encouraged new services, making it easy for them to get a foothold in the market with minimum government regulation.

3.1

3.1 *Community Antenna TV*

Broadcasting's most damaging competitor emerged from harmless attempts to improve television-station coverage.

Translators The television channel-allotment plan set forth in 1952 by the FCC in its *Sixth Report and Order,* as described in Section 2.11, left many white areas of the national coverage map—places where people could not receive television service. Even in large population centers viewers could get only eight to ten channels. Most people received three or four. As television became more nearly universal, it began to be regarded as a virtual necessity.

"white areas" left by TV allotment plan

At first, low-power **repeater transmitters** met some of the demand for service. They extended station coverage into fringe reception areas and into dark pockets cut off from normal reception by mountain ranges. The most common type of repeater, the **translator**, operates on a different channel from the originating station so as not to interfere with the originating station's signal. More than 5,000 translators were in operation by 1990.

Community Antennas Another signal-extender, **community antenna television (CATV)**, originally worked something like a translator, repeating the signal of a single station. Instead of propagating signals over the air to everyone in the coverage area, however, a CATV system delivers them by wire to individual subscribers. A CATV system using **wide band cable** can deliver signals from *several stations*, outdoing translators by giving eager subscribers a range of program choices.

CATV systems began appearing in 1949, almost as soon as regular broadcast television began. Community antennas on hilltops or on high towers, not affordable by the average viewer, obtained unobstructed line-of-sight signal paths to originating stations.

During their first decade, CATV systems remained primarily a local concern. Municipal governments granted cable operators franchises, permitting them to reach their subscribers by stringing cables on utility poles along public rights of way. Early multiple-channel cable systems carried only five or six channels, devoted solely to nearby television stations. Most systems served from a few dozen to a few hundred subscribers.

cable TV authorized by local franchises

Broadcasting welcomed CATV as long as it simply filled in unserved areas, beefed up fringe reception, and overcame local interference. Some stations eventually found their signals carried by dozens of cable systems that substantially enlarged their audiences.

Program Augmentation CATV operators soon realized that they could make their services more attractive and could charge higher subscription rates at little added cost by expanding their services beyond simply delivering programs from nearby television stations. Once installed, cables could easily carry additional program services. Cable operators therefore began to augment their services by using microwave relays to import signals from distant stations and even to originate their own programs locally. Such augmentation represented a fundamental change from CATV's original role.

program importation and local origination

By the mid-1960s, broadcasters began to see augmented CATV more as a dangerous predator than as a benign extender of their audience coverage. The growing practice of importing signals from distant cities tended to obliterate the normally fixed boundaries of broadcast markets. A network affiliate might find its programs duplicated in its own viewing area by a cable-delivered distant station affiliated with the same network but located in a different market.

This blurring of coverage boundaries undermined the concept of market exclusivity, under which broadcast programs had usually been sold. Program duplication added to CATV's tendency to fragment audiences, leaving broadcast stations with lower ratings and thus less appeal for advertisers.

Cable Regulation As cable's economic impact on broadcasting grew, the FCC began to intervene with protectionist rules. In 1962, the commission began using its power to license microwave relays as a justification for

FCC protects broadcast TV from cable TV inroads

regulating cable systems that imported signals from distant stations. Four years later, it extended regulation to all cable systems, beginning a brief period of pervasive control of cable.

The FCC soon required cable systems to carry all television stations in their systems' areas of coverage (the **must-carry rule**) and to refrain from duplicating network programs on the same day a network offered them. No new signals could be imported into any of the top 100 markets without a hearing on the probable economic effect existing broadcast stations might suffer. In 1968, the Supreme Court upheld this FCC intervention (US, 1968a).

As to cable-originated programs, broadcasters feared that networks of cable systems might outbid them for transmission rights to popular programs such as major sports events. They spread scare stories about **program siphoning**—the draining away of hitherto "free" broadcast programs to cable. Broadcasters warned that fans might have to start paying to receive Major League baseball. They also claimed that network news and local public-service programs would suffer if cable cut deeper into broadcast revenues.

definitive cable
regulations

Such tactics resulted in the FCC's so-called definitive cable regulations of 1972 (FCCR, 1972b). These rules severely restricted the type and number of signals that cable could bring into the largest cities. And cable operators had to provide, on request, **access channels** for local governments, educational institutions, and the general public.

Cable Deregulation   Only five years after the 1972 "definitive" rules appeared, however, an appeals court held that the FCC "in no way justified its position that cable television must be a supplement to, rather than an equal of, broadcast television" (F, 1977d:36).

cable regulation
stabilized by Cable Act
of 1984

This rebuff, plus a change in administration at the White House (and consequently in the FCC chair), led the FCC to reconsider. It began to remove itself step by step from cable regulation, eventually returning cable to the unregulated state in which it began, as detailed in Exhibit 12.9. The resulting vacuum gave Congress an open invitation to step in with new legislation. Eventually it did so, amending the Communications Act of 1934 with the Cable Communications Policy Act of 1984, which is discussed in detail in Section 12.10.

3.2   *From CATV to Cable TV*

As program augmentation grew and cable shed its regulatory constraints, CATV began to emerge as a full-fledged competitor for the broadcast audience. Exhibit 3.1 depicts the growth of cable. As the medium matured, the term *CATV* faded out (though it is still used in Europe) and the term *cable television* took over. The transformation of CATV into cable television depended not only on deregulation but also on the use of satellite relays.

EXHIBIT 3.1 Cable TV Growth Indicators, 1960–1990

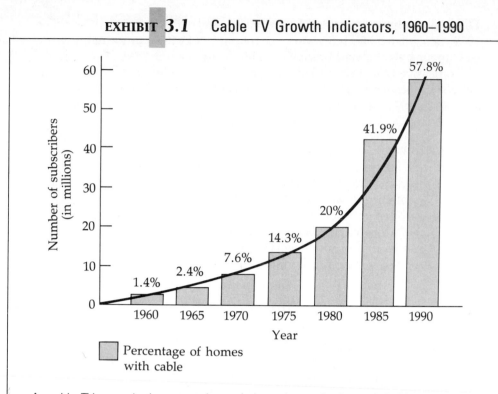

As cable TV grew, both system size and channel capacity increased. After 1975, pay cable spurred basic cable growth.

Sources: Christopher H. Sterling, *Electronic Media: A Guide to Trends in Broadcasting and Newer Technologies, 1920–1983* (Praeger Publishers, New York, 1984) pp. 28, 30. Copyright © 1984 by Christopher H. Sterling. Reprinted and adapted with permission of Praeger Publishers; 1985 and 1990 data from Warren Publishing, citing *Television and Cable Factbook*.

Domsat Relays   In the 1960s, *international* communication satellites came into use for broadcast relays, enabling television to bring foreign events to the television screen instantaneously. The demand for **domestic satellites (domsats)**—space stations designed for relaying programs *within* the country—was less insistent because a well-developed national system of microwave and coaxial-cable relays already existed.

But in 1972, a key FCC deregulatory move stimulated demand for domsats. The commission adopted an **open-skies policy**. It allowed any adequately financed and technically qualified business firm to launch satellites for domestic use (FCCR, 1972a).

Western Union's Westar I became the first American domsat in 1974. Such satellites operate as **common carriers**—point-to-point, rate-regulated communication services. They lease or sell satellite relay services, either to program distributors or to brokers who resell short-term access to users such as television-station news departments.

TVRO Antennas A second key satellite-related FCC decision, issued in 1979, deregulated the **television receive-only (TVRO) antennas**, used to pick up programs relayed by satellite. This decision eliminated a cumbersome and expensive licensing process, opening the way to widespread satellite use for relaying program services to cable systems—and soon to broadcast stations as well. In 1977, fewer than 200 cable systems had their own TVROs, but within a decade some 8,000 systems had them.

Superstations Domsats and TVROs thus gave cable systems a relatively efficient and inexpensive way of obtaining nationally distributed program services with which to attract new subscribers. However, the programs themselves still remained in short supply. Ted Turner, an innovative entrepreneur who disdained the traditional broadcast networks and had an almost mystical faith in cable's future, addressed himself to this problem. He invented the **superstation** as one way of relieving the shortage of cable programs. His colorful career as a maverick entrepreneur is outlined in Exhibit 3.2.

EXHIBIT 3.2   Ted Turner: "Captain Outrageous"

Ted Turner, board chair and president of Turner Broadcasting Systems (TBS), founded SuperStation WTBS, Cable News Network, Headline News, Turner Network Television (TNT, a satellite-to-cable program network), Turner Program Services, and two professional sports teams—the Atlanta Braves (baseball) and Atlanta Hawks (basketball).

Referred to variously as "Terrible Ted," "Captain Outrageous," and "The Mouth of the South," Turner is known for outspoken opinions, willingness to challenge the establishment, aggressive and entrepreneurial spirit ("Lead, follow, or get out of the way"), driving ambition ("My desire to excel borders on the unhealthy"), and ego (he once told an interviewer, "If I only had a little humility, I'd be perfect"). Physically, he is the prototype of the southern gentleman: tall, lanky, with silver-streaked hair and mustache, cigar-smoking, speaking with a

EXHIBIT **3.2** Continued

Georgia drawl. He loves the movie *Gone With the Wind* so much he named one of his five children Rhett.

Turner attended Brown University, where he was vice president of the Debating Union and commodore of the Brown Yacht Club. College yachting experience served him in good stead in 1977, when he won the prestigious America's Cup race. Brown threw him out of college twice and his fraternity once dropped him for burning down its homecoming display.

Turner began his business career as an account executive with his father's advertising company in Savannah, later joining the company's office in Macon, GA, as general manager. In 1963, he became chief executive officer of the various Turner companies with headquarters in Atlanta. His interest in broadcasting began with his 1970 acquisition of Atlanta's channel 17, then a failing independent operation. There he dreamed up the superstation concept six years later. The station beams its signal by satellite-to-cable relays, making its programs nationally available to millions of viewers.

On 1 June 1980, Turner launched Cable News Network (CNN), the first live, 24-hour-a-day, all-news cable network. Skeptics dubbed it the "Chicken Noodle Network", but by 1988 over 8,000 cable systems carried CNN to a potential 40 million homes. Millions more see it in over 50 foreign countries, and Turner modestly aims to blanket the entire globe. In 1981, Turner began a second cable-news service, now called Headline News, a continuously updated 30-minute cycle of hard news carried both by cable systems and by some television stations. In 1982, he formed CNN Radio, a 24-hour all-news cable network.

In 1984, Turner stumbled when he tried to compete with Music Television (MTV). His Cable Music Channel lasted only 36 days. MTV bought some of its assets for about $1 million plus free advertising on Turner's other cable services.

His biggest battle came in 1985 when he tried to take over the CBS broadcast network. Although he lost that fight, he came up within a year as the new owner of MGM's film library, including his beloved *Gone With the Wind* for use on his superstation and the projected TNT cable network. The purchase pushed TBS deeply into debt, forcing Turner to accept a consortium of large cable-system operators as partners. They received positions on his board of directors in return for their investment in TBS. Three years later he scheduled *Gone With the Wind* for the October 1988 debut of Turner Network Television (TNT). He promoted TNT as the first cable network designed expressly to challenge the three broadcast networks. Initially able to reach about 17 million homes, the service offered mostly movies but promised 200 original programs a year by 1992. Early projects included *The Story of Billy the Kid, The Story of Michelangelo,* the plays of William Shakespeare, and the histrionics of his newly acquired National Wrestling Alliance. To attract more viewers to both TNT and WTBS, Turner backed the colorization of black-and-white films from the MGM film vaults. This computer process, which adds color to old films, involved Turner in controversy with critics who accused him of ruining classic movies.

Source: Photo courtesy Turner Broadcasting System, Inc.

In 1970 Turner brought the lowest-ranked outlet in the five-station Atlanta television market, UHF channel 17, now called WTBS (for Turner Broad-casting System). Prevented by law from uplinking the WTBS signal to a satellite himself, in 1976 Turner set up Southern Satellite Systems (SSS) as a satellite-capacity resale company. Its primary role was to uplink WTBS programs, a schedule heavy with movies and sports, to a satellite for distri-bution to cable systems throughout the country.

WTBS becomes first superstation

Turner creates satellite-capacity resale company to relay his superstation programs

Turner charged nothing for his programs so as to entice cable-system operators to invest in TVROs with which to downlink WTBS programs from the satellite. Cable systems paid SSS 10 cents per subscriber per month for the relay service. Turner's eventual profit came from higher advertiser rates on WTBS, justified by the nationwide cable audience that it acquired as a superstation. By 1990, several thousand cable systems carried WTBS, representing a potential audience of some 50 million homes. Several other broadcasting outlets also became superstations.

Pay Cable   Domsats played a role in another major programming innovation—**pay cable**. Home Box Office (HBO) led this development in 1972. It introduced an advertising-free channel of superior entertainment for which subscribers paid a fee added to the charge for subscription to run-of-the-mill, advertising-supported channels. The latter became known as the **basic tier**.

HBO pioneers pay-cable service

Lack of cost-effective relay facilities held back pay-cable progress until 1975, when HBO leased a **satellite transponder**—the receive-transmit unit on a satellite. HBO offered its programs to any system in the country able to buy or lease a TVRO antenna. Satellite delivery reduced distribution costs and enabled simultaneous reception throughout the country—an essential condition for effective national promotion of the service. HBO's move from terrestrial to space relays transformed the cable business almost overnight.

Only a quarter of all cable systems carried a pay-cable channel in 1977, but by the mid-1980s, virtually all did. In the meantime, HBO had been joined by a dozen other pay-cable networks.

Encryption   Pay television, along with several noncable types of program material, created a need to prevent unauthorized persons from receiving service. Several kinds of **encryption**—signal-scrambling techniques—became available. Encryption distorts the signal so that only subscribers who have paid for decoding devices can receive pay programs. The device most widely used is called VideoCypher II.

cable industry's VideoCypher II scrambles TV signals

pirates bootleg descrambling devices

Suppliers of encryption devices constantly alter their codes to defeat pirates who peddle black-market decoders. But bootleggers can apparently solve even sophisticated encryption codes (sellers of bootleg descramblers hold international conferences to promote their wares). The companies affected by pirates try to reduce losses by prosecuting unlicensed dealers. In 1988, the first major case against an illegal dealer resulted in a $1.3 million fine and a three-year jail term.

Evolution of Cable Programs   Until 1980, cable remained basically parasitic, feeding off existing broadcast programs and motion pictures. In the 1980s, however, cable began to flex its programming muscle. HBO led the way with **cable-specific productions**—programs made especially for cable. It taped special on-stage performances, obtained rights to sports events, and commissioned original programs.

cable-specific productions

Ted Turner made a major contribution to cable-specific programming in 1980 by introducing Cable News Network (CNN)—a 24-hour schedule of news and news-related features. Turner spun off CNN Headline News 18 months later, another 24-hour service.

CNN spins off headline news service

CNN may have been inspired not only by HBO but also by a slightly earlier full-time, public-affairs cable service, Cable-Satellite Public Affairs Network (C-SPAN)—a cooperative effort aimed at cultivating good public relations for the cable industry. Founded in 1979 and based in Washington, C-SPAN covers House of Representatives and Senate sessions, congressional hearings, and other public-affairs events.

C-SPAN brings full-time cable TV public affairs service

Other cable-specific program channels followed. MTV (Music Television), which began in 1981, provides 24 hours of hit recordings with matching video images, hosted by video disc jockeys. The Weather Channel, which started in 1982, offers 24-hour weather and environmental programming. As the decade wore on, other networks unique to cable appeared—evangelical religion, country music, children's programs, home shopping, and other specialized formats.

MTV and other cable-specific services emerge

Thus, the 1975–1984 decade brought a revolution to cable programming. Still more program services followed. By 1990, cable-system operators could choose among more than 60 satellite-distributed basic program channels and over a dozen pay-cable services. Data on some of these networks can be found in Exhibit 6.4.

Enhanced Cable Services   3.3

Cable television potentially lends itself to a number of technological enhancements that add to its versatility. One such enhancement, **interactivity**, makes two-way communication possible and thus gives the viewer more options than merely switching channels.

Qube   Cable visionaries of the 1970s foresaw interactivity as the logical next step in the evolution of home communications. Customers would hold dialogues with persons at the other end of the cable. Teachers could interact with students, and the public could forward requests to—and receive replies from—stores, banks, public utilities, safety agencies, and others.

Starting in 1977, Warner Cable, a large **multiple-system cable operator (MSO)**, gave this type of interactive cable a thorough trial. It offered an interactive service called Qube on its Columbus, Ohio, system. Qube had ten special channels over which viewers could respond by means of a touch-pad. Though the experiment generated much interest, Qube failed to attract sufficient subscribers to warrant its high cost, and after three years of mounting losses Warner closed it down. Similar apathy greeted several other two-way experiments.

Pay-per-View   A more promising use of interactivity represents a return to the earliest experiments with pay cable, which envisioned subscribers paying for *each program* individually. This option was revived in 1984 with the introduction of **pay-per-view (PPV)**, a service that allows the viewer to order specific programs from the cable company at will.

Widespread use of home PPV depends on **addressability**—an efficient means for the headend to receive program orders and to turn PPV decoders on or off at individual addresses. A sophisticated addressable service permits the customer to use a touch-pad to communicate with a computer at the headend. The computer automatically responds to PPV requests, turning on the customer's decoder. The computer also carries out record-keeping and billing operations. PPV began to develop rapidly in 1988. By 1990, 9.3 million households could be reached by addressable cable.

Videotex   Another type of interactive home service can use the television receiver or other display terminals. Although not a cable television service, **videotex** is also a wired service, bringing text and graphics materials into the
how teletext differs from videotex

home via telephone cables. It differs from **teletext**, a one-way text/graphics service that piggybacks on the normal *broadcast* television signal, as described in Section 4.10.

Using the interactive feature of videotex, the viewer can gain access to numerous data bases and carry on many forms of correspondence. In the United States, however, test-marketing investments amounting to over $200 million have so far failed to generate sufficient subscriber interest. Proponents of videotex finally gave up trying to use the home-television receiver as a terminal, turning instead to the smaller market of home-computer terminals.

Minitel—successful French videotex service

Videotex has had considerable success in France, where the national tele-communications monopoly introduced the Minitel, initially as a substitute for the printed telephone book. Its subsequent success is discussed in Section 14.9.

3.4   *Niche Services*

Several alternative services supplement broadcasting and cable television in delivering programs to consumers. They fill specific needs, often called *niche markets*.

MDS/MMDS (Wireless Cable)   It sometimes happens that a specific small area or group of potential subscribers want television programs but cannot get satisfactory service from either over-the-air broadcasting or a cable system. A special wireless service called a **multipoint distribution service (MDS)** can fill this need. Because its role resembles that of cable television, MDS came to be called *wireless cable*.

MDS consists of a common-carrier delivery service, transmitting programs by microwave from one point to multiple reception points. The frequency band to which MDS is assigned limits its coverage to a range of only about 15 miles, and reception points must have a line-of-sight view of the transmitter.

Because they are common-carrier operators, MDS owners must contract out the programming function, often to HBO or some other pay-cable provider (in fact MDS is the only full-scale electronic entertainment medium in which the facilities owner may not program the service). However, as common carriers, MDS operators go through a less cumbersome licensing procedure than do broadcasters and cable operators. This advantage enables MDS to fill a market niche with minimum delay.

To enhance the ability of MDS to compete with cable, in 1983 the FCC authorized **multichannel MDS (MMDS)** in major markets. The FCC allows MMDS operators to cobble channels together from several other services, enabling them to offer up to about 20 program channels. This increase in channel capacity stimulated a boom in MMDS applications. The first MMDS service began operation in the District of Columbia area in December 1985.

MMDS competes head-on with cable television, making program suppliers reluctant to contract with MMDS operators. In any event, as cable continues to expand into the last of the major markets, it closes the window of opportunity for MMDS. The largest MMDS operator, MicroBand, petitioned for bankruptcy in 1989. In the future MMDS may be limited to servicing hotels and a few isolated niche markets not attractive to cable companies.

MATV/SMATV A second niche service of the 1980s is adapted to the television need of a building or group of buildings on a single piece of property. **Master antenna television (MATV)** and **satellite MATV (SMATV)** represent a special, limited-area type of cable television.

An MATV installation consists of a master television antenna on the roof of an apartment building, feeding programs to each unit in the building by means of a coaxial cable. Modern multiple-dwelling buildings usually come with suitable cabling already installed.

Satellite MATV adds a TVRO antenna to the installation, enabling the system to pick up satellite-distributed cable television services. The fact that SMATVs operate entirely within the boundaries of private property (usually an apartment or condominium complex) exempts them from both cable and broadcast regulations.

Cable-system operators, who naturally want to sign up as many households as possible, oppose the SMATV systems within their coverage areas. In fact, applicants for new cable franchises often press municipal authorities to assure them equal access to SMATV-equipped buildings. In 1990 several thousand MATV/SMATV operations existed (mainly in motels and large apartment buildings).

As a wired service, cable television has a family relationship to the telephone. The history of the telephone giant, AT&T, was interrupted in 1926 at the point in Section 2.5 when AT&T withdrew from radio broadcasting after a brief fling as a pioneer developer of the new medium. In the intervening years, AT&T continued to profit from broadcasting as the common-carrier supplier of network relays. In the 1970s, changing technology and competitive forces renewed telco (telephone company) interest in the entertainment media.

AT&T's longtime role as network relay provider

The Consent Decree

AT&T as regulated monopoly

AT&T, operating as a *regulated monopoly* under FCC supervision, had created a widely admired universal telephone service, the Bell System. It drew on long-distance profits (mostly from businesses) to subsidize local telephone service, keeping the rate for ordinary home users artifically low.

Competitors such as MCI, taking advantage of new technology and their ability to move faster than the vast Bell System bureaucracy, began nibbling at AT&T's long-distance monopoly. The newcomers complained that AT&T took advantage of its great size to hamper their efforts. These complaints revived the Justice Department's concern over the Bell System monopoly. In 1982, after an eight-year court battle, AT&T ended the costly antitrust suit by signing a consent decree, admitting no guilt but agreeing to accept court-ordered changes.

consent decree ends AT&T monopoly

In one of the biggest industrial breakups in history, AT&T divested itself of its 22 local operating companies, which thereafter became seven independent firms known as RBOCs (Regional Bell Operating Companies), more informally as "Baby Bells." At the same time AT&T withdrew from local telephone service, focusing on providing long-distance service in competition with MCI and others.

AT&T spins off BOCs ("Baby Bells")

Telco Media Competition

Meanwhile a technological development had opened up new vistas for telco operations. **Fiber-optic cable**, using light waves guided through hair-thin flexible strands of glass, offers advantages over both copper cable and radio. Its small diameter (as shown later in Exhibit 5.11) makes for easy installation, and it has enormous capacity as well as freedom from interference.

Fiber-optic cable is a natural for heavy-traffic telephone routes and for the main distribution routes of large cable television systems. More controversial are experiments that replace the telephone's traditional copper-wire connection to the individual home with fiber-optic cable. A score of small-scale telco experiments with such hookups are under way.

The vast capacity of fiber-optic cable invites the telcos to consider home delivery of services needing wide bands of frequencies, such as television, along with telephone services. However, under the provisions of the consent decree, the Baby Bells may supply only common-carrier services for the use

Baby Bells restricted to common-carrier roles

of others as information providers. They themselves may not become information providers. By the close of the 1980s, the telcos began pressing to loosen this restraint on their range of services. They wanted to get additional revenue from their huge investments in telephone networks by using them to carry more than telephone messages and data.

This potential threatened both the broadcasting and the cable industries. They united in opposing a broader scope for the telephone business. At the same time, the cable companies themselves foresaw that their cables might carry various kinds of home and business services other than entertainment—in competition with the telcos. Such overlapping of roles became a key policy issue in the evolving relationships among the broadcasting, cablecasting, and telephone businesses.

cable and broadcast TV unite to oppose telco TV

Communication Satellites 3.6

In Section 3.2 reference was made to the fact that domsats opened the way to efficient distribution of program services to cable systems. In addition to their role in relaying programs, satellites also have significant potential for delivering programs directly to consumers in the form of direct-to-home transmissions from direct-broadcast satellite (DBS) vehicles in space.

Satellite Relays

Starting with the introduction of transoceanic relays in the 1960s, satellites played an increasingly important role in news broadcasting. In the 1970s, when domsats became available, individual stations as well as networks began routinely employing satellite links to relay news events from the field.

use of satellites for international news

In 1978, public broadcasting pioneered in the use of satellites for distributing network programs to affiliates, as related in Section 7.2. Soon the commercial networks also adopted satellite relays. By the 1980s over a score of American domestic satellites were in use.

DBS Concept

A **DBS (direct-broadcast satellite) transmitter** can deliver programs to consumers without going through an intervening terrestrial station, as shown in Exhibit 3.3. Each terrestrial broadcast transmitter, relatively cumbersome and inflexible, reaches only a limited area. Hundreds of such transmitters must be linked to provide national network coverage in a large country such as the United States. A single DBS transmitter in space could serve the entire country.

In the long run, DBS transmitters pose a threat to both traditional broadcast television and cable television. They take advantage, as cable cannot, of broadcasting's unique ability to send programs to any number of receivers without physical connection. This ability enables reaching the most remote receivers with ease. Increasing the number of receivers reached adds nothing to transmission costs.

EXHIBIT 3.3 DBS: Direct-Broadcast Satellite Service

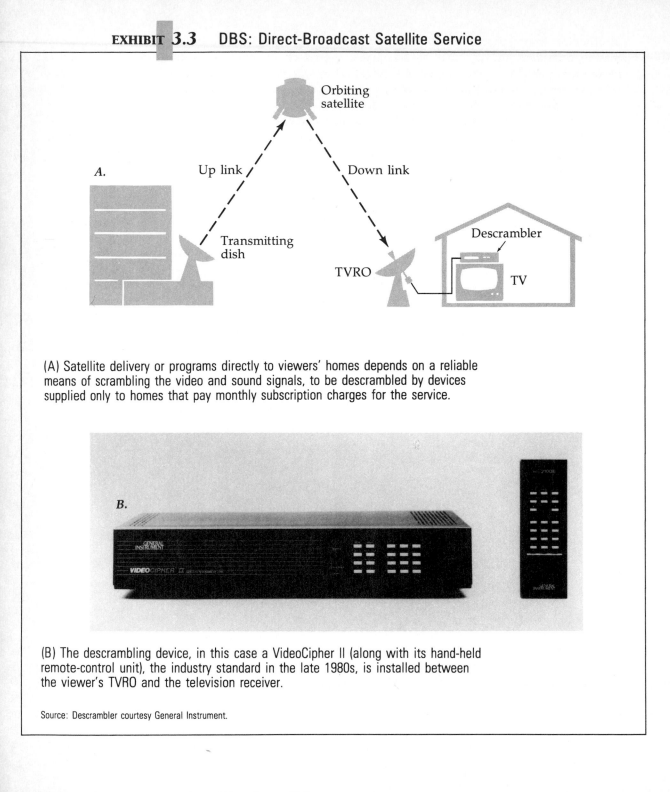

(A) Satellite delivery or programs directly to viewers' homes depends on a reliable means of scrambling the video and sound signals, to be descrambled by devices supplied only to homes that pay monthly subscription charges for the service.

(B) The descrambling device, in this case a VideoCipher II (along with its hand-held remote-control unit), the industry standard in the late 1980s, is installed between the viewer's TVRO and the television receiver.

Source: Descrambler courtesy General Instrument.

Ideally, a dish-shaped or flat antenna only a foot or less in diameter would pull in a wide range of program services from a DBS satellite. The antenna can be attached to the roof, a side wall, or a windowsill, or it can even be hidden in the attic. The ideal DBS service requires a more powerful satellite than those generally employed for relays. It also requires using the Ku band, a higher range of frequencies than the commonly used C-band that permits the use of smaller antennas.

C-band vs. Ku band satellites

DBS Services: Phase I

The FCC first received applications for DBS licenses proposing direct-broadcasting satellite service in 1980. It authorized commercial operations in 1982—a remarkably fast regulatory go-ahead for a new service. Critics questioned whether DBS, primarily of interest to audiences in uncabled rural areas and competing elsewhere with cable and established program sources, could recoup its costs.

The critics proved right. In 1984, United Satellite Communications (USCI) inaugurated America's first DBS service, using rented capacity on a Canadian satellite (*not* of the type ideally needed for DBS). USCI committed an estimated $178 million for equipment, marketing, programming, and customer servicing. Nevertheless, within a year, it shut down, having signed up only about 7,000 subscribers.

USCI suffered from the fact that the needs of many potential DBS customers had already been satisfied. Rural residents beyond the reach of stations and cable had already taken advantage of what might be called pseudo-DBS— backyard TVROs for **C-band-direct reception**. This term refers to the fact that the signals came from satellites using the C-band portion of the spectrum, which is set aside for relay purposes, not for direct-to-home reception. The fact that C-band satellites require larger and more expensive receiving antennas than higher-powered Ku-band DBS satellites had not discouraged backyard-TVRO enthusiasts.

backyard dishes enable "pseudo-DBS" service

C-band-direct reception

Until 1986, such backyard dish owners could view any satellite-borne programs they wished without paying subscription fees. They had access to over 200 channels of programming, including both the cable and the broadcast networks, news relays, and other private transmissions. After satellite relayers, led by HBO, began scrambling their signals, TVRO owners had to purchase a decoder box and pay a monthly subscription fee to view encrypted programs.

DBS Services: Phase II

By the end of the 1980s, technological advances had revived interest in true DBS. Once again, the FCC had applications on hand from potential DBS operators. They proposed services that would begin in the early to mid-1990s. Plans for new U.S. DBS projects drew on increasing experience with DBS systems in Europe and the Far East, where direct-to-home satellite services faced fewer competing terrestrial channels than the United States. Exhibit 14.10 gives some details on British DBS services launched in 1989 and 1990.

Early in 1990 a powerful American consortium consisting of NBC, Rupert Murdoch, Hughes Communications, and cable interests announced plans for

Sky Cable. The consortium planned to transmit over 100 channels. Such abundance (previous DBS projects could muster only 4 to 6 channels) would be impossible using conventional transmission technology. Nowhere near enough satellite transponders could be made available within the alloted DBS frequency band. Sky Cable counted on an as yet untried method of signal compression that, if successful, would double the output of satellite transponders. Other American DBS services were also in the planning stage as the 1990s began.

signal compression
needed to increase DBS
channels

3.7 *The Microelectronic Revolution*

Most of the new services reviewed so far in this chapter came into being because of the microelectronic revolution—fundamental changes in technology that opened up incredibly varied new ways of producing, storing, relaying, and delivering programs.

miniaturization and
computers make
satellites possible

For example, satellites would be impossible had not miniaturization reduced their size and weight to launchable proportions. And the complex calculation of their orbits and their telemetering signals depend on highly sophisticated computers using digitally processed information.

Before going further, a review of four interdependent lines of development that undergrid the microelectronic revolution will prove helpful:

- The invention of *solid-state devices* that take the place of vacuum tubes, including *transistors* and *integrated circuits.*
- The development of small *computers,* which in turn depend on large-scale integrated-circuit silicon chips.
- The substitution of *digital* for analog means of encoding signals (sounds, pictures, symbols).
- The tendency toward *convergence*—a coming together of hitherto separate media caused by the developments just mentioned, created novel configurations and new modes of communicating.

The discussion that follows deals with the history of these innovations. The specifics of the technology involved comes in Chapter 5.

Solid-State Devices   The history of electronics was left in Section 2.3 at the stage when de Forest's improvement of the vacuum tube had opened the way to broadcasting. For most audio and video uses, the fragile, bulky, power-hungry vacuum tube has long since given way to tiny blocks of solid crystal— the original of the term **solid-state devices.**

Bardeen, Brattain, &
Shockley invent
transistor

A trio of Bell Laboratories engineers—John Bardeen, Walter Brattain, and William Shockley—invented the first of these devices, the **transistor**, in 1947. It won them the 1956 Nobel Prize in physics.

transistors replace
vacuum tubes

The transistor manipulates electrons far more efficiently than the vacuum tube. Within a few years, transistors transformed much of the electronics

EXHIBIT **3.4** Microelectronics and Portability

B.

C.

D.

A.

A. The paper clip and pencil show the size of 1950s vacuum tubes in relation to 1960s transistors and current integrated-circuit chips. B. Cumbersome vacuum-tube portable radios required either large batteries or household electric power. C. Transistors began to replace vacuum tubes in the 1960s, leading to small, inexpensive portable radios. D. In the late 1970s tiny portable television-receivers using integrated circuits became available.

Source: Photos B and C courtesy Zenith Electronics Corporation; photos A and D by Janna Olson.

industry. The tiny portable radio, one of the first mass-produced products based on the transistor, appeared in 1954, quickly becoming the best seller in consumer product history to that date. It started an accelerating trend toward miniaturization, as suggested in Exhibit 3.4.

Computers   Transistors made possible the development of that prime electronic artifact of the late 20th century, the computer. Only computers could manipulate billions of information bits with the speed and intricacy needed for digital processing. The first large experimental electronic computer used some 18,000 vacuum tubes plus miles of wire. The tubes generated so much heat that attendants had to stand by to replace them as they blew out. Transistors solved the heat and size problem, at the same time enormously increasing computer speed and memory capacity.

Tiny computers remained impractical, however, as long as hundreds of separate transistors had to be meticulously wired together with hand-soldered connections. True miniaturization came with the invention of the **integrated circuit**—the computer chip. Examples are shown in Exhibit 3.4.

Chips are made of crystalline wafers, often silicon (hence the name Silicon Valley for the area south of San Francisco where much of the U.S. electronics industry is concentrated). Microscopically small electronic components and their connecting circuits are etched on such chips.

The chip's ability to concentrate computer components in a tiny space made possible the explosion of devices such as inexpensive digital watches and hand-held calculators. The personal computer followed, transforming the work scene during the 1980s.

bits and *bytes* mean high-quality digital transmission

Digital-Signal Processing   Computers have made digital *bits* and *bytes* household words. Both traditional radio/television broadcasting and cable television use *analog* methods of encoding signals for transmission. The hands of a clock tell time by the analog method, advancing gradually without abrupt transitions from one time to another. Analog encoding imitates (is *analogous to*) the natural patterns of things. But a *digital* clock tells times in *numbers*, advancing by discrete jumps from one number to the next.

analog vs. digital display

Analog methods seem like the natural way of representing things, perhaps because we have lived with them so long. But they are rapidly giving way to the seemingly more artificial digital methods, which enable previously undreamed-of technological feats.

Digital technology is described in Chapter 5. Suffice it to say here that digital processing involves breaking down electronic signals into tiny, numbered fragments of information. The numbers then become the content to be transmitted, recorded, and manipulated. The utter simplicity of a digital signal's make-up (just various combinations of only two digits) enables easy manipulation of signal content.

digital signal: the last word in simplicity

Viewers often see examples of such manipulation in the infinitely varied permutations of television graphics—pictures or designs that zoom in and out, swirl and twirl, break apart and reassemble, and so on. Switching around individually recorded digital-signal bits makes possible these dazzling video effects.

Digitizing makes possible many improvements and innovations in the handling of both video and audio signals—higher fidelity, copying without loss of quality, elimination of static and other sources of distortion, and mass production of highly sophisticated equipment. Formerly, such equipment had to be operated by trained professionals. Now amateurs can afford to buy and quickly learn to use recorders and cameras capable of producing virtually professional-quality results.

digital equipment makes amateur look professional

Many everyday appliances as well as communication equipment incorporate digitally processed functions—telephones, watches, calculators, and microwave ovens, for example. However, digital broadcast transmission presents problems. It would require either channels with much wider frequency bands than those used at present or advances in techniques of signal compression. Transmission from space is another matter. Japan has already experimented with digital satellite high-definition television, and digitally encoded radio signals are broadcast from space in Europe.

signal compression needed for digital broadcast transmission

Convergence   Digital processing provides a common electronic language that encourages **convergence**—interaction among formerly distinct modes of communicating. The telephone, broadcasting, cable television, motion pictures, printing, data storage and transmission, and even mail tend to encroach on each other's territory, creating new modes of communication.

Thus, distinctions among previously separate communication modes have grown less sharp, and new combinations constantly emerge. In this process of convergence, computers play a central role, bridging the gaps between functions and technologies. Convergence presents the broadcasting medium with unforseen challenges that may alter its nature or, conceivably, even eliminate it in its present forms.

New Era Broadcasting: Technology   3.8

In the new era of convergence, traditional broadcasting lost a substantial percentage of its audience to their services, but it also gained from improved technology. Satellites gave both radio and television networks cheaper, more flexible ways of relaying services to their affiliates. Stations also benefited from the availability of satellites for news gathering, both for local and for distant news. Receivers gained in quality and came equipped with many computerized improvements. Digital production equipment expanded the tools available to directors. Computer-assisted automation cut back on costs and increased efficiency.

digital components improve TV receivers

Receiver Improvements   Solid-state devices have made television receivers lighter, less demanding of power, and cheaper to operate. Television-sound reception, long a neglected element in receiver design, improved with stereophonic sound, which the FCC authorized in 1984. The first stereo sets needed adapters, but manufacturers soon marketed sets with built-in stereophonic capability.

Small computers using digital processing enhanced picture quality in **improved definition television (IDTV) receivers**. Advanced receivers also offered options such as freeze frames held in memory, zoom picture enlargement, special interfaces with cable services and videocassette tape recorders, and picture-in-picture (PIP) displays, pictures from more than one channel shown simultaneously.

Despite predictions that it may soon give way to more advanced technology, the bulky, power-hungry kinescope tube at the heart of the television receiver still offers the best method of displaying electronic pictures. The next expected major breakthrough in image display may be a flat, solid-state picture device that can be hung on the wall. Flat screens can already be found in tiny, portable receivers.

HDTV Large, wide screens will be one of the benefits of **high-definition television (HDTV)**, which will double picture quality. Japanese, European, and American versions compete for acceptance. A great deal hangs in the balance because if HDTV wins public acceptance it will eventually mean billions of dollars in the sale of new production, transmission, and reception equipment.

For that reason, in 1990 the FCC rather hastily adopted at least tentative goals for American HDTV standards so as to keep up with the Japanese and Europeans. It stipulated a target date of 1993 for development of a **spectrum-compatible simulcast system**. Its transmissions would be receivable on conventional receivers as well as HDTV receivers.

Cable, VCR, and DBS were already involved in HDTV demonstrations. Nonbroadcast services, not straitjacketed by the NTSC broadcast-television channel requirements, can forge ahead with their own HDTV version without waiting for the FCC to set broadcast standards. By 1988, several producers in the United States and abroad already had programs in preparation using HDTV cameras and recorders. This advanced equipment, employed as a "mastering medium," has economic and quality advantages over film.

Producers of HDTV programs convert them to the older television standards for broadcasting, retaining the master recordings pending the evolution of HDTV home receivers. Once these receivers become common, cable television and videocassette producers could move into HDTV production immediately.

Early in 1990, a consortium of major HDTV interests arranged to send an HDTV production of the Leonard-Duran boxing match by satellite from Las Vegas to a private showing in Los Angeles. This nonbroadcast event was the first U.S. commercial use of HDTV. It employed a system developed by an American firm, Scientific Atlanta.

Progress in Recording

Home Videorecording   Mass marketing of home videorecorders based on magnetic recording technology dates back to 1975, when Sony introduced the Betamax videocassette recorder (VCR) at an initial price of $1,300. Sony's monopoly ended in 1977 when Matsushita introduced the technically incompatible VHS format. Mass production quickly brought VCR prices down, as shown in Exhibit 3.5.

The VCR freed viewers from the tyranny of broadcast and cable schedules. Consumers can time-shift by copying and replaying cable and broadcast programs. Hollywood distributors recognized in the VCR a new market for movies. Soon VCR owners could buy or (more often) rent movies and other video material for home showing. By the late 1980s, purchase prices of many motion pictures on cassette had dropped to $30 and less.

time-shifting with VCRs

To keep VCR sales climbing, the manufacturers continually introduced new features. The machines have become marvels of computerized efficiency, capable of many more tricks than most users ever exploit.

In a related video/audio recording development, new technology enabled mass marketing of camcorders—hand-held video cameras with built-in recorders. Amateurs can produce such amazingly good pictures with camcorders that television stations routinely encourage them to send in news footage for use on the air, and network programs composed entirely of home-made videos became a popular fad in the early 1990s.

home-made videos on the air

EXHIBIT 3.5   Growth of VCRs, 1978–1988

Year	VCRs sold (thousands)	Average price	VCR households (thousands)	Percentage of TV homes	Titles available	Blank tape sales (thousands)
1978	402	$1,200	200	—	N/A	N/A
1980	805	1,080	840	1%	3,000	N/A
1982	2,035	900	2,530	3	4,000	$33,529
1984	7,616	680	18,880	11	7,000	133,088
1986	12,005	432	30,920	36	N/A	296,253
1988	10,748	377	51,390	58	N/A	296,947

By 1988, nearly 60 percent of the nation's homes had VCRs. As prices dropped, sales shot up. By the end of the 1980s, prices stabilized, with the least expensive VCRs costing under $300. At the same time tape rentals slowly began to give way to tape sales as prices of theatrical films on videotape dropped. Sales of blank tapes give an indication of the extent of off-air taping.

Source: Sales data from Electronic Industries Association; household and percent of homes with VCRs from Television Bureau of Advertising.

Compact Discs   A newer recording medium exploits two of the most advanced technologies: digital-signal processing and laser beams (the technologies involved are discussed in Section 5.5).

The first of these devices, the compact-disc audio recording (CD–A), achieves virtually perfect sound reproduction with neither surface noise nor distortion. By the late 1980s the CD had become "the most successful product introduction in consumer electronics history" (EIA, 1988: 31). CD sales surpassed sales of record albums in 1987; by 1990 about 18 percent of American homes had a CD player. Radio stations used CDs almost exclusively, though broadcast transmission still relied on the traditional analog method of signal processing.

The success of CD–A stimulated development of an entire family of products based on the same digital/laser technology. CD technology has been applied to motion pictures, stills, text, and data as well as sound. The full potentials of these versatile recording are still being explored. Their astounding capacity, quality, ruggedness, and versatility make them valuable for many applications beyond the entertainment field.

Digital Audio Tape   Analog audio-tape cassettes surpassed the sale of disc albums in the early 1980s and remain the most popular music-recording medium. Late in the decade, Japanese firms began marketing digital audio tape (DAT). However, American recording interests delayed its introduction into the U.S. market. They feared that the ability of DAT to make perfect copies of audio materials would undermine the sales of recordings. But in 1989 the industry agreed to introduce DAT machines equipped with a special chip that prevents making more than a single copy of a recording.

DAT recording equipment enters media market

3.10   *New Era Broadcasting: Economics and Politics*

Competing services and deregulation brought intense competition both within broadcasting and between broadcasting and newer services, dramatically changing broadcasting in the 1970s and 1980s.

Network Audience Loss   The most discussed fallout has been the decline of network broadcast television. As Exhibit 3.6 shows, since 1980 the estimated average prime-time audience share for the three traditional television networks has declined from 90 percent to 64 percent in 1990. This dropoff affects revenue, advertising, programs, and other aspects of the medium.

Nevertheless, though no longer unchallenged, broadcasting still draws the biggest audiences in the history of entertainment, still dominates national advertising, and still plays the major role in news dissemination and program making.

EXHIBIT 3.6   Decline in Network TV's Prime-Time Audience, 1980–1990

Season	Share	Season	Share
1980	90%	1986	76%
1981	85	1987	75
1982	83	1988	70
1983	81	1989	67
1984	78	1990*	64
1985	77		

Figures show combined three-network share of total prime-time television audience for each season (1980 indicates 1979–1980 season, etc.)

*Data for 1990 are estimated from various trade sources.

Source: Nielsen data as cited in *Channel Field Guide 1990,* p. 73.

Network Competition   In the 1970s, ABC improved its competitive position, gaining a line-up of affiliates equaling the line-ups of the two older networks. It expanded its evening news to a half-hour and went fully into color. Late in the decade, ABC led the network ratings for several seasons in succession.

NBC tried to move to the number-one slot by hiring away ABC's program chief, Fred Silverman, as president. But NBC remained in third place until former independent producer Grant Tinker took over the network presidency in 1980. Within five years he had piloted NBC into the top spot, where it remained for the rest of the decade.

The CBS story after 1970 centers on the search for William Paley's replacement. Paley restlessly hired and fired a string of potential successors. Finally Paley himself retired in 1983, leaving Thomas Wyman the CBS chief executive officer—only the second one in the network's 55-year history.

On the regulatory side, the FCC conducted its third (and probably last) investigation of the broadcast networks from 1978 to 1980. (FCC, 1980b). The Justice Department had previously dropped antitrust suits against all three networks after they accepted consent decrees that loosened their control over independent programmers and barred them from acting as sales representatives for their affiliates.

FCC's latest (and last?) network investigation

The latest study concluded that most FCC network rules merely restricted legitimate business interaction between networks and their affiliates without actually protecting the stations from network dominance. The study blamed an earlier commission's channel-allotment decisions for the continued dominance of the ABC/CBS/NBC triumvirate. So few markets have more than three VHF channel allotments that a fourth network faced an almost insurmountable barrier to obtaining a competitive line-up of affiliates.

EXHIBIT 3.7   Rupert Murdoch and the Elusive "Fourth Network"

In 1985, Australian publisher Rupert Murdoch became a United States citizen almost overnight in order to acquire Metromedia's six independent major-market television stations (WNEW–TV, New York; KTTV–TV, Los Angeles; WFLD–TV, Chicago; WTTG–TV, Washington, DC; KNBN–TV, Dallas; and KRIV–TV, Houston) and one network affiliate (WCVB–TV, Boston) for $2 billion. He resold WCVB–TV to the Hearst Corporation for $450 million but picked up another Boston station, WFXT–TV.

Having purchased half-ownership of 20th Century-Fox film corporation in 1984 for $250 million, Murdoch acquired the remaining half in 1985 (after the Metromedia deal) for $325 million. He thus gained complete control over a company with an extensive film library (including such hits as *Cocoon* and *Aliens*) and rights to numerous television series (*L.A. Law* and *M*A*S*H*, for example). In 1985 Murdoch announced plans to form a new national television network, Fox Broadcasting Company. A core of six O&O stations (reaching about 20 percent of all U.S. television households) served as the network.

Fox premiered in October 1986 with *The Late Show,* starring comedienne Joan Rivers. Rivers, who had been the primary substitute host on Johnny Carson's *Tonight Show* on NBC, had credited Carson for much of her success. She became the object of Carson's ire when she switched from friend and collaborator to competitor and challenger in his time period. However, the Rivers show lasted only seven months. Fox tried several other programs before giving up on the late-night time period altogether in order to concentrate on other parts of the day.

In its first season, Fox averaged between 2 percent and 6 percent of the national audience. Fox programs typically languished at the bottom of the Nielsen list, although some fared better.

The quality of the Fox affiliate line-up remained a problem. More than 120 stations carried Fox programming, but most were UHF, some were only low-power television stations, and nearly all were the weakest stations in their markets. The network lost about $80 million in its first year of operation, but Murdoch marched on.

His acquisition in 1988 of Triangle Publications (publisher of *TV Guide*) for $3 billion brought his U.S. magazine empire to about the same level as that of Time Inc., the largest magazine publisher in America. Indeed, Murdoch appeared well on his way to developing the most powerful communications empire in the world. He controlled 60 percent of metropolitan newspaper circulation in Australia, 36 percent of national circulation in Britain; he also had part-ownership in ten book publishers, and reached more than 13 million homes in 22 European countries with Sky Channel, a satellite broadcasting service for cable-TV viewers. He had interests in printing plants, real estate, an airline, even sheep farms. As if that weren't enough, in 1990 Murdoch joined a powerful consortium including NBC in a plan to launch a U.S. DBS service called Sky Cable in 1993.

Source: Photo courtesy The News Corporation Ltd. and Fox Broadcasting Co.

This barrier did not deter Rupert Murdoch, an international publishing tycoon with immense resources, as indicated in Exhibit 3.7. He launched the Fox network in 1985, the first such attempt at a fourth national television network since 1967, when efforts to launch the United Network failed within a month.

Fox network is launched

Actually, the initial limitations on the Fox network's size worked to its advantage. It escaped the financial-interest rule that prevents the full-service networks from producing their own programs. This technicality gave Murdoch freedom to use his 20th Century-Fox studios as a source of programs for the network.

Ownership Changes

In the meantime, the three established networks were going through traumatic corporate changes. After more than three decades of stable ownership, all three changed hands within a two-year period. This abrupt break with a thirty-year tradition coincided with retirement of long-time leaders, declining ratings, and weak financial performance.

ABC went first. In 1985, Capital Cities Communications announced that it would acquire American Broadcasting Companies, parent of the ABC network, in a friendly deal valued at more than $3.5 billion. The acquisition resulted in a conglomerate worth some $4.5 billion (the 1953 merger of ABC with Paramount Theaters had been valued at only $25 million). The combined firm had to shed its cable interests and several TV stations to meet FCC ownership rules.

ABC/Capital Cities merge

Within weeks after the Cap Cities/ABC announcement, Ted Turner revealed plans for an unfriendly takeover of CBS. He put together a complex deal valued at about $5 billion. Instead of cash, he offered CBS stockholders junk bonds (high-risk, high-yield debt securities backed by the resources of the target company) and stock in Turner Broadcasting. In exchange he sought a controlling two-thirds of CBS. The network managed to thwart Turner's takeover by purchasing 21 percent of its own stock from the general public. Turner withdrew his offer, but the battle left CBS deep in debt and torn by internal dissension.

Ted Turner attempts CBS takeover

Severe cutbacks followed, and management of the CBS network seemed relieved when Laurence Tisch, entertainment and investment conglomerate chairperson of Loews, obtained nearly 25 percent of CBS's stock. He edged out Thomas Wyman as the network's chief executive officer and brought back William Paley as figurehead chairperson.

William Paley's rerun as CBS chair

From 1985 to 1987, Tisch sold off virtually all the network's subsidiaries, including extensive publishing interests, culminating with the sale of Columbia Records (the world's largest record company) to the Japanese manufacturer Sony in 1988 for $2 billion.

NBC's turn came in December 1985. Its parent company, RCA, had been weakened by years of inept management and by huge losses from failed computer and videodisc ventures. RCA welcomed a friendly buy-out offer from General Electric. RCA, along with its NBC subsidiary, went for $6.28

GE takes over RCA/NBC

billion. It was the biggest nonpetroleum acquisition made in the United States up to that time. The sale made NBC part of an industrial conglomerate with annual sales of over $40 billion.

For months after the takeovers, news from the three networks seemed all bad. Profits fell, audience shares slipped, and employees by the thousand lost their jobs. From the public-interest standpoint, the network takeovers raised long-range concerns about increasing concentration of economic and editorial control in communications. The neutrality of their news operations seemed at risk when the networks came under the control of huge conglomerates whose military and other government-funded contracts could create conflicts of interest.

Network Programs   The national broadcast-television networks clung to the ideal of comprehensive programming, but during the 1980s their traditional commitment to serious news and public-affairs programs began to erode. Networks cut back on news-department budgets. Although the networks maintained their news leadership, broadcast journalism took on a more popularized slant, emphasizing entertainment as well as information. A new hybrid format emerged, derisively called **infotainment**.

The turnovers of ownership, the growth of huge, conglomerate corporations without commitment to the traditional public-service ideals of old-time network broadcasters, competition from cable, and deregulation that relaxed enforcement of public-interest standards all contributed to this decline.

decline in network standards

Radio Networks and Stations   The new GE/NBC management sold NBC Radio to Westwood One, Inc., which had bought the Mutual Broadcasting System in 1985. Thus the historic first and fourth radio networks came under common ownership. In other deals, NBC sold its owned-and-operated (O&O) radio stations, marking an end to a pioneer radio dynasty that had lasted nearly seven decades. Radio City, NBC's long-time New York home, no longer housed a radio network.

The traditional pattern of four full-service radio networks gave way to dozens of highly flexible specialized-service networks. The major radio chains offered affiliates a choice of several subnetworks, each tailored to fit in with a specific station format, such as Top-40 or news/talk.

FM overtakes AM radio

The intense competition did not prevent the number of radio stations from continuing its upward trend, dividing the listening audience into ever-smaller segments. The number of FM stations rose to match that of AM by the mid-1980s. By 1988, FM had three listeners for every AM listener. Looser FCC technical oversight had permitted erosion of AM signal quality. Under pressure from AM interests, the FCC began studying technical and ownership rule-changes to halt decline of the service as the 1980s came to an end.

Deregulation   In the late 1970s, broadcasters began arguing for **regulatory parity**, often described as a "level playing field." They wanted the FCC to remove rules that put them at a disadvantage in competing with newspapers, cable television, VCRs, and (potentially) DBS. In 1981, Congress extended the broadcast-license period from three to five years for television stations, seven for radio. The FCC dropped or simplified many of its broadcasting regulations.

The newer services also benefited from deregulation. In most cases, the FCC decided to regulate them either minimally or not at all, trusting the marketplace competition to keep all players in line. Thus, even after the removal of many rules, radio and television stations remained by far the most regulated of media. However, by 1990, the regulatory climate in Washington had changed, and movements were under way both to shore up the technical viability of broadcasting and to re-regulate its chief rival, cable television. Discussion of these developments is resumed in detail in Chapter 12.

broadcasting still the most regulated medium

Technology of Traditional Broadcasting

4 This chapter deals with broadcasting as it worked before the explosion of new technology in the 1970s and 1980s. The traditional technology is still basic and needs to be understood as background to recent developments covered in the next chapter. Readers without some knowledge of electronics may have to accept the more intricate concepts on faith, but the underlying concepts can be readily understood without technical background.

4.1   *Electromagnetism*

A basic natural force, **electromagnetism**, makes possible a host of communication services, among them broadcasting. All forms of electromagnetic energy share three fundamental characteristics:

properties shared by all forms of electromagnetic energy

- They radiate outward from a source without benefit of any discernible physical vehicle.
- They travel at the same high velocity.
- They have the properties of waves.

Radio Waves   The visible waves that ruffle the water when a stone is dropped into a pond are familiar. They radiate outward from the point of disturbance caused by the stone. Unlike water waves, radio waves have the ability to travel through empty space, going forth in all directions without benefit of any conductor such as wire. This *wirelessness* gives broadcasting its most significant advantage over other ways of communicating. Radio waves can leap over oceans, span continents, penetrate buildings, pass through people, go to the moon and back.

Light, a visible form of electromagnetic wave energy, illustrates some of the characteristics of radio waves. When an electric bulb is turned on, light radiates into the surrounding space, just as radio waves radiate from a transmitter. Light travels at the rate of 186,000 miles (300 million meters) a second, the common velocity of all electromagnetic energy. Both radio and light waves can be reflected—light from a mirror, radio waves from any large surface. Both lose energy as they travel away from a source, getting weaker with distance.

speed of light: 300 million meters per second

Radio and light differ, however, as to wavelength and wave frequency. Light waves have much shorter length and much higher frequency than radio waves.

Wave frequency refers to the fact that all electromagnetic energy comes from an oscillating (vibrating or alternating) source. In a radio transmitter, giant vacuum tubes cause the oscillation. The number of separate waves produced each second determines a particular wave's frequency. Differences in frequency determine the varied forms that electromagnetic energy assumes.

electromagnetic energy comes from an oscillating source

Wavelength is measured as the distance from the crest of one wave to the crest of the next. The waves that radiate out from the point of disturbance— the stone in the water or the radio transmitter—travel at a measurable velocity and have a measurable frequency and length.

Frequency Spectrum   A large number of frequencies visualized in numerical order constitutes a spectrum. The keyboard of a piano represents a sound spectrum. Keys at the left produce low-pitch sounds (low frequencies). Frequency (heard as pitch) rises as the keys progress to the right end of the keyboard. Columns 3 and 4 of Exhibit 4.1A show the frequencies and lengths

EXHIBIT **4.1**   The Electromagnetic Spectrum and Its Uses

A. Electromagnetic

phenomena	Examples of uses	Frequency ranges	Typical wavelengths
Cosmic rays	Physics, astronomy	10^{14} GHz and above	Diameter of an electron
Gamma rays	Cancer therapy	10^{10}–10^{13} GHz	Diameter of smallest atom
X rays	X-ray examination	10^{8}–10^{9} GHz	Diameter of largest atom
Ultraviolet radiation	Sterilization	10^{6}–10^{8} GHz	1 hundred-millionth of a meter
Visible light	Human vision	10^{5}–10^{6} HGz	1 millionth of a meter
Infrared radiation	Photography	10^{3}–10^{4} HGz	1 ten-thousandth of a meter
Radio waves	Radar, microwave relays, satellites, television, short-wave radio, AM and FM radio	300 GHz to 150 kHz	1 centimeter to 20,000 meters

In the examples from the top down, frequency decreases as wavelength increases. Radio occupies the lower frequencies; the higher the frequency (or the shorter the waves), the more dangerous the manifestations of electromagnetic energy become. But even some of them can be useful, as in the case of x-rays.

The following table breaks down the radio-frequency portion of the spectrum into large bands, as designated by international agreement. Low-frequency radio, a long-distance form of AM broadcasting, is used in Europe but not in the United States.

B. Name of frequency band	Frequency range	Broadcast-related uses
LF (low frequency)	30–300 kHz	LF radio (Europe)
MF (medium frequency)	300–3,000 kHz	AM radio
HF (high frequency)	3–30 MHz	Short-wave radio
VHF (very high frequency)	30–300 MHz	VHF TV, FM radio
UHF (ultra high frequency)	300–3,000 MHz	UHF TV, microwave relays, satellites
SHF (super high frequency)	3–30 GHz	Satellites
EHF (extremely high frequency)	30–300 GHz	Satellites

The bands grow progressively larger as frequency increases. Changes in frequency nomenclature avoid awkwardly long numbers: a kilohertz (kHz) = 1,000 Hz (hertz, or cycles per second); a megahertz (MHz) = 1,000 kHz; a gigahertz (GHz) = 1,000 MHz. Broadcasting uses only parts of these bands, which also accommodate many types of nonbroadcast services. Exhibit 4.12 shows the specific portions of the bands used by AM and FM radio and VHF and UHF television.

of waves in the electromagnetic spectrum. Notice that as frequency *increases,* wavelength *decreases.*

As frequency goes up, the practical difficulty of using electromagnetic waves for communication also increases. Frequencies suitable for radio communication occur near the low end of the spectrum, the part with the lower frequencies and longer wavelengths, shown in detail in Exhibit 4.1B.

Communication satellites employ the highest frequencies currently useful for broadcasting, mostly in the range of 3 gigahertz (3 *billion* oscillations per second) to 15 gigahertz. Even these frequencies are nowhere near as high as those of light.

4.2   *Wave Motion*

Sound energy differs from electromagnetic energy in fundamental ways, but sound too originates from oscillating sources and travels in the form of waves. Sound therefore helps to illustrate characteristics of waves in a tangible way. We can actually *hear* differences in frequency as differences in pitch, for example. Understanding the nature of sound also helps because sound quality and studio acoustics play a central role in broadcasting.

Sound Waves   A conversation between two people at a party illustrates the basic principles of sound-wave motion. When a speaker's vocal cords vibrate, they set molecules of air into motion in the form of waves. The airborne sound waves travel to the listener's eardrums, which respond by vibrating in step with the wave motion of the air molecules. Eardrum vibrations stimulate nerve fibers leading to the listener's brain, which interprets the vibrations as word sounds.

Eardrums, unlike broadcast receivers, cannot *tune out* other voices. Competing conversations may interfere with comprehension. When this happens, the speaker talks louder (producing stronger waves) to overcome the interference. Similarly in radio, increasing transmitter power can overcome interference from competing signals.

The party conversation illustrates basic concepts of wave motion. At each step in the sequence, **vibration** (alternation, oscillation) occurs. Vibration in one object (vocal cords) causes corresponding vibratory motion in other objects (air, eardrums). Vibrating air molecules travel invisibly from one point to another. Increased volume (transmission energy) overcomes interference from competing sounds.

The signal (word sounds) can also be transferred as energy patterns from one medium to another, altering form each time—from vocal chords to air to eardrums to nerves. The process of changing medium and form is called **transduction**.

Phase   As waves travel, they go through a cycle of motion. That cycle is conventionally visualized as a wheel (which is what *cycle* means). The up-and-down and forward motion of a point on the perimeter of a revolving wheel illustrates the basic wave attributes of *amplitude* and *velocity*. Exhibit 4.2 depicts these concepts.

As Exhibit 4.2 shows, waves go through opposite *phases* of motion. The two opposing phases of a wave cycle may be regarded as positive (plus) and

EXHIBIT **4.2**   Wave-Motion Concepts

Tracing the rise and fall of a spot on a wheel as it revolves illustrates the concepts of *cycle, phase, amplitude,* and *velocity.* With the axle level treated as zero amplitude, movement of the movement above the axle level represents the dot's positive phase; black dot below the axle is its negative phase.

   The curves to the right depict the factor of distance as the wheel travels, tracing a complete cycle of wave motion. The distance factor involves the concept of velocity, the distance traveled in a unit of time.

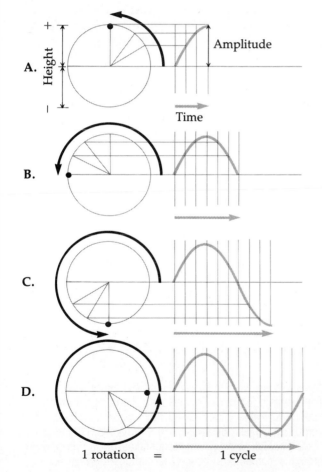

A. Starting at zero level, the dot moves to maximum positive amplitude in one quarter-turn.

B. In the next quarter-turn, the dot returns to zero level, completing one phase of its cycle.

C. In its next quarter-turn, the dot moves to its maximum point of negative amplitude.

D. In its final quarter-turn, the dot returns to its starting point, completing its second phase and one complete cycle.

Source: Diagram adapted from *Signals: The Telephone and Beyond* John R. Pierce. Copyright © 1981 by W.H. Freeman and Company. Reprinted with permission. *Signals: The Telephone and Beyond.*

negative (minus) aspects of the wave. The two opposing phases constitute a complete cycle. The number of complete cycles produced each second determines a wave's frequency, expressed in terms of cycles per second (cps).

When two waves of the *same* frequency coincide exactly, they are said to be *in phase*. If both waves have the same amplitude (strength), their amplitudes combine, doubling the amplitude of just one wave. Conversely, if two waves of the same amplitude that are exactly halfway (180 degrees) out of phase combine, they cancel each other completely. As a practical use of this fact, antinoise devices eliminate unwanted sounds by generating competing sounds 180 degrees out of phase with the unwanted sounds.

how phase differences affect sound quality

Phase has an important bearing on sound quality. A sound with a perfectly smooth, symmetrical waveform oscillates at a single frequency. It has a single tone—pure but uninteresting. Interesting sounds—pleasing voices, musical tones—consist of many different frequencies of varying amplitudes, all blended together. This blending produces a complex wave, irregular in pattern, as shown in Exhibit 4.3.

EXHIBIT 4.3   Complex Wave Analyses: Fundamental and Overtones

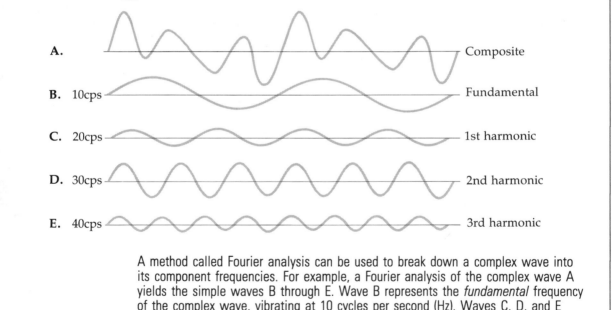

A method called Fourier analysis can be used to break down a complex wave into its component frequencies. For example, a Fourier analysis of the complex wave A yields the simple waves B through E. Wave B represents the *fundamental* frequency of the complex wave, vibrating at 10 cycles per second (Hz). Waves C, D, and E represent *harmonics* of that fundamental, waves with frequencies of 20, 30, and 40 Hz, respectively. Waves B through E combined produce the composite wave A.

Source: Diagram adapted from Paul Davidovits, *Communication* (New York: Holt, Rinehart & Winston, 1972), p. 129, Fig. 11-1. Used by permission.

Overtones   The frequency heard as "the" pitch of a sound is its **fundamental frequency**, or **fundamental**. The fundamentals of human speech have quite low frequencies, from 200 to 1,000 cps for women and from 100 to 500 cps for men. Complex sounds have overtones at higher frequencies. **Overtones** (also called **harmonics**) give sounds their distinctive timbres and are multiples of fundamentals. Middle C, for example, has a fundamental of 264 cps, with possible overtones at 528 cps, 792, 1056, and so on.

Differences in the distribution and amplitudes of overtones account for qualitative differences among sounds of the same pitch. One can tell a violin from a clarinet, even when they produce exactly the same note (frequency) at the same volume (amplitude), because their overtones differ. Overtones have pitches higher than their fundamental frequencies. Thus good sound equipment reproduces the higher sound frequencies. Hi-fi equipment has, among other things, the ability to capture overtones by reproducing sound frequencies up to 15,000 cps or higher.

hi-fi equipment and overtones

Attenuation   In traveling, sound waves **attenuate**, gradually lose their energy. Draperies, human bodies, clothing, and other soft, irregularly shaped objects increase attenuation by *absorbing* sound energy. Hard, flat room surfaces cause less attenuation by *reflecting* sound waves much as a mirror reflects light. Reflections cause **reverberations** or echoes (reverberations are echoes that are too closely spaced in time to be heard as separate sounds).

The shorter a wave's length, the more easily small objects block the wave's path. Long waves tend to "bend" around objects in their path. One can verify this fact by listening to music in another room or from around the corner of a building. As soon as one turns the corner into the area where the music originates, it immediately brightens because one begins hearing the shorter-wave sounds (that is, the higher-pitched sounds) that could not get around corners as readily as the longer-wave sounds.

personal experiment: frequency and sound transmission

Radio Waves   4.3

Though radio and sound waves behave in similar ways, they also have fundamental differences as to frequency, velocity, and the medium in which they travel.

Sound vs. Radio Frequencies   Limitations of the ear confine audible sound to an upper frequency ranging from 15,000 to 20,000 cps (people's hearing acuity varies a good deal, especially at the upper frequencies).

In contrast, the radio spectrum runs from a few thousand cycles per second into the billions. Radio waves travel at 186,000 miles per second—about

key number: highest frequency audible to humans

900,000 times the speed of sound in air. Finally, radio waves need no intervening medium, such as air, in which to travel. Indeed, they travel best in a total vacuum.

With reference to radio waves, the phrase "cycles per second" has been shortened by international agreement to *hertz* (named after a famous radio physicist discussed in Section 2.3 and abbreviated *Hz*). A hertz is a frequency of one wave-cycle per second. The number of hertz in the frequencies of the highest radio bands rises into the billions, making for awkwardly long numbers. Exhibit 4.1B shows how metric terms simplify these numbers and how names such as MF, HF, VHF, and UHF for the frequency bands were derived.

Naming Channels and Bands   As Exhibit 4.1 suggests, the location of any wave in the electromagnetic spectrum can be stated in terms of either its frequency or its wavelength. Confusingly, both ways of naming waves occur. For example, the term *microwaves* identifies a group of waves by their length, but the term *VHF* identifies a band by frequency. The number 600 (often abbreviated to 60) on an AM radio dial identifies a channel by frequency, standing for 600 kilohertz. The frequency bands used for international broadcasting are identified both by wavelength and by frequency— short waves (SW) and high frequency (HF).

The picture and sound components of television transmissions use different groups of radio frequencies. For the sake of convenience, television channels are identified by arbitrarily assigned channel numbers rather than by wavelength or frequency. For example, "channel 6" is a shorthand way of saying "a station using the 82- to 88-MHz channel, with a video carrier-wave frequency of 83.5 MHz and a sound carrier-wave frequency of 88.75 MHz."

Wave Radiation   The production of radio waves, like sound, depends on vibration (oscillation). But an electric current, rather than a physical object, oscillates. An oscillating current can be envisioned as power surging back and forth (alternating) in a wire, first in one direction (one phase), and then in the other direction (the opposite phase).

When current alternates in any electric circuit, even in the wiring of one's home, it releases electromagnetic energy into the surrounding space. The tendency of alternating current to radiate energy increases with its frequency—the higher the rate of alternation, the more radiation takes place. Dangerous radiations such as x-rays occur at frequencies far above radio frequencies. Nevertheless, even the much-lower-frequency microwaves used in some forms of communication (as well as in microwave ovens) can be harmful to humans exposed to unshielded, high-power sources of such waves.

A broadcast transmitter generates radio-frequency energy, feeding it to a transmitting antenna for radiating into the surrounding area. The basic emission, the transmitter's **carrier wave**, oscillates at the station's allotted frequency. It radiates energy at that frequency continuously, even when no sound or picture is going out.

Modulation refers to ways of imposing meaningful variations on a transmitter's carrier wave to enable it to carry programs.

Energy Patterns
Turning a flashlight on and off modulates the flashlight beam. A distant observer could decode such a modulated light beam according to any agreed-upon meaning. A pattern of short flashes might mean "All OK." A series of short and long flashes might mean "Having trouble. Send help." Modulation produces a *pattern* that can be interpreted as a meaningful *signal*.

When radio waves carry words, they consist of **amplitude patterns** (loudnesses) and **frequency patterns** (tones or pitches). Air molecules form pressure waves in response to the amplitude/frequency patterns of the words. A microphone responds to the air-pressure patterns, translating them into corresponding electrical patterns. The microphone's output consists of a sequence of waves with amplitude and frequency variations that approximately match those of the sound-in-air patterns.

Ultimately, those AF (*audio*-frequency) electrical variations *modulate* a transmitter's RF (*radio*-frequency) carrier, causing its oscillations to mimic the AF patterns. At last we have a **radio signal**—patterned variations in a carrier wave that convey meaning.

how radio signals are formed

Modulating by a sound signal involves frequencies in two widely different ranges—the low frequencies of the AF signal and the much higher frequencies of the RF carrier. The RF carrier could not depict the sound signal if the carrier frequency were near that of the sound frequency.

Sidebands
A specific radio frequency, not a channel or band of frequencies, identifies a station's carrier wave. For example, an AM station at 600 on the dial has a carrier wave of 600 kilohertz (600,000 cycles per second).

But modulation activates frequencies both above and below the carrier frequency. These adjacent frequencies constitute **sidebands**. The sidebands of the 600-kHz AM station include the five kHz above and five kHz below 600 kHz. The entire band of frequencies from 595 to 605 kHz make up the 600-kHz channel.

The upper (above 600 kHz) and lower (below 600 kHz) sidebands represent opposite *phases*—they simply mirror each other. Either one could convey all the information in the channel. Nevertheless, many radio services—for example, sound broadcasting—transmit both sidebands. That wastes spectrum space, but suppressing one of the sidebands would add considerably to the cost of both sending and receiving equipment.

why AM radio transmits both sidebands but TV only one

Some services, however, economize on spectrum usage by suppressing one of the sidebands. Television needs such wide channels that transmitting both sidebands would use up too much spectrum space and reduce the number of channels that could be put to use. Therefore one of the television signal's sidebands is suppressed, leaving only a vestigial lower sideband, as shown later in Exhibit 4.11.

Channel Width   In broadcast communication, **channel width**, or **bandwidth**, determines information capacity, much as a water pipe's diameter determines the rate at which water can be delivered. Broadcast stations need large pipes, or channels, because they must deliver large quantities of information without delay—in real time.

real-time messages need wide bands

A still-picture news service can use a narrow picture channel if it is willing to tolerate delay while each picture gradually builds up over time. A taxi radio-dispatching service needs real-time message delivery, but it can tolerate narrow channels because it needs only voice intelligibility, not voice quality. Radio broadcasting needs wide channels both for real-time delivery and for reproducing the overtones that involve the higher sound frequencies. Television broadcasting needs still wider channels in order to transmit both pictures and sound.

AM vs. FM   To repeat, *modulation* means imposing meaningful patterns on an otherwise unvaried stream of energy, a carrier wave. Broadcasting transmitters use either amplitude or frequency modulation. Exhibit 4.4 shows how they work. AM (amplitude-modulated) stations are called *standard* stations because the technology of amplitude modulation was developed before that of FM (frequency modulation). Television uses both types, AM for the picture signal and FM for the sound signal.

Electrical interference caused by lightning or machinery affects AM signals because the stray energy from interference distorts wave amplitude patterns. Listeners hear electrical interference as **static**. Overlapping signals from more distant stations on the same channel also easily distort AM signals.

why FM has less static

Electrical interference has no effect on FM patterns, which rely on changes in frequency rather than changes in amplitude. FM also rejects interference from other stations more readily than AM does.

Multiplexing   Two or more separate carriers can be modulated in the same channel, a form of **multiplexing**. The shortage of spectrum space makes multiplexing important as a spectrum-saving measure. Later in this chapter reference is made to multiplexing auxiliary signals in the FM channel and to multiplexing the sound signal and a color subcarrier in the television channel.

4.5   *Wave Propagation*

Modulated signals are piped from a transmitter to its **antenna**—the physical structure from which signals radiate into the surrounding space. The traveling of signals outward from the antenna is called **propagation**.

EXHIBIT **4.4** Amplitude vs. Frequency Modulation

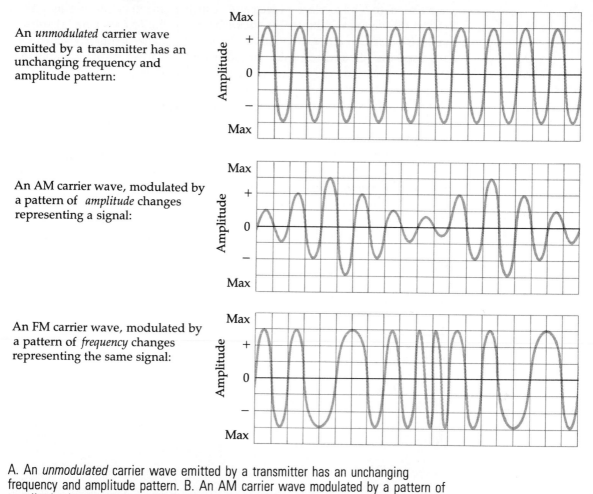

An *unmodulated* carrier wave emitted by a transmitter has an unchanging frequency and amplitude pattern:

An AM carrier wave, modulated by a pattern of *amplitude* changes representing a signal:

An FM carrier wave, modulated by a pattern of *frequency* changes representing the same signal:

A. An *unmodulated* carrier wave emitted by a transmitter has an unchanging frequency and amplitude pattern. B. An AM carrier wave modulated by a pattern of *amplitude* changes representing a signal. C. An FM carrier wave modulated by a pattern of *frequency* changes representing the same signal.

Sources: Diagram adapted from *Signals: The Telphone and Beyond.* By John R. Pierce. Copyright © 1981 by W.H. Freeman and Company. Reprinted with permission; also Federal Communications Commission.

Coverage Contours In theory, an omnidirectional (all-directional) antenna would propagate signals over a circular coverage area. In practice, coverage patterns usually assume uneven shapes. Physical objects in the transmission path, interference from electrical machinery and other stations, the time of day, and even seasonal sunspot changes can affect propagation distances and patterns.

The higher the frequency of waves, the more the atmosphere absorbs their energy and therefore the shorter the distance they can travel. Objects wider than a wave's length tend to block propagation, causing "shadows" in coverage areas. Later in this chapter, Exhibit 4.14 shows how large buildings cause "shadows" in television-station coverage. VHF, UHF, and still higher frequency waves (the ones used for FM and television broadcasting, microwave relays, and satellites) have such short lengths that relatively small objects can interfere with their propagation. In fact raindrops can block the shortest waves.

even raindrops can block waves

Such variables make for irregular coverage patterns. Engineers draw contours on maps by measuring signal strength at various points surrounding a transmitter. Contour lines link points of equal received signal strength. Exhibit 14.4 depicts contour lines in a satellite's footprint, indicating the minimum antenna size needed for good reception at various distances from the center of the beam.

Frequency-related propagation differences divide waves into three types: direct, ground, and sky waves. Each type has advantages and disadvantages that must be considered in matching frequency bands with service needs.

Direct Waves   At FM radio and television frequencies (that is, in the VHF and UHF bands), waves follow a line-of-sight path. They are called **direct waves** because they travel directly from transmitter antenna to receiver an-

EXHIBIT 4.5   Direct- and Ground-Wave Propagation

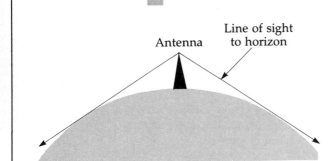 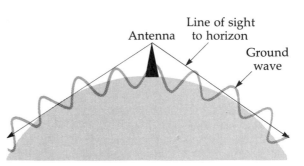

Direct waves travel straight out, like light, from small radiating elements atop an antenna support. Television antennas radiate their waves downward toward the reception area, blocking off radiation that would otherwise travel upward and outward into space. The distance to the apparent horizon limits the coverage area of direct-wave transmissions. One speaks of the "apparent" horizon because its distance varies in accordance with the heights of the sending and receiving antennas.

Ground waves travel along the surface of the Earth, whose electrical conductivity affects the distance they can travel. Given good soil conductivity and sufficient power, ground waves outdistance direct waves, reaching well beyond the horizon.

tenna, reaching only as far as the horizon, as shown in Exhibit 4.5. Line-of-sight distance to the horizon from a 1,000-foot-high transmitting antenna propagating over a flat surface reaches about 32 miles. The signal does not cease abruptly but after reaching the horizon, fades rapidly.

Engineers locate direct-wave antennas as high as possible in order to extend the apparent horizon. By the same token, raising the height of a *receiving* antenna also extends the horizon limit.

Ground Waves

AM radio uses medium-frequency (MF) waves. Waves in the MF band travel as **ground waves**, propagated through the surface of the Earth. They can follow the Earth's curvature beyond the horizon, as shown in Exhibit 4.5.

Ground waves have the potential for covering wider areas than do direct waves. In practice, however, a ground wave's useful coverage area depends on several variables, notably **soil conductivity**—the degree to which soil resists the passage of radio waves—which varies according to dampness and soil composition.

Sky Waves

Most radio waves that radiate upward toward the sky dissipate their energy in space. However, waves in the medium-frequency band (AM radio) and the high-frequency band (short-wave radio) when radiated upward tend to bend back at an angle toward the Earth when they encounter the ionosphere.

The ionosphere consists of several atmospheric layers located from about 40 to 600 miles above the Earth's surface. Bombarded by high-energy radiation from the sun, these layers take on special electrical properties, causing **refraction** (a gradual type of reflection, or bending back) of AM and short-wave signals. Refracted waves are called **sky waves**.

Under the right frequency, power, and ionosphere conditions, returning sky waves bounce off the surface of the Earth, travel back to the ionosphere, bend back again, and so on. Following the Earth's curvature, they can travel thousands of miles, as depicted in Exhibit 4.6.

The ionosphere's effectiveness varies with time of day and with frequency. AM broadcast stations produce sky waves only at night, extending their coverage areas after sundown. However, sky waves do not necessarily improve an AM station's effective nighttime coverage. Their intrusion may actually shrink it.

conditions essential for ionosphere reflection

Short-wave stations, however, are not limited to using a single carrier frequency as are AM broadcasting stations. They can switch frequency several times throughout the 24 hours of the day to take continuous advantage of the ionosphere's changing refractive abilities.

Antennas

Whichever type of propagation may be involved, antennas are needed, both to launch signals at the transmitting end and to pick them up at the receiving end. Antenna size and location can have a critical influence on the efficiency of transmission and reception.

Small antennas built into receivers suffice to pick up strong AM and FM signals. The higher the frequency, however, the more elusive the signal and the more essential an efficient antenna becomes—for radio perhaps a retract-

EXHIBIT **4.6** Sky-Wave Propagation

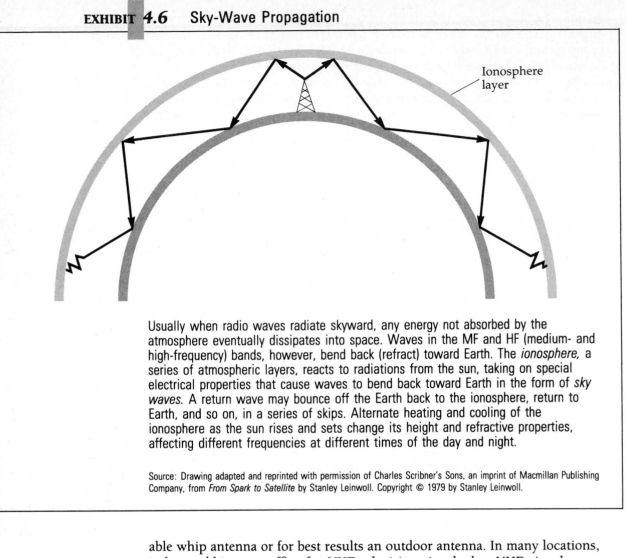

Usually when radio waves radiate skyward, any energy not absorbed by the atmosphere eventually dissipates into space. Waves in the MF and HF (medium- and high-frequency) bands, however, bend back (refract) toward Earth. The *ionosphere,* a series of atmospheric layers, reacts to radiations from the sun, taking on special electrical properties that cause waves to bend back toward Earth in the form of *sky waves.* A return wave may bounce off the Earth back to the ionosphere, return to Earth, and so on, in a series of skips. Alternate heating and cooling of the ionosphere as the sun rises and sets change its height and refractive properties, affecting different frequencies at different times of the day and night.

Source: Drawing adapted and reprinted with permission of Charles Scribner's Sons, an imprint of Macmillan Publishing Company, from *From Spark to Satellite* by Stanley Leinwoll. Copyright © 1979 by Stanley Leinwoll.

able whip antenna or for best results an outdoor antenna. In many locations, indoor rabbit ears suffice for VHF television signals, but UHF signals may require an outdoor antenna.

Transmitting antennas vary in size because for them to work efficiently their length must be mathematically related to the length of the waves they radiate. For example, channel 2 (VHF) television transmitters radiate 20-foot waves, but television channel 48 (UHF) waves are less than 2 feet long.

Directional Propagation A flashlight or an auto headlight focuses light into a beam. A reflector creates the beam by redirecting light rays that would otherwise radiate backward or sideways, reinforcing the rays that go in a forward direction. Transmitting antennas can also be designed for **directional propagation**—beaming reinforced signals in a desired direction. Directional propagation has value both for increasing signal strength in a desired direction and for preventing interference between stations.

Concentrating radio waves by means of directional propagation increases their strength. This increase, called **antenna gain**, can be many-thousand-fold.

Receiving antennas are also directional; this is easily demonstrated by turning a portable AM radio in different directions. Signals from a given station come in most strongly when the radio's built-in antenna points in the direction of that station's transmitter.

personal experiment: test antenna for directionality

Mutual Interference　4.6

The number of stations that can be licensed to operate in any particular community is limited by mutual interference between stations.

Cochannel Stations
The primary troublemaker, **cochannel interference**, comes from mutual interference between stations operating on the same channel.

Cochannel stations must be sited far enough apart geographically to prevent their coverage contours from overlapping. Separation rules must take into account the fact that signals too weak for useful reception by an audience may nevertheless cause cochannel interference. A station's **interference zone** therefore extends far beyond its service area.

In keeping with the U.S. policy of allowing as many local communities as possible to have their own stations, the Federal Communications Commission (FCC) makes cochannel separation rules as liberal as possible. The changing daytime vs. nighttime coverage areas of AM stations, caused by sky-wave propagation at night, complicate the problem. The FCC seeks to prevent such sky-wave interference by requiring many AM stations either to use lower power or to go off the air at night.

why some stations close down at night

Adjacent Channel Stations
In the vicinity of a transmitter, radio-frequency radiation is so powerful that sidebands spread far beyond the nominal channel limits, causing **adjacent-channel interference**. The possibility of such interference limits the number of stations that can be licensed in any one locality. Stations will not be found on consecutively numbered channels in a single market (as Exhibit 4.12 shows, some seeming exceptions to this rule occur: television channels 6 and 7 and 13 and 14 are consecutively numbered but their frequencies are not consecutive).

However, signal strength falls off rapidly beyond the immediate vicinity of the transmitter. Adjacent-channel stations therefore need to be separated only by about the radius of their service areas. For example, the FCC requires a minimum adjacent-channel separation of only 60 miles for VHF television stations but about 270 miles for VHF cochannel separation (distances for UHF stations are shorter).

AM Stations

As a broadcast-station class name, *AM* is somewhat misleading because the term means simply *amplitude modulation* and many services other than standard radio broadcasting use that type of modulation. The video component of the television signal, for example, is amplitude-modulated.

AM Band and Channels

to watch for: implementation of new AM channels

Until 1988, AM stations were allocated to the 535- to 1,605-kHz segment of the MF band, for a total AM bandwidth of 1,070 kHz. In 1988, by international agreement, the upper limit of the AM band was extended to 1,705 kHz. However, use of these new channels will be delayed while extended-tuning receivers are manufactured and sold. Although the FCC planned to start licensing stations in the new band in 1990, doubt remained as to the role they would play. The discussion that follows describes the AM band and channels as they existed before the new channels became available.

Ideally, sound-broadcasting channels would be wide enough to encompass the maximum range of overtone frequencies detectable by the human ear—a channel width of at least 15,000 Hz. However, spectrum conservation dictates using no more than the essential number of frequencies needed for each type of service. AM stations in the United States make do with a channel width of only 5,000 Hz.

meaning of numbers on AM dial

In practice, the FCC spaces AM channels 10 kHz apart. This spacing allows for 107 channels (that is, 1,070 divided by 10). A station's carrier-wave frequency, expressed in kilohertz, identifies its channel—540, 550, 560, and so on, up to 1,600 (receiver dials often drop the last zero). The 10-kHz spacing allows only 5 kHz for the actual signal, because one 5-kHz sideband contains all the useful information. Stations may modulate beyond 5 kHz on either side of their carrier frequencies if they can do so without causing interference, and many do. Nevertheless, AM's channel limitation makes it less satisfactory for music as compared to FM.

Channel and Station Classes

"clear" refers to channels, not stations

The FCC classifies AM channels as *local*, *regional*, and *clear*. By defining varying areas of coverage according to need, the FCC can license the maximum number of stations. Those on clear channels have been "cleared" of interfering cochannel stations, enabling distant sky-wave reception at night. Exhibit 4.7 explains the classification system further.

Sky-wave coverage also influences the FCC's station classification system. Again in the interest of licensing the maximum possible number of outlets, the FCC divides AM stations into four classes—Classes I, II, III, and IV (shown in relation to channel classes in Exhibit 4.7). Class I stations have dominant status on clear channels.

why not all stations on clear channels have clear sailing

Secondary stations on clear channels, designated as Class II, must avoid interfering with the Class I stations whose frequencies they share. Widely separated geographically from cochannel Class I stations, they often must also restrict their output by using directional antennas (sometimes with different patterns for night and day) and by either reducing power or closing down entirely at night.

Transmission   High AM radio transmitter power improves the efficiency of both ground-wave and sky-wave propagation, getting greater coverage and overcoming interference. Power authorizations for domestic U.S. AM broadcasting run from .25 kW (kilowatts), (250 watts), to a maximum of 50 kW (50,000 watts), as indicated in Exhibit 4.7.

range of kilowatt power for AM stations

The 50-kW ceiling is low relative to the maximum in other countries, which tend to favor fewer but more powerful stations. However, American broadcasting policy calls for licensing the maximum number of stations the market will bear. Limiting power to 50 kW prevents those with high power from getting too much of a competitive edge over weaker stations.

AM stations usually employ quarter-wavelength transmission antennas (waves at the lower end of the AM band are 1,823 feet long; those at the upper end, 593 feet). The entire steel transmitter tower acts as the radiating element.

why an AM tower's height reveals its frequency

In choosing sites for AM antennas, engineers look for good soil conductivity, freedom from surrounding sources of electrical interference, and distance from aircraft flight paths. Because ground waves propagate through the

EXHIBIT 4.7   AM Radio Station and Channel Classes

Station class	Power range	Channel class	Number of channels in class	Percentage of stations in class*
I	10–50 kW	Clear	60	1%
II	2.5–5 kW	Secondary clear	60	33
III	.5–5 kW	Regional	41	46
IV	.25–1 kW	Local	6	22

A large number of clear channels is needed because dominant Class I stations provide long-distance sky-wave reception and therefore have very wide spacing geographically. By the same token, only a small number of local channels is needed because many can occupy the same channel, prevented from interfering with each other by their low power.

Class I stations have A and B subclasses, with the I-Bs mostly on international (especially Mexican and Canadian) clear channels. Though Class II stations also occupy clear channels, they have secondary status and have to reduce power at night and use directional antennas to prevent their sky waves from interfering with the Class I stations on their channels.

For details on station and channel classes, see U.S. 47 CFR 73.21 ff. *Broadcasting/Cablecasting Yearbook* lists all AM stations by channel, location, power, and antenna pattern.

*Column does not add to 100 percent because of rounding.

EXHIBIT 4.8 AM Radio Transmitting Antenna

The entire steel tower of an AM radio antenna serves as a radiating element. For efficient propagation, the length of a tower must equal a quarter the length of the waves it radiates. Propagation also depends on soil conductivity, among other things. Heavy copper ground cables, buried in trenches radiating from the tower base, ensure good ground contact.

Source: Photo from Paul Will/Courtesy of Stainless Steel, Inc., North Wales, PA.

Earth's crust, AM antennas must be extremely well grounded, with many heavy copper cables buried in trenches radiating out from the base of the antenna tower. Exhibit 4.8 shows one of the AM antenna towers needed for directional propagation.

Low-power AM signals can be fed into building steam pipes or power lines, which serve as distribution grids. The signals radiate for a short distance into the space surrounding these conductors. Services using this propagation method are called **carrier-current stations**. Colleges and universities use carrier-current stations, which require no licensing.

Short-Wave AM Short-wave broadcasting, which also uses AM, has been allocated parts of the HF (high frequency) band between 6 and 25 MHz. The ionosphere refracts waves in this band both day and night, enabling round-the-clock coverage in target zones thousands of miles away from the originating transmitter.

The U.S. public makes little use of short-wave broadcasting. However, some foreign countries use short waves extensively for domestic services. A few privately operated American HF stations, mostly evangelistic religious outlets, broadcast to foreign audiences. Short waves are used most extensively by governments for international diplomacy, as discussed in Section 14.9.

The term *standard broadcasting* has become something of a misnomer because FM's inherently superior quality has enabled it to forge ahead of AM in numbers of both listeners and stations (counting both commercial and non-commercial stations in the total).

Bands and Channels

U.S. frequency-modulation broadcasting occupies a 20-MHz block of frequencies running from 88 to 108 MHz in the VHF band (Exhibit 4.1 identifies the band). This 20-MHz block allows for 100 FM channels of 200 KHz (.2 MHz) width. Later in this chapter, Exhibit 4.12 shows their spectrum location in relation to other broadcast channels.

key numbers: width of channels for FM

The FCC numbers FM channels 201 to 300, but licensees prefer to identify their stations by their midchannel frequency (in megahertz) rather than by channel number (88.1 for channel 201, 88.3 for channel 202, and so on). The first 20 FM channels are reserved for noncommercial educational use.

educational FM stations' dial location

The FM channel width of 200 kHz is generous—20 times the width of the AM channel. The extra width allows FM not only to transmit high-fidelity sound but also to include a stereophonic subcarrier. Subsidiary Communications Service (SCS) subcarriers can also be multiplexed in the FM channel to provide readings for the blind and background music for offices and stores, for example. An SCS service goes out simultaneously with the regular FM broadcast program but requires a converter attached to the receivers of its intended audience.

Transmission

The coverage area of an FM station depends on the station's power, the height of its transmitting antenna above the surrounding terrain, and the extent to which obtrusive terrain features or buildings block wave paths. In any event, FM uses direct waves, which reach only to the horizon.

Once determined by these factors, an FM station's coverage remains stable, day and night. This stability is one reason the FCC had an easier time preventing FM interference than it did AM interference.

FM coverage more stable than AM

The FCC divides the country into geographic zones and FM stations into three groups according to coverage area: Classes A, B, and C, defined in terms of power, antenna height, and zone. Class A power/height combinations enable a station to cover a radius of about 15 miles; Class B, about 30 miles; and Class C, about 60 miles (licensed only in uncrowded areas). The maximum power/height combination permits 100,000 watts (twice the maximum AM station power) and a 2,000-foot antenna elevation.

Reception

FM receivers with quality loudspeakers can reproduce the overtones essential for high-fidelity sound. That, plus FM's inherent immunity to static and interference, gives FM radio a significant quality advantage over AM radio.

FM's static-free reception is particularly noticeable in the southern part of the country, where subtropical storms cause much natural interference. FM also has an advantage in large cities, where concentrations of electrical machinery and appliances cause static.

In addition, FM radio has greater **dynamic range** (the loudness difference between the weakest and strongest sounds) than does AM, making for more realistic reproduction of music.

4.9   *Pictures in Motion*

It helps to approach broadcast television technology through a review of cinema, the original pictures-in-motion technology.

Picture Resolution   Most photographic systems represent scenes by breaking images down into many tiny **pixels** (picture elements). Basically, the size and distribution of pixels on the film stock limit **resolution**—the ability of film to depict fine detail. Film resolution (also called **definition**) equates with **information capacity** in electronic communication. Broadcast television pictures demand a broadband channel, one with the capacity to handle a great many pixels each second.

35 mm film: the
standard for theatrical
productions

Cinema quality standards vary according to the width of film stocks, stated in millimeters: 35 mm, 16 mm, and 8 mm. Along with some larger formats for wide-screen projection, 35 mm represents the professional theatrical standard. The intermediate size, 16-mm film, was originally the amateur standard, but television's great appetite for film hastened the evolution of 16-mm technology to the professional level. The less expensive 8-mm format became the amateur, home-movie standard. The quality of broadcast television approximates the quality of the current 8-mm standard.

In all cinema formats, some film area must be reserved for sprocket holes. Sprockets, the toothed wheels that pull film into position for exposure or projection, ensure accurate **registration**—the precise positioning of film frames in cameras for picture taking and in projectors for picture display. Some film area also has to be reserved for between-frame separation and (usually) for a soundtrack.

In electronic motion pictures, the frequency channel is the equivalent of the film stock. In terms of information capacity, channel width corresponds to film width—wider film equates with wider channel. Accordingly, television channels must be wide enough to permit reserving some frequencies for sound, frame separation, and other auxiliary information.

Frame Frequency   In cinema, what appears to be motion actually consists of still pictures (**frames**) projected in rapid succession. Each frame freezes the action at a slightly later moment than the preceding frame. The human eye retains the image of an object briefly after the object has been removed.

This image retention, called **persistence of vision**, blends together the images in successive frames. Thus the "motion" of motion pictures is actually an optical illusion.

no real motion in motion pictures

A fairly satisfactory illusion of natural motion occurs if a projector displays 16 frames per second (fps). At that rate, however, the track recorded along the edge of a sound film passes too slowly over the projector's pickup head for adequate sound quality.

It was found that increasing the frame rate to 24 fps made for satisfactory sound. The difference between the 16-fps silent standard and the 24-fps sound standard accounts for the jerkiness of silent films that are shown on modern projectors. Sound projectors change the projection rate from the original 16 fps to 24 fps—a 50 percent increase that speeds up the action to an unnatural degree.

key number: 24 fps— frame frequency for sound film

After each frame flashes on the screen, a moment of darkness ensues while the sprockets pull the next frame into position for projection. Although the 24 fps rate gives the illusion of continuous action, the eye still detects the fact that light falls on the screen intermittently. A sensation of **flicker** results.

An increase in frame frequency could overcome the flicker sensation, but because the 24-fps rate gives all the visual and sound information required, such an increase would waste film. Instead, projectors show each frame twice. Although the projector shows only 24 separate pictures per second, it throws light on the screen 48 times per second. This higher repetition rate gives the illusion of continuous illumination.

Television uses a similar trick. It illuminates the entire screen twice as many times as the number of complete pictures shown each second.

Electronic Pictures **4.10**

To achieve the illusion of motion without excessive flicker, television adapts the physical tricks of the cinema to the realm of electronics. Both media employ pixels, frames, registration, and a strategy for avoiding flicker.

Camera Pickup Tube   In the studio, a television-camera lens focuses the live televised scene on the face of the **pickup tube** within the camera. The pickup tube has two basic jobs: to break down the picture into many separate pieces (pixels) and to convert the light energy of each piece into electrical energy of corresponding strength.

Light-sensitive particles are densely scattered at random on the surface of a tiny rectangular plate within the tube. When an image falls on the plate, each particle reacts to the amount of light that strikes it, converting the light into an electrical equivalent and temporarily storing it.

The tube generates a microscopically small beam of electrons that sweeps back and forth across the back of the rectangular plate. When touched by the electron beam, each pixel discharges the energy it has stored. The

role of electron beam in TV camera

EXHIBIT **4.9**   TV Pickup Tube

A.

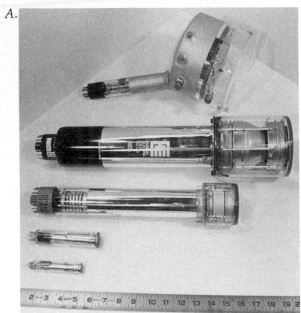

B.

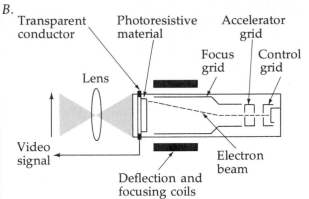

A. As technology improved, tubes became smaller. Commercial broadcasters first used the *iconoscope,* the odd-shaped tube at the top. Then *image orthicons,* with 3-inch and 4.5-inch faces, replaced iconoscopes. Smaller tubes such as the *vidicon* and *plumbicon* in turn replaced the image orthicon.

B. The main components and functions of the vidicon type of tube. A lens focuses the image on a photoresistive plate whose electrical resistance varies with the amount of light striking its surface. At the base of the tube, three components called grids help generate and shape the electron beam. As it leaves the focus grid, it enters magnetic fields created by coils surrounding the neck of the tube. Changes in the magnetic fields, caused by changes in the voltage fed to the deflection coils, sweep the electron beam back and forth in the prescribed scanning pattern. As the electron beam scans the rear side of the plate, it causes the electric energy stored in each pixel to flow to the conductor plate as an electrical voltage. The varying amplitudes of those voltages, led by a wire away from the plate, constitute the video signal.

Source: Photo by Frank Sauerwald, Temple University. Drawing adapted from A. Michael Noll, *Television Technology: Fundamentals and Future Prospects* Fig. 7–8, p. 67. © 1988 Artech House, Inc. Used by permission.

discharges are led away from the tube as electrical amplitude variations (voltages). Exhibit 4.9 gives more information on the process.

TV picture an illusion

Pickup tubes have been made in various shapes and sizes, as shown in Exhibit 4.9A. In principle, they work as described in Exhibit 4.9B. The tube has no moving part such as the film camera's revolving shutter and sprockets. The television camera needs no shutter, for the picture never exists as a complete frame; it occurs only as a sequence of pixels and lines. When the electronic equivalent of the pickup tube's pixel sequence reaches the receiver tube, persistence of vision blends the pixels into a seemingly unbroken image, as explained more fully in Section 4.13.

Scanning Standards   In U.S. television (standards differ from one country to another), the pickup tube's electron beam scans 525 lines per frame. The number of lines per frame affords a convenient way of stating a system's fidelity—its degree of resolution. Other key numbers affecting resolution are 30 per second (frame frequency) and 60 per second (field frequency).

key numbers: lines per TV frame and frames per second

The television camera cannot use the cinema's antiflicker strategy of repeating each entire frame twice. That repetition would double the size of the frequency channel—an unacceptable solution because of spectrum limitations.

Instead, television splits each frame into two parts, called **fields**. The electron beam illuminates the receiver screen from top to bottom for each field,

EXHIBIT 4.10   Video Scanning Sequence

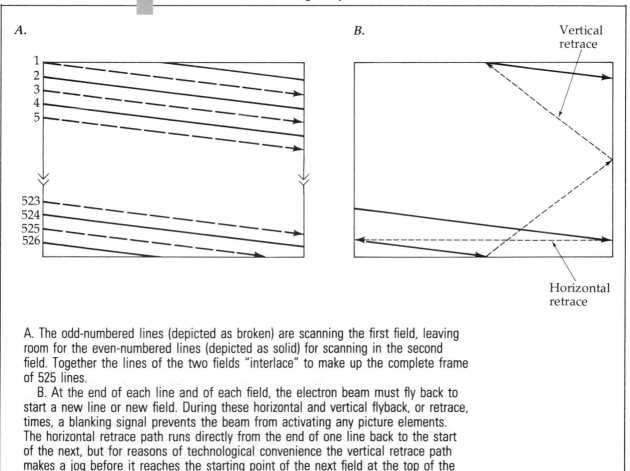

A. The odd-numbered lines (depicted as broken) are scanning the first field, leaving room for the even-numbered lines (depicted as solid) for scanning in the second field. Together the lines of the two fields "interlace" to make up the complete frame of 525 lines.

B. At the end of each line and of each field, the electron beam must fly back to start a new line or new field. During these horizontal and vertical flyback, or retrace, times, a blanking signal prevents the beam from activating any picture elements. The horizontal retrace path runs directly from the end of one line back to the start of the next, but for reasons of technological convenience the vertical retrace path makes a jog before it reaches the starting point of the next field at the top of the frame. The vertical retrace time, equivalent to the time needed to scan 21 normal lines, is called the VBI (vertical blanking interval). During the VBI, nonpicture information can be transmitted, such as closed captions and teletext.

but it picks up only *every other line* in the frame. This method, known as **offset**, or **interlace**, **scanning**, causes the electron beam to scan line 1, line 3, line 5, and so on, to the bottom of the field, then fly back to the top of the field to fill in lines 2, 4, 6, and so on, as explained more fully in Exhibit 4.10. Interlace scanning cheats the eye by presenting it with 60 *fields* per second, but only 30 *frames*. The eye fails to detect the fact that two fields are needed to complete a frame.

To review, the electron beam scans *60 fields* per second, each field consisting of every other line in a frame. Because it takes two fields to make up a single frame, the beam scans *30 frames* per second. The beam scans the 525 lines of pixels that make up each frame in 1/30th of a second. Instead of the sound-motion-picture rates of 24 fps, with each frame repeated once for 48 screen illuminations per second, television uses 30 (frame frequency) and 60 (field frequency).

relationship of TV frames to TV fields

Auxiliary Signals Several types of auxiliary signals occupy part of the television channel. Signals called **sync pulses** keep camera-tube scanning in step (synchronized) with receiver-tube scanning. Generated by a special timing device in the studio control-room (as shown in Exhibit 4.13), sync pulses ensure that each pixel in each line will appear on the receiver screen in the same location it had in the pickup tube.

Another auxiliary signal blanks out the scanning beam during **retrace** (also called **flyback**) **intervals**. The electron beam uses these intervals to fly back diagonally from the end of one line to the beginning of the next line (**horizontal retrace**) and from the bottom of one field to the top of the next field (**vertical retrace**). Exhibit 4.10 illustrates these retrace movements.

If the beam continued to pick up picture elements during its retrace movement, the orderly scanning sequence would be destroyed.

Teletext The vertical retrace time is called the **vertical blanking interval (VBI)**. Because no picture information goes out during the VBI, that transmission time (the equivalent of 21 picture lines) can be used to send additional information. The VBI has several uses, notably for **teletext**—still frames containing text and maps or drawings.

A television station equipped to transmit teletext stores up to about 200 pages (picture frames) of information and transmits them in rotation during the VBI. At the home receiver, the user may request specific pages by means of a key-pad. The key-pad activates a minicomputer in a teletext adapter. It "grabs" the requested frames as they go by in rotation. The computer then feeds them to the television screen for display.

A specialized form of teletext, **closed captioning**, superimposes captions over regular television programs for the benefit of the hearing impaired. Only viewers with a decoder can display the captions; hence the term "closed" for this type of teletext.

type of modulation used for TV sound

TV Sound U.S. television uses FM sound. The 100-kHz sound subchannel is located in the upper part of the television channel, as shown in Exhibit 4.11. Sound needs no synchronizing signals to keep it in step with the picture. Sound and picture occur simultaneously and go out in real time.

TV uses FM sound

Though half the size of the FM radio channel, the television sound channel is designed to respond to a sound range from 10 to 15,000 Hz. It also has room for subcarriers that enable multiplexing stereophonic sound and alternative language soundtracks within the channel.

Color TV The signal specifications for color television provide for **compatibility**—black-and-white (monochrome) receivers can reproduce a color signal without the aid of an adapter. Multiplexing permits adding the color

EXHIBIT *4.11*   The TV Channel

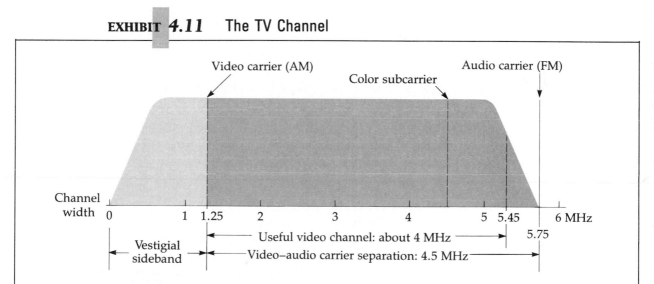

The architecture of the 6-MHz television channel. A vestigial lower sideband takes up the 1.25 MHz below the video carrier frequency. A subcarrier, higher in the video portion of the channel, conveys the color information.

When modulated by the black-and-white video (luminance) information, the main video carrier's upper sideband overlaps the sideband of the color subcarrier, but *interleaving* minimizes conflict. Uneven distribution of frequencies carrying the luminance signal makes such interleaving possible. If the teeth of a comb are visualized as the frequencies occupied by the monochrome information, the color information occupies frequencies represented by the spaces between the teeth.

A 100-kHz subchannel accommodates the audio information, located near the upper end of the channel. A buffer zone above the audio subchannel intervenes before the next higher contiguous 6-MHz channel begins.

Source: Adapted from 47 CFR 73.699.

component without enlarging the television channel. Exhibit 4.11 shows the position of the color subcarrier in the television channel.

TV primary colors differ from painters' primaries

The color camera picks up images in three designated primary colors. The primaries are red, green, and blue rather than the red-blue-yellow primaries familiar to artists. Filters separate the color components of images before they reach the camera tube. The various **hues** of the color picture depend on the proportional strengths of the primary colors in each pixel.

In addition to hue, color images also have a brightness attribute, **luminance**. The luminance component contains all the fine detail in color pictures, and it alone suffices for the black-and white receiver.

4.11 *TV Channels*

key number: size of TV channel

U.S. broadcast standards call for a 6-MHz television channel—600 times the width of an AM radio broadcast channel. Indeed, *all* the AM and FM broadcast channels together occupy less spectrum space than only four television channels. Exhibit 4.11 shows how the 6 MHz of the channel are utilized.

Channel Width and Resolution

TV picture quality compared with movie quality

Even with such wide channels, television achieves relatively low picture resolution by the standards of theatrical motion pictures and good-quality still photography. The average home receiver displays about 150,000 pixels per frame, but a projected 35-mm film frame contains about a million pixels.

Current television resolution standards represent a compromise between ideal quality and the lowest quality that most viewers can tolerate for continuous watching. Higher quality has to be sacrificed to avoid using too much spectrum space. The same spectrum-saving goal motivates the suppression of the lower sideband of the television picture signal, as shown in Exhibit 4.11. Among the improvements for the future, discussed in Chapter 5, high-definition television is expected to improve the current standard, known as NTSC (National Television System Committee, which recommended the standards adopted in 1952).

Location in Spectrum

Exhibit 4.12 shows the location of television channels in the spectrum relative to the location of channels used by the other broadcast services. An FCC table allots specific channels by number to specific towns and cities throughout the United States (the table can be found in 47 CFR 73.606, an official FCC rule listed under "Code of Federal Regulations" in the bibliography of this book). The map in Exhibit 2.10 gives an example, showing all the places to which one particular channel has been allotted.

Cochannel separation varies among three geographic zones (essentially, northern, midland, and southern) and between the two channel types (VHF and UHF). As an example of the VHF–UHF distinction, in Zone 1, stations

EXHIBIT *4.12*   Summary of Broadcast Channel Specifications

Broadcast service	Channel width	Number of channels	Channel identification numbers	Band	Allocated frequencies
AM (standard) radio	10 kHz	107[a]	54–160[b]	MF	535–1605 kHz[a]
VHF television	6 MHz	3	2–4[c]	VHF	54–72 MHz
		2	5–6	VHF	76–88 MHz[d]
FM radio	200 kHz	100	201–300	VHF	88–108 MHz
VHF television	6 MHz	7	7–13	VHF	174–216 MHz
UHF television	6 MHz	56[e]	14–69	UHF	470–806 MHz

This table consolidates scattered information in the text to enable comparing the primary channel specifications for all three broadcast services. Note that the television allocation is fragmented into four different frequency groups in two different bands.

[a]AM channels are denoted by midchannel frequenices at 10-kHz intervals—540, 550, 560, . . . , up to 1600. Receiver dials often omit the last zero, reading 54, 55, 56, and so on.

[b]The AM band was due to be expanded to 117 channels running up to 1705 kHz in 1990.

[c]Originally there was a channel 1, located at 44–50 MHz. However, it interfered with other services, and in 1948 the FCC reallocated that group of frequenices to nonbroadcast services but retained the original number scheme.

[d]Note that VHF channel 6 comes immediately before the start of the FM band. This proximity sometimes causes TV–FM interference.

[e]Because of the high demand for UHF frequencies by other services, not all the 56 UHF channels have been allotted to actual TV use.

on VHF channels must be about 170 miles apart, whereas those on UHF must be about 155 miles apart. Details of these rules can be found in 47 CFR 73.609–613.

TV Transmission   4.12

Synchronization   The **sync generator** keeps the camera pickup tube in step with the receiver display tube. Exhibit 4.13 shows the sync generator in relation to other control-room equipment. It generates precisely timed signals that activate the camera's deflection coils, causing the electron beam to go through its prescribed scanning motions.

coordination of picture-tube electron beam with pickup tube

The sync generator also inserts the blanking signals during retrace periods and synchronizes inputs from external picture sources such as recordings and network feeds. Synchronizing and blanking cues become part of the composite picture signal.

Combining Picture and Sound   The picture (video) and sound (audio) components go from the studio to the transmitter site as independent signals.

EXHIBIT 4.13   TV Station Operational Components and Signals

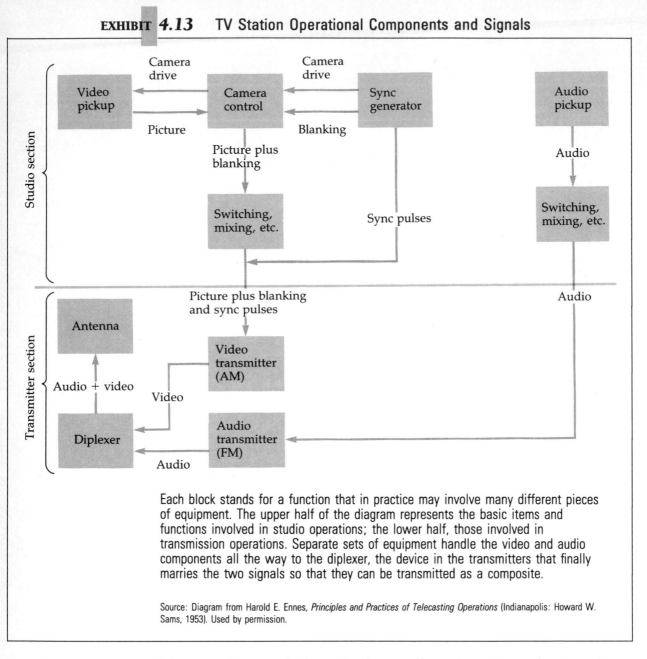

Each block stands for a function that in practice may involve many different pieces of equipment. The upper half of the diagram represents the basic items and functions involved in studio operations; the lower half, those involved in transmission operations. Separate sets of equipment handle the video and audio components all the way to the diplexer, the device in the transmitters that finally marries the two signals so that they can be transmitted as a composite.

Source: Diagram from Harold E. Ennes, *Principles and Practices of Telecasting Operations* (Indianapolis: Howard W. Sams, 1953). Used by permission.

The transmitter may be located miles away from the studio so that it can be near the antenna. At the transmitter, video and audio signals modulate separate audio and video transmitters.

A television station's power is usually stated in terms of the **effective radiated power (ERP)** of its *video* signal. The video transmitter operates on higher power than the audio transmitter because it has a much greater information load, requiring up to 20 times as much power.

Video and audio signals meet for the first time in the **diplexer**—a device that combines video and audio signals before feeding them as a composite signal to the antenna for propagation, as shown in Exhibit 4.13.

Propagation   Engineers elevate television-transmission antennas as high as possible—on mountain peaks, the roofs of tall buildings, or the tops of tall steel towers. The antenna towers themselves do not radiate signals as do AM towers. They only support the radiating elements, which are relatively small, in keeping with the shortness of television's VHF and UHF waves.

Television antennas propagate signals directionally. They cut off waves that would otherwise shoot off into space above the horizon, redirecting them at a *downward* angle, toward the line-of-sight coverage area.

why TV transmitting antennas propagate directionally

Objects in the propagation path block UHF waves more easily than they block VHF waves. Moreover, UHF waves attenuate more rapidly than VHF waves. The FCC therefore allows UHF stations to use very high power (up to 5 million watts) to compensate to some extent for the inherent coverage limitations of UHF waves. In setting television-power limits, the FCC uses a formula that takes antenna height into consideration. Details on power/height regulations can be found in 47 CFR 73.699.

A television station's coverage distance and the shape of its coverage area thus depend on several factors: transmitting antenna height and efficiency, obstructive terrain features, transmitter frequency, and effective radiated power. Exhibit 4.14 shows how obstructions can affect propagation.

factors that control TV signal coverage area

TV Reception   4.13

Antenna   The length of a transmitting antenna can be sized for the length of the antenna's specific carrier wave. Receiving antennas, however, must be designed to pick up many channels, often both VHF and UHF. At these frequencies, receiving antennas are highly directional. They must therefore point toward the transmitters. In areas where transmitters are located at widely different points of the compass, a rotatable outdoor antenna may be necessary.

Contour Grades   The FCC classifies television-station coverage in terms of Grade A and Grade B contours. A station's **Grade A contour** encloses the area within which satisfactory service can be received with ordinary antennas 90 percent of the time. Its **Grade B contour** encloses an area more distant from the transmitter within which reception is satisfactory only 50 percent of the time. These coverage contours have no meaning for cable television subscribers, who do not depend on over-the-air antennas for reception.

EXHIBIT **4.14** TV Propagation Paths

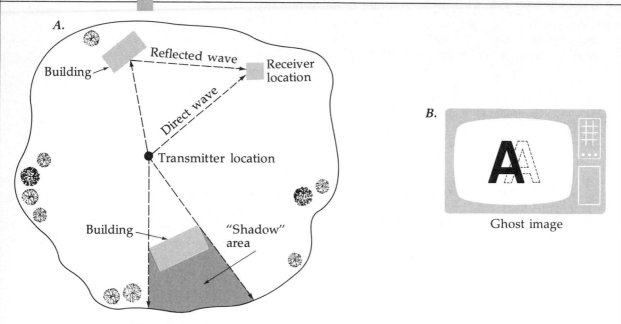

A. Hypothetical coverage pattern of a television station, showing some characteristics of direct-wave propagation. The waves carry only to the horizon; some may encounter surfaces that reflect signals; some may encounter obstructions that cause "shadow" areas in the coverage pattern.

B. When a receiver detects both a direct wave and a reflected wave, the reflected wave will have traveled over a longer path, therefore arriving at the receiver slightly later than the direct wave. When the receiver displays the signal of the delayed reflected wave, the image lags slightly behind that of the direct wave, appearing as a "ghost."

CRT Operation Like transmitters, receivers process the video and audio parts of the signal separately. In conventional receivers, the video information goes to a **kinescope**—a type of cathode-ray tube (CRT). This is the tube the viewer looks at as the receiver "screen."

TV picture tube as CRT, a class of vacuum tubes

On the inside face of the kinescope, pixels consisting of phosphorescent particles glow when bombarded with electrons. Within the neck of the kinescope resides an electron gun—a large analog of the one in the pickup tube. It shoots a beam of electrons toward the face of the tube. Guided by external deflection coils, the electron beam writes an image on the "screen" (actually the inner face of the tube).

The beam stimulates pixels that glow with varying intensities, depending on the strength of the beam. It lays down the image, line by line, field by

EXHIBIT **4.15** Color Kinescope Tube

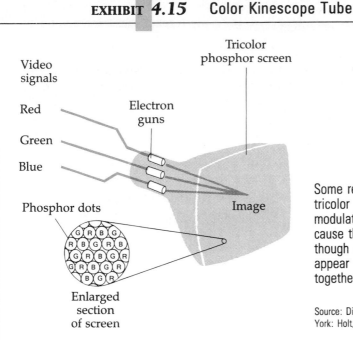

Video signals

Red

Green

Blue

Electron guns

Tricolor phosphor screen

Image

Phosphor dots

Enlarged section of screen

Some receiver tubes use three electronic guns and tricolor phosphor dots. Varying amplitudes in the modulated currents fed to each of the electron guns cause the dots to glow with varying intensities; though only the red, green, and blue primary colors appear on the kinescope face, the eye blends them together to make all the various hues.

Source: Diagram adapted from Paul Davidovits, *Communication* (New York: Holt, Rinehart & Winston, 1972), p. 114. Used by permission.

field, and frame by frame. The synchronizing signals originated by the sync generator in the studio activate the deflection coils, keeping the receiver scanning sequence in step with that of the pickup tube at the studio.

Color Reception Phosphors that glow in the red-blue-green primaries coat the inner face of the color CRT, arranged either as narrow parallel stripes or as triads of dots. Receiver circuits decode the television signal into components representing the energy levels of the three primaries in each pixel. Three streams of electrons, one for each primary, strike the tube face, using one or more electron guns, as shown in Exhibit 4.15.

Only the primary colors appear on the kinescope. The eye perceives varying hues in accordance with varying intensities of the primaries as delivered by the electron beams. One can confirm that only the primaries appear by looking at part of a color picture on the face of a kinescope with a small magnifying glass. Only dots or stripes in red, blue, and green will be visible.

personal experiment: test color TV for primaries

Program Recording 4.14

Broadcast stations, whether radio or television, obtain most of their programs from distant centralized sources, either as recordings or as network feeds. Program recording and networking therefore rank as essential elements of broadcasting technology. Here the familiar, conventional disc- and tape-recording technologies are described. Innovative recording methods are described in the next chapter.

Audio Discs   In traditional disc sound-recording, a stylus ("needle") responds via a microphone and amplifiers to the vibrations of sound in air. The vibrating stylus cuts a concentric groove in a revolving master disc. The stylus transforms the frequency and amplitude patterns of the original sound into deformations in the groove. Molds derived from pressings of master discs enable mass production of copies.

When a disc is played back, a pickup-head stylus rides in the modulated groove. It vibrates in keeping with the recorded pattern. The stylus movements generate a modulated electric current. After amplification, these analog voltages create sounds by causing vibrations in headphones or a loudspeaker.

Audio Tape   The mechanics of disc-and-stylus recording have obvious drawbacks. For example, the stylus causes wear and tear as it rides in the groove, and dust and scratches cause distortion. Nor does the system lend itself to home recording.

Magnetic-tape sound recording solved these problems, combining recording and playback functions in a single, portable unit. The magnetic recording medium is a flexible plastic tape coated with minute particles of a metallic compound. The smallness of the particles and the number available during each second, as determined mainly by the tape's width and velocity, limit a tape's storage capacity.

size and speed of magnetic tape determine sound quality

Master sound recordings on quarter-inch tape usually call for a tape speed of either 15 or 30 inches per second (ips). In sound broadcasting, a playback speed of $7\frac{1}{2}$ ips suffices. Lower speeds can be used for office dictation and other applications in which economy counts more than quality. Multitrack master recordings and other specialized tasks that call for high quality use wider tape.

In recording, the tape passes over a record head consisting of an electromagnet. Modulated current from a microphone modulates the magnetic field of the electromagnet, rearranging the tape's metallic particles into corresponding analog patterns. On playback, the tape passes over another electromagnet, which responds to the stored patterns on the tape by generating a modulated electrical current that actuates the loudspeaker. A third electromagnet, the erase head, can be used to neutralize the stored patterns so that the same tape can be used repeatedly.

how a tape cassette differs from a tape cartridge

Reel-to-reel magnetic-tape recorders leave each reel separate and accessible. Cassettes and cartridges enclose the tape in a housing. A cassette houses two hubs, one for the feed reel, one for the takeup reel. After playing, the cassette must be rewound or, in the case of half-width recording, the cassette can be flipped over to play a second "side."

A cartridge, or cart, contains an endless tape loop that repeats itself, using a single hub. Stations record commercial spots, jingles, promotional announcements, musical pieces, and other program elements on carts, each one containing a single item. Inaudible cues recorded on the tapes tell the playback unit to stop at the end of an item and to recue the tape for subsequent replay. Carts can be activated by a computer in a preprogrammed sequence, or a DJ or control operator can activate them by pushing buttons.

Videotape Recording   In order to handle the increased information load of television, videotape recorders (VTRs) must pass tape over the record/

EXHIBIT 4.16   Videotape Recording Formats

A. Transverse Quadraplex Format.

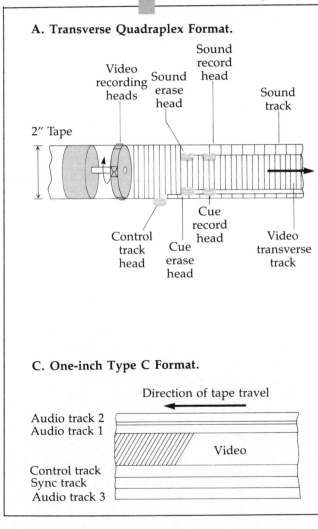

B. Helical Format.

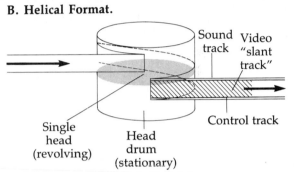

A. Four video recording heads mounted on a rapidly spinning wheel, shown at the left, lay down transverse tracks across the width of the 2-inch tape. Sound is recorded longitudinally along one edge, auxiliary information along the other edge.

B. Tape spirals around a large, stationary drum. Within the drum, the video recording head spins on a revolving disc, making contact with the tape as it slips over the drum's smooth surface. Because of the spiral wrap, the tape moves slightly downward as well as lengthwise, so that the combined movements of tape and recording head produce a slanting track, as shown. Some helical recorders use two heads; some use different wraparound configurations.

C. An example of one of the larger formats. Still narrower VTR tapes are used—$\frac{3}{4}$-inch, half-inch, 8-mm, and even quarter-inch.

Source: Drawings courtesy Ampex Corporation.

playback heads at an extremely high speed. The original quadruplex VTRs achieved an effective tape-to-head velocity of 1,500 inches per second by using four revolving recording heads that lay down a track transversely, across the width of 4-inch tape, as depicted in Exhibit 4.16A. Simpler, less expensive professional videotape recorders use narrower tape with a modified head-to-tape configuration, as shown in Exhibit 4.16B.

transverse tracks on tape increase head-to-tape velocity

Home videotape recorders in the form of videocassette recorders (VCRs), costing about 1 percent of the original quadruplex professional VTR price, enable the consumer to play and copy programs with nearly professional quality. Older models record sound along the edge of the tape, as in the format shown in Exhibit 4.16B and C. More recent models incorporate high-quality stereophonic sound, interleaving slant tracks for sound with the picture tracks.

role of home VCRs

VCRs depend on the user's home television set for playback display but contain their own tuners to enable recording off the air while the owner watches a different program on the set. VCRs can also record the output of home video cameras (camcorders) and can display rented or purchased feature films that have been transferred to tape.

Equipped with many sophisticated computer-assisted features, such as the ability to be programmed days in advance to pick up a sequence of shows on different stations, modern digital VCRs are one of the most versatile and popular of ancillary consumer electronic communication products. Some provide "windows" (to monitor as many as nine channels at once on the screen), freeze-frame storage, and a "mosaic" function that changes the image into patterns of colored squares.

EXHIBIT 4.17   Coaxial Cable

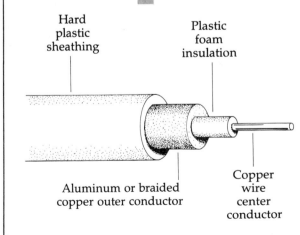

| Hard plastic sheathing | Plastic foam insulation |
| Aluminum or braided copper outer conductor | Copper wire center conductor |

Coaxial cable gets its name from the fact that it has two conductors with a common axis: a solid central conductor surrounded by a tubelike hollow conductor. The radio energy travels within the protected environment of the space between the two conductors. Cable television relies on this type of conductor, as do many terrestrial relay links that convey television signals, telephone calls, data, and other types of information.

Source: Drawing adapted from illustration in Walter S. Baer, *Cable Television: A Handbook for Decision Making* (Santa Monica, CA: The Rand Corporation, 1973), p. 4. Used by permission.

Networks, like recordings, represent a centralized source of programs. Essential to networks are the relays that distribute programs from network headquarters to affiliated stations.

Wire/Cable Relays   Any point-to-point or point-to-multipoint linkage, whether by wire or radio, can function as a relay. A relay's channel capacity determines which types of material the relay can distribute.

The original broadcast radio-network relays used wire telephone circuits. When equalized to compensate for the faster attenuation of the higher audio frequencies, telephone wires suffice for radio programs.

telephone wires as radio relays

EXHIBIT 4.18   Microwave Relay Antenna Designs

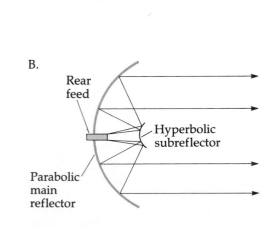

A. An outlet ("front feed") positioned in front of the dish-shaped parabolic main reflector delivers the radio waves, which are then reflected outward in a narrow beam resembling that of a searchlight. B. A variation of the parabolic main reflector directs the energy from the center of the reflector toward a small subreflector that sends the waves back to the main reflector for transmission. C. Dish-shaped reflectors lose efficiency because the feed tube or subreflector cuts off part of the outgoing beam. The horn reflector avoids this problem.

Source: Drawings from Graham Langley, *Telecommunications Primer*, 2nd ed, 1986. Reprinted by permission of Pitman Publishing, London.

However, telephone wires cannot pass the broad band of frequencies required for television. The radio energy tends to radiate from the wire, dissipating rapidly. Coaxial cable prevents much of this loss, conducting a broad band of frequencies through an enclosed space. Coaxial cable has two conductors, a solid wire running down the center of a hollow metal tube. A nonconductive material insulates the center wire from the tube, as shown in Exhibit 4.17. Attenuation still occurs, but repeater amplifiers inserted at intervals compensate for the loss.

Microwave Relays A second traditional relay method uses radio waves in the form of microwave links. Microwaves vary in length from 1 meter down to 1 millimeter. Microwave relays usually employ the UHF band (only a portion of which is allocated to broadcast television channels).

enormous microwave ERP achieved by a directional beam

UHF waves in the range used by microwave relays attenuate rapidly in the atmosphere. However, when focused in a narrow, concentrated beam, the waves from a microwave transmitter attain an effective radiated power increase of a hundred-thousand-fold. Exhibit 4.18 shows how microwave antennas focus radio energy. Microwaves concentrated in this way can travel about 30 miles without excessive attenuation.

number of microwave repeaters needed to span U.S.

Accordingly, a microwave relay system uses a series of towers spaced about 30 miles apart, each with a line-of-sight view of the next and the previous tower. Repeater equipment on one tower receives transmissions from the previous tower, amplifies the signals, and retransmits them to the next tower in the series. It takes more than a hundred towers to span the continental United States from coast to coast.

Although still in use, the traditional recording and relay technologies described in this chapter have been supplemented by newer, more efficient methods. New program-delivery systems have also developed, competing with traditional broadcasting. These innovations are the subjects of the next chapter.

Technological Innovation and the Future of Broadcasting

The preceding chapter described the steady development of traditional broadcasting technology from 1920 to 1970. After 1970, electronic media technology entered an innovative era of rapid change. This chapter focuses on innovations—some already in use, others still in experimental and planning stages—and their impact on traditional broadcasting. The public welcomed new methods of program delivery because they overcame three technical limitations of traditional television broadcasting:

- The short range of VHF/UHF television signals, which limits station coverage.
- The spectrum shortage that puts a cap on the number of stations that can be licensed in any one community.
- The confinement of each broadcasting station to a single channel, which limits program choice.

Cable television offered solutions to these technical drawbacks, making possible the reception of dozens of programs where before only a few could be received.

5.1   *Cable TV*

A cable television system sends its many programs through an enclosed environment, that of coaxial cable—a special pipelike conductor of the type shown in Exhibit 4.17. Such a cable can carry a wide band of frequencies—as many as 400 MHz (compared to the 6 MHz required for one single television program). Because coaxial cable guides its signals through an enclosed space, its signals neither cause nor receive significant over-the-air interference.

Coaxial cable was originally introduced as a means of distribution. It provided a broadband pathway for relaying broadcast television network programs and other signals that need wider frequency bands than ordinary wires can carry, as described in Section 4.14. Expensive to install, coaxial cable first served only heavily trafficked relay routes. Its cost made it seem impracticable as a widespread means of delivering programs to individual homes. Cable television changed this perception. Cable-system operators discovered that people will pay so much in subscription fees to receive programs over cable that sufficient income can be generated to defray the high capital costs of running cable to every subscribing home. Thus coaxial cable became a

hybrid distribution/delivery medium. It distributes programs via trunk lines throughout a service area and delivers them via drop lines to individual homes.

Cable Channels   Cable television uses the same type of radio-wave energy as broadcast television, enclosing it in coaxial cable instead of propagating it through space. Exhibit 5.1 shows how cable systems utilize the broad band of frequencies fed through a 60-channel coaxial cable.

The fact that coaxial-cable signals offer no interference to existing over-the-air services means that cable television can employ dozens of VHF channels both above and below the portion of the VHF band used for broadcasting. These frequencies are denied to over-the-air broadcasters because they have

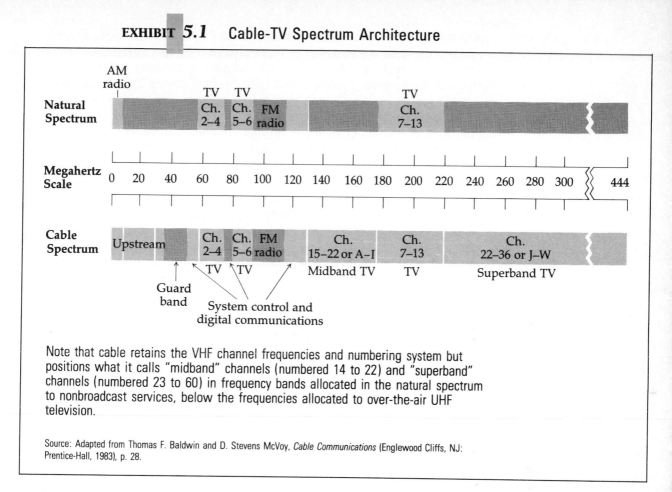

EXHIBIT 5.1 Cable-TV Spectrum Architecture

Note that cable retains the VHF channel frequencies and numbering system but positions what it calls "midband" channels (numbered 14 to 22) and "superband" channels (numbered 23 to 60) in frequency bands allocated in the natural spectrum to nonbroadcast services, below the frequencies allocated to over-the-air UHF television.

Source: Adapted from Thomas F. Baldwin and D. Stevens McVoy, *Cable Communications* (Englewood Cliffs, NJ: Prentice-Hall, 1983), p. 28.

been assigned to nonbroadcast over-the-air services. Although broadcast television is limited to only 12 VHF channels, cable television uses as many as a hundred.

All radio energy attenuates (weakens) as it travels, but it attenuates much faster in the enclosed cable environment than in the atmosphere. Moreover, the higher the frequency, the more drastic is the attenuation. Because of the high attenuation rate of the higher band of broadcast television frequencies, the UHF band, cable systems use only VHF channels.

Even in the VHF range, signals lose half of their strength traveling through a mere 200 feet of cable. Booster amplifiers must be inserted in the cable at frequent intervals to keep the signals up to strength. The battle against attenuation therefore adds considerably to the cost of the cable itself.

battle against attenuation

Subscribers to systems with 12 or fewer channels use the VHF tuners in their television receivers to switch from one cable channel to another. Systems with more than 12 channels require an adapter unit that has its own tuner for channel switching. The adapter ignores the receiver's UHF tuner, using cable-specific VHF channels not available to over-the-air television. Exhibit 5.1 shows the numbers assigned to these channels by cable systems.

Only older receivers need an external adapter containing the expanded VHF tuner. Cable-ready receivers have built-in cable tuners. Whether located in an adapter or built into the receiver, the cable tuner gets access to the receiver circuitry by feeding the viewer's channel selections into the receiver's regular over-the-air tuner (usually through channel 2, 3, or 4).

As Exhibit 5.1 shows, cable television assigns no video signals to the segment of the VHF band allocated to FM radio broadcasting. It reserves those frequencies for cable delivery of audio services. Cable firms obtain audio programming from subcarriers on satellite-delivered television channels as well as from radio broadcast stations.

audio programs on cable

Cable-TV System Components   A cable television system assembles programs from various sources at the system's control center, the **headend**. The programs consist of over-the-air signals of both nearby and distant television stations, material produced or procured locally by the individual cable system, and programs relayed to the system's headend by satellite-to-cable networks.

Besides reception facilities, a headend contains equipment for reprocessing the incoming signals, equalizing them, and feeding them to a **modulator**— a transmission device for sending the signals over the system's coaxial-cable distribution/delivery network. The cable operator positions program services on the system's array of channels, arbitrarily assigning a channel number to each service. This practice accounts for the fact that cable subscribers sometimes find that a channel 9 television station, for example, might come in on cable channel 12.

positioning service on cable channels

Also at or near the headend may be found local-origination facilities. They can vary in complexity from simple automated alphanumeric news-and-weather displays to full-scale production studios.

From the headend, the cable system distributes programs throughout its service area via a coaxial-cable network. Cable distribution/delivery networks have a tree-and-branch pattern. As Exhibit 5.2 shows, trunk cables distribute signals to branching feeder cables that carry the signals to clusters of houses, where still lighter drop cables deliver the signals to individual subscribers. A headend can distribute programs over a radius of about five miles. Because of attenuation, covering wider areas requires subsidiary headends. They receive the programs via special supertrunk coaxial cable, fiber-optic cable, or microwave relay.

cable TV's tree-and-branch distribution pattern

Where possible, cable firms mount distribution cables on existing utility poles. Within large cities, however, the cables must go underground in conduits and tunnels. It costs too much to install cable over long distances to reach thinly scattered populations in remote areas. This unserved rural market creates a ready-made audience for the direct-broadcast satellite services discussed in the next section.

EXHIBIT 5.2   Cable-TV System Plan

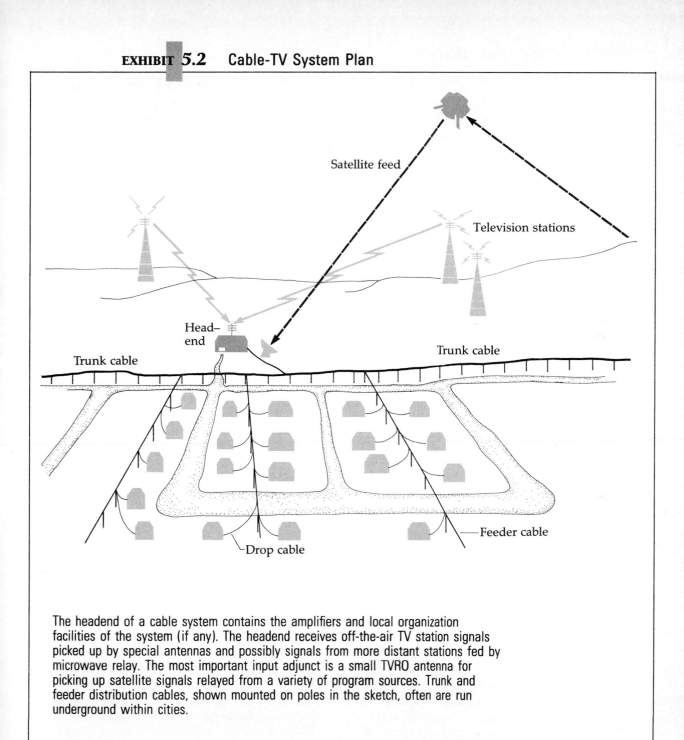

Satellite feed

Television stations

Head-end

Trunk cable

Trunk cable

Feeder cable

Drop cable

The headend of a cable system contains the amplifiers and local organization facilities of the system (if any). The headend receives off-the-air TV station signals picked up by special antennas and possibly signals from more distant stations fed by microwave relay. The most important input adjunct is a small TVRO antenna for picking up satellite signals relayed from a variety of program sources. Trunk and feeder distribution cables, shown mounted on poles in the sketch, often are run underground within cities.

Like coaxial cable, satellites first served a relay function and only later began to deliver programs directly to consumers. The great majority of satellite traffic still consists of relays, such as network programs relayed to affiliates and on-the-spot news events relayed to studios. But improvement in satellite technology promises an increase in another hybrid—direct-broadcast satellite (DBS) services.

DBS as a hybrid service

Satellite vs. Microwave Relay Distribution

Microwave relay networks depend on ground-based towers spaced every 20 miles or so. They cannot span oceans. Live transoceanic television first became possible only when international communication satellites began to function as relay stations in space. Far beyond the Earth's attenuating atmosphere, a single satellite has line-of-sight access to some 40 percent of the globe's surface, as suggested by Exhibit 5.3.

Although often likened to microwave towers thousands of miles in height, communication satellites differ fundamentally from the older relay technology. A microwave repeater links one specific location with only two others—the next sending and receiving points in the relay network. A satellite, however, links a group of relay stations (the satellite's receive/transmit units) to an unlimited number of receiving Earth stations. Adding more Earth stations adds nothing to transmission costs, whereas linking up new destinations in microwave relay networks does add to costs.

satellites are distance-insensitive relays

Satellites also have the advantage of being distance insensitive. They can reach Earth stations at any distance within the satellite's **footprint** (coverage area). Distance adds no transmission expense as it does with microwave networks. In addition, microwave signals lose quality as they go through scores of reamplifications in being passed on from one repeater station to the next. But satellite relays amplify a signal only once before sending it down to an Earth station.

Geostationary Orbit

If satellites moved across the sky like the sun and moon, receiving antennas would need costly tracking mechanisms to keep them pointing toward the moving signal source. But satellites can be positioned so that they remain stationary with respect to their target area on the Earth below. Once a receiving antenna has been adjusted to point in the right direction, it needs no further attention.

why satellites in orbit don't fall toward Earth

Satellites that appear to stay in one location above the Earth operate in **geostationary** (or **geosynchronous**) **orbit**—an orbital position directly above the equator at a height of about 22,300 miles. At that height, objects revolve around the Earth at the same rate that the Earth turns on its axis. Moreover, the centrifugal force tending to throw a satellite outward into space cancels the gravitational force tending to pull it back to Earth, keeping it suspended in space.

EXHIBIT 5.3   Geostationary Satellite Orbit

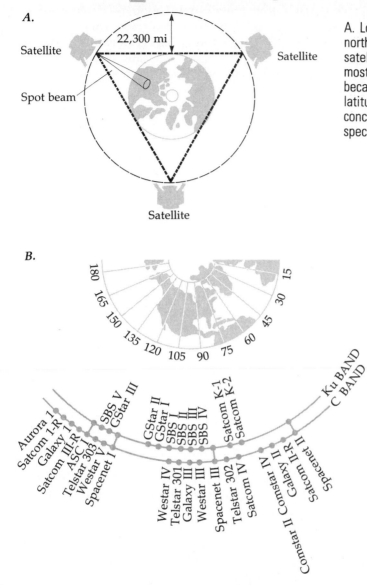

A.

22,300 mi

Satellite

Satellite

Spot beam

Satellite

A. Looking down from space on the Earth's north pole, one can see how three equi-distant satellites poised above the equator could "see" most of the Earth's surface (only "most" because satellite signals fade out at polar latitudes). Signals can be intensified when concentrated in a *spot beam* directed at a specific region.

B.

B. Each satellite has its assigned position, expressed in degrees of a half-circle either east or west of the prime meridian at Greenwich, in the segment of the geosynchronous orbit approximately in the longitude of the target area. Because the orbital segment allotted to the United States is so crowded, Ku-band satellites are shown at a different height than the C-band satellites; actually, all occupy the same orbit, 22,300 miles above the equator. Note that the Aurora 1 occupies the position farthest west, at 143°; Spacenet II occupies the position farthest east, at 69° west. The linkages between bands for Spacenet I and others indicate that those satellites carry both Ku-band and C-band transponders. The drawing shows the U.S. satellites and their positions as of mid-1989.

Source: (Satellite orbital locations); "Satellite Guide to the Sky," *Broadcasting*, 18 July 1988, p. 44. Used by permission.

The geostationary orbit consists of an imaginary circle in space. Satellites in that enormous orbit, some 22,300 miles above the equator, actually move through space at about 7,000 miles per hour. From the perspective of an observer on Earth, however, they seem to stay in one place, keeping in step with the Earth as it rotates. In practice, geosynchronous satellites tend to drift out of position, but ground controllers can activate small on-board jet thrusters to nudge a satellite back to its assigned orbital slot.

how satellite slots are identified

Through the International Telecommunication Union (ITU), the nations of the world have agreed to allot each country one or more specific slots in the geosynchronous orbit for domestic satellites. The ITU identifies positions in degrees of longitude, east or west of zero longitude, called the *prime meridian*. Zero longitude is arbitrarily located at Greenwich, England. Exhibit 5.3 shows the slots occupied by U.S. domestic satellites.

Allotments in the segments of the orbit suitable for looking down on areas of high traffic density, such as continental North America, are in high demand. This demand has created a potential slot scarcity. It resembles the spectrum shortage that limits the number of frequencies that can be allotted to stations and hence the number of stations that can go on the air.

Spectrum Allocations   Like Earth-based transmitters, satellite transmitters need internationally allocated transmission channels. Satellites used in broadcasting transmit on microwave frequencies between 4 and 17 GHz, most of them in the 4- to 6-GHz region (C band) and the 12- to 17-GHz region (Ku band). Most of the existing communication satellites use the C band. More powerful satellites, intended primarily for direct reception by small home antennas, use the higher-frequency Ku band.

C-band vs. Ku-band satellites

In areas of heavy terrestrial microwave usage, ground-based services often interfere with Earth stations receiving C-band signals. Ku-band signals escape this drawback. But Ku-band waves are so short that raindrops in heavy downpours can interfere with their propagation.

downlinking

Each satellite needs two groups of frequencies, one for uplinking (on-board reception) and one for downlinking (on-board transmission). These frequency groups must be far enough apart in the spectrum to prevent interference between uplink and downlink signals. Thus satellite frequency allocations come in pairs—4/6 GHz, 12/14 GHz, and so on—and the lower frequencies are used for downlinking.

The downlink frequency bands must be large enough to accommodate a number of different channels for simultaneous transmission by the satellite's **transponders**—combination receive/transmit units. Most relay satellites carry 24 transponders. Each transponder can transmit two television channels, making a capacity of 48 television channels per satellite (or many more narrowband channels such as those for telephone or radio transmissions).

Transmission/Reception   Satellite transmitting antennas focus their output into beams to create footprints of varying size. Exhibit 5.4 shows an example. The narrower the beam, the higher is the power within the footprint, because directionality causes signal gain.

satellite beams

A satellite downlink beam is strongest at its center, growing progressively weaker at reception points farther out. Viewers located at points near the margins of footprints therefore need larger-diameter antennas than those

EXHIBIT **5.4** Satellite Footprints

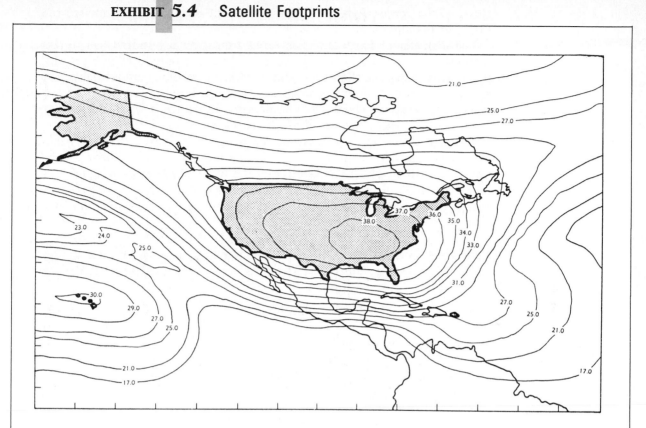

A satellite's *footprint* is depicted on a map in terms of various levels of signal strength. The inner contour defines the satellite's *boresight,* its area of maximum signal strength, where the smallest receiving antennas can be used. The outermost contour defines its *beam-edge* power, the region beyond which satisfactory reception cannot be expected even with large receiving antennas. The numbers associated with contour lines are signal-strength measurements.

The map shows one of the footprints of Westar IV, a Hughes Communications C-band domestic satellite, located at 99° west longitude. The continent looks foreshortened because the satellite views the United States from a point far to the south, a position above the equator in the vicinity of the Galapagos Islands. Note that this particular transponder emits two beams, a relatively wide beam that focuses on the eastern portion of the United States mainland and a smaller one directed at the Hawaiian Islands. Among Westar IV's users are the PBS and CNN networks.

Source: Map courtesy Hughes Communications, Inc.

closer to the center. Exhibit 5.4 shows how the signal weakens toward the footprint margins.

The diameter of Earth antennas varies from over a hundred feet to less than one foot. The bowl-shaped antennas of receive-only satellite Earth stations, such as the one shown in Exhibit 5.5, have become familiar sights, but rectangular satellite receiving antennas also exist. Round plate antennas and rectangular squarials about a foot in diameter, as shown in Exhibit 5.7 (page 145), may become the standard for direct-broadcast reception in homes.

The signals captured by a satellite receiving antenna are extremely weak. They therefore need beefing up by a special high-quality amplifier—a **low-noise amplifier (LNA)**. LNAs magnify the incoming signal strength by as much as a million times. The LNA feeds the satellite signal to a **downconverter**, which translates the high satellite frequencies into the lower frequency range used by television receivers.

Satellite Construction   Communication satellites need five essential groups of hardware components. Their locations are shown in Exhibit 5.6A (page 142).

major components of satellites

- *Transponders,* the receive/transmit units that pick up programs, amplify them, and transmit them back to Earth.
- *Antennas* for receiving uplink signals and transmitting downlink signals (both program material and telemetering information).
- *Power supplies,* consisting of arrays of solar cells and storage batteries.
- *Telemetering devices* for reporting the satellite's vital signs to, and for receiving instructions from, the ground controllers.
- *Small jet thrusters* for moving the satellite, orienting it, and holding it in its assigned position, activated on command from ground controllers.

Orientation matters vitally to a satellite because its antennas must always point in the target direction and its arrays of solar collectors, located on the satellite's body or on extended wings, must be positioned to receive direct rays from the sun. The solar collectors provide electricity to operate the satellite. They also charge on-board batteries that take over during periods when the Earth's shadow interrupts sunlight.

why satellites require such little power

Satellites operate at extremely low power relative to terrestrial relays—power per transponder varies from about 10 watts to 400 watts (the higher power for Ku-band satellites designed for direct-broadcast reception). Most satellite transmitters use no more wattage than ordinary electric light bulbs, though their power is enhanced by directional radiation.

It may seem paradoxical that, despite atmospheric absorption, satellites send signals such great distances with so little power. However, for most of their 22,000-mile journey, satellite signals travel through the near vacuum of space. When at last they encounter the Earth's relatively thin atmospheric envelope, they pass almost straight down through it, experiencing little attenuation. Terrestrial radio signals, in contrast, travel nearly parallel to the Earth, impeded by atmospheric absorption along their entire route.

EXHIBIT **5.5**   TVRO Earth Station

The relatively inexpensive *television receive-only* (TVRO) Earth station (antenna) shown here concentrates the weak satellite signal into a narrow beam directed at a small second reflector mounted on the tripod. This secondary reflector beams the signal into a horn at the center of the TVRO dish, from which it is fed, still as a very weak signal, to a low-noise amplifier (LNA).

Source: Photo from Eric A. Roth.

Satellite Launching   Most commercial U.S. communication satellites have been launched from Cape Canaveral in Florida by NASA (National Aeronautics and Space Administration). NASA is a government agency charged with the development of aviation and space travel.

NASA's role in launching satellites

Launching involves two phases: a powerful rocket vehicle overcomes the initial drag of gravity and air resistance, carrying the satellite into low orbit. After being released from the rocket, the satellite's own, less powerful, onboard rockets propel it into the high, geostationary orbit. Exhibit 5.6B (page 143) illustrates the sequence of events.

After NASA switched from giant unmanned launch rockets to reusable winged vehicles called *shuttles,* television viewers became familiar with the spectacular televised launches. The shuttles carry satellites in their holds for the first phase of the journey. When the shuttles reach their low-orbit stations, they release their satellite payloads, which then fire their on-board rockets to reach geosynchronous orbit.

how shuttles launch satellites

Following the 1986 *Challenger* shuttle explosion that killed six crew members and a civilian passenger, the U.S. government reserved future shuttle launches for military and scientific satellites. Since then, commercial communication satellites have been launched on American private rockets and from overseas sites operated as commercial enterprises by Chinese, European, and Soviet governments.

EXHIBIT 5.6   Satellite Construction

Many cable-network channels use the Galaxy series of domestic satellites, built by the Hughes Aircraft Company. A Galaxy starts out only about 9 feet long at launch because some of its fragile components are retracted to avoid damage during the trauma of the lift-off. Once in space, the satellite extends its antennas and the lower solar panel, reaching a length of nearly 22 feet.

Construction features shown in drawing A include:

Telemetry and command antenna—The receive/transmit antenna sends performance data to the ground control center and receives commands from the center.

Antenna feeds and antenna reflectors—Feed horns direct signals for transmission toward reflectors, which redirect the signals back toward Earth. Reflectors function like the microwave antennas depicted in Exhibit 4.18.

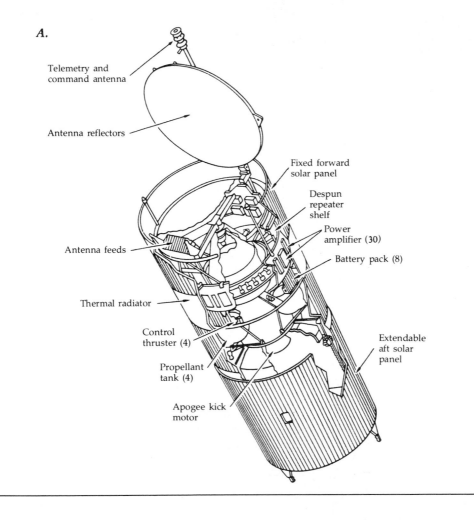

A.

Telemetry and command antenna

Antenna reflectors

Antenna feeds

Thermal radiator

Control thruster (4)

Propellant tank (4)

Apogee kick motor

Fixed forward solar panel

Despun repeater shelf

Power amplifier (30)

Battery pack (8)

Extendable aft solar panel

EXHIBIT 5.6   Continued

Fixed forward and extendable aft solar panels—Cylindrical panels hold the solar cells that convert sunlight into electric energy to power the satellite. The sleevelike lower panel at first surrounded the main body of the satellite; after launch it extended downward to expose the upper panel.

Power amplifiers—Galaxy I, II, and III use TWTAs (traveling-wave tube amplifiers) for on-board signal amplification. Note that Galaxy has 30 amplifiers but only 24 transponders. Spare TWTAs must be carried because they are a satellite's most vulnerable component. The newest Galaxy will use solid-state amplifiers.

Despun repeater shelf—To give the satellite gyroscopic stability, the solar panels spin at about 50 revolutions per minute. The shelf supporting the transponders and antennas is "despun" by revolving at the same rate in the opposite direction. This motion cancels the rotation, enabling the antennas to keep pointing in the desired direction.

Battery pack—Solar panels charge storage batteries, the satellite's only power source when its solar cells temporarily cease functioning as the satellite passes through the Earth's shadow.

Thermal radiator—About two-thirds of a satellite's power is lost in the form of heat. Unless dissipated by radiation into space, the heat would build up internally and destroy the satellite.

Control thrusters—A satellite tends to drift out of its assigned orbital slot. Control thrusters, activated on command from the Earth, nudge it back into position.

Propellant tank—The liquid propellant needed by the control thrusters represents a significant portion of the satellite's weight and plays a major role in limiting a satellite's life span: once its control thrusters stop functioning, a satellite cannot be maintained in orbit.

Apogee kick motor—The satellite's on-board rocket motor gives it the final "kick" to move it out of its initial "parking" orbit into geosynchronous orbit, as shown in diagram B.

Sources: Satellite drawing courtesy Hughes Communications, Inc.; orbital sequence drawing from Bruce R. Elbert, *Introduction to Satellite Communication*, p. 262. © 1987 Artech House, Inc. Used by permission.

B.

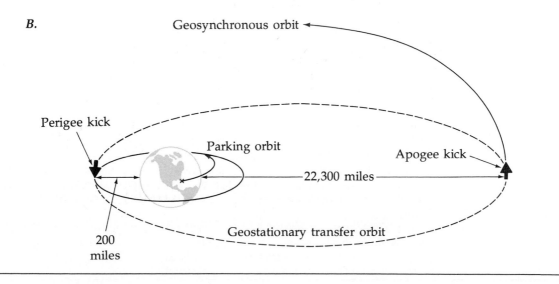

Direct-Broadcast Satellite Service Cable television systems, broadcast stations, and other satellite-relay users can afford relatively large, relatively expensive TVROs (television receive-only antennas). Large antennas compensate for the low power of C-band satellite transponders. An unexpected bonanza for TVRO antenna manufacturers came when hobbyists, high-tech enthusiasts, and people hungry for video programs but beyond the reach of either television stations or cable began buying TVROs. They found they could intercept C-band satellite-relay signals with somewhat smaller, less expensive "backyard dishes."

role of TVROs in direct-broadcast satellite transmission

About 2 million such dishes on the order of 6 to 10 feet in diameter had been installed in the United States by 1989. They can pick up as many as 150 different programs from domestic and foreign satellites, most of them private relays, such as news feeds, not intended for public consumption. Such home pickups became known as **C-band direct reception** because the general public received the signal directly from the satellite rather than from an intermediary cable system or broadcast station. Theoretically, private users should have waited for Ku-band direct-broadcast satellite vehicles designed

EXHIBIT 5.7 DBS Reception: C-Band Direct vs. Ku-Band

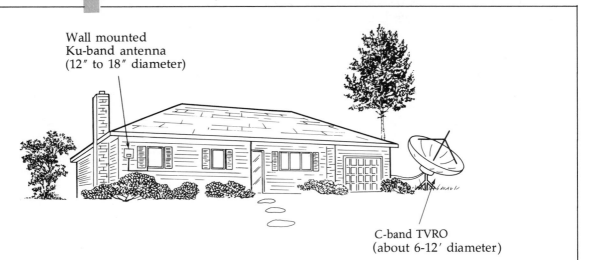

Wall mounted
Ku-band antenna
(12″ to 18″ diameter)

C-band TVRO
(about 6-12′ diameter)

Relatively small receive-only television antennas (TVROs) enable homeowners to receive satellite signals directly, without the need of being within reach of a terrestrial television station. This satellite-to-home service began in an unplanned way when hobbyists set up TVROs in their backyards to pick up relay signals never intended for public reception. This kind of satellite reception came to be known as *C-band direct*.

True DBS (direct-broadcast satellite) services employ higher power and shorter wave-length *Ku-band* frequencies, enabling the use of much smaller antennas suitable for mounting on the side or roof of a house.

specifically for easy reception by means of home antennas 3 feet or less in diameter.

The uplink leg of a DBS transmission acts in the manner of a broadcast relay, sending signals from a distribution point to the equivalent of a broadcast station. The downlink leg acts as a broadcasting station, delivering programs directly to consumers without the need for terrestrial transmitters. The shortness of the Ku-band waves and the high power of DBS transponders favor the use of receiving antennas suitable for mounting on private dwellings—in some cases only a foot in diameter but in any case not more than 3 feet. Exhibit 5.7 compares C-band direct reception with Ku-band DBS reception.

Eight orbital positions have been allotted to the United States for direct-broadcast satellites, only three of which fall at points in the orbit suitable for covering the entire country. Frequency allotments provide for the equivalent of 32 television channels on each satellite, making a total of 256 DBS channels. That may seem a high number, but each company planning a DBS service expects to offer large numbers of channels in order to compete effectively with cable television. Sky Cable, a DBS project announced in 1990 by a consortium that included NBC, hoped to offer over a hundred channels, doubling the limited channel potential by means of **signal compression**— a technique for crowding more information into a channel than normal modulation methods permit.

number of U.S. DBS channels available

Digital-Signal Processing 5.3

Satellites rely heavily on digital-signal processing. Broadcasting, however, is based on an older processing method that creates signals analogous (similar) to original sounds and images. Analog processing imitates nature. For example, the continuously rotating hands of the clock imitate the movement of the shadow on a sundial. A digital timepiece, however, tells time directly in numbers, jumping from one number to the next. Digital signals bear no resemblance to natural forms because they consist entirely of digits—simple strings of numbers.

clock hands vs. numbers: analog vs. digital

Sampling Digital processing can be likened to cutting up a picture (the analog signal) into thousands of tiny pieces, selecting every other piece, assigning a digital number to each of those pieces representing its amplitude, transmitting the numbers, then using the number to reassemble the picture with every other piece missing. If the pieces are tiny enough, the absence of the missing pieces will not be noticed.

Cutting up the original analog signal and leaving out some pieces is done by high-speed sampling. Each sample consists of a short pulse of energy, proportional in strength to the amplitude of the original signal at that point. Each energy pulse is then **quantized**—labeled with a number representing the momentary amplitude of the analog signal.

Encoding

Encoding   The numbers attached to each sample are encoded by converting them from the decimal number system (0, 1, 2, 3 . . . through 9) into the binary number system (0 and 1 only). Computers have made the binary system familiar along with the acronym *bit,* which stands for *binary digit.*

decimal and binary numbers compared

Numbers expressed in binary digits consist of nothing more than strings composed of only two digits. They are conventionally expressed as "zero" and "one" but can also be regarded as equivalent to "on" and "off."

As an example, the output of a microphone consists of an analog signal, a continuously varying electrical amplitude (that is, voltage). A digital processor samples this continuous amplitude pattern, breaking it down into a series of small, discrete amplitude values. An encoder quantizes each value by assigning it a number in binary form representing its momentary amplitude. The digitized output consists of a string of "power off" signals (zeros) and "power on" signals (ones).

Bit Speed   The capacity of a digital channel is measured in terms of **bit speed**—the number of bits per second that the channel can handle. Digitally processed signals inherently need wider channels than the same signals in analog form. Sampling takes place many thousand times per second. Those thousand are in turn multiplied by the number of binary digits it takes to quantize each one. Exhibit 5.8 shows how expressing a three-digit decimal number digitally results in 15 binary digits. An analog telephone channel requires a bandwidth of only about 3 kHz. When converted to digital code, however, a telephone call requires a 32-kHz transmission channel to accommodate its bit speed of 64,000 bits per second.

why digital signals need wide channels

Exhibit 5.8 goes into more detail for those interested in exploring digital processing further. It suffices to sum up here by saying that digital processing converts a continuous signal into a series of samples that are given numerical values encoded as binary numbers.

Advantages   The extreme simplicity of digitized signals protects them from the many extraneous influences that distort analog signals. A digital signal cannot be distorted or misunderstood as long as the elementary difference between "off" and "on" can be discerned. In contrast, each new manipulation of analog signals lowers their quality. Recording, relaying, and other processing of analog information inevitably introduce noise, causing quality loss. However, each new digital copy of a digitally encoded sound or picture is in effect an original.

digital recording: each playback matches the original

The fact that digitally processed information exists as binary digits means that the stored signal can be taken apart and reassembled at will in infinitely varied forms. A signal distorted by static can be cleaned up; ghosts in television pictures can be eliminated. The possibilities for manipulation are endless.

Application to Broadcasting   The high bit-speed requirements of digital processing limit its applicability to over-the-air broadcast transmission and reception. The current broadcast channels could handle only a fraction of

EXHIBIT 5.8 More About Digital-Signal Processing

Digital-signal processing has become so pervasive in contemporary life that it's worth a little effort to learn how it works.

Actually, digital-signal processing began with the first of the electrical communication systems, the 19th-century telegraph. Telegraph operators sent messages in Morse code by means of an on/off key that controlled electricity going down the telegraph wire. The code consists simply of varying lengths of "on" and "off," presented to the ear or eye as dots, dashes, and spaces, which in turn represent letters of the alphabet, punctuation marks, and numbers.

Modern digital-signal processing also employs simple on/off signals. They represent the elements of a *binary code,* a two-digit number system that requires only two code symbols, conventionally written as 0 and 1. All communication content can be reduced to nothing more than strings of zeros and ones.

A system that communicates digitally needs to make only one elementary distinction. "On" and "off" differ so obviously that they leave little chance for ambiguity. That simplicity makes digital signals extremely "rugged"—able to withstand external interference and imperfections in transmission and copying systems.

The familiar ten-digit *decimal* system (0 through 9) is used in everyday life. In that familiar system, the values of digits depend on their *positions* relative to one another, counting from right to left. Each new position increases a digit's value by a multiple of 10.

Thus the number 11 means (counting from right to left) one 1 plus one 10 (1 + 10 = 11). The binary code also relies on position, but each digit's position (again counting from right to left) increases by a multiple of 2. Thus in binary code the decimal number 11 becomes 1011, which means (counting from right to left) one 1 plus one 2 plus no 4 plus one 8 (1 + 2 + 0 + 8 = 11). Here's an example converting the decimal numbers 4, 6, and 3 to binary form:

$$
\text{Multipliers:} \qquad 8 \quad 4 \quad 2 \quad 1 \quad 0
$$

$$
\text{Binary numbers:}
\begin{cases}
01000 = 0 + 4 + 0 + 0 + 0 = 4 \\
01100 = 0 + 4 + 2 + 0 + 0 = 6 \\
00110 = 0 + 0 + 2 + 1 + 0 = 3
\end{cases}
$$

As the examples indicate, it takes more digits to express a number in the binary system than in the decimal system. Thus, although the simplicity of digital transmissions makes them less subject to error, they need larger channels than analog transmissions.

Conversion of an analog signal to a digitized signal involves *quantizing* the analog signal, that is, turning it into a number sequence. Quantizing consists of rapidly sampling an analog waveform and assigning a binary numerical value to the amplitude of each momentary item in the sample. The higher the sampling rate, the greater is the fidelity of the digitized signal. There is an equation for calculating the sampling rate necessary to avoid distortion; it usually calls for sampling thousands of times per second.

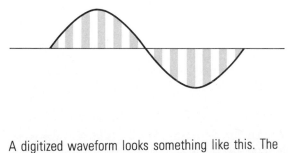

A digitized waveform looks something like this. The dark bars indicate the points at which the wave's amplitude is sampled.

the bits per second that digital versions of broadcasts would require. However, cable television, MMDS, recordings, and DBS present no such barrier to the use of larger channels. Broadcasters eagerly await further technical developments that could make it possible to broadcast digitally.

In the meantime, digital processing plays an increasingly important role in every aspect of program production. Studios use digital sound and video recording, cameras, effects generators, and many other types of equipment. Before the output from these digital components can be transmitted, it has to be fed to an interfacing device—a **coder-decoder**, abbreviated **codec**. A codec decodes the binary signals for transmission over analog circuits. Personal computer owners who use their computers for communication have become familiar with a similar device, the modem (modulator-demodulator). It provides an interface between the digital output of a computer and the analog capability of telephone lines.

The basic circuitry of television receivers is inherently analog, but the performance of newer receivers has been much enhanced by the addition of digitally processed features. An improved-definition television (IDTV) receiver converts incoming analog signals into digital form. It stores them in a computer that can eliminate ghosts, save individual frames, and show more than one picture at a time. Interlace scanning in ordinary receivers often works imperfectly because of scanning-line overlaps in successive fields. By retaining one field in memory for 1/60th of a second, an IDTV receiver can display both fields simultaneously, perfectly synchronized.

IDTV receivers improve reception

Radio receivers, too, can incorporate digitally processed features. Radio data system (RDS) transmissions have a subcarrier whose digital signals activate a small window in receivers. The window displays the call letters of the station being received, the current program format, and other information. Tuners can even be programmed to search the dial for a station broadcasting in a desired format.

5.4 *Solid-State Devices*

The developments mentioned in the previous section rely not only on digital processing but also on a variety of components that manipulate electrons far more cheaply and efficiently than do electron tubes. These components bear the family name **solid-state devices**. They profoundly affect all aspects of electronic technology.

Vacuum Tube as Forerunner   The predecessors to solid-state devices were the vacuum tubes. They manipulate electrons within a glass enclosure from which nearly all the air has been evacuated. Vacuum tubes are bulky, power-hungry, and easily damaged. A rack of equipment containing scores of tubes generates so much heat that artificial cooling has to be used.

drawbacks of vacuum tubes

Before the invention of solid-state devices, tubes performed the essential jobs of signal detection, amplification, and transmission, as well as many other electronic functions. For most applications, they have now almost entirely given way to solid-state devices. Ironically, however, computers—those most digitized, chip-reliant of artifacts—still use cathode-ray tubes similar to television kinescope tubes for image display.

Transistors   The solid-state revolution started with transistors, which manipulate electrons in a small piece of solid crystal instead of within the relatively large vacuum chamber of a tube. Transistors are also known as semiconductors because although they conduct electricity, they do so selectively. Transistors are made of silicon, a common crystalline element. The crystals are specially treated to control the flow of electrons in prescribed ways.

transistors function as semiconductors

Integrated Circuits   The second generation of solid-state devices, integrated circuits, combine (integrate) many transistors and other circuit components on silicon chips. The very large-scale integrated circuit (VLSIC) consists of hundreds of thousands of transistors and other components, along with their microscopic connections—etched on a single chip a quarter of an inch square.

Cramming complex electronic components into such tiny spaces enables miniaturization, indispensable for the microcomputers that reside in practically every modern technically sophisticated device, from satellites to wrist watches.

VLSICs fit sophisticated technology into tiny spaces

ENG (electronic news gathering), for example, depends on miniaturization. It enabled covering news events outside the studio with lightweight, portable equipment. The key to ENG development, the **time-base corrector**, uses a microcomputer to supply accurate synchronization without recourse to the sync generator at the studio. Before the time-base corrector became available synchronizing errors plagued remote operations, showing up as jittery pictures, skewing, and color breakup.

Solid-State Receivers and Cameras   Most television receivers still rely on the cathode-ray tube (the CRT or kinescope tube) for picture display. However, researchers are exploring several technologies for producing flat screens that could be hung on a wall.

Flat screens can already be found in tiny, portable television receivers and in laptop computers. One type uses LCD (liquid crystal display) technology. It employs liquid crystal molecules that exist in an ambiguous liquid/solid state. They change from opaque to transparent when hit with an electric charge, altering the amount of light reflected by each pixel. Reliance on reflected light makes the LCD passive as compared to the CRT, whose phosphor coating actively emits light. Several other alternatives to the CRT are also under development.

Solid-state cameras, however, are already widely used. The amateur video photographers' camcorders are CCD cameras, and manufacturers are rapidly switching to CCD studio cameras. In place of the pickup tube, these cameras employ an image sensor called a **charge-coupled device (CCD)**. It consists basically of an integrated-circuit chip incorporating thousands of transistors, one for each pixel.

Compared to cameras equipped with the traditional pickup tube, CCD cameras are inexpensive, highly reliable, small, and able to withstand rough treatment.

5.5 *Digital Recording*

The combination of solid-state devices, digital processing, and computers has revolutionized both sound and picture recording. One group of such recorders also incorporates laser beams as pickup devices.

Laser/Digital Sound Recording   The word *laser* compresses into a welcome acronym the formidable name *light amplification by stimulated emission of radiation*. A laser produces an intense beam of light at a single frequency. The incredible density and narrowness of laser beams give them unique advantages as a means of reading digitally encoded information by reflection.

In the audio compact disc (CD), the most highly developed of the laser/digital group of playback devices, a laser beam takes the place of the traditional audio-disc stylus pickup. Instead of a groove, the disc carries a track consisting of millions of microscopic pits. The pits interrupt an otherwise shiny, reflective surface. A laser beam reflected or not reflected from the disc, in accordance with the location of the pits, provides binary on/off signals—a digital code. Exhibit 5.9 outlines the way the CD playback works.

The laser beam has no wear-and-tear effect on the disc surface as does a stylus on the grooves of conventional album discs and "singles." CDs are sealed in plastic covers that are transparent to the laser beam. This protection makes them virtually impervious to damage. They have enormous storage capacity, recording an hour's stereo sound on a $4\frac{3}{4}$-inch disc—smaller than a 45-rpm stylus recording holding only three or four minutes of music. Best of all, they reproduce sound with uncanny perfection.

Laser Video   The laser recording principle used in the CD audio disc has also been applied to text and picture recording. An entire family of CD video applications is evolving, as indicated in Exhibit 5.10. Promising as these developments are, so far laser recordings remain a playback-only medium. The recording process is too intricate and costly for the mass market. Laser recordings have therefore not outmoded magnetic tape, with which it is just as easy to record as to play back.

laser video: home
playback but no
recording

EXHIBIT 5.9 Compact-Disc Playback System

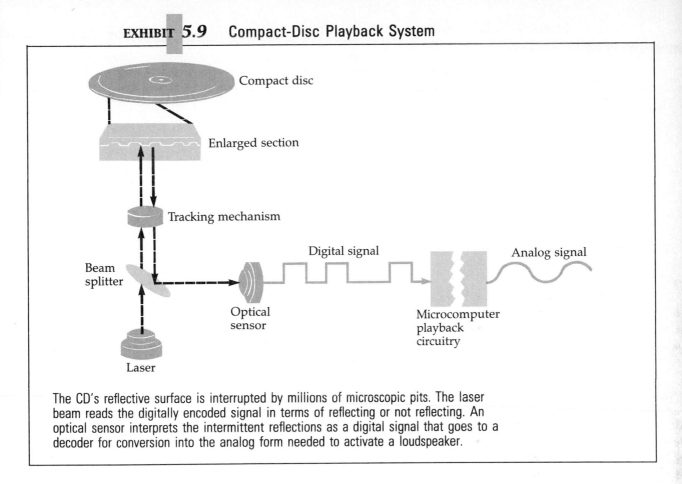

Compact disc

Enlarged section

Tracking mechanism

Digital signal

Analog signal

Beam splitter

Optical sensor

Microcomputer playback circuitry

Laser

The CD's reflective surface is interrupted by millions of microscopic pits. The laser beam reads the digitally encoded signal in terms of reflecting or not reflecting. An optical sensor interprets the intermittent reflections as a digital signal that goes to a decoder for conversion into the analog form needed to activate a loudspeaker.

Digital Tape Digital processing has been adopted for most professional sound and television recording. Three video recording standards have evolved:

- The D1 standard provides the best picture quality because it handles the color and brightness components of the signal separately, each within its own channel.
- D2 uses composite color, which means that it multiplexes both color and brightness in a single channel in the manner of the analog broadcast signal.
- D3, the newest standard, which also uses composite color, reduces tape width from ¾-inch to ½-inch, making it more adaptable for lightweight field equipment.

The output of digital videorecorders and of digital audio tape (DAT) must be converted to analog form for reproduction on loudspeakers and on receiver screens and for transmission over the air.

EXHIBIT 5.10 Digital/Laser Disc Options: A Case of Convergence

Optional form	Content	Primary market
CD–Audio	Sound	Home
CD–Interactive	Sound, picture, and text	Home and education
CD–Video	Sound and motion pictures	Home
CD–ROM	Data	Professional and business

The family of CD (compact disc) recording formats represents a good example of convergence—the merging of several technologies and types of communication material. These formats share the advantages of high fidelity, resistance to damage, and large capacity. They also share the limitations of high production cost and playback-only capability.

CD–Audio is a well-known high-fidelity music playback medium, the most highly developed of the CD family.

CD–Interactive recordings can accept queries and give answers when linked to a computer. This interactivity makes them promising as a training tool.

CD–Video comes in several sizes, capable at one extreme of playing back a music video, at the other extreme a feature film.

CD–ROM uses the computer term "read only memory." CD–ROM's enormous memory for digital data gives computer users access to a variety of reference works. For example, a single small disc can contain the contents of an entire, multivolume encyclopedia.

5.6 *Fiber-Optic Cable*

Although satellites have taken over most relay functions, for some applications cable has come back into favor in the new form of fiber-optic conductors. Their high capacity makes them ideal for handling digitally processed information.

wideband capacity of fiber-optic cable

In fiber-optic cable, hair-thin strands of extremely pure glass convey modulated light beams. Exhibit 5.11 shows an example of such a cable. The tremendously high frequency-range of light (from 1 million to 10 million gigahertz) enables using a bandwidth in the thousands of megahertz. A single glass filament has more than 600 times the information-carrying capacity of a coaxial cable.

EXHIBIT 5.11 Fiber-Optic Cable

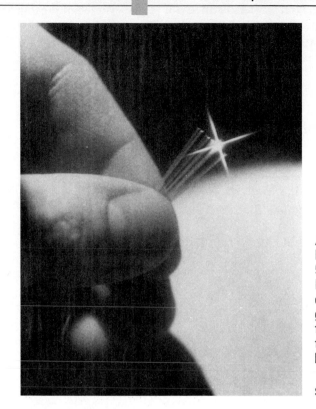

An AT&T fiber-optic cable made up of five pairs of hair-thin glass strands (each pair can carry about 50,000 telephone calls) transmitted on beams of laser light. Capacity is limited not by the small size of the fibers but by the speed of the lasers that generate the information-bearing light beams and the light detectors at the receiving end. Currently, these components can send and receive 3.4 billion bits of information per second.

Source: Photo from AT&T.

The bundle of frequencies present in ordinary light will not travel efficiently through an optical fiber. Instead, lasers or light-emitting diodes (LEDs) must be used to generate light beams consisting of a very narrow band of frequencies.

The modulated light does not run straight down the glass fiber as does water through a pipe. Instead, it reflects back and forth within the fiber. For this reason, fiber-optic glass must be extraordinarily pure, devoid of impurities that would randomly change the angle of reflection.

Fiber-optical cables have many advantages as relay links, especially for those carrying very heavy traffic. Little loss occurs from attenuation, reducing the number of repeater amplifiers required. The cables are small in size and light in weight. They neither radiate energy to interfere with other circuits nor receive interference from the outside. And the glass of which cables are made is one of the cheapest and most abundant of natural materials.

Transatlantic fiber-optic cable has been in use since 1988. In that year a consortium dominated by AT&T opened TAT-8, a 4,000-mile transatlantic

TAT-8 fiber-optic cable links U.S. and Europe

submarine fiber-optic cable. A single fiber in the TAT-8 cable can handle 8,000 telephone circuits. TAT-9 was planned for 1991. Wideband cable facilities offer an alternative to INTELSAT and other satellite systems for transoceanic television relays. Fiber optics, used principally for high-density telephone traffic, are increasingly employed in the trunk lines that distribute cable television.

5.7 *High-Definition Television*

The advances described in the preceding sections paralleled the interest in improving television-picture quality. The NTSC broadcast standard, dictated by the state of technology in the 1940s, has always suffered from comparison with the picture-resolution standard of theatrical films.

HDTV Concept   High-definition television (HDTV) closes the gap between the technical quality of broadcast television and motion pictures. It at least doubles the current broadcast NTSC number of scanning lines per frame—from 525 to 1,050 or 1,125, depending on the specific HDTV system. This increase in line frequency boosts traditional television's 250,000 picture elements (pixels) to 1 million—a fourfold improvement in resolution. HDTV also changes the picture aspect ratio to a wide-screen format, as shown in

EXHIBIT *5.12*   TV Aspect Ratios

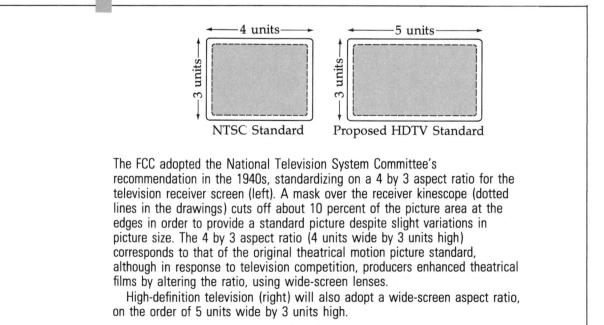

NTSC Standard   Proposed HDTV Standard

The FCC adopted the National Television System Committee's recommendation in the 1940s, standardizing on a 4 by 3 aspect ratio for the television receiver screen (left). A mask over the receiver kinescope (dotted lines in the drawings) cuts off about 10 percent of the picture area at the edges in order to provide a standard picture despite slight variations in picture size. The 4 by 3 aspect ratio (4 units wide by 3 units high) corresponds to that of the original theatrical motion picture standard, although in response to television competition, producers enhanced theatrical films by altering the ratio, using wide-screen lenses.

   High-definition television (right) will also adopt a wide-screen aspect ratio, on the order of 5 units wide by 3 units high.

Exhibit 5.12. These changes would bring television up to the quality of the best 35-mm motion pictures. In fact, distributors of theatrical movies will be able to use satellite relays to deliver HDTV movies to television projectors in movie theaters throughout the country. Such relays will eliminate the cost of exhibition prints—the reels of film that now have to be printed and physically transported to each of thousands of movie theaters.

HDTV potential for movie theaters

Ideal viewing of conventional 525-line television calls for a seating distance of at least six times the picture height; moving closer can cause eyestrain because the viewer's eye strives to see nonexistent detail. HDTV allows comfortable viewing at a distance of only three times the picture height and can also be viewed at a wider angle from the screen than can existing television. HDTV permits multiple sound tracks, not only for stereophonic sound but also for sound in several languages.

Compatibility The millions of receivers already existing in the world, sometimes referred to as the "installed base," represent an investment by the public that cannot be simply discarded. The FCC has made compatibility a requirement for approval of a U.S. HDTV standard.

A compatible HDTV system enables normal reception on existing sets from the same source that supplies HDTV reception on newly marketed high-definition sets. The compatibility constraint means that terrestrial broadcast HDTV will probably have to employ two channels. Current sets would pick up the signal from one of the two; high-definition sets would pick up the two channels and combine their output. The two channels may employ two transmitters, or a single transmitter might radiate a composite signal, only part of which would be decoded by NTSC receivers, as illustrated in Exhibit 5.13.

compatible HDTV requires two channels

Channel Size Spectrum shortage dictates that the HDTV signal must be compressed to fit the existing 6-MHz broadcast channel or must find a second supplementary channel in another part of the spectrum. A third possibility, applicable only to direct-broadcast satellite transmission, is to use a single, wider channel in the higher-frequency ranges where spectrum space still exists.

Although signal compression is already possible up to a point, it cannot yet squeeze a 30-MHz HDTV signal into the traditional 6-MHz broadcast channel. Additional auxilliary channels, possibly only 3-MHz in width, working in tandem with existing channels, appear to be the more likely solution.

Proposed Standards Japanese engineers have made the most progress with HDTV, experimenting extensively with a 1,125-line picture having a 9-to-16 aspect ratio. This system is not compatible with NTSC standards but is envisioned as a direct-broadcast satellite service.

The NHK, Japan's public-service broadcasting network, has proposed this system, along with several variants, all based on MUSE. The acronym stands for multiple sub-Nyquist sampling encoding (the name Nyquist identifies a

Japan's MUSE system

EXHIBIT 5.13   Two HDTV Proposals: Augmented vs. Simulcast

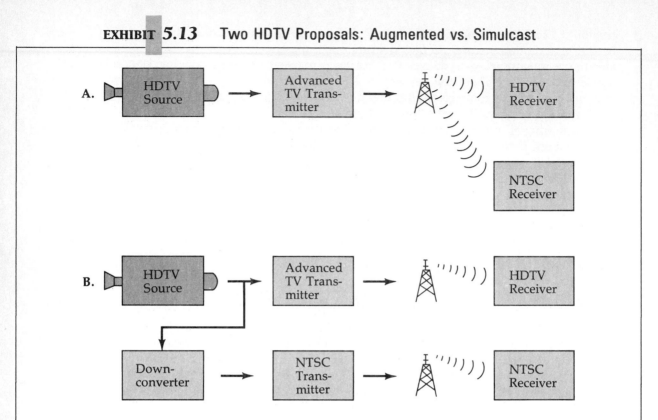

Two HDTV methods proposed by Japan's public broadcasting authority, NHK. NTSC (National Television System Committee) refers to the current U.S. system.

A. A common HDTV studio output goes to a single transmitter whose signal can be picked up as ordinary television by NTSC-type receivers. The transmitter broadcasts the added information to provide the wide-screen, 1125-line picture over a supplementary channel. This is the "augmented" HDTV type rejected as a goal by the FCC.

B. A common HDTV studio output is separated into HDTV and NTSC components for broadcast by separate transmitters on separate channels. This is the "simulcast" type of HDTV, stipulated as a goal by the FCC.

formula for calculating the minimum number of samples required for digital processing).

The MUSE family of HDTV standards includes a compatible method to meet the FCC's requirements for a U.S. system. Exhibit 5.13 sketches the essential elements of two MUSE terrestrial broadcasting proposals, one of which meets the FCC's minimum requirements for consideration as a U.S. standard.

The European Community also actively promotes HDTV standards. Its proposals complicate international agreement by preferring a 50 frames-per-

5 / Technological Innovation and the Future of Broadcasting

second/1250-lines standard, instead of the NTSC 60-frames standard. This difference comes from the fact that the frequency of alternating electrical current in Europe is 50 Hz in contrast to 60 Hz in the United States.

European vs. U.S. HDTV standards

American proposals, lagging somewhat behind the Japanese and European, come from several groups, notably the David Sarnoff Research Center and NBC. Two levels of image improvement that fall short of true HDTV were being touted by American interests in 1990:

TV improvements that are evolving toward HDTV

1. Improved-definition television (IDTV) would tinker with the NTSC system to get better *apparent* definition but would not have fundamental changes. The IDTV receiver is described in Section 5.3.
2. Enhanced-definition television (EDTV) would improve definition without going as far as HDTV, possibly acting as a bridging technology to ease the transition from NTSC to true HDTV.

Where to from Here?   The outlook as this book went to press made the following scenario seem likely for the near future:

- Most major television production studios will probably adopt a single international HDTV production standard.

HDTV's immediate future

- Facilities for HDTV viewing will become available in specialized public settings.
- The FCC's policy of ensuring that HDTV broadcasts will be receivable on old sets may encourage viewers to hang on to their old sets and even to replace them with improved-definition receivers, rather than buying the more expensive HDTV type.
- Though high-definition receivers may soon become available in the homes of innovators for the showing of HDTV videotapes and even HDTV cable television and MMDS "wireless" cable channels, the mass market for full HDTV may lag behind, postponing the day when over-the-air HDTV broadcasting becomes available.

Commercial Operations

The sources of revenue that make electronic media possible exert a controlling influence over them. In a national system as heavily dominated by advertising as that of the United States, an examination of the media's financial operations, including the role of advertising, has obvious importance for understanding media behavior and program output. This chapter focuses on commercial operations, leaving the special financial problems of public broadcasting to the next chapter.

Basic Economic Units

Exhibit 6.1 summarizes the dimensions of the commercial and noncommercial broadcasting and cable industries in relation to the total audience potential. The individual outlet—nearly 12,000 stations and over 10,000 cable television systems—forms the basic economic unit of these industries.

stations and cable systems as local retailers of programs

These 22,000 units function as local retailers, delivering programs directly to consumers. The phrases *local station* and *local cable system* often occur, but in fact all stations and systems are local in the sense that all are licensed or franchised to serve specific local communities.

Despite the localism of licenses and franchises, economic efficiency favors centralization of station/system ownership and program production. Still more

EXHIBIT *6.1*   Dimensions of the Broadcast/Cable Industry

Commercial AM stations	4,950
Commercial FM stations	4,192
Educational FM stations	1,390
Total radio stations on the air	10,532
Commercial VHF TV stations	547
Commercial UHF TV stations	523
Noncommercial VHF TV stations	121
Noncommercial UHF TV stations	218
Total TV stations on the air	1,409
VHF LPTV stations	300
UHF LPTV stations	324
Total low-power stations on the air	624
Television network affiliates	
ABC	220
CBS	193
NBC	207
Fox	122
PBS	336
Cable systems	10,172
Total U.S. population	245.1 million
Total U.S. households	92.0 million
Total U.S. television households (TVHH)	90.4 million

Note: The data given here were representative for 1989.

Source: *Broadcast Marketing & Technology News,* National Association of Broadcasters, Dec. 1988; *Broadcasting,* 28 Nov. 1988, 27 Feb. 1989, 6 Mar. 1989, 8 May 1989, 22 May 1989, and 29 May 1989; Miami *Herald,* 5 Oct. 1988; and *Broadcasting/Cablecasting Yearbook 1988.*

efficiency comes from vertical integration—common ownership of production, distribution, and delivery facilities. The large organizations that result increasingly dominate the media economy.

Broadcast Stations 6.2

Definition   In the United States, the traditional commercial broadcast station can be defined as an entity (individual, partnership, corporation, or nonfederal governmental authority) that

- Holds a license from the federal government to organize and schedule programs for a *specific community* in accordance with an approved plan.
- Transmits those programs *over the air,* using designated radio frequencies in accordance with specified technical standards.
- Carries commercial messages that promote the products or services of profit-making organizations, for which the station receives compensation.

attributes of a broadcast station

Within limits, an individual owner may legally control more than one station, but each outlet must be licensed separately to serve a specific community. Moreover, each license encompasses both transmission and programming functions. A station therefore normally combines three groups of facilities: business offices, studio facilities, and transmitter (including an antenna and its tower). Usually all facilities come under common ownership, although in a few cases stations lease some or all of them.

Station Functions   All commercial stations need to perform four basic functions: (1) general and administrative, (2) technical, (3) programming, and (4) sales.

General/administrative functions include the services that any business needs to create an appropriate working environment—services such as payroll, accounting, housekeeping, and purchasing. Services of a specialized nature peculiar to broadcasting usually come from external organizations, such as engineering-consulting firms and program syndicators. For a network affiliate, the main such external contract is with its network.

Technical functions, usually supervised by the station's chief engineer, center on transmitter operations, which must follow strict FCC rules, and the maintenance and operation of studio equipment.

Program functions involve planning and implementation. Major program-planning decisions usually evolve from interplay among the programming, sales, and management heads. Because most stations produce few programs locally, the program department's main job is to select and schedule prerecorded programs.

News, although a form of programming, usually constitutes a separate department, headed by a news director who reports directly to top

special status of news in station organization

management. This separation of news from entertainment makes sense because of the timely nature of news and the unique responsibilities news broadcasting imposes on management.

Sales functions divide into local and regional/national aspects. Station sales departments have their own staff members to sell time to local advertisers. To reach regional and national advertisers, however, a station usually contracts with a national sales representative who acts for the station in out-of-state business centers. A network affiliate benefits from a third sales force, that of its network. Exhibit 6.2 suggests some of the tasks routinely performed by a television sales manager and other executives.

EXHIBIT 6.2   A Day in the Lives of TV Executives

	GENERAL MANAGER	PROGRAM DIRECTOR	GENERAL SALES MANAGER	NEWS DIRECTOR
8:30	Open mail; dictate letters and memos.	Check Discrepancy Reports for program and equipment problems; take appropriate action.	Check Discrepancy Reports for missed commercials; plan make-goods.	Meet with Assignment Editor and producer; plan the day.
9:30	Discuss financial statements with Business Manager.	Call *TV Guide* with program updates.	Local sales meeting; discuss accounts and quotas.	Meet with Union Shop Steward; discuss termination of reporter.
10:00	Call group headquarters regarding financial status.	Prepare weekly program schedule.	Accompany local account executive on sales calls.	Read mail; screen tape of last night's 11:00 PM news.
10:30	Meet with civic group angry about upcoming network program.	Select film titles for Saturday and Sunday late movies.	More sales calls.	Discuss noon news rundown with show producer.
11:00	Call network; ask for preview of questionable show.	Meet with Promotion Manager regarding *TV Guide* ad for local shows.	Call collection agency; discuss delinquent sales accounts.	Meet with Chief Engineer regarding SNG failure.
12:00	Lunch with major advertiser.	Lunch with syndicated program saleswoman.	Lunch with major advertiser.	Monitor noon news; lunch at desk.
2:00	Department heads meeting.	Department heads meeting.	Department heads meeting.	Department heads meeting.
4:00	Meet with Chief Engineer regarding new computer system in master control.	Meet with producer/director to plan local holiday special.	Prepare speech for next week's Rotary club meeting.	Meet with producer and director; plan rundown of 6:00 PM newscast.
6:00	Dinner with Promotion Director job candidate.	Attend National Academy of Television Arts & Sciences annual local banquet.	To airport; catch flight to New York for meeting with National Sales Rep.	Monitor 6:00 PM news.

Not all television station executives work 10- or 12-hour days, but many do, especially as competition from cable and the other new media increases.

EXHIBIT **6.3**   Station Functional Organization

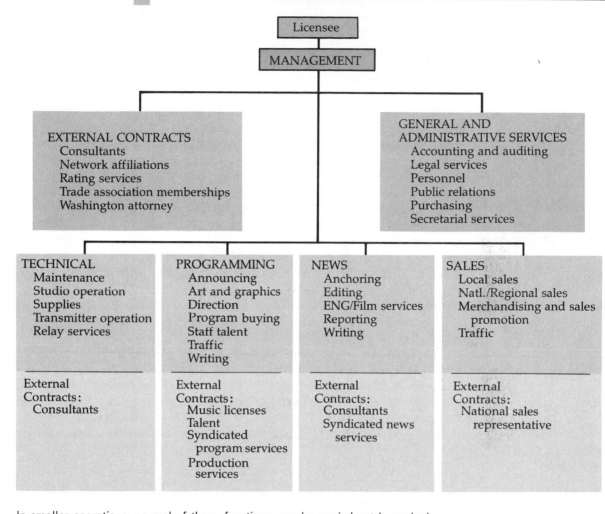

In smaller operations, several of these functions may be carried out by a single employee. Stations also vary widely as to the types and the extent of the services they obtain under contract from outside sources.

One job straddles the program and sales functions—that of the traffic department. It coordinates sales with program operations, preparing the daily **program pre-log** (usually called simply the **log**), which schedules facilities, personnel, programs, and announcements. Traffic personnel ensure fulfillment of advertising contracts and arrange for **make-goods**—the rescheduling of missed or technically inadequate commercials. Traffic maintains a list of **availabilities** (or **avails**), keeping sales personnel up-to-date on commercial openings in the schedule. Traffic usually fills unsold openings with public-service or promotional announcements.

Exhibit 6.3 charts some of the subordinate functions that fall under the four main headings. References in the exhibit to external contracts indicate the extent to which stations depend on specialized external agencies. They obtain not only most programs from external sources but also the expertise of outside consultants. These experts advise on financial, management, programming, promotional, sales, technical, and legal problems.

role of consultants in station operations

Station Groups   Like other business enterprises, broadcasting can benefit from economies of scale. A company owning several stations can buy programs, supplies, and equipment in bulk and spread the cost of consultants and attorneys across several stations, sharing experiences and new ideas.

Were it not for legal constraints, large chains of commonly owned stations would doubtless have evolved, just as in the newspaper business. Newspapers need no licenses and are protected by the First Amendment from government oversight. Broadcasting, however, does operate under license and Federal Communications Commission oversight.

legal status of newspapers compared to that of stations

The FCC prevents undue centralization by limiting broadcast ownership (with some minor exceptions) to a maximum of 12 AM, 12 FM, and 12 television stations per individual or group owner. Within these limits, the trend is toward concentration of station ownership. In 1988, group owners held 90 percent of the stations in the 100 largest markets.

All of the stations owned by a group do not necessarily affiliate with the same network—or for that matter with any network. Stations owned by the networks themselves, known as network **owned-and-operated (O&O)** stations, are the exceptions. Each national television network's O&O group reaches between 20 and 25 percent of the nation's television households, assuring ABC, CBS, and NBC their own prestigious outlets in major markets.

6.3   *Broadcast TV Networks*

Definition   FCC rules dealing with television affiliation agreements define a network as "a national organization distributing programs for a substantial part of each broadcast day to television stations in all parts of the United States, generally via interconnection facilities." More specifically, the FCC defines a network as an entity "which offers an interconnected program service on a regular basis for 15 or more hours per week to at least 25 affiliated television licenses in 10 or more states" (47 CFR 73.658).

only 3 "full-service" TV networks

Only three major national full-service commercial television networks meet these definitions—ABC, CBS, and NBC. The Fox Broadcasting Company is attempting to form a fourth national network but as of 1990 had achieved nowhere near full-service status. However, Fox did plan to exceed the 15-hour limit in the foregoing definition late that year. In addition to the three full-service networks and the emergent Fox network, over a hundred regional and part-time networks are in operation.

In this section, the focus is on the three national full-service television networks: ABC, CBS, and NBC. Each of the three has about 200 affiliates, through which they can reach virtually all the television homes in the United States.

Like stations, networks vary in their organizational structure, yet each must fulfill the same four basic functions as stations—administration, programming, engineering, and sales. Networks, however, enjoy the luxury of a much higher degree of specialization than do stations. NBC, for example, has separate units to handle operations, entertainment, news, sports, the television network, and NBC owned-and-operated stations.

Affiliation   About 60 percent of all full-power commercial television stations affiliate with a major network. Most function as **primary affiliates**—the only affiliate of a given network in a given market. **Secondary affiliates** share affiliation with more than one network. For example, Butte, Montana, has only two stations, one a primary affiliate of CBS, the other a primary affiliate of NBC; both also have secondary affiliations with ABC.

Most of the 200-plus stations that affiliate with a network do so under contract—each network has only about a half-dozen O&O stations. A network agrees to offer an affiliate the network's programs before offering them to any other station in the same market. The affiliated station, in turn, agrees to *clear* time for the network schedule. However, it has the right to decline to carry specific programs. An affiliate devotes up to approximately 65 percent of its schedule to its network.

affiliates not obligated to carry network programs

Networks pay affiliates compensation for their time, in exchange for which they offer affiliates four valuable services:

- A structured schedule of *network programs*.
- *Simultaneous program distribution* so that the service can be received by all affiliates at the same time.
- An *advertising environment* that appeals to local advertisers.
- A *sales organization* that finds national clients to purchase network advertisements that occupy part of the affiliates' commercial time.

An affiliation contract sets the terms of network compensation. On the average, the dollar actually received as network compensation by an affiliate amount to only about 15 percent of the affiliate's theoretical network hourly base rate. In the late 1980s, the three major networks combined paid their affiliates about $400 million a year to carry their programs.

This compensation represents a surprisingly small percentage of the gross revenues of network-affiliated stations—on the average, less than 5 percent. But stations measure the value of affiliation less in terms of compensation than in terms of the audiences that network programs attract. Affiliates profit from the sale of commercial spots in the 90 seconds or so the network leaves open for affiliate station breaks in each prime-time hour of network

network programs attract audiences for local shows

programming and the seven or eight minutes per hour made available at other times of the day. Moreover, the stations' own programs (whether locally produced or purchased from distributors) benefit from association with popular and widely promoted network programs.

Network Regulation

FCC does not license networks

Network Regulation   Unable to control networks directly (because it does not license them), the FCC regulates them indirectly through rules governing the stations they own and the contracts affiliates make with them.

The FCC's network regulations were originally intended to ensure station autonomy and to prevent the networks from becoming the overwhelmingly dominant force in broadcasting. For example, regulations prevent network contracts from forcing stations to clear time for network programs. However, as network power waned with the increasing strength of competing media, the FCC became less heavily concerned with network dominance. This reversal is discussed in more detail in Section 12.11.

Nevertheless, the FCC still prevents national networks from engaging in the distribution of non-network programs (syndication) and from owning entertainment programs. The Fox network initially escaped these limitations. It has not yet achieved full-scale network status under the FCC rules (as explained in defining *network* early in this section). Fox has ownership ties with a program producer (20th Century Fox) and program exhibitors (the Fox O&O stations), as described more fully in Exhibit 3.7—a classic case of vertical integration. In order to avoid complying with the network rules when it planned to exceed 15 hours a week, Fox obtained a temporary waiver of the 15-hour rule (for the 1990–1991 television season).

Clearance   With or without FCC regulation, networks and their affiliates experience a somewhat uneasy sharing of power, complicated by political and economic factors too subtle for contracts to define. In one sense the networks have the upper hand. Affiliation plays a vitally important role in an affiliate station's success. However, without the voluntary compliance of affiliates, a television network amounts to nothing but a group owner of a few stations rather than the main source of programming for some 200 stations.

The complex relationships between networks and their affiliates hinge on the act of **clearance**—the contractual agreement by an affiliate to keep clear in its program schedule the times the network needs to run its programs. An affiliate might fail to clear time or might pre-empt already cleared time for several reasons. Network public-affairs and other nonentertainment offerings usually get low ratings and therefore most often fail to get clearance. Sometimes stations skip low-rated network programs in favor of syndicated shows simply to keep audiences from flowing to the competition. Often a station wants to increase the amount of commercial time available. It can run more commercials than the network allows by substituting a syndicated program or a movie. Only infrequently do affiliates pre-empt network time in order to run locally produced programs.

why affiliates pre-empt network shows

Networks rely on affiliates not only to carry their programs but also to carry them *as scheduled*. Delayed network broadcasts erode national ratings. Moreover, networks need simultaneity of coverage to get the maximum benefit from promotion and advertising. When they run national campaigns on the air and in newspapers announcing a program's scheduled time, they count on its actually appearing on the air at that time.

In practice, affiliates accept about 90 percent of all programs offered by their networks as scheduled, most of them on faith. Stations can demand advance screening of questionable programs but usually feel no need to do so, despite the fact that, as licensees, stations rather than networks have the ultimate legal responsibility. Because most television programs come in series, affiliates know their general tone, so the acceptability of future episodes can usually be taken for granted.

Thus affiliates have little or no direct influence over the day-to-day programming decisions of their networks. In the long run, however, they have powerful leverage. Network programming strategists take serious note of the feedback that comes from their affiliates.

power of affiliates over networks

Changing Network/Affiliate Relations   Starting in the late 1980s, when rising costs and increasing competition combined to weaken ABC, CBS, and NBC, the traditional network/affiliate relationship began to crack under the strain. Affiliates felt that network compensation failed to reflect the true value of their time to their networks. The networks increased the amount of precious advertising time available to themselves in their schedules, a move resented by their affiliates. Pre-emptions reached all-time highs, costing the networks millions of dollars in lost revenues.

Affiliates came to feel less dependent on their networks when satellite relays and electronic news gathering (ENG) equipment began giving them alternative sources of program materials. For example, by 1990 about a quarter of NBC's affiliates subscribed to the cable news source, CNN. To counter this drift, NBC announced plans to expand its existing intermittent affiliate news service to a 24-hour schedule.

ENG makes affiliates more independent of networks

Competition from Independents   Approximately 400 stations, most of them UHF, are known as **independents.** They have no full-service network affiliation, although they may be affiliated with Fox or one of the regional networks. Independents at first offered little threat to the networks. As a group they lost money until 1975, when they first averaged a small profit.

The FCC's **prime-time access rule (PTAR)** had played a major role in turning some independents into profit-makers. Starting in 1971, PTAR gave independents their first chance to counterprogram effectively against network affiliates in the 7:00 to 8:00 P.M. (Eastern and Pacific time) period. They gained the advantage of rerunning network series during that hour, a program option that PTAR denied to affiliates in the major markets, as explained more fully in Section 8.2.

Other factors favoring independent stations included their coverage of live sports events, their success in outbidding affiliates for popular syndicated program series, their aggressive promotional campaigns, and their establishment of the Association of Independent Television Stations (INTV) in 1972.

continued dominance of TV network affiliates

Despite the loss of some business to independents, network affiliates continue to dominate television viewing. Affiliation with a national network remains one of the most valuable assets a television station can have.

6.4 *Cable TV Organization*

Cable/Broadcast Comparison   The economic organization of cable television systems and networks differs substantially from that of broadcast stations and networks. Municipal franchises for cable systems impose fewer restrictions than do FCC licenses for broadcasters.

allegiance to audience: cable TV vs. broadcasting

Cable systems depend on subscriber fees for 95 percent of their revenue. A cable system therefore owes allegiance only to the television households in its franchise area that choose to subscribe (in 1989 as high as 89 percent of the households in Palm Springs, for example, but averaging only about 57 percent of all television households in the country).

monopoly status of cable systems

A commercial broadcaster, in contrast, depends almost entirely on advertisers and has a legal obligation to serve the total audience in its market area, which is usually much larger than that of a cable system. Large cities often divide their municipal areas into several different cable franchises. Cable systems outnumber commercial television stations nearly 10 to 1. Whereas most viewers can tune in a number of local radio and television stations, almost without exception they can subscribe to only a single cable system.

Cable-System Organization   By the late 1980s more than 10,000 **cable systems** (the basic units of the industry) served 23,000 communities in the United States. Three out of four cable subscribers had access to 30 or more channels; 15 percent could see 54 or more; some could view more than 100. Whether small, with a few hundred subscribers, or large, with thousands, each cable system performs the same four basic functions as do broadcast stations, as described in Section 6.2.

However, a cable system's *technical* functions differ from those of a broadcast station. Broadcast technicians' jobs end when the signal leaves the transmitter—listeners/viewers are on their own when it comes to arranging for reception. Cable technicians must be concerned with the integrity of both the sending and the receiving aspects of the system. Often this division of responsibility results in a distinction between inside- and outside-plant personnel.

outside- vs. inside-plant cable technicians

The inside group operates and maintains the complex array of equipment at the headend, which receives programs by various means from program suppliers and processes the signals for delivery via coaxial cables to subscribers. The outside group installs and services subscriber cable connections, converters, and often pay-per-view units—a critically important job because the subscriber always has the option of abruptly discontinuing a technically unsatisfactory service.

As for the *programming* function, cable systems start with a more even playing field than broadcasters because the distinction between network affiliates and independents does not exist in cable. Nor does broadcasting's elaborate symbiotic relationship between an affiliate and its sole network exist for cable.

Typically, cable systems fill their channels with programs from both broadcasting stations and cable networks. The general manager of smaller systems makes program decisions, usually in consultation with the marketing director. Some cable systems produce local programs, often on channels programmed by community or educational organizations. Although a few cable companies have made a commitment to locally produced news, most systems defer to broadcast radio and television in this expensive and personnel-intensive area.

Cable system *sales* operations might better be called *sales and marketing*. Although some systems sell commercial time on some of their channels, marketing the cable service to subscribers ranks as the all-important function that brings in most of the revenue in the form of monthly subscriber fees.

importance of marketing to cable TV

The cable system marketing department tries to convince nonsubscribers to subscribe and current subscribers not to disconnect. The marketing department's customer service representatives interface with the public, answering telephones for eight or more hours a day, responding to complaints from subscribers and questions from potential customers. A system's ability to handle these contacts promptly and skillfully can have a profound effect on its financial success and ultimately even on whether it keeps or loses its franchise.

MSOs

Cabling large urban areas far exceeds the financial means of small-system operators. Firms large enough to make the initial capital investments are not likely to be attracted by the limited potential of a single franchise. Thus emerged a trend toward **multiple-system operators (MSOs)**—firms that gather scores and even hundreds of systems under single ownership. Such firms have the resources to bid for high-cost, politically intricate cable franchises in metropolitan areas. Cable regulations, unlike broadcasting regulations, place no limit on the number of systems or subscribers that may be served by a single MSO.

Some 350 MSOs operate in the United States. The largest, Tele-Communications Inc. (TCI), has more than 12 million subscribers. Impressive though that number may seem, even TCI serves less than 14 percent of all television homes. By contrast, the largest television station-group can reach nearly 25 percent.

Vertical Integration

Cable television often involves ownership links with related businesses such as program production and magazine publishing. This type of linkage is called **vertical integration.** Regulations prevent a high degree of vertical integration in broadcasting, but the less heavily regulated cable-TV industry resorts to it increasingly. In the late 1980s, nearly 32 percent of all cable systems had ties with broadcast interests, more than 20 percent with program producers, and approximately 18 percent with newspapers. Tele-Communications Inc. (TCI) provides the best example. TCI operates the nation's largest MSO. It also owns parts of a program producer (United Artists), several cable networks (Black Entertainment Television, the Discovery Channel, American Movie Classics, the Fashion Channel), and a satellite program distribution service (Netlink USA). TCI also owns part of

TCI: largest MSO as media conglomerate

EXHIBIT 6.4 Examples of Satellite-Distributed Cable Networks

Selected basic channels		
Name *(Owner and launch date)*	*Homes reached* *(millions)*	*Content*
Entertainment & Sports Programming Network (ESPN) (Capital Cities/ABC, 9/79)	53.4	College and NFL football, college basketball, auto racing, golf, other sports
Cable News Network (CNN) (Turner Broadcasting System, 6/80)	52.0	24-hour in-depth news
USA Network (Paramount Pictures, MCA Inc., 4/80)	49.7	Broad-based entertainment, sports
CBN Family Channel (Christian Broadcasting Network, 4/77)	47.5	Family entertainment, comedies, westerns, children's shows, religious programs
Music Television (MTV) (MTV Networks, Viacom Int. Inc., 8/81)	48.2	24-hour music videos, with interviews and concerts; some original programming
C-SPAN (non-profit corporation of cable companies and others, 3/79)	46.6	Live coverage of U.S. House of Representatives, public-affairs programs, congressional hearings
Selected superstations		
Name *(Owner and launch date)*	*Homes reached* *(millions)*	*Content*
WTBS (Turner Broadcasting System, 12/76)	50.5	Family programming, including classic movies, sitcoms, sports
WGN (The Tribune Co., 10/78)	29.0	Children's shows, sports, syndicated programs, movies

an already vertically integrated program producer/distributor/station owner—the Turner Broadcasting System, as detailed in Exhibit 3.2.

Cable-TV Program Operations 6.5

Cable systems carry most broadcast television stations whose signals cover their franchise areas. Beyond that, they draw on three main types of centralized program providers: basic cable networks, superstations, and pay-cable networks. Exhibit 6.4 gives data on a representative selection of these providers.

Basic-Cable Networks For their minimum subscription fee, cable systems usually offer a group of channels comprising the locally available

EXHIBIT 6.4   Continued

Pay services		
Name *(Owner and launch date)*	*Subscribers* *(millions)*	*Content*
Home Box Office (HBO) (Time Inc., 11/72)	17.0	Movies, variety, sports, specials, documentaries, children's programming
Showtime (Viacom, 7/80)	6.7	Movies, variety, comedy specials, Broadway adaptations
Selected home shopping networks		
Name *(Owner and launch date)*	*Subscribers* *(millions)*	*Content*
Home Shopping Network I & II (Home Shopping Network Inc., 7/85)	77.0	Electronics, jewelry, housewares, clothing, cosmetics, health products, collectibles
Cable Value Network (CVN Companies Inc.)	20.0	Electronics, tools, jewelry, toys, clothing
Selected pay-per-view networks		
Name		*Addressable homes (millions)*
Request Television (11/85) and Request-2		5.1
Viewer's Choice I (10/84) and Viewer's Choice II (11/85)		5.5
Playboy at Night		2.6
Groff PPV		1.2
Jerrold's Cable Video Store		1.0

Source: Data from *Channels 1990 Field Guide.*

television-station programs plus some **basic cable networks.** Most of the basic networks derive the bulk of their revenue from the sale of advertising.

A cable system pays only a small copyright fee for the re-transmission of broadcast stations. For basic cable network programs, a cable system pays a fee to each network that it carries, based on the number of subscribers to the system. Fees may range from 1 cent to 25 cents per subscriber per month. A basic cable network sells commercial spots to its own advertising clients and usually leaves about two minutes of advertising time each hour for local sale by the cable systems that carry it.

Advertising-supported cable networks have smaller staffs than ABC, CBS, or NBC, and they reach smaller audiences. They maintain commercial sales departments but also must devote major attention to selling *themselves* to cable systems. Unlike the major broadcast television networks, they have no assurance of finding affiliates because so many cable networks compete for outlets.

Superstations   A few broadcast stations, notably Ted Turner's WTBS in Atlanta, schedule programs designed especially to be attractive to cable systems. Distributing their programs by satellite nationally, they became hybrid broadcast station/cable network combinations known as **superstations.**

Cable operators include superstations in their basic package of channels, paying a few cents per subscriber per month to defray superstation satellite relay costs. The superstation's cut of the pie comes from increased advertising rates, which are justified by the cumulative size of the audiences it reaches through cable systems. A score of superstations exist, the two largest of which are listed in Exhibit 6.4.

Some cable systems also carry the signals of radio superstations, notably Chicago's Beethoven Satellite Network (WMFT), a classical music station. It is heard on several hundred cable systems serving over a million subscribers.

Before superstations altered the rules, copyright holders charged fees for rented syndicated programs based on each broadcast station's local market. These markets, well-defined by ratings companies, extend over a station's immediate coverage area. Originally, syndicators licensed WTBS to cover only the Atlanta market. As a superstation, however, WTBS now reaches audiences in hundreds of other markets. In many of these markets television stations had already paid fees for the *exclusive* right to broadcast the very same programs that cable systems import from superstations.

In response to complaints about the inequities created by duplicate television-program distribution on superstations, the FCC reimposed its previously abandoned **syndication exclusivity (syndex)** rule in January, 1990. Syndex requires any cable system, on request, to delete from its schedule any superstation programs that duplicate programs for which local-market television stations hold exclusive rights.

It was anticipated that the trouble and expense of blacking out duplicate programs might make cable-system operators reluctant to carry superstations.

WTBS planned to meet this threat with a blackout-proof schedule, free of syndicated programs subject to exclusivity clauses.

blackout-proofing avoids syndex problems

Pay-Cable Networks   Subscribers pay their cable systems additional fees to receive **pay-cable networks.** In exchange for the added fee, the subscriber gets superior entertainment (usually recent movies) without commercial interruption. Pay-cable subscription fees, devoted to a single channel, accumulate large sums, enabling pay-cable networks to buy high-priced program materials. Pay-cable fees average about $10 per month for each so-called premium channel. The cable operator negotiates the amount of the fee with the network, usually splitting proceeds 50/50. Data on leading pay-cable networks are given in Exhibit 6.4.

Included under pay-cable are pay-per-view (PPV) networks. Instead of paying a flat fee for PPV services, subscribers pay a separate fee for each program, much as they would at a box office.

Advertising Basics 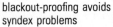 6.6

Unlike cable television, broadcasting in the United States operates primarily as an advertising medium. Dependence on advertising colors every aspect of broadcast operations. As Exhibit 6.5 indicates, broadcast television ranks as the largest *national* advertising medium, though newspapers surpass television in total advertising volume. Radio comes forth in *total* advertising dollars, after direct mail but ahead of magazines. Advertising on cable, although rapidly increasing, remains small relative to advertising on other electronic media.

broadcast TV is biggest national ad medium

Local, National-Spot, and Network Ads   Broadcast advertising falls into three categories, defined in terms of coverage area and image: local, network, and national spot.

Local advertising comes mostly from fast-food restaurants, department and furniture stores, banks, food stores, and movie theaters. When such local firms act as retail outlets for nationally distributed products, the cost of local advertising may be shared by the local retailer (an appliance dealer, for example) and the national manufacturer (a maker of refrigerators). This type of cost sharing, known as **local cooperative advertising,** or just **local coop,** supplies radio with a major source of its revenue. It also leads to some shady deals known as *double billing*, described in Section 6.8.

When a station connects to a national network, it instantly becomes a medium of national advertising. For national advertisers, **network advertising** has significant advantages:

advantages of TV commercials for advertisers

- The advertiser can place messages on more than 200 stations of known quality, strategically located to cover the entire country.

EXHIBIT *6.5*   Advertising Volume of Major Media: Local vs. National

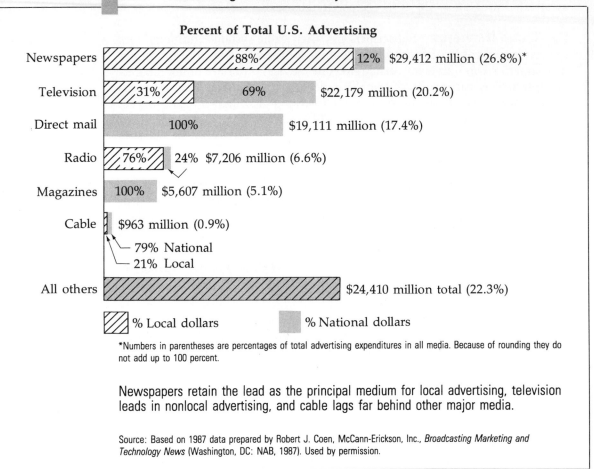

Percent of Total U.S. Advertising

Newspapers   //// 88% //// 12% $29,412 million (26.8%)*

Television   // 31% // 69% $22,179 million (20.2%)

Direct mail   100% $19,111 million (17.4%)

Radio   // 76% // 24% $7,206 million (6.6%)

Magazines   100% $5,607 million (5.1%)

Cable $963 million (0.9%)
— 79% National
— 21% Local

All others   //// $24,410 million total (22.3%)

//// % Local dollars   ▓ % National dollars

*Numbers in parentheses are percentages of total advertising expenditures in all media. Because of rounding they do not add up to 100 percent.

Newspapers retain the lead as the principal medium for local advertising, television leads in nonlocal advertising, and cable lags far behind other major media.

Source: Based on 1987 data prepared by Robert J. Coen, McCann-Erickson, Inc., *Broadcasting Marketing and Technology News* (Washington, DC: NAB, 1987). Used by permission.

- Advertising can be placed on all those stations with a single transaction.
- The advertiser has centralized control over commercial messages and assurance that they will be delivered in the chosen times and in a preferred program environment.
- The advertiser benefits from sophisticated network market research.
- The advertiser gains prestige from the very fact of being on a national network.

national spots are an alternative to network advertising

Despite those advantages, some national advertisers find networks too costly or too inflexible. They have the option of using **national-spot advertising.** Advertisers using national-spot advertising work through their advertising agencies and stations' national sales representatives to assemble ad hoc collections of nonconnected stations. The commercial announcements go out

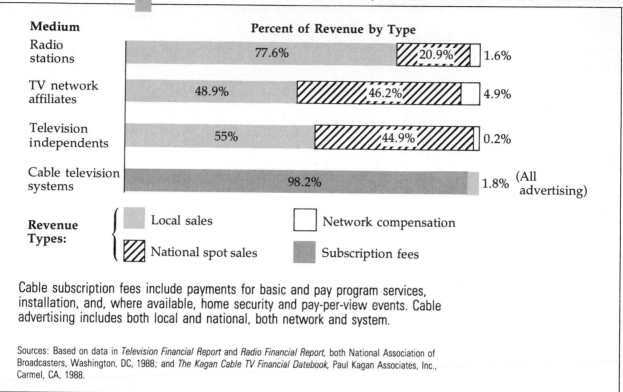

EXHIBIT 6.6 Broadcast Station/Cable System Commercial Revenue Sources

Medium	Percent of Revenue by Type
Radio stations	77.6% — 20.9% — 1.6%
TV network affiliates	48.9% — 46.2% — 4.9%
Television independents	55% — 44.9% — 0.2%
Cable television systems	98.2% — 1.8% (All advertising)

Revenue Types: { Local sales   Network compensation
National spot sales   Subscription fees }

Cable subscription fees include payments for basic and pay program services, installation, and, where available, home security and pay-per-view events. Cable advertising includes both local and national, both network and system.

Sources: Based on data in *Television Financial Report* and *Radio Financial Report,* both National Association of Broadcasters, Washington, DC, 1988; and *The Kagan Cable TV Financial Datebook,* Paul Kagan Associates, Inc., Carmel, CA, 1988.

to the chosen stations by mail or by satellite. As Exhibit 6.6 shows, television depends heavily on national-spot sales.

National-spot advertisers can choose from several program vehicles—station-break spots between network programs, participating spots in local or syndicated programs, and sponsorship of either local or syndicated programs. National spot thus enables advertisers to capitalize on audience interest in local programs, something the network advertiser cannot do. Exhibit 6.7 shows that the largest national advertisers use spot and network in combination to achieve better coverage than either could yield on its own.

Pros and Cons   As an advertising medium, broadcasting has unrivaled access to all family members under the changing circumstances of daily living. Moreover, car and portable radios allow broadcasting to compete with magazines and newspapers as an out-of-home medium. Above all, the constant availability of broadcasting as a companionable source of entertainment and information gives it a great psychological advantage.

EXHIBIT **6.7**   Media Mix of Top Advertisers

			Percent of expenditure allocated to:							
Rank	Advertiser	Total est. ad expend. (millions)	Network TV	Spot TV	Network radio	Spot radio	Network cable	News-paper	Maga-zines	Other
1	Philip Morris	$1,558	21	7	*	2	1	3	16	50
2	Procter & Gamble	$1,387	27	17	2	*	2	*	6	46
3	General Motors	$1,025	27	10	2	3	*	17	15	26
4	Sears, Roebuck	$887	18	3	6	2	*	NA	2	NA
5	RJR Nabisco	$840	25	4	*	1	2	2	13	53

*Less than 1 percent
NA = Not available

Even Philip Morris, prohibited by law from advertising its cigarettes on radio or television, sells other products in sufficient quantity to warrant allocating more than 20 percent of its ad budget to the networks. Among these five firms, only three spent much on cable. "Other" advertising includes the large direct-mail category.

Source: Based on 1987 data reported in *Advertising Age,* 28 Sept. 1988. Reprinted with permission.

However, commercials must make their point quickly. Normally, radio commercials last 60 seconds, and most television commercials 30 seconds, though there is a growing trend toward 10- and 15-second spots. Even the longest spot cannot duplicate the impact of a large printed department-store ad or a printed supermarket ad with clip-out coupons. Listeners or viewers cannot clip out broadcast ads to consult later. Nor can broadcasting compete effectively with the classified sections of newspapers, despite attempts with want-ad and home-shopping programs.

advantages of print ads

A broadcasting station has a limited commercial **inventory,** as the openings for commercials in its program schedule are called. Its single channel allows it only 24 hours of "space" each day. Moreover, only so many commercials can be crammed into the schedule without alienating the audience. Print media, in contrast, can expand advertising space at will without alienating readers, simply by adding pages.

Broadcasting also suffers the drawback of being unavailable to advertise some products. Congress forbade cigarette advertising, and most broadcasters find it expedient to ban voluntarily such products as hard liquor, X-rated movies, and condoms.

Integrating Ads into Broadcasts   Most broadcast advertising takes the form of announcements, or spots. Advertisers usually prefer **scatter buying**— spreading their spots over several programs. That avoids risking too much on any one program and gains exposure to varied audiences.

Some programs have natural breaks where spots can be inserted without interrupting the flow—between rounds of a boxing match or between record cuts on a radio show, for example. In other cases the break must be artificially contrived. The art of writing half-hour situation comedies includes building the plot to suspenseful break-off points for the insertion of commercials. Viewers often complain about the arbitrary interruptions of theatrical feature films, whose scripts do not, of course, provide seemingly natural climaxes in the action every 10 minutes to accomodate commercial breaks. Some viewers also object to television time-outs during football games, taken for the convenience of advertisers.

As a matter of both law and custom, stations make **station breaks**—interruptions in programming for the insertion of **identification announcements (IDs).** Commercials inserted during these interruptions are called **station-break announcements.**

Networks interrupt their program feeds periodically to allow affiliates time to insert mandatory IDs. They also leave time for affiliates to insert commercial announcements sold by the stations to local or national-spot advertisers. Because of their close association with popular network programs, commercials inserted in these **network adjacencies** are especially valuable.

Two quasi-commercial types of announcements also occur at the junctures where commercials appear. **Promotional announcements (promos)** call attention to future programs of networks and stations. Most broadcasters consider on-air promotion their most effective and cost-efficient audience-building tool. **Public-service announcements (PSAs),** though they resemble commercials, are broadcast without charge because they promote noncommercial organizations and causes. PSAs give traffic departments a way of fulfilling public-service obligations and, along with promos, serve as fillers for unsold commercial openings.

noncommercial commercials

The time devoted to clusters of commercial and other announcements at station breaks, once limited to a minute or two, has constantly edged upward. Advertisers as well as audiences often complain of this proliferation, which is referred to as **commercial clutter.**

Cable TV Advertising   Cable-system operators face more complexities than do broadcasters when inserting commercial messages in their programs. They have to deal with many channels, each with different requirements for advertising insertions. Some systems use computer programs triggered by electronic signals originated by cable networks to insert locally sold commercials automatically into cable-network programming. However, such hardware has often proved unreliable, sometimes rolling commercials late or even not at all.

problems for cable ads

Perhaps more than anything else, lack of adequate statistical information about cable audiences has impeded the growth of cable advertising. Cable's multiplicity of program choices so fractionalizes its audience that few channels attract viewers in sufficient numbers to yield statistically valid measurements.

Rating services supply audience information for only a few of the most popular national cable networks.

cable advertising accounts for less than 1% of U.S. total

Nevertheless, cable advertising is growing rapidly. Exhibit 6.5 shows that cable advertising revenue reached nearly a billion dollars by 1987, though that still amounts to less than 1 percent of the nation's total advertising. National cable networks accounted for about 80 percent of cable's ad revenue.

6.7 Advertising Rates

Two sets of variables affect the price of broadcast advertising time, one set relatively stable, one relatively dynamic. Station managers have *no* day-to-day control over *market size, station facilities* (frequency, power, antenna location), and *network affiliation,* if any. Station managers *do* control *programming, promotion,* and *sales.* Good management can lure demographically desirable audiences away from competitors by offering attractive programs supported by effective promotion, and an efficient sales department can lure advertisers away from competitors with persuasive arguments and solicitous attention.

Cost Per Thousand (CPM)　No standard formula for setting appropriate broadcast rates exists. Market forces, however, eventually tend to bring prices into line. The industry uses **cost per thousand (CPM)** as the main test for comparing the relative cost of advertising. CPM is the cost of reaching 1,000 (represented by the Roman numeral "M") household or other defined targets.

CPM is calculated by dividing the cost of a commercial by the number of homes (in thousands) that it reached. Advertisers typically pay an average CPM of under $10 for a prime-time spot on one of the three major television networks.

CPM enables comparing media costs

CPM calculations enable comparing the cost of advertising on one medium with the cost on another, one station with another, and one program with another. They also enable a station or network to guarantee a specific CPM in advance, promising to reimburse the advertiser should the actual audience fall below the predicted level. This is called selling advertising *on the come.* CPM measurements depend, of course, on reliable audience-size information—one more reason that ratings play such a dominant role in programming strategies.

Price Variables　Broadcast advertising depends for its effectiveness on cumulative effect. A buyer therefore normally contracts for spots in groups (a spot schedule). Prices vary according to the number of spots purchased (quantity discounts) and other variables, such as

- *Time classes.* Typically stations divide their time into specific dayparts, and even subclasses of dayparts, with different prices for each.

- *Spot position.* For an assured place in the schedule, advertisers are willing to pay the premium rate charged for **fixed-position spots. Run-of-schedule (ROS) spots** may be scheduled by a station anywhere within the time period designated in the sales contract.
- *Pre-emptibility.* Stations charge less for pre-emptible spots, which advertisers buy on the understanding that their contract will be canceled if a higher-paying customer turns up.
- *Package plans.* Stations offer at discount a variety of packages, which may include several spots scheduled at various times and on various days.

A television station may offer more than a hundred different prices for spots, using a device known as a **rate grid.** For example, it might list 20 different time periods or program titles down the left side of its grid. Across the top it might list 6 different rate levels, numbered I through VI. This arrangement would create 120 cells or boxes into which specific prices can be entered. Rate levels can be defined quite arbitrarily, enabling the station to quote six different prices for the same spot. Such a grid gives sales personnel great flexibility in negotiating deals without having to resort to under-the-table rate cutting.

The rate for the same television-spot position in the same program may change over the course of a single season if the audience for the program rises or falls significantly. In 1988 the cost for one showing of a 30-second network spot in a regular prime-time television program averaged about $100,000. Ad rates cover time charges only, not the cost of producing the commercials. Radio-network ad rates range widely, influenced by daypart and audience reach. In the late 1980s, the average spot on the Westwood One network cost $900 and on ABC more than $1,000.

Cable-TV Ad Rates   Cable advertising rates vary according to three levels of audience potential: single system, interconnected systems, and networks. In 1989, about 20 percent of all cable systems accepted local ads. Rates for 30-second commercials ranged from as little as $2 up to $400 and sometimes higher.

Interconnected cable systems differ from cable networks. A network may reach thousands of systems throughout the nation, but system interconnection involves a relatively small number of systems within a limited geographic region. Such a region is called a **cable market of opportunity (CMO).** A CMO may represent anywhere from about 55,000 subscribers, as in the Fort Wayne, Ind., area, to more than 2 million, as in the New York City area. Several spots inserted locally into programs of selected advertiser-supported cable networks in the Fort Wayne CMO cost as little as $24, whereas a single spot in a sporting event shown in the New York City CMO costs $2,000.

cable systems interconnect to facilitate ad sales

Cable networks and superstations, although national in scope, do not necessarily command the highest advertising prices. In 1988, less than 3 percent of U.S. television households tuned in to WTBS during prime time, although it is the highest-rated cable program service. WTBS charged from $800 to

$15,000 per spot. Commercials on MTV averaged $2,500, and in 1988 USA sold spots in syndicated reruns of *Miami Vice* and *Murder, She Wrote* for an average of $5,500 each.

Alternative Ad Buys   Some types of ad-buying deals, used by both broadcasters and cable operators, fall outside normal rate practices.

- In a **trade deal** (also called a **tradeout**), a station or cable system exchanges commercial time for an advertiser's goods or services.
- In **barter deals**, stations exchange advertising time for programs. These are discussed in detail in Section 8.2.
- **Time brokerage** refers to the practice of selling time in blocks to brokers, who then resell it at a markup. Foreign-language programmers often buy brokered time.
- **Per inquiry (PI) deals** are favored by mail-order firms on some cable networks and in cut-rate time periods on television stations. They commit the advertiser to pay not for advertising time but for the number of inquiries or the number of items sold in direct response to PI commercials.

6.8   *Advertising Standards*

Advertising raises touchy issues of taste, legality, and social responsibility. Both legal standards and voluntary self-regulatory standards influence what may be advertised and what methods may be used.

Government Regulation   The Communications Act makes the FCC responsible for ensuring that broadcasters operate in the public interest. Specifically, Section 317 of the act requires reasonably recognizable differences between radio/television commercials and programs. A station must disclose the source of anything it puts on the air for which it receives payment, whether in money or some other "valuable consideration."

This **sponsor identification rule** attempts to prevent deception by disguised propaganda from unidentified sources. Of course, anonymity is the last thing commercial advertisers desire. But propagandists who use **editorial advertising** (sometimes called **advertorials**) may not always be so anxious to reveal their true identity; nor do those who make under-the-table payments to disc jockeys or others for on-the-air favors wish to be identified. Outright deception in advertising comes under Federal Trade Commission jurisdiction.

no FCC standards for amount of commercial time

Contrary to popular opinion, the FCC never set a maximum number of commercial minutes per hour of programming. Until 1981, FCC license applications and renewal forms required applicants to state the number of commercial minutes per hour they planned to allow or had allowed in the past. The FCC then might ask applicants who exceeded the usual time standards to justify the excess. Neither the FCC nor any other authority ever suggested any time limits for commercials on cable television.

Program-Length Ads   The FCC once prohibited what it called **program-length commercials**—productions that interweave program and noncommercial material so closely that the program as a whole promotes the sponsor's product or service. The FCC lifted the ban on program-length commercials in 1981 for radio and in 1984 for television. Earlier commissions had reasoned that the FCC licensed stations primarily to broadcast programs, not advertising. The 1980s commission left the choice of content up to the licensee, subject mainly to the economic discipline of the marketplace.

A flood of program-length commercials, by then known also as **infomercials,** ensued, often touting merchandise of questionable value. Ads for medical nostrums, kitchen gadgets, astrology charts, and the like overran the less desirable hours on both broadcast and cable television.

Some advertisers spent as much as it would take to produce legitimate half-hour talk programs on slick program-length ads. The Federal Trade Commission forced some particularly outrageous ads promoting a diet and an impotency cure off the air, and in 1990 a congressional committee held hearings on the infomercial trend. Despite the aura of sleaze surrounding infomercials, they continued on the rise. Some even began to achieve respectability—"Slick Superblurbs go Upmarket," as a trade journal put it (Robins, 1990).

Taboo Products   Some perfectly legal products and services that appear in print and billboards never appear in the electronic mass media. This double standard reflects the fact that special restraints are imposed on broadcasting and, to a lesser degree, on cable because they come directly to the home, accessible to all.

Congress banned the broadcasting of cigarette ads in 1971. The most conspicuous example of self-imposed advertising abstinence is the refusal to accept commercials for hard liquor, though beer and wine are acceptable. On rare occasions hard-liquor ads have been broadcast, but most broadcasters decline to carry liquor ads for fear of giving ammunition to opponents of wine and beer advertising.

ad standards for in-home media differ from standards for other media

Self-Regulation   The ban on liquor ads is an example of the voluntary self-regulation codified by the National Association of Broadcasters (NAB). Its radio and television codes, though full of exceptions and qualifications, set nominal limits on commercial time. For example, NAB allowed radio 18 minutes per hour; and it allowed network-television affiliates 9.5 minutes in prime time, 16 minutes at other times.

In 1984, the Justice Department charged that the NAB standards, even though only voluntary, violated antitrust laws by urging limits that reduced competition. The NAB promptly disbanded its Code Office, apparently relieved to be rid of a thankless task. By 1990, however, a move developed in Congress to restore the option of industry self-regulation by exempting the NAB codes from the antitrust law.

NAB codes discontinued

Meanwhile, the three major television networks, and some group broad-casters, had begun dismantling their individual program and advertising codes. The networks had separate departments, variously called Continuity Acceptance, Broadcast Standards, and Program Practices. In the late 1980s, ABC and CBS cut back the number of employees assigned to standards and practices departments from about 85 per network to about 28. NBC eliminated its department entirely. Advertisers, agencies, and others expressed fears that these moves might result in an overall lowering of standards. Adverse public reaction, they felt, could be followed by attempts at governmental intervention.

Cable networks have not felt it necessary to pay much attention to self-regulation. For example, ABC Television's commercial standards guidebook is about an inch thick, but ESPN (80 percent owned by Cap Cities/ABC) prints its standards on a single page. Most cable networks issue no written standards at all.

Unethical Practices   Aside from issues of advertising length and content, four specific types of unethical advertising practices in broadcasting have proved particularly troublesome: plugola, payola, double billing, and clipping. In the past, they triggered both FCC and congressional action.

A conflict of interest occurs when a station or one of its employees uses or promotes on the air something in which the station or employee has an undisclosed financial interest. This practice, called **plugola,** usually results in an indirect payoff. A disc jockey who gives unpaid publicity to her or his personal sideline business is an example.

Direct payments to the person responsible for inserting plugs usually constitutes **payola.** It typically takes the form of under-the-table payoffs by recording-company representatives to disc jockeys and others responsible for putting music on the air.

Local cooperative advertising sometimes tempts stations into **double billing.** Manufacturers who share with their local dealers the cost of local advertising of their products must rely on those dealers to handle cooperative advertising. Dealer and station may connive to send the manufacturer a bill for advertising higher than the one the dealer actually paid. Station and dealer then split the excess payment.

Clipping occurs when affiliates cut away from network programs prematurely, usually in order to insert commercials of their own. Clipping constitutes fraud because networks compensate affiliates for carrying programs in their entirety with all commercials intact.

In keeping with deregulation policy then in vogue, in 1986 the FCC redefined billing frauds as civil or criminal matters, not FCC violations. It left the networks to solve clipping problems on their own by bringing suit against offending stations—a cumbersome procedure at best. The commission did say, however, that it would consider false-billing charges when judging a licensee's character during licensing proceedings.

Local-Level Broadcast Sales   As noted in Section 6.7, one of the dynamic variables that can affect the success of a commercial station is the efficiency of its sales operation. Most television sales departments employ a general sales manager, a local (and sometimes also a national) sales manager, account executives, and support staff. The number of account executives (a fancy name for salespersons) varies from station to station. About six salespeople usually suffice for a medium-market television station. At some stations a sales assistant or even a secretary does all the support work; some include research specialists and commercial writers on the sales staff.

Sales managers hire, fire, and train salespersons, assigning them a list of specific advertisers and ad agencies as contacts. Beginning salespeople sometimes start without benefit of such an account list. They must develop their own accounts by consulting the Yellow Pages and making cold calls on potential new advertisers.

Salespeople usually work on a commission basis, keeping a percentage of all advertising dollars they bring to the station. This arrangement gives them an incentive and the opportunity to raise their income without waiting for the traditional annual raise.

In addition to the personal qualities needed for success in any sales job, an account executive needs one indispensable sales tool—the ability to use audience research. He or she must reduce the myriad numbers contained in rating reports to terms understandable to a client and must present them to show the station in the best possible light. Armed with these data (often displayed in attractive brochures), along with a list of commercial availabilities supplied by the traffic department, their local rate card (if one exists), and information on the advertising needs and history of each prospect, the salesperson sallies forth to do battle.

role of audience research in sales

National-Spot Sales   Stations and cable systems gain access to national advertising business through national sales representative firms (*reps* for short) and, in the case of affiliates, network sales departments. Some stations also have regional reps for non-national sales outside the station's service area. A rep contracts with a string of stations, acting as an extension of the stations' own sales staff in the national and regional markets. Television reps have only one client station in any one market, whereas radio reps often have more than one.

role of reps

Reps perform many services other than sales. Their national perspective provides client stations or systems with a broader view than that of local markets. Reps often advise clients on programming, conduct research for them, and act as all-around consultants. In return for their services, rep companies collect a commission of 8 to 15 percent on the spot sales they make for their clients.

The 1980s saw the introduction of a new way of selling national-spot television advertising—the **unwired network.** Under this concept, companies buy commercial time, usually in bulk and at a discount, from television stations throughout the United States. Then they sell it, at a markup, to national advertisers. One such organization, Independent Television Network, offers a package of spots in prime-time movies on independent stations around the country, selling time on many stations in a one-invoice transaction. Traditional sales reps strongly oppose the unwired-network concept, viewing it as a threat to their exclusive national representation of client stations.

Cable Ad Sales   Advertising-supported cable networks deliver relatively small audiences compared with the three major broadcast networks. However, some advertisers target the specialized audiences attracted by cable's dedicated channels (sports fans who watch ESPN, for example).

how time-buyers line up cable networks for ads

Because of cable networks' limited audience reach, advertisers are likely to place commercials on several different networks. Dealing with several networks can be a bothersome task. Time-buying organizations, such as Cable One, solve this problem by negotiating deals on behalf of advertisers for spots on all, or any combination of, cable networks.

Advertising Agencies   All regional and national advertisers and most large local advertisers deal with the media through advertising agencies. Agencies conduct research; design advertising campaigns; create commercials; buy time from cable systems, broadcast stations, and cable and broadcast networks; supervise the implementation of campaigns and evaluate their effectiveness; and, finally, pay the media on behalf of the advertisers they represent.

Agencies become intimately familiar with each client's business problems, sometimes even assisting in the development of new products or the redesigning and repackaging of old ones. The ad agencies that handle large national accounts mix their clients' buys among the major media, as indicated in Exhibit 6.7. Advertising agency media directors decide on the media mix.

payments to ad agencies

Ad agencies traditionally receive a 15 percent commission on billings, the amount charged by the advertising media. An agency bills its client the full amount of advertising time charges, pays the medium 85 percent, and keeps 15 percent as payment for its own services.

Variations in payment method arise because a firm's own advertising department may do some of the work or may retain specialist firms to do specific jobs, such as research, time buying, or commercial production. Some agencies accept less than 15 percent commission or charge fees in addition to commission; some work on a straight fee basis; and some work on a cost-plus basis.

In any event, the fact that the media allow a discount on business brought to them by agencies creates an odd relationship: the agency works for its client, the advertiser, but gets paid by the medium in the form of a discount on time charges. The travel business operates similarly. A travel agency works, at least theoretically, for the traveler but gets paid by the hotel or airline in discounts on charges.

Proof of Performance   After commercials have been aired, advertisers and their agencies need evidence to show that contracts have been carried out. Broadcast stations log the time, length, and source of each commercial when broadcast. These logs provide documentary proof of contract fulfillment. The sales department relies on logs when preparing proof-of-performance warranties to accompany billing statements. At many stations, computers do the logging automatically. Some stations also make slow-speed audio recordings of everything they air as backup evidence in the event of a dispute.

Advertisers and agencies can get independent confirmation of contract fulfillment by subscribing to the services of Broadcast Advertising Reports (BAR), a firm that conducts systematic studies of radio and television commercial performance. BAR checks on commercials by recording the audio portion of television programs in 75 markets, sending the recordings to central offices for processing. It also assigns operatives to actually view commercials in some markets.

how airing of ads is verified

The A.C. Nielsen Company began testing a monitoring service in 1986, using computer technology to recognize each television commercial's unique combination of images and sounds. In 1988, Arbitron announced a similar service.

Subscription-Fee Revenue   6.10

In sharp contrast to broadcasting, cable television relies on monthly subscription fees for about 90 percent of its revenue. Some small cable systems charge a single monthly rate. Others divide their channels into several tiers of program services, charging a separate fee for each tier.

Fixing Fee Levels   Under the Cable Act of 1984, the municipalities that franchise cable systems have no authority to regulate fee levels as long as a cable system has "effective competition" in its franchise area. The FCC set the minimum competitive standard extremely low—only three television stations need be receivable within the cable system's service area. Hardly any systems operate in areas with fewer than three television stations. In 1990, the FCC announced plans to consider raising its effective-competition standard. Doing so would give at least some cities the right to regulate subscription rates.

cable TV subscription fees virtually unregulated

Most cable systems offer their *basic* service for a monthly fee varying from a few dollars to about $25, averaging $15. Some systems pull the more popular ad-supported networks such as MTV and ESPN out of the basic package to offer them as an *expanded basic* service at extra cost.

The next level of service includes pay-cable channels, such as HBO. By 1990 nearly 30 million homes—more than half of all cable households—subscribed to pay cable. Usually, subscribers must pay a separate fee for each pay service they select at the average rate of about $10 per service per month.

In addition to monthly fees, most cable systems also charge a one-time installation fee and may also add a connection charge when a subscriber elects to add a new pay-cable channel. To induce homeowners to sign up, cable operators frequently offer reduced charges or waive them altogether.

Pay-Per-View
Cable systems equipped to use addressable converters offer **pay-per-view (PPV)** programs. The one-time PPV charge allows viewers to see a movie or a special event, such as a major boxing match or a rock concert. In 1989, PPV subscribers ordered more than 30 million programs, and typically paid about $4 for each movie and about $15 to $25 for each special event.

Individual cable systems—in this context called *standalones*—sometimes negotiate the right to a PPV event and then produce it themselves. Alternatively, national program services acquire PPV rights to programs and distribute them to cable systems. The program services and the cable systems split the revenue.

By 1988 more than 14 million homes had addressable PPV hardware. Between 500,000 and 600,000 of those home paid approximately $35 each to watch the 91-second heavyweight championship fight between Mike Tyson and Michael Spinks on 27 June 1988, producing more revenue for promoters and rights holders than did that year's Super Bowl on network broadcast television.

Niche Services
The services that satisfy small audience niches—MMDS, SMATV, and TVROs—showed little prospect of attaining financial significance.

In the late 1980s MMDS monthly subscriber fees averaged about $15 plus installation. Late in 1989, however, Microband Companies, Inc., the largest "wireless-cable" owner, filed for bankruptcy. MMDS services had attracted fewer than 100,000 viewers.

SMATV operators, who often divide their channels among a basic service and one or more tiers, charge subscribers from about $6 to $20 a month. A full package of basic services and additional tiers came to around $35. Some building owners operate SMATV systems themselves, offering the service free or at cost to entice new tenants.

Home TVRO installations can subscribe to packages of cable channels from Showtime and others. Each household pays $400 or so for a decoder to unscramble cable-network signals., The 1988 Showtime package offered TVRO owners 13 basic cable networks, plus Showtime or the Movie Channel, for $17.95 a month. Eastern Microwave packaged the signals of three superstations for as little as $36 a year.

The number of people employed in an industry usually gives some indication of its importance. According to that yardstick, the electronic media have relatively little importance. However, the social significance of the media lends them far greater weight than their small workforce suggests.

Employment Levels   Exhibit 6.8 gives employment statistics for the non-network units of the broadcast and cable industries. They employ in the aggregate some 600,000 people full-time. By way of comparison, one lone manufacturing corporation, General Motors, employs more than 900,000 people.

However, many specialized creative firms undergird the media, producing materials ranging from station-identification jingles to prime-time entertainment series. Such firms offer more opportunities for creative work than the media themselves—performing, writing, directing, designing, and so on.

Many other media-related jobs are found in nonprogram areas. These include jobs in advertising agencies, sales representative firms, program-syndicating organizations, news agencies, common-carrier companies, and audience-research organizations.

jobs in non-program media work

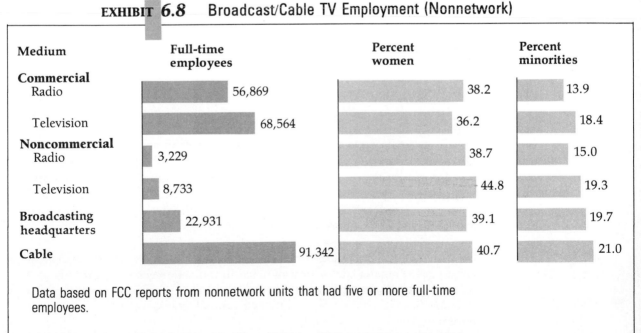

EXHIBIT 6.8   Broadcast/Cable TV Employment (Nonnetwork)

Medium	Full-time employees	Percent women	Percent minorities
Commercial Radio	56,869	38.2	13.9
Television	68,564	36.2	18.4
Noncommercial Radio	3,229	38.7	15.0
Television	8,733	44.8	19.3
Broadcasting headquarters	22,931	39.1	19.7
Cable	91,342	40.7	21.0

Data based on FCC reports from nonnetwork units that had five or more full-time employees.

Source: FCC, *Broadcast and Cable Employment Trend Reports*, Washington, DC, 13 Jan. 1989 (broadcast) and 29 Dec. 1988 (cable).

Aside from the major television networks, most broadcast and cable organizations have small staffs. The number of full-time employees at radio stations ranges from fewer than 5 for the smallest markets to about 60 for the largest, with the average being 15. Television stations have between 20 and 300 employees. A typical network affiliate employs about 90 and an independent station about 60 full-time people.

Cable systems average about 30 full-time employees but range from family-run systems in small communities (with perhaps 5 or 6 employees) to large-city systems with staffs of well over 100. Cable MSO headquarters units average about 55 full-time employees.

Salary Levels

The huge salaries reported in gossip columns go to top performing and creative talent and executives who work mostly at network headquarters and the production centers of New York and Hollywood.

Average salaries for jobs at most stations and cable systems rank as moderate at best. Typically, those working in sales earn the highest income at broadcasting stations. At the department-head level, general sales managers usually make the most money and traffic managers the least. Program managers fall somewhere in between. Exhibit 6.9 offers a more detailed analysis of managerial salaries.

News jobs rank among the better-paying nonsupervisory positions in television. A 1989 survey conducted for the Radio-Television News Directors Association found that television news reporters earned a median annual salary of $19,240; anchors earned between $34,000 and $47,000. Radio paid reporters $13,000 and anchors about $16,000. Median annual salaries for television and radio news directors showed a similar disparity, with TV at $42,000 and radio at $18,000.

Fair Employment

The FCC enforces Equal Employment Opportunity (EEO) Act standards for broadcast stations, cable systems, and headquarters operations with five or more employees.

In its annual employment study of all broadcast stations with five or more employees, the FCC reported that in 1988 women occupied more than 38 percent of all jobs, up from 32 percent in 1979. Perhaps more important, women represented 31 percent of the employees classified as "officials and managers" (up from 23 percent in 1979) and 49 percent of those classified as "sales workers" (up from 31 percent in 1979).

Unionization

At the networks, the national production centers, and most large-market network-television affiliates, unionization generally prevails. Not so at the smaller-station and cable-system levels. The fragmentation of the industry into many units, mostly with small staffs, makes unionization impracticable.

In small operations, staff members often have to handle two or more jobs that in a union shop might come under different jurisdictions. For example, a small radio station cannot afford to assign two employees to record an

EXHIBIT 6.9 Average Annual Salaries of TV and Radio Station Managers

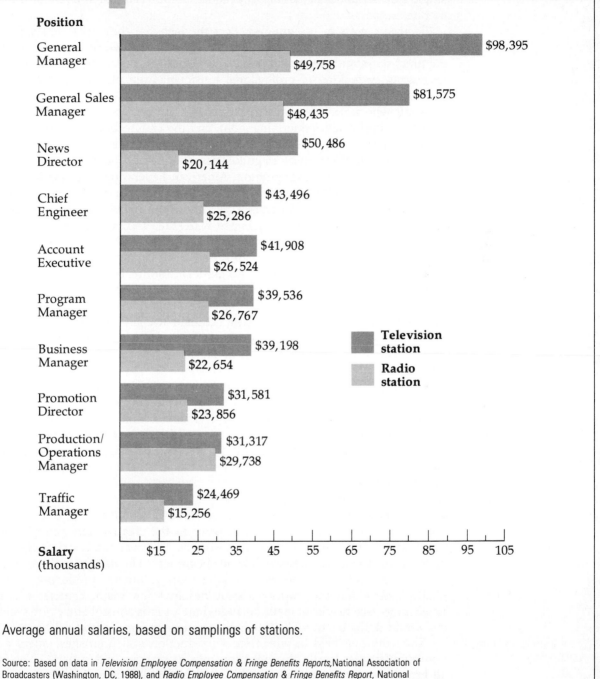

Position

Position	Television station	Radio station
General Manager	$98,395	$49,758
General Sales Manager	$81,575	$48,435
News Director	$50,486	$20,144
Chief Engineer	$43,496	$25,286
Account Executive	$41,908	$26,524
Program Manager	$39,536	$26,767
Business Manager	$39,198	$22,654
Promotion Director	$31,581	$23,856
Production/ Operations Manager	$31,317	$29,738
Traffic Manager	$24,469	$15,256

Salary (thousands): $15 25 35 45 55 65 75 85 95 105

Average annual salaries, based on samplings of stations.

Source: Based on data in *Television Employee Compensation & Fringe Benefits Reports,* National Association of Broadcasters (Washington, DC, 1988), and *Radio Employee Compensation & Fringe Benefits Report*, National Association of Broadcasters (Washington, DC, 1988).

interview, paying one as a technician to operate the equipment and the other as a performer to do the talking. If need be, the job can just as easily be done by one employee.

Electronic mass media unions reflect the fact that they draw on types of personnel first unionized in older industries—electrical work, music, motion pictures, stage, and newspapers. Thus the American Federation of Musicians represents every kind of professional musician, from players in symphony orchestras to pianists in bars.

People who work in broadcasting and cable can be grouped into two broad categories, the creative/performing group and the craft/technical group. Unions divide along similar lines; those representing the former usually avoid the word *union,* calling themselves guilds, associations, or federations.

The first pure broadcasting union, American Federation of Television and Radio Artists (AFTRA), began (originally as AFRA) in 1937, representing that universal radio performer, the announcer. Most of the creative/ performing unions, however, originated with stage and motion-picture workers. Examples include the Writers Guild of America (WGA), the American Guild of Variety Artists (AGVA), and the Screen Actors Guild (SAG).

The creative unions have played a significant though belated role in forcing recognition of technological developments. The fact that filmmaking contracts had no provisions covering television kept most feature films off the air in the 1950s. SAG struck in 1960, when Ronald Reagan was president of the union. The goal was to force higher scales for residuals, the payments made to performers and others for repeat showings of recorded programs on television.

New technology issues triggered strikes in 1980–1981. They involved several unions that fought over the income from the sale of recorded programs to the pay-television, videocassette, and videodisc markets. The same issue played a role in 1985 and 1988 Writers Guild strikes. Guild members also wanted greater creative control over their products. The 1988 strike lasted 22 weeks, causing a delay in the start of the fall television season and a further drop in network audiences.

Job Opportunities   Surveys of students enrolled in college electronic media programs indicate that most want to work in the creative/performing area, especially in on-camera or on-mike positions. The oversupply of candidates makes these the *least* accessible jobs for beginners. The delegation by broadcast stations and cable systems of creative work to outside production companies means that such work concentrates in a few major centers, where newcomers face fierce competition and where unions control entry. Job seekers would do better to look elsewhere, as suggested in Exhibit 6.10.

News, the one field in which local production still flourishes, offers an exception to the dearth of production jobs at stations and systems. Nearly all broadcast stations and some cable systems employ news specialists.

Sales offers another employment area likely to expand. All commercial networks and stations, as well as a growing number of cable systems, employ

EXHIBIT *6.10* Advice to Job Seekers

The International Radio and Television Society, The Radio-Television News Directors Association, and The National Association of Television Program Executives commissioned the Roper Organization to conduct a survey of media executives' attitudes concerning the educational preparation received by students seeking careers in broadcasting and cable. Some examples of their opinions:

- Entry-level job applicants often have unrealistic career expectations. They expect too high a starting salary, they expect to advance too quickly, and they come to the job with a misguided impression of the industry.
- Recent college graduates will find their best opportunities in *sales* (cited by 49 percent of those responding), *news* (cited by 32 percent), and *production* (28 percent).
- Nonacademic considerations receive more weight than academic and formal credentials when broadcasters evaluate a candidate for an entry-level position. They regard as most important the applicant's *general presentation, writing skills and style, experience in the industry, and hands-on experience* in actual work situations.
- Nearly three-fourths of the respondents ranked a four-year undergraduate education as either *essential* or *important*. They placed less importance, however, on a graduate degree.
- Two-thirds of the executives considered a journalism or a communication degree as an important consideration in evaluating a prospective employee; almost half felt that way about a liberal arts background.
- Broadcasters generally expect students to come to the job knowing the *basic* elements required for work in the industry—*writing skills,* the *basics of broadcasting, knowledge of equipment operation,* and *communication skills.*

Not everyone agreed with all the findings. For example, Professor Robert O. Blanchard, chairman of the Department of Communication at Trinity University, argued that:

The worlds of the media professionals and mass communication educators overlap only minimally. The obsession of professionals, by nature, is with the present or, more likely, with the immediate past . . . What they do is based on what worked, or didn't work, last season. The university tradition reflects concern with identifying, assessing and transmitting enduring skills, principles and values, and understanding what they hold for the future . . . The future for us is symbolized for our times with the advent of the 21st century, where today's students will be living and working most of their adult lives. It will be conceptual skills and principles and values, not last season's entry-level skills, that will guide them through our fast-changing and expanding information society. (Blanchard, 1988).

Source: The Roper Organization Inc., "Electronic Media Career Preparation Study," Executive Summary, Dec. 1987. Used by permission. Photo from J.G. Zimmerman/FPG.

salespeople. Advertising agencies and national sales representative firms offer entry-level employment opportunities. Nevertheless, personnel directors frequently complain that college-trained job applicants fail to comprehend the financial basis of the industry.

As technologies proliferate and competition intensifies, so does the need for creative and effective promotion. Stations, systems, and networks have to promote themselves and their products both to the public and to potential advertisers. Cable networks use promotion extensively to persuade cable systems to buy their offerings.

About two-thirds of all jobs in cable fall in the technical category, but marketing, market research, and advertising have high priority. The need for creative people will also increase as more cable systems gear up for public-access and local-origination programming.

Corporate Video   Applicants who look only to broadcasting and cable for entry-level jobs seriously limit their employment opportunities. Virtually every large organization that has contact with the public uses the electronic mass media in one form or another. Opportunities for production and writing jobs exist at manufacturing and retail firms, religious institutions, educational and health organizations, foundations, government agencies, the armed services, and specialized production companies.

Many such organizations make extensive in-house use of closed-circuit television. Chrysler has a network to distribute training videos. The Ford Motor Company produces daily newscasts, complete with field reporters, for its Ford Communications Network, beaming them by closed-circuit to 180,000 employees in 270 factories and offices in North America. The Automotive Satellite Television Network provides 40 hours of programming each month to about 3,000 car dealers. Some 60 firms operate such networks.

These and others in the rapidly growing field of corporate video apply broadcast techniques to productions dealing with job-skills training, management development, sales presentations, and public relations. Such nonbroadcast uses of television require trained personnel for production, direction, writing, studio operations, program planning, and other tasks that originated as occupational specialities of broadcasting.

6.12 *Investments and Profits/Losses*

The broadcast and cable industries, though not as capital intensive as such giants as the automobile business, nonetheless require high capital investments for constructing new facilities or acquiring and maintaining existing ones.

Investments   Radio-station construction costs range from $50,000 for a

simple, small-market AM or FM outlet to several million dollars for a sophisticated station in a major market. Full-power, major-market television facilities may cost tens of millions. Upgrading operations with new technologies such as satellite news-gathering vans and newsroom computer systems call for additional capital outlays in the hundreds of thousands.

However, broadcasting and to some extent cable have reached the point where investment in new facilities has come to a halt. Now the more likely route to ownership is through purchase of existing facilities.

Such factors as market size and location, format (in the case of radio), network affiliation (in the case of television), and competitive position in the market influence asking/offering prices for stations. As a rule of thumb, an FM or AM/FM combination should sell for about 2.5 times the station's annual cash flow (revenue minus operating expenses). For a standalone AM station, the price should be closer to 1.5 times cash flow. Formulas for estimating prices for television stations include multiplying gross revenue by 2.5, cash flow by 12, and the number of the station's viewers by $2,050.

pricing formulas for selling stations

As for satellite-to-cable networks, initial success led to an oversupply, followed by mergers and acquisitions. For example, in 1985, Viacom (a major MSO, programmer, and syndicator) acquired full ownership of Showtime/TMC and of MTV Networks (operator of three basic cable services, MTV, VH-1, and Nickelodeon). This purchase, estimated at $690 million, made Viacom the largest cable programmer and the only programmer with significant stakes in both basic and pay-cable services.

The high prices paid for stations, cable systems, and networks reflect the fact that, on the whole, the electronic mass media have been exceedingly profitable. There was a grain of truth in the cliché that a broadcasting license conferred a license to print money. By 1990, however, station prices seemed to have peaked.

"a license to print money"?

Profits and Losses   In 1985, network revenues fell slightly for the first time since 1971; yet even in that year the three networks attracted more than $8.3 billion in advertising and produced profits exceeding $1 billion. By 1987, however, total ABC/CBS/NBC net revenues had dropped to $6.8 billion. All three major networks embarked on an austerity program, cutting budgets and laying off personnel. Meanwhile, the emergent Fox network struggled to stay in the race, losing about $90 million in its 1988 fiscal year and projecting losses at about $20 million in 1989. These setbacks seemed to be part of a broad, though uneven, pattern of retrenchment.

In 1987, according to National Association of Broadcasters research, the average *independent television station* in the 10 largest markets produced a $5.5 million pretax profit, but independents as a group showed an average pretax loss of about $130,000. The average *FM radio station* showed a 1987 pretax profit of about $63,000, but the typical full-time *AM station* reported a loss of nearly $20,000.

Cable television went from an aggregate $200 million loss (1982) to an estimated $279 million profit (1987). Though newer systems with high construction costs and low subscriber penetration experience sizeable losses, at least initially, many of the established systems generate handsome profits.

By the mid-1980s the subscriber growth rates of *pay cable networks* had slowed. Some suffered a net subscriber loss, some even went under. By that time, the home videocassette recorder played an increasingly important role in competition for the video dollar. Toward the end of the decade, in fact, it was estimated that twice as many American families owned VCRs as subscribed to a pay-cable service.

Only the strongest *advertiser-supported cable-program networks* were profitable. MTV and CBN turned the corner by 1984. Superstation WTBS had been profitable for several years, but Turner's CNN and CNN Headline News remained in the red until 1986. *Pay-per-view,* despite high expectations and some single-event successes, still had a long way to go to reach maturity.

6.13 *Critique: Bottom-Line Broadcasting*

From the public-interest standpoint, stations, cable systems, and networks *need* to earn profits. When they operate at a loss, their public-service programs tend to suffer. Moreover, the lowering of standards by money-losing firms can be contagious. Their rivals tend to reciprocate by lowering their standards in order to compete in the marketplace.

effects of focus on
short-term profitability

But obsessive concern for short-term profitability has its dangers, too. Federal deregulation and permissive interpretation of antitrust laws have encouraged media acquisitions, mergers, takeovers, and consolidations. These transactions focus so single-mindedly on profit they that produce what has been referred to as the *bottom-line mentality*—executive preoccupation with profit-and-loss statements to the exclusion of all else.

Cable television, not explicitly required to operate in the public interest, has made little or no effort to modify profit-driven goals. Broadcasting, which does have a public-interest mandate, and which FCC rules formerly kept mostly in the hands of professional broadcasters, fell increasingly under the control of conglomerate officials with no broadcasting background.

Trafficking in Stations The FCC's antitrafficking rule was designed to prevent station-trading at the expense of public service. It required the holder of a broadcast-station license to keep it for a minimum of three years before requesting its transferral to a buyer. Deletion of this rule in 1982 enabled new licensees to make quick entrances and exits into and out of the broadcasting business for the sake of overnight profits.

what leveraged buyouts
are doing to industry

First-time broadcast buyers began to specialize in leveraged buyouts of television stations. These deals involve buying up stock to gain a controlling interest in target firms. To do so, they incur huge debts that have to be repaid out of profits, leaving little money for quality programming. Increasingly, stations turned to quick and easy sources of income—program-length commercials, titillating shows exploiting sex and violence, tabloid pseudo-news shows, and the like.

Network Changes   The mighty networks were not immune. In the mid-1980s, new management took over at ABC, CBS, and NBC. Cutbacks in operating budgets caused the layoff of between 2,000 and 3,000 employees and the early retirement of others. This new austerity took its heaviest public-service toll in the area of network news. News-division budgets, roughly $85 million for each network in 1980, had grown to $300 million by 1986. This $900 million three-network total loomed especially large when viewed in the light of news-division revenues of only $830 million.

At House of Representatives hearings, Congressmen Dennis Eckart of Ohio and John Bryant of Texas asserted that, "The wave of cutbacks and layoffs that is sweeping all three networks is alarming. . . . The American people deserve to know what the bottom line is where their news programming is concerned." Eckart said, "In this rush for profits, the public interest has been trampled on." Bryant added, "The root of my concern is that these corporate takeovers have made America's principal source of information the subject of giant corporate poker games" (quoted in *Broadcasting*, 1987).

impact of corporate takeovers on network news

Making an unprecedented public criticism of his own network, Dan Rather, *CBS Evening News* anchor and managing editor, wrote a piece for the *New York Times* headlined "From Murrow to Mediocrity?" Rather pointed out that Chairperson Tisch "told us when he arrived that he wanted us to be the best. We want nothing more than to fulfill that mandate. Ironically, he has now made the task seem something between difficult and impossible." He added,

> news is a business, but it is also a public trust. . . . We have been asked to cut costs and work more efficiently and we have accepted that challenge. What we cannot accept is the notion that the bottom line counts more than meeting our responsibilities to the public. Anyone who says network news cannot be profitable doesn't know what he is talking about. But anyone who says it must always make money is misguided and irresponsible. (Rather, 1987)

Noncommercial Operations

7 Most of this book deals with commercial radio and television, which form the backbone of broadcasting in America. But in the United States, as in most countries, commercial broadcasting's overwhelming emphasis on light, mass-appeal entertainment fails to meet the full potential of the medium. The profit motive alone cannot be counted on to fulfill all the national cultural, educational, and informational needs that broadcast media could ideally serve. Hence arose the concept of **noncommercial broadcasting**—motivated by public-service goals rather than by profit.

7.1 From "Educational Radio" to "Public Broadcasting"

What is known today as *public broadcasting* started as a more narrowly defined service devoted explicitly to education. When license applications boomed in the 1920s, educational institutions joined in the rush. Most of these pioneer not-for-profit stations operated on a shoestring for only a few hours a week.

no AM channels reserved for education

AM Radio   With broadcasting's growing financial success in the late 1920s, commercial interests began to covet the AM channels tied up by educational licenses. Some schools surrendered their licenses in return for promises of airtime for educational programs on commercial stations—promises that faded with the rising value of commercial time.

Educational stations that held on found themselves confined to low power, inconvenient hours (often daytime only, of limited value for adult education), and constantly changing frequency assignments. In 1927, 98 noncommercial AM stations were in operation, but by 1945 they had dwindled to about 25.

Reserved Channels   The decline in educational AM stations confirmed what some had said from the first: educational interests should not be expected to compete with commercial interests for broadcast channels, and the government should have set aside a certain number of AM channels exclusively for educational use.

When the Federal Communications Commission came into being in 1934, it reviewed the proposal to reserve AM channels. But the commission accepted the commercial owners' assurance that they would give ample free time for education. As the stations that gave up their licenses for promises of time had already discovered, such promises never seemed to work out in practice.

The FCC finally endorsed the **reserved-channels principle** when it had an opportunity to allocate a brand-new group of channels in 1941—those for FM radio. In its final FM-allotment plan in 1945, the commission reserved the lower portion of the FM band exclusively for educational use. It consists of the 20 channels (of the 100 total) running from 88 to 92 MHz.

FM channels reserved as a group

The first noncommercial educational FM stations depended almost totally on local programs. They had neither a well-developed system of program exchange nor a network to help fill out station schedules. Their experience, of course, repeated that of commercial stations in the early 1920s—local resources alone simply could not provide adequate programming. Networking was as essential for noncommercial as for commercial broadcasting.

The appearance of television on the scene in the late 1940s stimulated a new campaign for reserved channels. It was considerably more intense than the previous radio campaigns, because television attracted more attention. Educators and foundations foresaw far greater possibilities for educational television than they had for educational radio.

During the FCC's 1948–1952 freeze on new television-station applications, commercial interests made a concerted effort to block the educators' campaign. But a wide spectrum of educational and cultural groups—the Joint Committee on Educational Television (JCET)—combined into a counter-lobby. As part of its pro-reservations exhibits JCET prepared a content analysis of existing television programming (less than a hundred commercial television stations were on the air at the time). Analysis showed conclusively that commercial stations and networks did little to put television at the disposal of education and culture. JCET sounded a warning: if the forthcoming channel allotments failed to reserve channels for educational use, a once-in-a-lifetime opportunity would be lost.

The FCC took notice. Its *Sixth Report and Order,* which ended the freeze in 1952, provided for 242 reserved educational-television (ETV) channel allotments, 80 VHF and 162 UHF. Many more were added in later years, making possible the present level of 349 public-television stations on the air.

TV channels are reserved city by city

ETV Constituency   Educational-radio leaders had kept the faith over many lean years, largely ignored in the seats of power. During the fight to achieve ETV channel reservations, however, the noncommercial-broadcasting constituency grew larger and more diversified. The glamour of the new medium attracted national educational, cultural, and consumer groups that previously had taken little notice of educational-radio broadcasters.

The miscellaneous grouping of enthusiasts developed conflicting views about the form educational television should take. One group took the words "educational television" to mean a broadly inclusive cultural and information service. Another took them to mean a new and improved audiovisual device, primarily important to schools and formal adult education. Some, following the model of commercial broadcasting, favored a strong national network and a concern for audience building. Others, expressly rejecting the commercial model, focused on localism and service for more limited, specialized audiences. Some wanted to stress high culture and intellectual stimulation. Others wanted to emphasize programs of interest to ethnic minorities, children, and the poor.

varied views on role of educational TV

A New Beginning   For its first dozen years, ETV developed slowly, long on promise but short on performance. Exhibit 7.1 shows the growth rate. The few stations on the air depended on underfunded local productions and filmed programs of limited quality and interest. Their broadcast day lasted about half the length of commercial-station schedules.

By 1959, the stations had formed a program cooperative, National Educational Television (NET). It provided a few hours a week of shared programs, delivered to the cooperating stations by mail. Though a step in the right

NET: forerunner of PBS

7.1 / From "Educational Radio" to "Public Broadcasting"   **195**

EXHIBIT *7.1*   Growth of Public Stations, 1925–1990

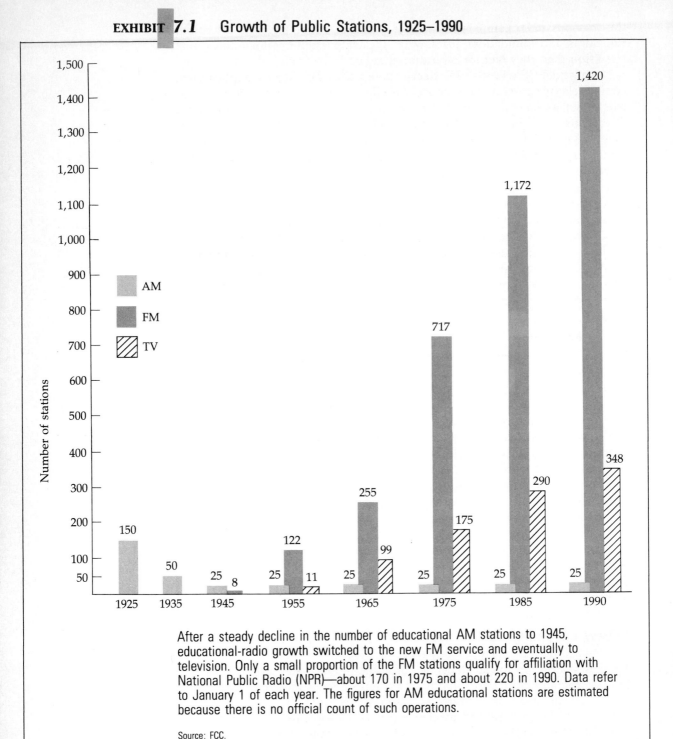

After a steady decline in the number of educational AM stations to 1945, educational-radio growth switched to the new FM service and eventually to television. Only a small proportion of the FM stations qualify for affiliation with National Public Radio (NPR)—about 170 in 1975 and about 220 in 1990. Data refer to January 1 of each year. The figures for AM educational stations are estimated because there is no official count of such operations.

Source: FCC.

direction, NET still fell far short of meeting the enormous program needs of the noncommercial service.

During the mid-1960s, a nonprofit foundation stepped into this bleak picture, hoping to transform it with a dynamic vision. The Carnegie Foundation felt ETV needed well-articulated national goals, topnotch public relations, and leadership at the federal level.

To generate highly visible recommendations for achieving these goals, the foundation set up the Carnegie Commission on Educational Television (CCET). The commission was made up of nationally known figures from higher education, media, business, politics, and the arts. In its watershed 1967 report, *Public Television: A Program for Action,* The Carnegie Commission proposed that Congress establish a national "corporation for public television."

Carnegie Commission proposes public TV in 1967

The CCET deliberately used the word *public* rather than *educational* to disassociate its proposals from what many had come to regard as the "somber and static image" projected by the existing ETV services. It also chose the word *public* to emphasize its recommendation for an inclusive service embracing not only formal instruction and classroom television but also a broad cultural/informational service intended for the general public.

reason for term "public" broadcasting

Six months after the 1967 Carnegie Commission report came out, its basic recommendations were enacted into law as part of President Lyndon Johnson's Great Society legislative program. It has survived to this day.

National Organizations   7.2

The migration of ETV into the national political arena and its transformation into public television succeeded in bringing it to public attention. In solving some problems, however, the Carnegie Commission created others. The public-television stations were often highly individualistic. They made uneasy, sometimes even acrimonious, partners with their federal allies in Washington.

Corporation for Public Broadcasting   Congress set the Carnegie Commission's keystone recommendation in place with the Public Broadcasting Act of 1967 ("broadcasting" because Congress added radio at the last moment). The new law became part of the Communications Act. It created the Corporation for Public Broadcasting (CPB), a quasi-government organization whose key role is to funnel money into projects supportive of the nation's public broadcasters.

The Carnegie Commission had recommended that the president of the United States appoint only half of the CPB board. Congress, however, gave all the appointive power to the president. Congress also declined to legislate the long-term federal funding that the Carnegie Commission had recommended. These two departures from the plan left CPB at the mercy of presidential politics. Unfortunate consequences followed, as detailed in Exhibit 7.2.

Congress leaves CPB subject to politics

EXHIBIT 7.2 Politics and the CPB

Incidents during two conservative presidential administrations illustrate the difficulty of insulating a broadcast service from politics when it depends on government for substantial economic support. Section 398 of the Communications Act, added by the 1967 public broadcasting law, tries to prevent political influence by expressly forbidding any "direction, supervision, or control" over noncommercial broadcasting by officials of the U.S. government. This legal detail did not stop the Nixon administration in the 1970s nor the Reagan administration a decade later from manipulating CPB for its own ends.

When the Public Broadcasting Service (PBS) network began beefing up its news and public-affairs programing around 1970 by hiring former commercial-network personnel, the White House took umbrage. Regarding the PBS network as far too

liberal, the administration objected to public television's concern with national affairs when, according to the administration's interpretation, it should be focusing on *local* matters. This view struck a chord with some of the station managers, who were already resentful of the increasing centralization of program decision making by PBS and CPB. In 1973, the administration sent a more direct message when President Nixon vetoed a two-year funding measure for CPB. Several board members—ironically, all presidential appointees—resigned in protest. Long-range federal funding legislation did not finally pass until 1975.

By 1981, when the Reagan administration took office, the CPB board, never high on the priority list of political appointees, had become fertile ground for political games. Reagan appointed several hard-right conservatives to the CPB board. In 1986, during a dispute with Reagan-appointed CPB chair Sonia Landau over a proposed trip to the Soviet Union to trade programs, CPB president Edward Pfister resigned. Less than a year later, Pfister's replacement also left CPB, which had developed a reputation for constant political infighting. Another Reagan CPB appointee advocated making a content analysis to determine whether public-television programming leaned too far to the left. Opponents of the study felt that its sponsors merely wanted to send a signal to public broadcasters and they should adopt a more conservative agenda. The study never materialized, but the legally mandated political impartiality of CPB had been seriously undermined.

Source: Photo from Joan Shaffer/Courtesy CPB.

The Public Broadcasting Act gives CPB such tasks as

- Making grants and contracts for obtaining and producing high-quality programs from diverse sources
- Helping to set up network interconnection.
- Encouraging development of new public-broadcasting stations.
- Conducting research and training.

CPB itself may not own or operate stations. Congress emphasized that the stations should retain local autonomy, remaining free to select and schedule programs according to local needs. The last thing Congress wanted was to create a centralized, federal broadcaster.

The act directs CPB to do its job "in ways that will most effectively assure the maximum freedom . . . from interference with or control of program content or other activities." Nevertheless, some stations regarded the very existence of a federal agency dispensing federal funds as a threat. The issue of local versus federal control has continually stirred up controversy between CPB and the stations.

key issue: local vs. federal control

Public Broadcasting Service
CPB launched the network in 1969–1970, calling it the Public Broadcasting Service (PBS). PBS is deliberately fashioned to differ considerably from the commercial-network model. PBS operates the interconnection facilities, but the all-important task of program selection remains a station prerogative.

A weak national network had in fact been a Carnegie report recommendation. Though the report stressed the vital importance of network interconnection, it also warned against tight centralization of program control. Public broadcasting was expected to have "a strong component of local and regional programming." It would "provide the opportunity and the means for local choice to be exercised upon the programs made available from central programming sources" (CCET, 1967: 33).

As time proved, it was unrealistic to downgrade the national network's programming role, even though doing so was desirable to avoid the over-centralization typical of commercial networks. The Carnegie Commission failed to anticipate the practical problems of asking the national public-broadcasting network to lay out a smorgasbord of programs from which affiliates would pick and choose at will (public broadcasters tend to avoid the term *affiliate* because of its commercial connotations, but it is used here for convenience).

The commercial experience had shown that a network needs the strong identity that can come only from a uniform national program schedule—identical key network programs available to everybody in the nation at the same time of day. But station licensees—zealous to protect their local identity, operating under varied ownership and funding patterns, and profoundly suspicious of political interference from Washington—resisted that type of network. They sided with "their" organization, PBS, against CPB in the battles over program philosophy that followed.

PBS barred from strong central control

The present PBS operational role was delineated by Lawrence Grossman, PBS president from 1976 to 1984. Grossman came from, and later returned to, commercial broadcasting. Previous PBS heads had come from public-service and public-broadcasting backgrounds. Grossman reshaped PBS closer to the commercial model. He put primary emphasis on programming. PBS offices blossomed with wall-size displays contrasting PBS offerings with the commercial networks' schedules, suggesting that at last PBS leadership had begun to think competitively. Grossman pushed the use of original American productions, relying less heavily on British material than had his predecessors.

In the late 1980s, PBS programs went to 327 affiliates—virtually all the noncommercial public-television stations on the air. The 35-member PBS board included representatives from station boards and professional station managers. The staff totaled about 300, divided among offices in the Washington area, New York, and Los Angeles.

By 1989, PBS had begun to heighten the impact of its prime-time schedule by ensuring that at least one public-TV station in each market carried the national programs from 8 to 10 P.M. Sunday through Friday. The 10 to 11 P.M prime-time hour Sunday through Friday and all Saturday evening hours remained under local control. Thus a degree of network centralization was achieved without depriving the stations of ample local decision-making opportunities.

PBS Program Selection

how PBS differs from commercial networks

Commercial television networks pay compensation for their affiliates' time. PBS affiliates, however, pay their networks varying levels of dues. An affiliate's dues depend on its budget and market size. PBS produces no programs of its own. It provides a distribution service for programs produced by others, selected mainly by the member stations.

how station program cooperative works

Program selection takes place through a democratic funding mechanism— the Station Program Cooperative (SPC). PBS offers a list of proposed programs for the coming season, categorized as follows:

- Programs fully underwritten by business corporations or foundations.
- Programs only partially funded by those sources.
- Programs that are proposed for production but that so far lack financial support of any kind.

PBS carries programs from the second and third categories only if a sufficient number of stations votes for (and agrees to share in the cost of) those programs.

The stations make their choices in a series of voting rounds, rather like an auction. Stations base their commitments first on what they can afford. Next they judge which programs are likely to appeal to local viewers and to local underwriters (mostly corporate sponsors). As an example, the 1987 SPC realized station funding for some 900 program hours at a total cost of nearly $50 million.

PBS Satellite Interconnection

On the engineering side, public television has been notable for leading the commercial sector in the development and adoption of technical innovations. Especially noteworthy was its early adoption of satellite relays for distributing network programs.

satellite relays help preserve local autonomy

Benefits derived from satellite interconnection include better-quality reception; the ability to relay signals both eastward and westward as well as variously within given regions; transmission of several signals at a time to allow stations simultaneous choice among several programs; and cost savings. In fact, the satellite actually earned some money through the sale of excess capacity to other users. During 1978, public-television stations disconnected themselves one by one from the terrestrial network and began using network satellite interconnection—the first national television network to do so.

Twenty-one ground stations uplink programs to the satellite. The uplink facility near Washington, DC, provides the main PBS feed. Secondary uplinks serve regional networks from centers in Colorado, Nebraska, Florida, South Carolina, and Connecticut.

In 1988, PBS invited bids for a replacement satellite costing an estimated $240 million. The new satellite, expected to be in orbit by 1992, will include Ku-band transponders. Although these transponders cost more initially, the higher-frequency Ku-band signals will be receivable on smaller receiving antennas. They will also be adaptable for possible future high-definition applications. Late in 1988, Congress authorized $200 million toward the replacement satellite. The stations will be responsible for raising the rest of the capital.

second-generation PBS satellite

National Public Radio

In 1970, CPB set up the radio equivalent of the PBS network—National Public Radio (NPR). The public-radio stations had no qualms about a network that provides both interconnection and programs. As a second Carnegie Commission report said of NPR in 1979:

> Unlike the situation in public television, the public radio stations have been quite willing to have national program production and distribution centralized and under the financial oversight of CPB. Public radio stations supported the creation of NPR from the beginning, and they retain control over it through its board. Sorely underfinanced, the stations have recognized the benefits of centralizing program functions. (CCFPB, 1979: 61)

public radio more amenable than TV to strong network

CPB sets standards for NPR members chosen from the pool of 1,425 (the 1990 number) potential radio affiliates. The criteria for acceptance as a CPB-qualified radio station include the following minimum requirements:

qualifications for NPR affiliation

- FM power of at least 3,000 watts.
- At least one production studio with a separate control room.
- At least five full-time employees.
- An 18-hour daily operating schedule.
- An annual budget of at least $150,000.

NPR furnishes affiliates about 22 percent of their program schedule. In addition to producing and obtaining programs, NPR operates the satellite interconnection, piggybacking on the PBS network circuits. NPR has 21 circuits and more than 300 uplinks. It feeds 12 program channels, giving affiliates ample opportunity to match programs to local needs.

Risky financial management caused a money crisis at NPR headquarters in the mid-1980s. Strained relations with its affiliates followed. Things took a turn for the better when CPB began sending its radio-program funds directly to the stations instead of through NPR. The stations in turn support NPR by subscribing to (paying for) the programs they use. Station payments range from $25,000 to over $300,000 annually. This arrangement means that if

NPR program funding

NPR programs fail to please affiliates, NPR makes no money—a healthy impetus toward financial responsibility.

American Public Radio   A second public radio network, American Public Radio (APR), began in 1981. It was formed by Minnesota Public Radio chiefly as a showcase for Garrison Keillor's popular *A Prairie Home Companion.* Its schedule also includes original musical performances and *MonitoRadio,* a half-hour weeknight news and feature program produced by the *Christian Science Monitor* newspaper.

By 1985, APR claimed to be the largest public-radio network. It provides more than 200 hours of material each week to 327 affiliates. Unlike NPR, APR affiliates with only one station in a market. It does not produce programs as NPR does but acquires them, mostly from its member stations.

7.3   *Public Stations*

Both public-radio and public-television stations vary enormously in size, resources, goals, and philosophy. Though all are licensed by the FCC as "noncommercial educational" stations, some flirt with commercialism and many play no discernible formal educational role.

Television   In general, four classes of owners hold the licenses to public-television stations. The four groups differ and even conflict in their concepts of noncommercial broadcasting.

States and municipalities hold about 38 percent of the licenses, which totaled 349 in 1990. Many belong to state educational networks, usually programmed by the station located at the state capital or other key origination point. The southern states in particular chose this means of capitalizing on educational television. Alabama, for example, began building a state network in 1955 that now has nine stations.

differing public-TV
ownership patterns

Institutions of higher learning own 25 percent of the stations. They often complement educational-radio stations of long standing and are closely tied to college curricula. For example, the University of Wisconsin's WHA, one of the AM survivors from the early 1920s, was joined in 1954 by WHA–TV.

Public-school boards hold licenses for 4 percent. Their stations naturally focus on in-school instructional programs, many produced by and for the local school system. The low numbers of such stations reflect the failure of public television to live up to its early promise as a major adjunct of formal education. In fact, as school budgets became tighter, several school stations have left the air or been transferred to other licensees.

Community foundations control a third of the outlets. The licensees are nonprofit foundations set up especially to operate noncommercial stations. They recruit support from all sectors—schools, colleges, art and cultural organizations, foundations, businesses, and the general public. Usually free of obligations to local tax sources, they tend to be politically more independent than stations that depend for revenue on local or state tax dollars.

The four ownership structures, with their differing funding mechanisms and program goals, differ correspondingly in their approach to educational/public television.

Radio   In general, the four-way television-ownership pattern just described also applies to noncommercial-radio licensees. However, radio stations are so much cheaper to build and operate than television stations that room is left for more varied types of ownership. Radio stations licensed to educational institutions are often run by students for students with minimum interference from the institutional authorities.

The latter are often Class D stations—a 10-watt class authorized by the FCC to encourage the takeup of reserved FM channels (the minimum power in other classes is 100 watts). By the 1970s, several hundred low-power FM noncommercial stations had gone on the air.

class D radio stations

In time the existence of these minimal-power stations impeded the growth of a strong NPR network. Frequencies that could be better used were occupied by "electronic sandboxes," as one critic put it—mere playthings instead of genuine program providers. Faced with growing demand for public-radio licenses, in 1978 the FCC ordered 10-watt stations either to raise their power to a minimum of 100 watts or to accept a secondary status on commercial FM channels.

Funding Public Broadcasting   **7.4**

Most countries have some form of public broadcasting—a radio/television service funded either not at all or only partly by advertising revenue. In all such cases, the national government ensures a large part of the funding. Sometimes the money comes directly from tax revenues, but in Western democracies it comes more often from license fees on receiving sets. Though relatively exempt from appropriation uncertainties, license-fee income still depends on government enforcement of the licensing law.

A way of dramatizing the financial plight of public broadcasting in the United States is to consider that its revenue from all sources in a sample year amounted to $4.70 for every person in the country. In that same year commercial television alone grossed over $92 per person. Exhibit 7.3 looks at the question comparatively, suggesting how little federal government support goes to public broadcasting through CPB in contrast with central-government support in three other democratic systems that also have both commercial and noncommercial services.

EXHIBIT **7.3** Public-Broadcasting Funding Levels: A Four-Nation Comparison

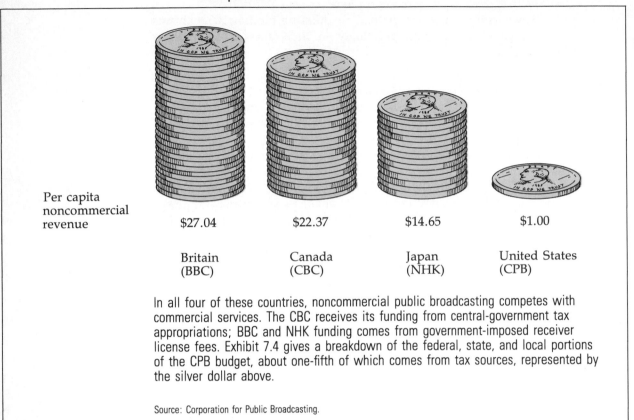

Per capita
noncommercial
revenue

$27.04	$22.37	$14.65	$1.00
Britain (BBC)	Canada (CBC)	Japan (NHK)	United States (CPB)

In all four of these countries, noncommercial public broadcasting competes with commercial services. The CBC receives its funding from central-government tax appropriations; BBC and NHK funding comes from government-imposed receiver license fees. Exhibit 7.4 gives a breakdown of the federal, state, and local portions of the CPB budget, about one-fifth of which comes from tax sources, represented by the silver dollar above.

Source: Corporation for Public Broadcasting.

Nonprofit Foundations   Public broadcasting derives its funds from a wide variety of sources, as indicated in Exhibit 7.4. Each source brings different obligations with its funding, and each has its own biases.

foundation support for early public TV

For example, during ETV's formative years, its chief support came from an arm of the Ford Foundation, the Fund for Adult Education (FAE). As the name suggests, the FAE had an explicit educational agenda. Its areas of specific concern were American history, social anthropology, international under-standing, and community self-development. Naturally those became ETV's topics of concern as well. The economic power of the fund virtually dictated the nature of the program service.

The FAE's parent organization, the Ford Foundation, played crucial roles in securing reserved TV channels by helping JCET prepare for FCC hear-ings. It supplied early stations with substantial equipment grants and provided a small core of nationally distributed programs to strengthen initial schedules. And it aided research on television education. Without the backing of the

EXHIBIT **7.4** Public Broadcasting Revenue by Source

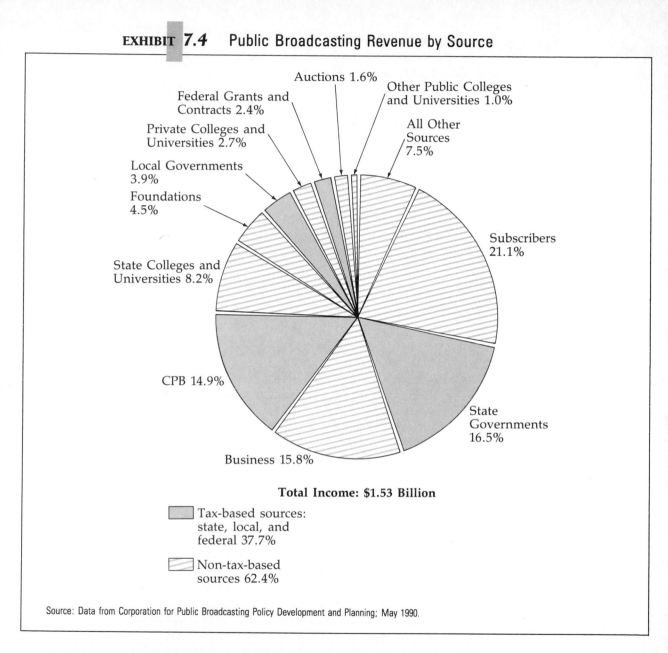

Auctions 1.6%

Other Public Colleges
and Universities 1.0%

Federal Grants and
Contracts 2.4%

All Other
Sources
7.5%

Private Colleges and
Universities 2.7%

Local Governments
3.9%

Foundations
4.5%

Subscribers
21.1%

State Colleges and
Universities 8.2%

CPB 14.9%

State
Governments
16.5%

Business 15.8%

Total Income: $1.53 Billion

Tax-based sources:
state, local, and
federal 37.7%

Non-tax-based
sources 62.4%

Source: Data from Corporation for Public Broadcasting Policy Development and Planning; May 1990.

Ford Foundation, educational television might not have survived its first decade. Other foundations and support groups also came to the aid of ETV in the 1950s, but the Ford support was crucial.

Even after 1963, when federal grants to buy equipment began, Ford continued to strengthen the national program-distribution effort and supported stations with direct grants. However, the foundation had planned to furnish only start-up grants to help a station or a service run for a few years in the hope that permanent means of support would evolve. By 1983, when its direct role had been largely phased out, Ford grants to noncommercial broadcasting had totaled more than $300 million.

Annenberg/CPB project

In 1981, the largest *single* gift ever made to public broadcasting came from Walter Annenberg, then publisher of *TV Guide*. He gave $150 million, spread over 15 years, to fund a CPB project to create innovative college-level courses and programs. The Annenberg/CPB project annually funded projects selected from proposals by dozens of applications. Some are aired on public-television stations. Because of income-tax problems the project had to be terminated after ten years, but in that time it supported many significant program initiatives.

Government Grants

Government Grants   From the beginning of educational FM broadcasting in the 1940s, local and state governments supported it at the station and state-network levels. By the mid-1960s, such tax funds amounted to about half of all public-broadcasting income. However, faced by ever-increasing budget problems, state support declined to about 30 percent of total system revenue by the mid-1980s. Local government support (mainly through school boards) fell to under 5 percent.

extent of state/local government support

At the outset, the federal government gave no financial assistance at all. Federal legislative recognition first came with the Educational Television Facilities Act of 1962. It granted up to a million dollars of federal money to stations in each state, subject to their matching federal dollars with money from other sources—one federal dollar for each dollar raised locally. This act, extended and revised, continued to assist equipment and facilities purchasing for public broadcasting into the 1980s, despite Republican administration attempts to close the program down.

federal support requires matching funds

Commercial Noncommercial Broadcasting

Commercial Noncommercial Broadcasting   The temptation for noncommercial broadcasters to contradict their premise by tapping advertising revenue has been ever present. Even when the JCET was pleading with the FCC to reserve noncommercial educational-television channels, some educational broadcasters lobbied unsuccessfully for educational stations operating on a *nonprofit* commercial basis.

A successful stratagem for drawing on advertising revenue without using actual commercials takes the form of **corporate underwriting.** Instead of buying commercial time, underwriters of public-broadcasting series pay the production costs of specific program series of their choice. In return, they get brief on-the-air acknowledgments of their support, including display of their trademarks. For example, petroleum giant Mobil Corporation has derived valuable name recognition and image building from underwriting the prestigious PBS series *Masterpiece Theatre*. Sometimes several firms share the underwriting costs of a series. Affiliates also seek local underwriters to defray the subscription costs for PBS series. The FCC imposes limits on the length and content of underwriting announcements.

In 1986, corporate underwriting paid 37 percent of PBS's annual budget for original programs. Some critics question such heavy reliance on commercial funding sources. Naturally, commercial underwriters are more likely to support *Masterpiece Theatre* than hard-hitting, controversial documentaries about industrial pollution. A case in point may be the problem Boston's public television station, WGBH, faced in obtaining underwriting for the series *Vietnam: A Television History*. The controversial series triggered hostile commentary from conservatives, though it won several awards and the highest rating among documentaries in 1983. It took WGBH over six years to find underwriters for the $5.6 million it needed to produce the series.

role of corporations in underwriting original productions

Experiments with Direct Advertising   Pushing further into commercial noncommercialism, Congress established the Temporary Commission on Alternative Financing for Public Telecommunications (TCAF) in 1981. Its mission was to supervise an experiment with commercials on noncommercial stations. Commission members included U.S. senators, members of Congress, and public-broadcasting representatives. It was chaired by an FCC commissioner.

In January 1982, 10 public-television stations volunteered to take part in a 15-month trial of direct on-air advertising. Public-radio stations decided not to participate. The legislation authorizing the test forbade interrupting programs with commercials, limited them to two minutes in length, and ruled out advertising political, religious, or other ideological points of view. WTTW–TV in Chicago earned the most advertising income of the 10 participating stations—more than $1 million in 1982–1983, or nearly 10 percent of its revenue that year.

direct advertising experiment

Following the test, the TCAF reported favorably on advertising support but conceded that most public-television stations would *not* carry advertisements, even if permitted to do so. The TCAF cited local/state legal restrictions, reluctance to compete with local advertising media, and concerns about long-term adverse effects on the character of public broadcasting. The commission added that, although the experiment alleviated immediate concerns about the impact of advertising, no experiment could ensure that advertising would not eventually alienate subscriber, underwriter, and government support (TCAF, 1983).

In 1984, the Senate Communications Subcommittee held hearings on resumption of the experiment. Several station executives argued for the proposal, but CPB witnesses opposed it, as did the National Association of Broadcasters. Eventually Congress shelved the idea, at least for the time being.

Also in 1984, the FCC, perhaps influenced by the TCAF recommendations, authorized **enhanced underwriting.** It allows stations to sell 30-second announcements mentioning specific consumer products but without the direct sales pitch of regular commercials. The four-station New Jersey public television network, for example, permitted advertisers to talk about products, services, and business locations but drew the line at statements about product

variations on underwriting

superiority. Enhanced underwriting increased New Jersey Network's income from corporations threefold in three years—to $900,000 in 1985. New York City's WNET–TV began selling 30-second **general support announcements** for between $1,000 and $1,500 each. They could include the company logo, location, brand and trade names, and a description of a product or service. Fudging on the enhanced-underwriting guidelines led the FCC to warn that it would enforce the limitations spelled out in its rules.

Critics deplore creeping commercialization in public television. After all, public broadcasting's primary justification is that it furnishes *alternatives*— programs not likely to appeal to advertisers but nevertheless useful and desirable. To the extent that pleasing advertisers motivates *both* services, the argument for public broadcasting is weakened.

Local Contributions   About a quarter of public-broadcasting revenue comes directly from local sources. Federal appropriations (and often national foundation grants) trickle down only when stations match federal grants. The desperate scramble to match proffered federal money forces local fund raisers to push membership/subscription drives to the saturation point. Polls indicate that many viewers detest marathon fund-raising drives (derisively called *begathons*). On-air auctions of donated goods and services (much of them from commercial sources) promote the givers so blatantly as to amount to program-length commercials.

Other devices considered (and in some cases actually used) to raise funds locally, and to some extent nationally, include

- Selling commercial rights to market merchandise associated with programs. The Children's Television Workshop defrays a large part of *Sesame Street*'s production costs from such sources.
- Offering closed-circuit seminar services to businesses on a profit-making basis. PBS gets a royalty on "companion" books that sometimes parallel its program series. Its 1990 five-part Civil War series is an example.
- Selling newly produced programs to commercial television or pay cable for initial showing before release to public television.
- Renting station facilities (usually studios) to commercial producers.
- Selling videotapes and other items to viewers.
- Trading a reserved educational channel for a less desirable commercial channel for a price. Such channel reclassification requires FCC approval. The history of channel-reservation struggles makes it ironic that noncommercial broadcasters would even consider turning back hard-won reservations to the commercial sector. The FCC has withheld approval of such trades in many cases.
- Acquiring assured tax-based revenue by charging commercial broadcasters a tax on profits, a receiver licensing fee, or a spectrum-use fee.
- Selling access to FM subcarrier or TV vertical blanking interval for commercial use.

In sum, public-broadcasting executives have to serve too many masters and spend an inordinate amount of time on fund raising. The year-to-year uncertainties of congressional appropriations, corporate underwriting, and local membership drives make it impossible for public broadcasters to plan rationally for long-term development.

Public Broadcasting Program Sources 7.5

This section deals with the sources, rather than the nature, of public-broadcasting programs. Programs as such are discussed in Chapter 9. Ideally, sources of public-broadcasting programs would differ from those of commercial broadcasts. But all broadcasting suffers from the inordinate demands that competitive schedules make on talent and budgets. PBS often schedules feature films and syndicated series obtained from the same distributors that commercial stations use. However, PBS and its stations produce more experimental programs, more documentaries, more literary/artistic/cultural material, more local shows, and certainly more instructional and explicitly educational telecasts than does any commercial network and its affiliates.

Stations as Producers   Several production-oriented stations act as creators of network series for PBS. Among the contributing producer-stations, WGBH–Boston, WNET–New York, and KQED–San Francisco stand out. Each has a long history of creative innovation in public television. WGBH introduced Julia Child's *The French Chef,* for example, one of the first nationally recognized public-television series. Washington, DC, station WETA supplies timely news and public-affairs programs, receiving direct support from CPB, among others. In 1986, nearly 38 percent of all public-television programs came from such major producer-stations, often in the form of cooperative productions with foreign partners.

producer-stations as major program source

Independent Producers   PBS buys about a tenth of its programs from independent producers. Some have complained that the public network should buy more. They argue that a service dedicated to enhancing program diversity should be especially supportive of innovative producers. Congress agreed. When it extended the CPB appropriation in 1988, it required CPB to fund a new Independent Production Service specifically to ensure more commissions for independent producers.

Congress mandates more independent production

One independent producer has done very well indeed—the nonprofit Children's Television Workshop (CTW). It won international fame for *Sesame Street* and subsequent children's series. The *Sesame Street* series began in 1969 with initial funding from government and foundation grants. By the late 1980s, ancillary commercial ventures, such as merchandising items using the program name and characters, defrayed two-thirds of its budget. CTW even produced a pay-cable series to generate revenue.

The CTW productions, though educational, come in the guise of home entertainment. Public stations also have a mission to provide more formal classroom instruction for schools. Many stations produce in-school programs locally. They also draw on several centralized libraries of instructional materials. Notable examples include the Agency for Instructional Television in Bloomington, Indiana, and the Great Plains National Instructional Television Library of Lincoln, Nebraska. They produce, archive, and distribute series of instructional programs for all levels of education.

Foreign Imports   Public television draws heavily on foreign, especially British, sources. One of PBS's most successful long-running series, *Masterpiece Theatre,* is produced by British independent (commercial) television. The coproducer, Boston's WGBH, selects the material and produces the opening and closing "book-end" remarks by Alistair Cooke.

Radio Program Sources   The typical public-radio station affiliated with NPR or APR takes about two-fifths of its weekly airtime from those networks and from syndicated sources. Station-produced local programs consist mostly of recorded music. Public stations tend to specialize in the commercially less salable music genres such as jazz and traditional folk music.

7.6 *Critique: Rethinking Public Broadcasting*

By the 1990s, public broadcasting had to face a fundamental question: does it still have a definable, defensible mission in the new electronic media landscape?

Program Diversification Role   Supporters of public broadcasting have traditionally claimed as one of its major benefits the scheduling of enriching program types not usually available on commercial stations—the fine arts, music, dance, foreign-language films, serious drama, and in-depth public-affairs discussions. Proponents also argue that public broadcasting can better meet the needs of ethnic minorities and children than can commercial broadcasting.

localism as distinctive
public-broadcasting role

Many also see public stations as the last bastion of localism. Public broadcasters interact with their communities, scheduling many hours of school-board and municipal council meetings, interviews with local personalities, coverage of the local/state political scene, and showcasing local talent. And of course defenders also see the noncommercial service as a necessary relief from the ever-increasing intrusion of advertising matter into commercial-network, station, and cable-system programs.

In rebuttal, critics point to the fact that specialized cable networks, VCR tapes, and other new program sources have co-opted public broadcasting's primary claim to uniqueness. Entire cable channels are dedicated to children,

ethnic programs, natural science, news and commentary, and other specialized program areas.

Some critics even challenge use of the term "public" television. They claim role of the public
the public actually has no more control over noncommercial than over
commercial broadcasting. In both cases, professional managers make the
decisions.

Audience Size and Composition   Critics also fault public television for
its failure to attract large audiences. They say that public television's vaunted
fine arts and high culture merely serve privileged groups that could easily
afford such material without resorting to publicly supported broadcast channels. They liken tax support of public broadcasting, limited though it is, to
the government subsidies that once sustained the luxury passenger liners that
only the rich could afford to patronize.

Critics hark back to the explicitly educational origins of public broadcasting. They point to *Sesame Street* as an example of what public broadcasting
can and *ought* to be doing—teaching primarily, entertaining incidentally.

Deregulatory Viewpoint   Much of this critique arises from the philosophy
of deregulation. Deregulation-minded critics dismiss the funding issue as little
more than a red herring. They blame public broadcasting's problem on its
lack of audience appeal rather than its lack of money. They see the funding
crisis as a *result* of the system's limitations rather than a cause of its problems.
Given the increasing number of viewing and listening options available to
most people, critics argue, **narrowcasting** (programs deliberately aimed at
a limited audience segment rather than at the mass audience) has to find
support from its own audiences in some form of direct subscription.

Similar attacks on public broadcasting have surfaced in other countries,
stimulated by a market-oriented, laissez-faire approach to media regulation.
Even so widely esteemed a service as that of the BBC has come under attack.
The conservative party in power condemns it as elitist and lacking in fiscal
responsibility. Some conservatives want to deprive the BBC of its assured
receiver license-fee income and let it sink or swim as a subscription service.

In Europe, as in the United States, these attacks raise an enduring basic
issue. Should all broadcasting be regarded as a purely economic undertaking, broadcasting: primarily business or culture?
a business like any other, trading in programs instead of soap, shoes, or soft
drinks? Or should it be regarded as a significant part of a nation's culture?
Must everything depend on that shibboleth of free marketers, consumer choice?
Not every consumer chooses to attend the great museums, galleries, and
libraries that public funds support in locations not so distant from ghettos,
yet few would advocate dismantling all such cultural treasures and diverting
their government grants to public housing.

As the 1990s began, leaders of the national public-service broadcasting
organizations prepared for profound reassessment. CPB had a five-year plan
in the making, constantly under revision. NPR undertook an in-depth review

of its role and its options. PBS tightened control over the public network's prime-time program scheduling, seemingly modeling itself more closely on the national commercial networks than before. As competition for audiences and funds increases, commercial broadcasting becomes ever more inclined to cater to the lowest common denominator of mass taste. This tendency would seem to make public broadcasting's counterbalancing influence all the more important. Yet the same competitive pressures also affect public broadcasting, tending to edge it closer to commercialism.

Programs and Programming Basics

Ask anyone for a personal opinion about programs, and, quite properly, every listener/viewer proves to be an expert on the subject. This chapter, however, deals not with personal preferences but with anticipating group preferences. Professional program specialists try to reach groups—large or small, depending on how they define their target audiences. They use the art of **programming**—creating a structured *service* by choosing and scheduling program items in sequence to attract the audience targeted by their particular network, station, or channel.

Programs can be produced locally for single-market consumption, or they can be produced centrally for multimarket national and even international consumption. This chapter deals primarily with centrally produced programs—the ones that fill national broadcast and cable network schedules and also most local broadcast-station and cable-system schedules. The chapter tells what they cost, where they come from, what they are called, how they are scheduled, and how they are promoted.

8.1 *Program Costs*

programs as "product"

Programs abound, but they must be both affordable and relevant to the programming goals of particular schedules. Programmers never end their search for what they refer to as usable *product*—a term, derived from the motion-picture industry, that gives a hint of the programmer's neutral point of view as to program quality.

Audience Targeting As the numbers of stations, cable systems, and networks grew, many program services gave up aiming at the mass audience that was the original target of broadcasting. The term *narrowcasting* came into vogue, suggesting a specific alternative goal. Cable networks such as CNN, MTV, Nickelodeon, and Home Shopping deliberately limit their appeal to specific audience segments. Radio stations adopt rigid musical formats (a particular radio format may repel most listeners but nevertheless prove irresistible to a narrow audience segment).

Advertisers influenced the trend toward narrowcasting. They are not inclined to pay to reach people who have no money to spend on their products or no interest in buying them. The need to target people willing and able to pay the bills, whether as advertisers or as subscribers, has led to **audience targeting** and segmentation throughout the electronic media.

Even though noncommercial broadcasting and pay cable sell no advertising, they also target specific audience groups. They try to attract audience segments most likely to support them by paying subscription and membership fees. Public television favors programs that appeal to middle-to-upper-income, well-educated families. Pay cable tends to select movies that attract women and families with children.

audience demographics and psychographics

The major broadcast television networks target the largest groups of viewers. Some cable networks target the same broad audience; others program for more narrowly defined groups. Each service defines audiences in terms of demographics (age range and gender) or psychographics (lifestyle and interests). Targeting women 18 to 34 years is a demographic goal; targeting sports fans is a psychographic goal.

Radio has further refined the process of targeting by using **segmentation**—defining extremely narrow subsets of the potential radio audience. Radio usually segments audiences in both demographic and psychographic terms: teenagers-who-want-to-hear-only-hit-songs or 25-to-44-year-old-adults-who-prefer-the-music-of-the-1960s, for example.

Parsimony Principle   The salient fact about programs is their high cost. the programming problem Product that can attract audiences of adequate size and desirable composition costs so much that filling all the channels continuously with brand new—not to mention "good"—programs would be economically impossible.

To cope with high program costs, writers, producers, and programmers resort to a variety of strategies based on what might be called the **parsimony principle.** This iron rule dictates that program materials must be used as sparingly as possible, repeated as often as possible, and shared as widely as possible.

Sparing use of material means, for example, stretching a dramatic plot over many episodes instead of burning it up in a single performance—the technique of the soap opera. Often material collected for a news feature is released in a series of minifeatures. An expensive live sports event is not programmed as a single item: it is stretched to the utmost, with a pre-game show, time-outs on the playing field for commercials during the game, half-time interviews, and a post-game wrap-up. Advertisers are sought to buy commercials in each part.

Repeated use is illustrated by the standardization of openings, closings, and transitions in daily newscasts, quiz shows, weekly dramatic series, and the like. And of course movies and television series replay endlessly over time—in fact, pay-cable networks repeat the same movie at several different times on the same day.

Shared use is best illustrated by networks, which enable the same programs to appear on hundreds of different stations and thousands of different cable systems. Such sharing by stations and systems spreads high costs among many users, bringing prices down to a reasonable level for each. The sharing does not stop there, because network entertainment programs reappear in syndication (the mechanics of which are explained later in this chapter); this enables further sharing worldwide among stations, cable systems, and networks.

Close monitoring of any station, network, or cable service discloses the personal experiment: monitoring services for repetition parsimony principle constantly at work.

From Prime Time to Any Time   The best-known entertainment programs, those that demand the heaviest outlay, are shown in **network prime time,** 8 to 11 P.M. Eastern time. Of the nearly $4.5 billion that the three major broadcast networks spend each year on programs, about $3 billion goes for prime-time shows alone. Budgets on that scale put enormous pressure on those who conceive, develop, and schedule the programs. Networks spend

EXHIBIT **8.1**   Prime-Time Series: From Concept to Air

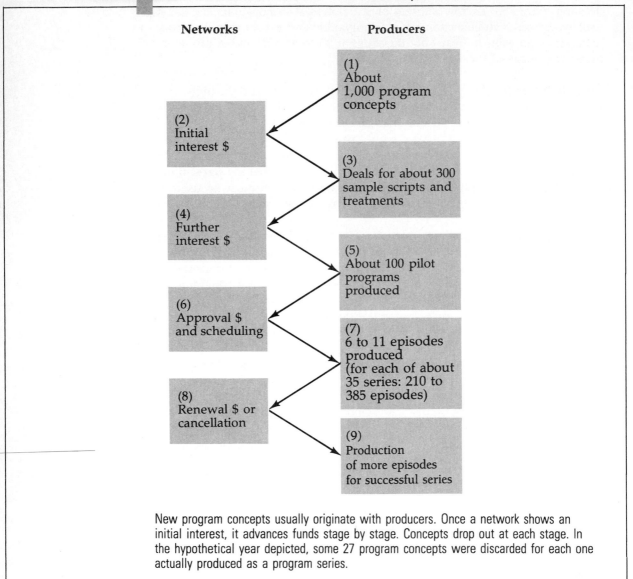

Networks   **Producers**

(1)
About
1,000 program
concepts

(2)
Initial
interest $

(3)
Deals for about 300
sample scripts and
treatments

(4)
Further
interest $

(5)
About 100 pilot
programs
produced

(6)
Approval $
and scheduling

(7)
6 to 11 episodes
produced
(for each of about
35 series: 210 to
385 episodes)

(8)
Renewal $ or
cancellation

(9)
Production
of more episodes
for successful series

New program concepts usually originate with producers. Once a network shows an initial interest, it advances funds stage by stage. Concepts drop out at each stage. In the hypothetical year depicted, some 27 program concepts were discarded for each one actually produced as a program series.

more than $150 million each year just on **pilots,** or prototypes, for new entertainment series. Only a quarter of them survive long enough to go on the air as first episodes in series. Exhibit 8.1 depicts the high attrition rate in the progress from program concept to on-the-air product.

As Exhibit 8.1 indicates, the networks leave the production of most prime-time entertainment series to outside studios. This fact has an important bearing on the parsimonious ways of the program market.

Deficit Financing   The television broadcast networks warded off a threatened antitrust suit by agreeing to accept severe limits on both their in-house production and their outright purchases of entertainment programs. The rationale of the agreement, embodied in the FCC's 1972–1973 **financial interest rule,** is discussed in Section 12.5.

Outside companies produce network programs, then license networks to use them for a limited number of showings (usually two). In the late 1980s, the license fees that producers charged the commercial networks for a one-hour prime-time drama or action/adventure program averaged $850,000 per episode. Higher-priced series, such as *Dallas* or *Miami Vice,* cost over $1 million an episode.

producers license networks to show major entertainment series

High as such payments may seem, they rarely cover the full cost of production. Producers of prime-time entertainment series count on subsequent resale fees to bring in the profits. This maneuver, known as *deficit financing,* capitalizes on the peculiar dynamics of the program market. Initial showing by the broadcast networks enhances the future resale value of a series. Exposure on ABC, CBS, NBC, or Fox confers recognition and a ratings track record.

After reverting to their producers, such shows become known as **off-network programs.** They go on to earn handsome profits when licensed for exhibition by broadcast stations, cable systems, cable networks, and foreign broadcast systems. In fact, the staggering profits that can be made from the distribution of entertainment programs have caused some of the major movie studios in Hollywood to pay more attention to distributing television programs than to producing them.

high profitability of the program distribution business

Syndication   8.2

The distribution method just described, known as **syndication,** offers both a supplement and an alternative to networks as a mechanism for financing centrally produced, high-cost product. Syndication occurs worldwide wherever broadcasting or cablecasting exists.

The FCC defines a *syndicated television program* as

> any program sold, licensed, distributed, or offered to television stations in more than one market within the United States for noninterconnected [that is, non-network] television broadcast exhibition, but not including live presentations. [47 CFR 76.5(p)]

In practice, programmers classify as syndicated all *nonlocal* programs not currently licensed to a network, whether live or not, including movies.

movies as syndicated product

How Syndication Works   Rather than *selling* programs, the syndicator *licenses* the buyer (actually the lessee) to use a syndicated product (program or series). The license permits a limited number of *plays* within a limited time period. After the license period expires, the programs return to the syndicator, who can recycle them over and over again.

Syndicated distribution resembles network distribution insofar as the same programs go to many outlets. But syndication differs both as to financial arrangements and as to timing. After a station pays for a license to broadcast a syndicated program, it may schedule the program at any time according to the station's needs. Network affiliates, however, contract to broadcast programs in exchange for compensation and normally carry them at network-stipulated times. Syndicators need no permanent relay interconnection with a chain of affiliates; they send their programs by various means and to various stations according to market demand.

difference between distribution by network and by syndication

Major television syndication firms usually operate as units within vertically integrated companies—firms engaged in several related activities. The leading syndicator is a subsidiary of Warner Brothers, which comprises production studios and broadcast stations as well as syndication sales. MCA, another major syndicator, has cable-network as well as studio and broadcasting interests.

Long-lived syndicated television series run season after season for decades, replayed scores of times. *I Love Lucy* (1951–1956), the quintessential off-network syndicated series, dates back to pre-color days and has been syndicated in virtually every country in the world. At times as many as five *Lucy* episodes have been available on the same day in a single U.S. city.

In syndication, the highly popular network shows, such as *The Cosby Show* and *Three's Company,* reach most of the 200-plus U.S. markets. This reach rivals the networks' national coverage. Hit programs made especially for syndication, such as *Wheel of Fortune* and *Entertainment Tonight,* also appear in nearly 200 markets, but the majority of made-for-syndication programs reach only about half of the television markets in any one season.

strongest syndicated shows equal network coverage

Television syndicators showcase new productions at annual meetings of the National Association of Television Program Executives (NATPE) and at other national and international program trade fairs. The two major rating services, Arbitron and Nielsen, document the track records of syndicated programs already on the market, issuing special reports on the size and composition of the audiences attracted by current syndicated series.

Syndication Exclusivity (Syndex) Stations may obtain from distributors **syndication exclusivity (syndex)**—the sole right to show a product within the buyer's own broadcast market for the term of the syndication deal. Cable networks, especially superstation networks, often distribute the same programs, bringing them into markets where broadcast stations have paid extra for local exclusive rights to the self-same programs. That duplication, of course, divides the audience and diminishes the programs' value to the broadcast station.

Responding to this program-duplication dilemma, in 1990 the FCC reintroduced its syndication exclusivity (syndex) rules (it had rescinded them eight years earlier in the first wave of deregulation). Syndex rules empower broadcast television stations to force cable systems in their coverage areas to delete duplicate syndicated programs to which the stations hold exclusive rights. Cable systems must go to the expense of temporarily blacking out the offending superstation or other network service, substituting another program or an explanatory slide.

Syndex rules do not apply to two affiliates of the same network carried by a cable system or to very small cable systems, nor are all syndication contracts exclusive. In fact, obtaining exclusivity increases the price of syndicated programs; sometimes stations prefer foregoing exclusivity for the sake of a lower price.

Prime-Time Access   Another FCC rule, the **prime-time access rule (PTAR),** gave syndicators a boost. Before 1971, the three major commercial television networks filled nearly all the best evening hours of their affiliates' schedules. This network monopoly left little opportunity for producers to sell programs aimed at the national market but not good enough (or lucky enough) to be selected for network exhibition. On affiliated stations, only the fringe hours (late afternoon and immediately following prime time) remained open for syndicated material. Of course, independent stations have prime time available, but in the early 1970s they could not afford to pay for recently produced, high-quality syndicated shows (later, some could, partly because of PTAR help). rationale for PTAR

In part to enlarge the market for producers of new programs, the FCC adopted PTAR, effective in 1971. It limits network entertainment programs to no more than three of the four prime-time hours—the evening hours when the television audience reaches maximum size and hence when stations can pay the most for non-network programs. As defined by the FCC, **prime time** consists of the four evening hours between 7:00 P.M. and 11:00 P.M. Eastern and Pacific time (one hour earlier in Central and Mountain time zones, with variations during daylight-saving time).

In practice, the networks had already abandoned the 7:00 to 7:30 P.M. slot to their affiliates. PTAR therefore gave the affiliates only the additional prime-time half-hour between 7:30 and 8:00 P.M. One daily half-hour may not seem like much for the networks to surrender. However, multiplying that half-hour of access time by the 260 weekdays in a year and by the 150 affiliates in the top-fifty markets yields an annual large-audience weekday market of 39,000 half-hours on major stations. PTAR therefore gave a significant new incentive to producers and distributors of non-network programs. number of prime-time access half-hours created by PTAR

With PTAR, the entire 7:00 to 8:00 P.M. hour became known as **access time.** Affiliates in the top-50 markets can fill access time with either locally produced programs or nationally syndicated non-network programs, but they may not schedule either regular network feeds or former network programs. The FCC makes certain exceptions in the case of nonentertainment programs as detailed in Exhibit 8.2.

Individual broadcast stations pay varying prices for licenses to show off-network and other centrally produced programs. Syndicated program prices

EXHIBIT **8.2**   PTAR: Access vs. Network Time

The prime-time access rule (PTAR) is intended to give television producers outside the limited circle of network program makers a chance to sell programs during at least one of the four top-audience hours. As the FCC put it, PTAR aims

> to make available for competition among existing and potential program producers, *both at the local and national levels,* an arena of more adequate competition for the custom and favor of broadcasters and advertisers. (FCCR, 1970: 326, italics added)

The networks chose the 7:00 to 8:00 P.M. EST hour as the one to give up—known thereafter as *access time.* The rule also forbids affiliates in the top-50 markets to schedule off-network syndicated programs in that hour.

The FCC aimed to give more producers a chance to create prime-time *entertainment* programs, but not to discourage network nonentertainment programs. It

therefore built several exceptions into PTAR, allowing the top affiliates to accept the following types of network offerings during access time:

- Children's, public affairs, and documentary programs
- Broadcasts by political candidates.
- Reports of fast-breaking and on-the-spot news events.
- Regular network newscasts if adjacent to one-hour affiliate news or public-affairs programs.
- Runovers of live sports events.
- Feature films.

On Saturdays, however, only feature films are excepted because when the FCC adopted PTAR, affiliates favored Saturday evening for locally produced public-affairs programs, which the commission wished to encourage. The accompanying table summarizes the rule and its exceptions.

	Days of Week	
Time Period	*Sunday through Friday*	*Saturday Only*
Local access time 7:00–8:00 P.M. EST and PST 6:00–7:00 P.M. MST and CST	No network programs with exceptions noted and no off-network programs on affiliates in top-50 markets	No network programs except for feature films on affiliates in top-50 markets
Network prime time 8:00–11:00 P.M. EST and PST 7:00–10:00 P.M. CST and MST	All affiliates may accept all network programs	

Source: 47 CFR 73.658 (k).

depend on such factors as the station's market rank and the programs' prior ratings performance. For a newly released off-network hit, major-market stations might pay $10 million for the right to four showings each of 100 episodes. Small-market stations might pay as little as $100,000 for the same rights.

Barter Syndication   Because program costs are high, stations sometimes run short of ready cash with which to buy syndicated programs. Distributors and stations therefore work out deals for trading advertising time for programs. The practice, known as **barter syndication,** has become well established.

As bartering evolved, two basic types emerged: **straight barter deals,** in which the syndicator and station divide the commercial minutes, and **partial barter deals,** in which the station pays for programs partly in cash and partly in commercial time. Distributors sell most weekly first-run syndicated shows on a straight barter basis, with varying divisions of the commercial time between station and distributor. For example, in its 1990 listings, Paramount offered the weekly hour-long first-run syndicated show *Entertainment This Week* in a straight barter deal: Paramount presold 6 commercial minutes in each program, leaving 3 for each bartering station to sell on its own.

In 1990, distributors offered most current first-run **stripped** (as contrasted to weekly scheduling) **shows** on a cash-plus-barter basis. For example, King World offered the game show *Jeopardy* for cash plus two 30-second commercials. The top first-run syndicated talk shows such as *The Oprah Winfrey Show* were sold for cash plus four 30-second spots. cash-plus-barter deals

Barter reached new heights when some syndicators adopted it for some of the most prestigious off-network shows. Viacom broke all revenue records in 1988 with the first such off-network series, *The Cosby Show.* Affiliates bought it on a cash-plus-barter basis, mostly as the all-important lead-in show to their early evening news. The first sale of the *Cosby* series in syndication generated more than $600 million for Viacom, at least $100 million of which came from the presale of a single minute of barter time.

Radio Syndication   Syndication and barter syndication also operate in radio. Satellites are used by radio syndicators to relay news, sports, and entertainment material to stations. Programmers distinguish between **syndicated formats** and **syndicated features.** A station might buy the use of a ready-made syndicated country-music format, for example, supplementing it with syndicated news and entertainment features from other sources. Thus stations can create unique programming mixes from commonly available syndicated elements. Radio feature material is often bartered, whereas syndicated formats are usually cash deals.

Program Types   8.3

As the previous sections indicate, programs can be classified according to their method of distribution as *local, network,* and *syndicated.* This section deals with other classification methods based on

- *Content,* in terms of a broad two-way division into entertainment and information.

- *Scheduling,* in terms of frequency ("strip scheduling") and time of day ("prime-time soap opera").
- *Format,* in terms either of individual programs ("the talk format") or of entire services ("the all-talk radio format").
- *Genre,* usually in terms of content ("the sitcom genre") but sometimes in terms of target audience ("the children's genre").

Entertainment vs. Information   Most programs qualify primarily as entertainment. However, information programs receive special attention and deference because they enhance the electronic media's social importance. A hybrid class of programs such as *A Current Affair* became trendy in 1989. They earned the name **infotainment** because they take on the aura of information programs but aim primarily at entertaining. Legitimate information programs have two main subtypes, news and public affairs.

sports programs: primarily information or entertainment?

Some people argue that sports programs should be classed as information rather than as entertainment. However, programmers regard sports as primarily entertainment. Network sports departments differ in purpose, style, and types of personnel from news departments.

Dayparts   Two programs of the same type that are scheduled in two different times of day take on different colorations. Prime-time programs have distinctive qualities, as do other programs associated with specific schedule positions. Thus a daytime soap opera differs from a prime-time soap opera, and prime-time sports shows usually differ from weekend sports shows.

For scheduling purposes, programmers break the 24-hour day into blocks they call **dayparts**. Radio programmers generally divide the day into *morning drive, midday, afternoon drive, night,* and *overnight* segments. Morning and afternoon drive periods have the largest audiences for most radio stations.

In television, broadcast and cable network programmers divide the day as shown in Exhibit 8.3. *Network prime time,* the most important segment, commands the largest audiences. *Access time,* the prime-time hour preceding network prime time, gives syndicators and station programmers their only shot at large audiences. During that hour, the prime-time access rule bans networks from scheduling entertainment programs. The rationale for prime time and the rules governing it are explained more fully in Exhibit 8.2.

Formats   A program may have a "quiz-show format." A cable channel may have a "home-shopping format." CNN has an all-news format, ESPN an all-sports format, MTV a music-video format, and so on. The term **format** can refer either to the organization of a single program or to the organization of an entire service. Most radio stations have adopted distinctive formats, such as MOR (middle-of-the-road) music, classical music, or all-news.

Television stations and broadcast television networks tend not to adopt single formats because they need to appeal to a broad audience. As a single-channel service, a station cannot afford to narrow its audience to the followers

EXHIBIT **8.3**   TV Dayparts

6-7 AM	Early Early Morning
7-9 AM	Early Morning
9-12 NOON	Morning
12-1 PM	Noon
1-4 PM	Afternoon
4-6 PM	Early Fringe
6-7 PM	News Block (varies)
7-8 PM	Access
8-11 PM	Prime Time
11-12 MID.	Late Fringe
12-2 AM	Late Night
2-6 AM	Overnight

The length of the TV news block varies from market to market and station to station, running as long as two or three hours on some major-market TV stations and as short as an hour elsewhere.

of one particular format. Cable can afford such specialization, however, because it is a multiple-channel service.

Genres   In the context of programs, **genre** usually denotes a type of content. Familiar entertainment genres include the situation comedy, the game show, the Western, and the soap opera. Some genres are defined in terms of target audience rather than content. Children's shows, for example, can take many different forms—not only cartoons and action/adventure drama but also news, discussion, quiz, and comedy.

Programmers identify a program by genre as a shorthand way of conveying a great deal about its probable length, seriousness, subject matter, visual approach, production method, and audience appeal. Hybrid programs are sometimes given combined names such as *dramedy* (a drama/comedy hybrid) and *docudrama* (a documentary/drama hybrid).

8.4 *Entertainment Program Sources*

Individual broadcast stations and cable systems obtain nearly all their entertainment programs ready-made from networks (if they are affiliated) and syndicators. The broadcast and cable networks and syndicators, in turn, obtain most of their new entertainment shows from Hollywood studios and independent producers.

In-house production by stations, cable systems, and networks consists mostly of news and sports programs (discussed in Sections 8.7 and 8.8). The television networks produce some entertainment shows in-house—mainly

EXHIBIT 8.4   TV Series Produced by Major Hollywood Studios

Studio	Programs for Broadcast Networks	Programs for First-Run Syndication and Cable Networks
Warner Brothers	China Beach, Growing Pains, Murphy Brown, Night Court	Superior Court, People's Court, Mama's Family, Gumby, She's the Sheriff
Paramount	Cheers, Dear John, Dolphin Bay, Family Ties, MacGyver, Mission Impossible	The Arsenio Hall Show, Entertainment Tonight, Star Trek: The Next Generation, Webster
Walt Disney	The Magical World of Disney, The New Adventures of Winnie the Pooh	Live with Regis and Kathie Lee, Win Lose or Draw, Siskel & Ebert, Chip'N'Dale's Rescue Rangers
20th Century Fox	Have Faith, L.A. Law, Mr. Belvedere, Hooperman	9 to 5, Small Wonder, P.M. Magazine, Hour Magazine
MCA/Universal	Almost Grown, Coach, Miami Vice, Murder, She Wrote, Columbo	Out of This World, My Secret Identity, The Morton Downey Jr. Show
Columbia	Police Story, Designing Women, Married. . . .With Children, Who's the Boss?	Wheel of Fortune, Jeopardy
MGM/UA	thirtysomething, 48 Hours, Knightwatch, Dream Street	Twilight Zone, Group One Medical, Kids Inc.

Source: Data from *Channels' Field Guide 1989*, p. 85. Copyright 1988, Channels Magazine. Reprinted with permission.

soap operas and specials. *Moonlighting,* a prime-time series produced by ABC, was a rare exception to the usual pattern of obtaining prime-time shows from major Hollywood studios and independent producers. The fact that the cable networks rely almost entirely on the same sources as the broadcast networks for their entertainment programs contributes to both program shortages and the overall lack of program diversity, despite the fact that cable has greatly increased the number of channels available.

Producers of original entertainment fall into five creative groups:

- The seven major Hollywood film studios, known as the Hollywood majors or the Big Seven (listed in Exhibit 8.4). The word *studio* implies a large-scale, permanent production facility.
- A few smaller Hollywood studios, below the "major" rank.
- About a dozen major independent producers.
- Many other smaller, more specialized independent producers.
- Foreign syndicators distributing to the United States.

Some original programs, seen mostly on cable networks and public television, come from other countries.

Major Studios   The seven Hollywood majors listed in Exhibit 8.3 have familiar movie-studio names, such as Paramount and 20th Century Fox. Best known to the public for feature films made originally for theatrical release, they also produce a less expensive type of film, made-for-TV movies. In addition, they produce program series made especially for broadcast and cable television networks. Exhibit 8.4 lists examples of such series.

Hollywood majors produce made-for-TV movies

By definition, theatrical feature films normally reach audiences first through motion-picture theaters. Thereafter distributors release them successively to pay cable and the other electronic media at intervals governed by windows of availability, as shown in Exhibit 8.5. Despite the exhibition priority enjoyed by movie theaters, the movie studios make more money from television, cable, videocassette, and foreign rights than from American theatrical exhibition. Feature films are a staple item in broadcast and cable network schedules and even in some individual broadcast station schedules. They have the advantage of filling large blocks of time with material that has strong audience appeal, especially for the young female subaudience that advertisers often target.

Independent Producers   At least half of the prime-time series shown on network television come from the second major force in television program production, the independent producers. They range in size from large firms such as Spelling and MTM, which usually have several series in production simultaneously, to smaller producers with only a single series under contract at any one time. In the 1970s, independent producers created some of the most innovative television series, such as *All in the Family, The Mary Tyler Moore Show,* and *Dallas.* Feature films and daytime television series, however, remain largely the province of the Hollywood Big Seven.

EXHIBIT **8.5**   Movie Windows of Availability

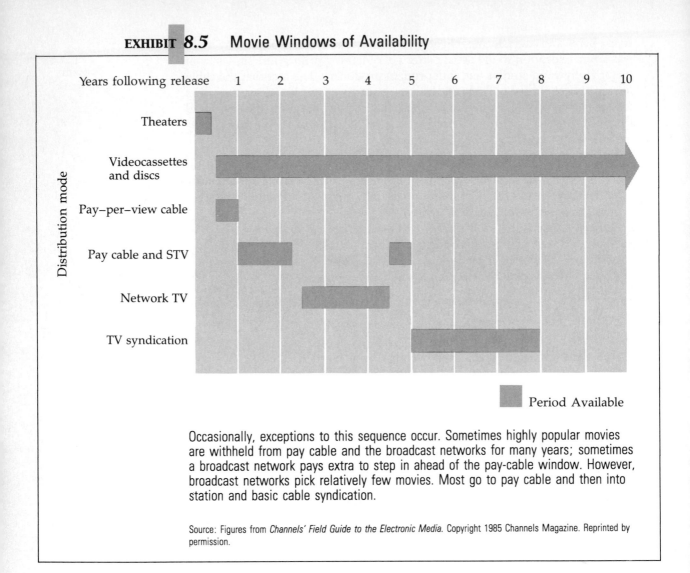

Occasionally, exceptions to this sequence occur. Sometimes highly popular movies are withheld from pay cable and the broadcast networks for many years; sometimes a broadcast network pays extra to step in ahead of the pay-cable window. However, broadcast networks pick relatively few movies. Most go to pay cable and then into station and basic cable syndication.

Source: Figures from *Channels' Field Guide to the Electronic Media.* Copyright 1985 Channels Magazine. Reprinted by permission.

Independent producers usually lease production facilities from the big studios to reduce overhead costs. The savings allow independents to charge lower license fees, which give them a special advantage in competing for network approval of proposed new prime-time series. Independents also avoid the unwieldy decision-making structures of the traditional movie studios.

Made-for-Cable Programs   The growth of pay-cable networks created an insatiable demand for movies, their staple offering. The leading pay-cable network, HBO, alone consumes more than 200 movies a year.

pay-cable investments in
movie production

To increase their program supply, to gain control over content and costs, and to create a distinctive image, pay-cable networks co-finance movies with

EXHIBIT 8.6   Prices of Off-Network Syndicated Programs, 1987–1991

Off-net Series	Syndicator	Estimated price per episode	Year available
Alf	Lorimar	$1,500,000	1991
The A-Team	MCA	950,000	1987
Cheers	Paramount	1,650,000	1987
The Cosby Show	Viacom	4,800,000	1988
Family Ties	Paramount	1,400,000	1987
Growing Pains	Warner Brothers	910,000	1989
Head of the Class	Warner Brothers	950,000	1990
Hill Street Blues	Victory/MTM	1,100,000	1987
Kate & Allie	MCA	1,200,000	1988
Mama's Family	Lorimar	515,000	1988
Night Court	Warner Brothers	1,100,000	1988
Perfect Strangers	Lorimar	1,500,000	1991
Silver Spoons	Columbia/Embassy	1,200,000	1987
Webster	Paramount	1,400,000	1988
Who's the Boss?	Columbia/Embassy	2,500,000	1989

producers. This investment gives them **exclusivity**—the right to show the product first on cable. A few of the movies co-financed by cable, such as *On Golden Pond* and *Sophie's Choice,* also had some box-office success in theaters. HBO's parent corporation is Time-Warner Inc., a magazine publisher and cable MSO. It became Hollywood's largest financial backer of movies in the 1980s.

Each year, basic as well as pay-cable services increase their investments in production activities. They develop made-for-cable dramatic and comedy series and variety programs for first-run cable use and, on average, underwrite production of at least 10 percent of their schedules annually. In 1988, for example, cable networks committed more than $500 million for original productions—a substantial sum, though still small compared to the $2 billion the broadcast networks spend for producing original series (out of $4.5 billion for all types of programs). About one-third of Showtime's schedule and nearly half of the Disney Channel's programs consist of original cable material. Some of the new products qualify as true cable-only programs; others merely add episodes to existing television series, as happened in the case of *Fame* on the pay-cable network Showtime.

Made-for-cable programs help to counteract the image of cable as a mere parasite on broadcast television. They also make good cable's promise to enhance program diversity. Moreover, original productions help one cable service to distinguish itself from another and to gain subscribers seeking new program options.

News Sources

A markedly different atmosphere surrounds the creation of new programs. By assuming the serious function of conveying news and information, broadcasters took on a more important role than that of merely entertaining. They became, in effect, sharers with the print media in the Western world's tradition of press freedom. However, not all broadcasters cared that much about being part of a great free-speech tradition if doing so interfered with another great American tradition—that of making money through free enterprise. But in time, news programs changed from money losers into moneymakers, ensuring the survival of broadcasting's special role as a bearer of information as entertainment.

News Agencies   Long before broadcasting and cable, newspapers established news-collecting agencies, the news field's equivalent of program syndicators. More than a hundred news services are available to the U.S. electronic mass media. Many are specialized, such as the Her Say News Service (women's news) and Intrigue Associates ("curious news items"). The major news agencies such as Associated Press, United Press International, and Reuters are international in scope and offer services especially tailored for the electronic media.

A news syndicator formed to meet the needs of nonaffiliated television stations, Independent News Network (INN), was launched in 1980. Stations subscribing to the INN service get packaged half-hour newscasts, live via satellite, each day. INN feeds its newscasts to the stations during the hour preceding network affiliates' late-evening newscasts.

Network News   Although the broadcast networks rely on outside producers for most of their entertainment programs, they retain tight control over most news and public-affairs production.

Each commercial broadcast television network operates a news division separate from its entertainment division, each employing about 2,000 people. Each also supports its own foreign news bureaus in the major world capitals, staffed by correspondents with in-depth knowledge of the regions they cover. In 1988, NBC became part-owner of Reuters international news service in order to reduce its foreign bureau costs while still maintaining a strong international news presence. Until that move, the American television networks had always competed head-on with the international news services.

Most cable networks, in contrast, specialize in either information or entertainment. Only a few of the largest provide comprehensive programming comparable to that of the broadcast television networks.

Ted Turner made the risky decision to launch a full-time news service, Cable News Network (CNN), in 1980. He aimed at making CNN the fourth major television news operation, providing both domestic and international news in direct competition with ABC, CBS, and NBC, using far smaller resources.

At first the Cable News Network was treated as a joke (some translated CNN as "Chicken Noodle Network"), but Turner's brashness paid off. CNN teams rapidly earned parity with the major broadcast news teams. They began receiving White House press notices, participating in pooled coverage, obtaining major interviews, and securing space for cameras, crew, and reporters at political conventions and other such events on a par with the broadcast networks. With CNN's success came even further cable specialization, with entire channels devoted to particular news genres such as finance, sports, and weather.

CNN achieves parity with broadcast networks

Local News   National and international news is the natural province of networks, local news the province of stations. But stations have increasingly expanded their coverage beyond local and regional news. They have many sources to call on beyond those of their local staffs and local regional news services.

Both television and radio affiliates can obtain what amounts to syndicated television news services from their own networks. Provided by the networks' news divisions, these services feed hard news and features over regular network relay facilities during hours when these facilities carry no scheduled network programs. Affiliates can record these feeds, selecting items for later insertion in local newscasts. They can obtain the right to record regular network news programs as sources of stories for insertion in local programs.

Affiliates and independents alike can draw on the established news agencies, AP, UIP, and others. With the advent of electronic news gathering (ENG) during the 1970s, local television news teams could fill longer newscasts and provide more on-the-scene coverage of both local and distant events. Only 3 percent of the commercial television stations used ENG in 1973; by 1989, 90 percent used it, mostly in conjunction with satellite relays.

Sports Program Sources   8.6

Networks   On-the-spot coverage of sports events is not controlled by the financial interest rules, and the broadcast networks at one time produced these shows themselves. They eventually found that specialists could produce sports for them at lower cost. However, the networks still produce the most prestigious live sports events such as the World Series, regular-season NFL football, and the Super Bowl. Broadcast and cable networks invest heavily in such major events.

specialist sports producers take over from networks

As examples, ABC and NBC paid a total of $1.2 billion for the rights to Major League baseball in the six years 1984 through 1989. All three broadcast networks and ESPN shared three years of NFL professional football (1988 through 1990) for $1.4 billion. NBC agreed to pay $401 million for the 1992 Summer Olympics in Barcelona, Spain. CBS bought the rights to four years of Major League baseball in the early 1990s for $1 billion and the rights to

rising cost of sports rights

seven years of college basketball for another billion. Such fees are justified both by the revenue and the prestige that come from being the exclusive carrier of "mega-events." The networks can also afford to go all-out on production facilities for these key events—numerous cameras, instant-replay machines, gigantic booms and cranes, and other specialized equipment—and still make a handsome profit.

Aside from mega-events, the networks rely increasingly on specialized sports production companies. Cable networks and individual broadcast stations also employ such firms (though the sports cable network, ESPN, produces most of the games it carries). In addition to paying production fees, the networks purchase the national rights to the events and pay their own announcers' salaries and travel expenses.

Sports Sponsorship Advertisers gave up most program sponsorship long ago, but the practice has revived for some lesser sports events. Sponsorship means that the advertiser obtains the rights to broadcast or cablecast the event and controls the program.

The network carrying a sponsored sports event supplies only play-by-play and color announcers. Sponsors hire nearby television stations or sports production houses to do the rest of the production work. They also often participate in lining up celebrity guests, promoting the program, and even selling tickets. They sometimes also recover some of their expenses by selling spots to other advertisers and peddling subsidiary coverage rights to the event to radio stations and cable systems.

Both networks and advertisers benefit from this division of labor. Sponsors retain control of costs and ensure maximum promotional value; networks gain hundreds of program hours of minor sports events too risky financially for them to cover by themselves.

8.7 *Network Schedule Strategies*

Whatever their program sources, stations and networks strive to structure their selections into coherent schedules. Effective scheduling requires, among other things, coordinating program types and production tempos to complement typical audience activities.

For example, during the busy early-morning period, listeners/viewers get ready for their day's activities at work, at school, in the home, or at play. This period calls for light, up-tempo treatment of news, weather, traffic reports, and short entertainment features. A more relaxing tempo and longer program units suit the less structured evening period.

Audience Flow Schedulers try to draw audience members away from rival channels and to prevent rival channels from enticing away members of their own audience. These efforts focus on controlling **audience flow**—the movement of viewers or listeners from one program to another. Flow occurs mostly at the junctions between programs or, on radio, after one block of songs ends and before the next begins. Audience flow includes both **flowthrough** (on the same stations or channel) and **outflow** or **inflow** (to or from competing programs).

Audience research can measure the extent and direction of audience flow. Such data give programmers guidance on how to adjust schedules and program types to retain audience members and gain new ones at the expense of opposing channels.

However, remote-control channel selectors and VCRs have made tracking television-audience flow more difficult. Over two-thirds of all households have videocassette players, and three-quarters have remote-control channel selectors. A special vocabulary has evolved to describe how some audience members use these devices: they *graze* through the available channels, *zap* unwanted commercials, *jump* between pairs of channels, *flip* around to see what's happening on nearby channels, and *zip* through the boring parts of prerecorded cassettes. Not all viewers take advantage of this new freedom, however, and programmers continue to employ scheduling strategies designed to influence audience flow.

The unique continuousness of the electronic mass media differentiates them from other media, whose products reach consumers only at intervals, coming in individually packaged physical units—a videocassette, a compact disc, an edition of a newspaper or a book, or an issue of a magazine. Only broadcasting and cable television afford the consumer an instantaneous choice among several continuously flowing experiences.

continuousness: unique attribute of electronic mass media

Specific Strategies   Taking into account the schedules on competing channels, programmers adjust their own program schedules, fine-tuning them to take advantage of opponents' weak points. Following are some typical scheduling strategies used by networks (broadcast and cable) and by individual systems and stations to exploit audience flow.

- **Counterprogramming** seeks to attract the audience toward one's own station or network by offering programs different from those of the competition. For example, an independent station might schedule situation comedies against evening news programs on the network affiliates in its market.
- **Block programming** seeks to maintain audience flowthrough by scheduling programs with similar appeal next to each other—for example, by filling an entire evening with family-comedy programs.
- **Stripping** tries to create viewing habits by scheduling episodes of a series at the same time every day of the week.
- A **strong lead-off** seeks to attract the maximum initial audience by starting a daypart with a particularly strong program in the hope of retaining the audience for subsequent programs

- A **hammock** tries to establish an audience for a new program, or to recover the audience for a show slipping in popularity, by scheduling the program in question *between* two strong programs. Flowthrough from the previous (lead-in) program should enhance the initial audience for the hammocked program, and viewers may stick with the weak (or unfamiliar) show in anticipation of the strong following program, bolstering the audience for the hammocked program.
- **Bridging** attempts to weaken the drawing power of a competing show by scheduling a one-hour (or longer) program that overlaps the start time of the competing show.
- **Repetition** is a pay-cable strategy that makes it convenient for viewers to catch a program, such as a movie, because repeat showings are scattered throughout the schedule.

- **Stunting** seeks to keep the opposing networks off-balance in the short term by such tactics as making abrupt schedule changes, opening a new series with an extra-long episode, and interrupting regular programming frequently with heavily promoted specials. Networks resort to stunting especially during the February, May, and November ratings periods.

Prime-Time Arena

The main arena of broadcast network rivalry is the weekly 22 hours of network prime time—the three hours from 8:00 P.M. to 11:00 P.M. each night of the week in the Eastern and Pacific time zones, an hour earlier in the Central and Mountain time zones, plus an extra hour from 7:00 P.M. to 8:00 P.M. on Sundays (EST/PST).

Prime time affords the major networks access to the largest and most varied audiences of any medium. It therefore calls for the programs with the broadest appeal. Because the networks pay so much for prime-time programs and because they need scheduling maneuverability, they normally run prime-time series weekly. If they scheduled all of prime time with *daily* half-hour series, each network would have only six weeknight programs to schedule, giving too few chances for exploiting scheduling strategies.

In other dayparts, however, the broadcast networks strip most of their shows—scheduling the same series at the same time, Monday through Friday. Network morning talk programs, soap operas, and evening newscasts, for example, occur at the same times each weekday.

Cable-Network Strategies

In the early 1980s, most cable networks showcased their best product in dayparts *other* than prime time. They contented themselves with reaching demographic subgroups in prime time. But by the mid-1980s, the largest cable networks, such as ESPN, WTBS, and USA Network, began to compete head-on with the broadcast networks for the prime-time mass audience.

Basic cable networks commonly adopt habit-forming strategies to build loyal audiences. The broad-appeal cable services strip their programs across the board both in daytime and in prime time. USA Network and Lifetime, for example, stripped costly off-network series such as *Miami Vice* in prime time, hoping to draw viewers away from the broadcast stations and to build a cable-watching habit among first-time viewers. ESPN, the sports network, strips a daily sports quiz show and a sports talk show. MTV strips videos, and Nickelodeon strips cartoons.

Pay-cable networks rely heavily on the strategy of repetition, scheduling repeat showings of their movies and variety shows in various time periods, cumulatively building audiences for each program. Each movie plays at varying start times on different days. A movie may be recycled as many as a dozen times a month. For this reason, and also because cable program guides come out once a month and cable companies need to encourage monthly subscription renewals, the pay networks plan their schedules in monthly cycles.

Pay cable also uses the bridging strategy, scheduling across the start times of other programs. HBO and Showtime movies, for example, usually start at 8:00 P.M., bridging the 9:00 P.M. station break. This is the period with the largest number of people watching television. If a movie ends before 10:00 P.M., HBO usually adds filler material to complete the hour in order to start a new program when viewers may be hunting for something to watch at station-break time. Sometimes the pay-cable networks try to get the jump on the broadcast networks by starting their movies earlier in the evenings (at 7:00 or 7:30 P.M.). This strategy works best when broadcast schedules have been disrupted by late-running sports or political programs.

how pay-TV uses bridging strategy

Station Schedule Strategies 8.8

TV Stations   On the average, the major broadcast television networks fill 70 percent of their affiliates' schedules. A network affiliate therefore has limited opportunity to use the strategies previously described, but the few that it can use are important in getting maximum results from the nonnetwork 30 percent of its schedule. The affiliate programmer's most important decisions concern the choice of programs for the early fringe and access dayparts (see Exhibit 8.3).

how much of a TV affiliate's day comes from its network?

Programmers at independent stations have charge of their total schedule. Their chief strategem, counterprogramming, capitalizes on the inflexibility of the affiliate's schedule because of its prior commitment to network programs. For example, an independent station can schedule sports events at times when affiliates carry major network shows. Networks can afford to devote prime time to only a few top-rated sports events of national interest. Independents, however, can schedule sports events of local interest, even during prime time.

how independents exploit counter-programming

Most of the 630 or so full-service network affiliates and the nearly 400 independent commercial stations (nearly half of which are Fox affiliates) utilize stripping on weekdays. Saturday and Sunday programs are scheduled only weekly. Monday-through-Friday stripping of syndicated and local programs has three advantages for stations. First, daily same-time

program stripping strategy

EXHIBIT **8.7** Radio Station Music Format

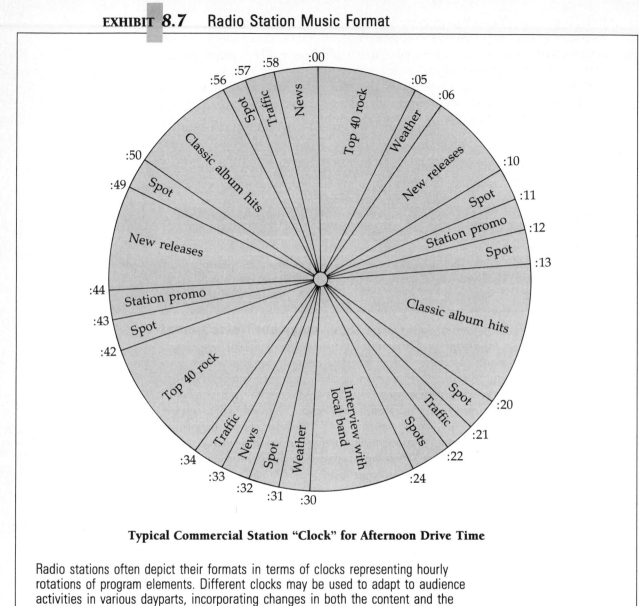

Typical Commercial Station "Clock" for Afternoon Drive Time

Radio stations often depict their formats in terms of clocks representing hourly rotations of program elements. Different clocks may be used to adapt to audience activities in various dayparts, incorporating changes in both the content and the tempo of presentation.

scheduling encourages the audience to form regular viewing habits, such as the 6:00 P.M. news habit. Second, a single promotional spot can publicize an entire week's schedule for a given time slot. Finally, purchasing many episodes of a syndicated series in a single transaction earns quantity discounts from syndicators.

The practice of stripping off-network programs "across the board" (the way daily scheduling looks on a display board) led to an enormous demand for television series with many episodes already "in the can." Stripping ideally requires 130 episodes for a half-year run. Off-network series that have generated such large numbers of episodes have, by definition, earned good ratings on a network over more than one season. They therefore command the highest prices among syndicated series. As Exhibit 8.6 suggests, a series with a large number of episodes can earn millions of dollars in aggregate revenue for syndicators in a single season.

number of episodes needed for effective stripping

Most series that had very long runs as original shows on the networks date back to the 1960s and early 1970s. Such hits as *Gunsmoke* and *Marcus Welby, M.D.* seemed to run forever. But later, competition made schedules more volatile. The networks nervously canceled shows at the first signs of weakening ratings. Runs became shorter, building up too few episodes for strip scheduling over the long period needed for the best results.

Radio Stations   Radio stations use counterprogramming, stripping, and blocking strategies even more than television stations do. Most radio stations schedule their program elements, whether songs or news items, in hourly rotations, creating 60-minute cycles. As the day progresses, the hourly pattern is altered by daypart to match changing audience activities. Exhibit 8.7 shows an hourly plan for a Top 40 format.

Program Promotion   8.9

Having the best programs in the world means little if audiences don't know about them. Promotion therefore ranks as a major aspect of programming strategies.

On-Air Promotion   Broadcast stations and broadcast/cable networks consider on-air promotional spots the most cost-efficient way to make their programs known. Station breaks between programs usually contain promos for upcoming shows. Stations and broadcast networks also air **teasers**—brief mentions of upcoming news stories—in the hour preceding newscasts.

HBO schedules elaborately produced billboards of upcoming programs as filler between the end of one show and the start of the next. Cable systems often dedicate one or more channels *entirely* to program listings. There are even companies that specialize in producing cross-promotional announcements for cable services. For example, Prime Time Tonight schedules promotional spots for several cable networks on such basic cable services as the Weather Channel and CNN.

cable networks use cross-promotion

Promotion via Other Media   To reach nonviewers, networks and stations advertise in newspapers and magazines, on radio, on outdoor billboards, and

EXHIBIT **8.8** *TV Guide:* Changing Role

Every week about 20 percent of all U.S. television households turn to *TV Guide* to see what's on television, to decide what to watch, and to read articles and gossip about the television and cable industries. *TV Guide* comes in a distant third, behind weekly TV supplements and daily listings in newspapers, as the source of program information most frequently cited by viewers. But these local publications cannot match *TV Guide*'s estimated national readership of 42 million.

Walter Annenberg (later a U.S. ambassador to Great Britain) combined three local weekly television program guides to create the first edition of *TV Guide* in 1953. He began with 10 regional editions and a circulation of 1.5 million subscribers. By 1988 the magazine offered 106 regional editions with a circulation of about 17 million (down from its 1977 peak of nearly 20 million), the highest of any magazine. Each of the regional editions offers the same national pages of articles and news, plus special pages inserted for that region's cable and station program listings. Nearly half of all *TV Guide* copies are sold at newsstands, mostly in supermarkets.

Media baron Rupert Murdoch took control of *TV Guide* in 1988 when he paid $3 billion for its parent company, Triangle Publications. Murdoch already owned half of *TV Guide*'s Australian counterpart, *TV Week*.

TV Guide is designed for readers, not for the electronic media. Indeed, the magazine includes stories critical of the industry, though under Murdoch it is gaining more of a fan magazine image and dwelling more on personalities. A look at some of its earlier contributing authors supports its claim of occasional serious journalism: Arthur Schlesinger, Jr., Pulitzer Prize–winning historian; Lee Loevinger, former FCC commissioner; Alvin Toffler, author of *Future Shock* and *The Third Wave*; Alexander Haig, Jr., former secretary of state.

Each week, television stations throughout the country send in upcoming program schedules, and each week editorial representatives of the magazine call stations to update program information. Often, through its direct contacts, *TV Guide* learns of

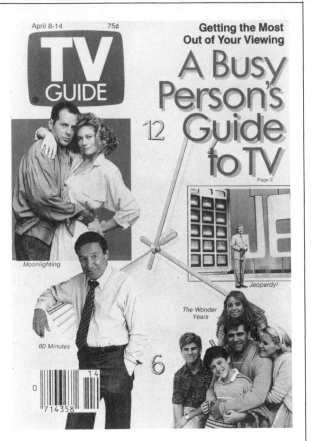

network program changes before the network's affiliates do—an occasional source of embarrassment to the stations and a subject for acrimonious network/affiliate discussions. The magazine's computers store summaries of more than a quarter of a million syndicated episodes and some 36,000 movies. When a station or network tells *TV Guide* it plans to show a certain episode of a series on a certain day, the editors call up the appropriate summary for inclusion in the listings.

in other media. Radio stations promote television programs, and television stations carry spots promoting radio stations—all paid advertising unless the services are co-owned.

Cable systems mail customized program guides to their subscribers or offer subscriptions to cable-network program guides (Arts & Entertainment has one, for example, available at $18 a year). A cable-only magazine, *Cable Guide,* has nearly 8 million subscribers, the most of any generic cable-only program guide. Owners of home satellite dishes turn to magazines such as *Satellite Orbit* to find out which transponders carry which services.

specialized program guides

The most widely recognized printed source for program information, *TV Guide,* publishes a hundred different editions weekly within the continental United States, as well as many localized editions in other countries. Exhibit 8.8 tells more about this uniquely successful publication. But even *TV Guide* cannot provide full details on all available programs for viewers with access to dozens of channels.

This chapter has introduced some industry code words that programmers often use: *audience targeting, syndication, exclusivity, financial interest rule, prime-time access, format, genre, audience flow,* and *stripping.* These terms frequently recur in the discussion of actual programs that follows in the next chapter.

Programs: Network, Syndicated, Local

Programs readily fall into three broad categories—network, syndicated, and locally produced. Subcategories are based on paired differences: prime time vs. other times, radio vs. television, broadcast television vs. cable television, first-run syndication vs. off-net syndication, network affiliates vs. independents, and entertainment vs.

information content. Altogether, this chapter describes nearly a score of separate program subcategories. Each subcategory has its own characteristic audience, its own production, distribution, and delivery method, and its own type of content.

9.1 *Prime-Time Network TV Entertainment*

The best-known and most popular programs appear on television networks in prime time. They consist mostly of light entertainment. Prime-time entertainment network programs come as weekly series, with a sprinkling of movies and occasional one-time specials. A series can run for an indefinite number of episodes. Those with eight or fewer episodes are known as **miniseries.**

difference between series and miniseries

Movies include both theatrical feature films and made-for-TV movies. After being shown in movie theaters, feature films are licensed for release to networks and other outlets in sequence, as shown in Exhibit 8.5. Outside producers create made-for-TV movies on commission from the networks. They are shot in two-hour lengths in the style of feature films but have lower budgets and are adapted to the limitations of the small television screen.

differences between movies and made-for-TV-movies

Audience Share   During the 22 hours a week of television network prime time, ABC, CBS, and NBC vie for huge audiences—larger than any in the previous history of entertainment. For nearly three decades (until the early 1980s) the three broadcast networks captured more than 90 percent of the prime-time viewing audience.

By the late 1980s, under the impact of cable networks, improved programming by independent stations, and widespread use of home VCRs, the combined audience share for ABC, CBS, and NBC in prime time had decreased to around 65 percent, as shown in Exhibit 3.6. A fourth network, Fox Broadcasting Company, had also emerged, dividing the prime-time network share four ways instead of three.

Despite the decline in their audience share, the broadcast television networks still draw the most massive audiences of any media. The rise and fall of their prime-time programs makes headline news. And after their contractual network runs, those same programs travel throughout the world as syndicated off-network shows.

Situation Comedies   Among the television prime-time series, situation comedies (sitcoms) are the staple product. Sitcoms such as *The Cosby Show, A Different World,* and *Roseanne* topped the charts in the late 1980s. Hit sitcoms command 30 to 40 percent of the viewing audience. They tend to earn higher ratings than hour-long dramas.

Writers of situation comedies create a group of engaging characters who find themselves in a particular situation—usually a family setting. Plots spring from the way the characters react to a specific new source of tension injected into the situation week by week. The characters have marked traits that soon become familiar to the audience: habits, attitudes, quirks, and mannerisms.

Family settings work well, but sitcoms also take place in other situations—the tavern of *Cheers,* for example (family-like in its way). *The Cosby Show* presents a traditional family situation—handsome middle-class father and mother, adorable kids representing typical age groups having typical problems. A contrasting family situation presents less conventional characters and problems. Sitcoms increasingly probe the boundaries of acceptable home viewing. In *Kate & Allie,* two divorced women with children attempt to make a go of a fatherless, two-mother household. Families with a single father (*Dear John*), with multiple fathers (*My Two Dads*), and no fathers (*Golden Girls*) have provided offbeat situations.

personal experiment: define the "situations" in your favorite sitcoms

A variant sometimes referred to as the *slobcom* (a play on the word *sitcom*) depicts less-than-ideal family situations. The family in the Fox network's *Married . . . with Children* features unhappy housewife, a husband who fails as a provider, and outrageously undisciplined children. ABC's *Roseanne* features an aggressively earthy, blue-collar family—a far cry from the idyllic family situations of traditional sitcoms.

Spin-offs and Clones

A program with a new angle instantly begets brazen imitations. Programmers speak of such copies as spinoffs and clones. A **spin-off** stars secondary characters from a previous hit on the same network, placing the characters in a new situation. *The Cosby Show,* for example, spun off *A Different World.*

A **clone** closely imitates an already popular program on another network, changing only the stars and details of plot and setting. Hour-long dramas tend to spawn clones. Attempts to capitalize on the success of *Magnum P.I.,* the number-three-prime-time show of the early 1980s, led to at least five clones in a single year, including *Hunter* and *Miami Vice* (only those two survived to become successes in their own right).

In the early 1980s, producers began injecting comedy elements, formerly the province of sitcoms, into action/adventure shows. Series such as *Magnum P.I.* and *Moonlighting* included lighthearted comic scenes. The late-1980s shows *thirtysomething* and *Beauty and the Beast* added nostalgia and fantasy to the mix. Critics referred to some of these shows as **dramedies**—hour-long blends of drama and comedy.

Crime Shows

Police, lawyer, and detective dramas such as *Dragnet* and *Perry Mason* peaked in the ratings around 1960. Then they faded until the mid-1980s, when a new breed of more authentic crime show captured top ratings. *Hill Street Blues* and *Cagney and Lacey* represent a trend toward crime dramas dealing with tough social issues, using multilayered plots involving many characters.

The newest breed of crime dramas such as *L.A. Law* uses character-oriented plots, focusing on personal moral dilemmas. Shows like *Miami Vice,* in contrast, feature action-oriented gunfights and car chases but do not depict the older simplistic, black-and-white view of the world in which good guys stay good guys and bad guys have no redeeming qualities. As another contrast, *Murder, She Wrote* features sanitized homicide mysteries, usually set in upper-class surroundings, with a well-bred, middle-aged mystery writer as the unlikely detective.

Movies

feature-film prices for TV showing

Movies   By the 1970s, the television networks were paying increasingly astronomical prices for licenses to exhibit hit feature films. In the mid-1980s, ABC set a new record by paying $15 million for the right to air *Ghostbusters,* even though it had already played for two years in theaters and on pay cable. By 1989, however, VCRs and pay cable had devalued network showings of movies to the point that the average network licensing fee dropped to about $3 million a showing.

Nevertheless, both broadcast and cable networks still pay huge fees for the biggest hits—movie blockbusters. These costly films rarely earn back their full rental fees in advertising revenue but can be useful for clobbering the opposing broadcast networks during February, May, and November **sweep weeks**—periods when ratings services collect viewing data in all markets nationwide.

Typically, a broadcast network's rental fee for a single showing of a major theatrical feature would more than pay for producing a brand-new, modest-budget, made-for-TV-movie. Sets, props, and locations in movies made for television need not be lavish because the small screen loses so much detail. In recent seasons, the top made-for-TV movies commanded higher audience shares than any televised theatrical movie. By 1990, two-thirds of network movies were in the made-for category. They also sometimes served as pilots for prospective prime-time network series.

By the mid-1980s, the major pay-cable networks—HBO, Showtime, and Disney—plunged heavily into the financing of made-for-pay movies. Made-for-pay production contracts give cable networks **première exclusivity**—the right to air the films first. In addition, pay-cable networks invest increasingly in original drama series, musical variety shows, and nightclub comedies. Nevertheless, pay cable still relies on feature films as its bread-and-butter entertainment.

Miniseries

Miniseries   *Roots,* a 14-hour adaptation of a best seller about the evolving role of blacks in American life, ran for eight successive nights in 1977. It started a trend toward miniseries. At the time, experts doubted the drawing power of the subject matter and its ability to sustain viewership for so many hours, but *Roots* took them by surprise. The audience increased for each episode, breaking all records on the eighth night. A western miniseries, *Lonesome Dove,* scored a similar surprise success in the late 1980s. Miniseries proved able to compete well against pay-cable movies and to attract new viewers, especially upscale professionals, who may otherwise watch little entertainment television.

how many "made-for-TVs" surpass theatrical films?

origin of miniseries

Prime-Time Entertainment on PBS   Public television once occupied a unique position in a programming game dominated by commercial interests. The commercial broadcasting networks claimed they could not afford to schedule cultural and other special-interest programs. Intellectually challenging drama, nature films, science documentaries, minority-appeal shows, and fine arts such as ballet and opera became the exclusive domain of PBS, the public-television network.

This pattern changed with the development of thematic cable networks in the 1980s. As cable grew, thematic networks bought up more and more of the available cultural and documentary programs. The Discovery Channel, for example, specializes in nature films and science documentaries; Black Entertainment Network specializes in comedy and music featuring black performers; Bravo and the Arts & Entertainment cable networks specialize in fine arts, foreign drama, and films with artistic appeal.

rise of thematic cable networks

Nevertheless, public television's long-running *Masterpiece Theatre* still gives Americans a glimpse of British television drama at its best. In the 1970s, miniseries based on real events became a mainstay of *Masterpiece Theatre,* starting with *The First Churchills*. Historical fiction, drawing on novels rather than on the lives of real people, proved even more popular.

The PBS series with the widest appeal, *Upstairs, Downstairs,* detailed the doings of a turn-of-the-century Edwardian family (upstairs) and its servants (downstairs) for four successive seasons. Long after its original airing, the series continues to be popular in noncommercial reruns. In the late 1980s, Australian producers began contributing to *Masterpiece Theatre* with successes such as *A Town like Alice*. More programs from other countries were expected to get their first U.S. exposure on public television during the 1990s.

In response to criticism that too much public-television fare came from Britain, PBS developed *Great Performances,* a showcase for major American performers, playwrights, and musicians, often taped live before theater audiences. These performances helped to build U.S. audiences for opera and ballet.

Non-Prime-Time Network TV Entertainment   9.2

Although the broadcast networks put their best creative efforts into prime-time programs, daytime programs yield a higher profit margin. The extraordinarily high production costs and the smaller number of commercial minutes in prime-time shows make them less efficient revenue earners.

daytime profit margin greater than prime time

Daytime programs air about seven more commercial minutes an hour than prime-time programs—as many as sixteen commercial minutes each hour. Constant switching of soap-opera plot lines from the doings of one character to those of another accommodates interruptions that would be intolerable in most dramas.

Dayparts Network non-prime-time breaks down into the dayparts depicted in Exhibit 8.2. A characteristic type of program tends to occupy each daypart:

- Networks fill the early-morning daypart with newscasts and talk, weekends with sports, both discussed later in this chapter.
- Soaps, games, and talk shows dominate daytime network television just as they once dominated daytime network radio.
- The most important afternoon hour on broadcast network television starts at 3:00 P.M., when daytime viewing reaches its highest level. At that hour, young children returning from school swell the stay-at-home audience. Network revenues depend heavily on the programs scheduled at that hour.
- Late-night fare consists mostly of talk and comedy/variety programs.

why daytime serial dramas are called "soap operas"

Soap Operas In the early days of radio, soap companies often sponsored daytime serial dramas whose broad histrionics earned them the nickname "soap operas." This genre is a classic case of the frugal use of program resources. Notorious for their snail-like pace, soaps (as they came to be called)

EXHIBIT 9.1   *Generations:* Soap Opera in a New Vein

Although *Generations* uses the endless plot lines, the dramatic closeups, and the pregnant pauses of the usual soap opera, it differs from most soaps not only in its racial balance but also in using less heavy-handed music and tackling unromantic topics. Episodes have focused on such concerns as getting better grades and preparing for a first job, problems more likely to turn up in situation comedies than in soaps. *Generations* targets the young and the new soap viewers, especially those of high school and college age.

Source: Photo from NBC, Inc.

use every tactic of delay to drag out the action of each episode. They minimize scenery costs, relying heavily on head shots of the actors in emotion-laden one-on-one dialogue.

However, contemporary soaps respond to changing public tastes. They sometimes have story lines based on once-taboo subjects such as drug addiction, social diseases, and family violence. Women and members of minority groups began appearing in more varied roles by the mid-1970s. In 1989, NBC began *Generations,* a trailblazing soap featuring close relations between a black family and a white family. Exhibit 9.1 gives more details.

Changes in audience composition encouraged soap-opera writers to deal with controversial topics and new social roles. First *General Hospital* and then *The Young and the Restless* stimulated a faddish interest on the part of younger viewers, including males, during the 1980s. ABC launched the promotion *My Time for Me* during the summer of 1988 to lure young viewers during the school vacation. College and high-school students prefer soaps and sports to the prime-time hits.

Soap operas have highly successful counterparts on ethnic and foreign-language cable networks. The two competing U.S. Spanish-language cable/broadcast networks, Univisión and Telemundo, feature imported *telenovelas.* These enormously popular soap operas reach tens of millions of viewers throughout the Hispanic world. In contrast to American soaps, which endure for decades, *telenovelas* burn themselves out in a few months. Though primarily entertainment, they often also carry educational messages, typically promoting socially approved conduct and family values.

Game Shows   Another classic parsimonious format, audience-participation game shows, became a staple of network radio more than a half-century ago. One of the cheapest formats, the game show costs little in time, talent, effort, and money once a winning formula has been devised and a winning emcee selected. Talent expenses are limited to the host's salary and, in some cases, fees for show-business personalities, who usually work at minimum union scale because of the publicity value of game-show appearances.

Both networks and producers profit from the enhanced commercial content of game shows. The giveaway format justifies supplementing the normal daytime limit of 16 minutes or so of advertising spots with additional **plugs**— short paid-for announcements on behalf of advertisers who donate prizes and other services such as transportation and wardrobe items. The prizes come free of charge from advertisers, who write them off as business expenses.

The top game show of the 1980s, *Wheel of Fortune,* benefits both from the suspense element of the wheel's unpredictable stopping places and from the winning talent combination of emcee Pat Sajack and his assistant, Vanna White. She won celebrity status for a unique talent—that of "letter turner." As she herself candidly admits, her primary role is simply to look beautiful while turning blocks on a board displaying the letters that contestants choose in their efforts to complete the words of a phrase or title.

Most games run the half-hour length favored by the syndication market (that length fits into the access time slot and enables flexible scheduling). The broadcast networks schedule game shows in the late morning. Basic cable networks such as WTBS and USA Network usually counterprogram them with off-network situation comedies. Cable then turns this formula around, counterprogramming the broadcast networks' afternoon soaps with syndicated first-run game shows or movies. In addition, affiliates typically purchase first-run game shows to schedule in access time.

Magazine Shows   In the 1950s, programmers began extending network television into hitherto unprogrammed early-morning and late-evening hours, a radical move at the time. In those days, as a chronicler of the period wrote, "Morning television was available here and there, but watching it was a taboo. . . . It was acceptable to listen to morning radio, but like sex and alcohol, television was deemed proper only after sundown" (Metz, 1977: 33). For these innovative shows, NBC developed the **magazine format**—a medley of short features bound together by a personable host or group of hosts. *Today,* NBC's pioneer early-morning magazine show, started in 1952.

Throughout the 1980s, the *Today* show shared the 7:00 A.M. to 9:00 A.M. morning spotlight with the *CBS Morning News* (in various guises) and ABC's successful *Good Morning America. CBS Morning News* counterprogrammed by sticking closer than its competitors to hard news in a traditional news format.

Talk Shows   Closely related to the magazine shows, the talk show resembles an essay more than it resembles a magazine. It emphasizes the talker's personality, which colors the interviews and other segments of the show. NBC's *Tonight,* a late talk-show companion to the morning magazine show, started in 1954 as a showcase for the comic talents of Steve Allen. After a series of other hosts, including Jack Paar, Johnny Carson took over in 1962. Carson became the perennial leader in late-night ratings. He was not seriously challenged for two decades. Then David Letterman and later Arsenio Hall began to gain ground, partly by virtue of attracting younger late-night viewers.

specialized talk shows
of cable TV

Talk shows fill a lot of time on cable television networks. Lifetime, for example, specializes in talk programs, carrying a dozen or so on health, consumer services, and the like. On Sundays, Lifetime devotes its schedule entirely to medical programs, both talk/interviews and documentaries, aimed at physicians and other medical practitioners. In addition to *Larry King Live,* CNN regularly schedules talk shows on money management, as well as news interviews and discussions. Religious networks rely heavily on inspirational talk programs, sports channels on sports talk segments.

Music   Except for *American Bandstand,* which was one of the first television hits, the visual medium paid little attention to contemporary popular music. That changed in 1981 with the formation of Music Television (MTV) as a basic cable network. MTV quickly became a 24-hour rock-video powerhouse.

MTV targets teens and young adults aged 14 to 24. A co-owned network, Video Hits One, targets adults aged 25 to 49.

Music videos are visual accompaniments to popular songs. They originated as promotional gimmicks to boost the sale of recordings. On MTV they became a television genre in their own right. As promotional tools, videos came free of charge to stations and networks. But MTV changed the ground rules in 1984 by *paying* for Michael Jackson's much-publicized *Thriller* video, bartering with the record company for exclusive rights to air the Jackson video. This precedent demolished music videos as a source of free program material.

MTV's success had wide ramifications. As one commentator put it,

> the fast pace and kaleidoscopic style of music video has ricocheted across popular culture, changing the way people listen to music and leaving its frenetic mark on movies, television, fashion, advertising and even TV news. (Pareles, 1989)

Music videos had another unexpected side effect: they tend to undermine the impact of commercials on other programs. Teenage television viewers use their remote controls to jump to MTV when the program they are watching reaches a commercial break. A music video lasts just about the right length to bridge a commercial "pod" in the temporarily abandoned program.

MTV as refuge from commercials

Home Shopping   Not all viewers find commercials boring, at least those that appear on home shopping networks. The cable Home Shopping Network and its several broadcast clones market consumer items such as clothing, jewelry, home appliances, and novelty ware, claiming that bulk purchasing and low overhead cost enable drastically reduced prices compared to in-store prices. A cable system carrying a shopping network receives a percentage of each sale consumated in its service area.

Such nonstop commercialism represents a radical break with the broadcasting tradition. The pre-deregulation FCC enforced an arm's-length relationship between programs and advertising by penalizing stations for program-length commercials—programs that so interwove commercial and noncommercial content that audiences could not tell one from the other. The FCC reasoned that full-time advertising violated the public interest by displacing normal program functions.

recurrent theme: program-length commercials

Cable systems, however, can devote one or more channels exclusively to program-length commercials without denying subscribers the normal program services available on their other channels. Even some broadcast stations, freed by deregulation from this traditional restraint, schedule syndicated home shopping programs.

Network TV Sports   9.3

For enthusiasts, sports give television and radio ideal subjects: real-life events that occur on predictable schedules but nevertheless are full of suspense.

Professional football and Major League baseball attract about a third of the audience. The numbers of viewers for other sports fall off rapidly. For the general audience, comedy and drama have wider appeal. Super Bowl football and World Series baseball, however, rank among the all-time hit programs. These exceptional events have elements of pageantry that appeal to a broad audience.

unique demographics of sports audiences

Network television strategists value sports programs mainly because they appeal to middle-class males, a demographic group not well reached by most other programs. The ability of sports to capture such elusive consumers justifies charging higher-than-normal advertising rates for commercials on sports programs.

Evolution of Network Sports   In the late 1960s, ABC's search for differentiation from its rival networks led to an all-out emphasis on sports. ABC had pioneered the weekend sports anthology genre with its long-lived *Wide World of Sports* in 1961. By combining highlights of several sports events into a single program, the anthology genre avoids boring audiences with over-long coverage of minor sports or games that have only regional appeal. ABC also introduced such novelties as instant replay, the controversial commentary of Howard Cosell, *Monday Night Football* (starting in 1970), and extensive Olympic coverage. A decade after ABC introduced the genre, the Nashville Network adapted the sports anthology for its country-music cable audience, originating such shows as *American Sports Cavalcade*. By 1990, the combined broadcast/cable rights payments for on-the-spot sports events exceeded a billion dollars annually.

origin of sports anthology genre

In the meantime, however, both professional and college football ratings, once a sure thing, began to decline. Sports fans increasingly divided their attention among dozens of televised sports events. Typically, national broadcast networks now carry professional football games and the end-of-season play-offs and championship games in other sports, leaving regular-season events to cable networks and local stations.

Two networks responded to their declining sports audience by purchasing stock in cable networks. Cable ownership gave them additional outlets for their sports programs. In 1984 ABC bought the outstanding shares of ESPN (originally Entertainment and Sports Program Network), an all-sports basic cable network. This 24-hour cable network carries first-rank sports events, including NFL football and Major League baseball. It furnishes full-length coverage of events that ABC cannot schedule in their entirety. This kind of broadcast/cable network pairing enhances bidding power for the rights to sports events.

Following the ABC/ESPN success, in 1989 NBC also moved into basic cable to create supplementary sports and news outlets. It bought Tempo TV and SportsChannel America (jointly with Cablevision). SportsChannel America introduced high-school sports to national television in 1990, an innovative step that expands the pool of televisable sports events.

CBS surprised the television industry by spending more than $1 billion on Major League baseball rights for the early 1990s and $243 million for the 1992 Winter Olympics. CBS had not carried baseball for decades and last televised an Olympic competition in 1960. From 1990 to 1993, CBS planned to televise 12 regular-season Major League baseball games, the All-Star Game, both league championship series, and the World Series. CBS protected its position by demanding exclusive rights to baseball on weekends and most weeknights, prohibiting cable networks, superstations, and local broadcast services from competing for the baseball viewer. Carrying these events would give the CBS network the prestigious sports image previously held first by ABC and then by NBC. Exhibit 9.2 shows how the network sports picture has changed.

Mega-events in the sporting world attract adult audiences that otherwise view little television. The Olympic Games, for example, capture millions of light television viewers. The networks now pay far more for the Olympics than they can recoup in advertising revenues, counting on them to enhance their worldwide images, to keep the premier events off cable and competing broadcast outlets, and to promote other programs. Events such as the World Series and the Super Bowl serve the same functions, especially because they

sports mega-events attract new viewers

EXHIBIT 9.2 Trends in Broadcast TV Network Sports Coverage

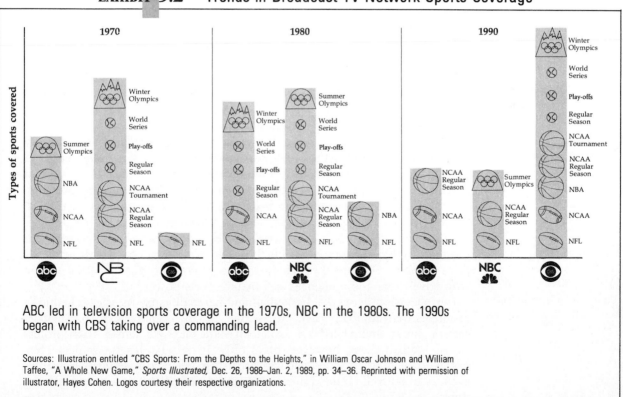

ABC led in television sports coverage in the 1970s, NBC in the 1980s. The 1990s began with CBS taking over a commanding lead.

Sources: Illustration entitled "CBS Sports: From the Depths to the Heights," in William Oscar Johnson and William Taffee, "A Whole New Game," *Sports Illustrated,* Dec. 26, 1988–Jan. 2, 1989, pp. 34–36. Reprinted with permission of illustrator, Hayes Cohen. Logos courtesy their respective organizations.

normally occur just as the broadcast networks add new shows to their fall and winter line-ups.

Cable and PPV Sports

Increases in rights charges for sports events forced the gradual emigration of many outstanding sports events to pay cable, which can afford the high costs. Despite its relatively small subscribership, HBO, for example, receives stable, predictable revenue that handily covers the costs of sports rights.

Events such as championship boxing and wrestling have strong appeal for relatively small but intensely devoted and willing-to-pay audiences. Such events can be profitably scheduled on national pay-per-view (PPV) television. PPV programs are seen mostly by means of addressable cable technology in homes, bars, and hotels.

future of PPV

Special sports events, particularly horse and car races, are expected to move increasingly to pay-per-view in the 1990s. Over half of U.S. homes had cable service in 1990, but only about one-third had pay cable. Only about one-fifth of homes could receive PPV programs. The number of PPV homes will rise, but some homes will never have cable service or backyard dishes. It is unlikely that most people will have home access to PPV during the 1990s. It remains to be seen whether direct-broadcast satellite (DBS) services, for which ambitious plans exist, will alter this expectation.

Scheduling Sports

The seasonal nature of sports events and the limited control that stations and networks have over their timing give rise to scheduling complications. ABC made a daring innovation in 1970 when it started scheduling *Monday Night Football* in network prime time. This scheduling risked devoting a long stretch of extremely valuable time to a single program with only selective audience appeal. Moreover, once the football season ended, replacement programs had to be found.

With the ABC Monday night exception, all three broadcast networks try to keep sports out of prime time. Regular-season sports generally get lower ratings than entertainment programs in prime time but capture the largest audiences on weekends. Football's weekend scheduling offers no problem. College football games appear on Saturdays. Professional football appears on Sundays on two networks, which alternate coverage of the two leagues.

In the late 1980s, ESPN also carried a weekend package of late-season NFL games and college games, generally those the commercial broadcast networks did not want. Gaining the rights to these games enhanced ESPN's stature with advertisers and audiences as a major sports power.

baseball & basketball harder to schedule than football

For television networks, basketball and baseball cause messier scheduling problems than football. Each professional baseball team plays 162 regular-season games, and each NBA basketball team plays 82 games. Each professional football team, however, plays only 16 regular league games. Thus professional football lends itself to broadcast television-network schedules because of both the limited number of games played and convenient playing times.

However, a few regular-season baseball games appear on the broadcast networks. ABC and NBC carried Major League games mostly on Monday nights and weekends in the late 1980s, though they generated less revenue than the rights cost. Nonetheless, CBS picked up Major League baseball rights for 1990–1993. Professional NBA and NCAA college basketball play-offs and championships appear on the broadcast networks on weeknights during the spring. Otherwise, basketball is seen mostly on cable networks.

Issues in Sports Broadcasting   Television has increased the popularity of sports and opened new opportunities for professional sports careers. The downside, however, is that the enormous fees exacted for television rights have brought up troubling ethical issues:

- Astronomical player salaries, induced by television stardom, invite searching press attention into attendant scandals.
- The millions of dollars in television rights fees that go to colleges have heightened the temptation to commercialize recruiting, to tolerate low graduation rates among players, and to manipulate college and NCAA rules.
- Television influences event scheduling and even how some games are played. Stations and networks sometimes try to overcome the unpredictability of sports events by staging them expressly for television—a practice that is innocent enough when the event is clearly labeled as staged, less innocent when the manipulation is concealed.
- Over the protests of fans, East Coast games are played under lights in order to maximize audiences on Pacific time in the West. Also controversial is the delay of college basketball start times to 9:30 P.M. so that ESPN can carry double-header games on weekends. Such late starts mean that players and student fans reach their dorms as late as 2 or 3 A.M.
- Referees call arbitrary time-outs about every 10 minutes to accommodate advertising spots with football and basketball games. Such artificial breaks interrupt a team's momentum and undermine coaching strategies.
- Teams and sports associations often insist on controlling the hiring of play-by-play and color announcers. Critics regard such control as an illegal surrender of broadcaster responsibility for programs.
- Critics deplore beer sponsorship of televised college games, which inappropriately links the consumption of alcoholic beverages with the enjoyment of sports by underage college students.

Children's Network TV Programs   9.4

Most television programs fall into recognized genres: situation comedies, movies, soap operas, game shows, sports. The children's program category, however, encompasses virtually all genres. Though cartoons dominate the children's category, most adult programs have their counterparts in children's programs.

Commercial Broadcasting　Each commercial broadcast network programs six or seven hours of children's television weekly, mostly on Saturday mornings and mostly consisting of animated cartoons. More than 4 million children watch the three networks regularly on Saturday mornings.

Children's programs earn less than 10 percent of broadcast television's advertising revenues, but they run at times that might otherwise go unsold. Consequently, the networks value the Saturday-morning child audience highly. They even fine-tune the children's program line-up in accordance with ratings just as they fine-tune prime-time shows.

program-length
commercials for kids

Toy, candy, and cereal manufacturers support most commercial children's programs. Ice cream, soda pop, chewing gum, snacks, fast food, movies, video games, record companies, and bicycle manufacturers—all market directly to children on television. Many syndicated children's shows essentially consist of program-length commercials. When companies such as Mattel, Hasbro, and Tonka originate a line of toys, they usually sponsor television series featuring the toys. Examples of recent commercial-laden series are *California Raisins* and *Teenage Mutant Ninja Turtles.*

Cable TV　Nickelodeon, Viacom's acclaimed cable network for children, originates several weekly hours of cable-specific, high-quality children's programming. The programs avoid violence as entertainment and present a broad range of role models. Nickelodeon's total of 13 hours a day of children's programs targets young children in the mornings and teens in the late afternoons.

Long-running favorites on Nickelodeon include *Mr. Wizard, Against the Odds,* and *You Can't Do That on Television.* In addition to regular series and movies, Nickelodeon imitates adult special programs with specials such as *Pop Warner's Football Superbowl,* highlighting the annual high-school football championships.

Cloning adult programs at a level appealing to children has proved popular with Nickelodeon's viewers, as have reruns of *Lassie* and *Dennis the Menace.* Its average audience amounts to a quarter-million children at any one time—small compared to the 3 million or so that watch Saturday-morning broadcast network cartoons, but a significant number nevertheless. In the evenings, Nickelodeon shifts to *Nick at Nite,* which schedules mostly off-network reruns and dance shows.

USA Network also schedules programs for children, mostly syndicated cartoons or old off-network sitcoms. Discovery Channel targets older children with original adventure and science programs, including shows on technology, history, and world exploration. About a third of Discovery's schedule consists of nature programs, which draw the network's highest ratings.

On pay cable, the Disney Channel programs for children in the daytime and for the family in the evenings. This premium service draws on the large Disney-studio library of films and off-network television series from the 1950s and 1960s. It also originates several new adventure series for older children and feature films for all ages.

Public Broadcasting

In the late 1960s, all three commercial networks turned down the concept for television's most celebrated children's program—*Sesame Street.* An independent, nonprofit corporation, Children's Television Workshop (CTW), launched the series on public broadcasting in 1969.

Sesame Street appeared just as the transition from educational to public television took hold, bringing the first large audiences to PBS. It targeted disadvantaged children, previously ignored by television, helping to prepare them for reading and writing. Research proved that children who watched *Sesame Street* learned to read more quickly and easily than other children.

Sesame Street's unique achievement

For the first time, CTW brought all the technical resources of television as well as all the capabilities of educational research to bear on a children's series. The programs capitalize on children's familiarity with commercial television by simulating commercials ("This segment of *Sesame Street* has been brought to you by the letters A and L and the numbers 3 and 7 . . . ").

No series on either commercial or public television has been given as much scheduled air time as *Sesame Street.* By the 1990s, it had taken on classic status as the pre-eminent program for three- to five-year-olds. CTW recycles segments of old episodes into new episodes, taking a kind of interchangeable-parts approach to production that stretched the series into its third decade.

CTW branched out with *The Electric Company* for older children, drawing on the production methods and research strategies of *Sesame Street* but using more advanced reading concepts. In 1980 CTW began a daily science program, *3-2-1 Contact,* and later *Square One TV,* a math series for young children. As in *Sesame Street,* segments in these series can be pulled out of their original contexts and reused in later episodes.

Unfortunately, not all children have access to *Sesame Street* and other high-quality PBS programs. Public television is available to more families than cable television but still fails to reach about a quarter of American households.

Issues in Children's Television

Children have such easy access to television, they consume so much of it, and it exerts such a powerful hold on their attention that society has a special stake in the quality of the programs made especially for them.

Most countries regulate children's programs in considerable detail; some forbid advertising to children altogether. The FCC, however, while paying lip service to the importance of children's programs, has resisted attempts to regulate them, as related in Section 12.14. Advocates such as Action for Children's Television raise such issues as these:

complaints against children's TV

- The inappropriateness of much television viewed by children in terms of their needs and vulnerabilities.
- The negative impact of violent and aggressive program content.
- The absence of a wide range of suitable role models on television.
- Exploitation of children by advertisers especially by those that encourage consumption of candy and sugar-coated cereals.
- The shortage of age-specific programs, especially for very young children.

Network TV News and Public-Affairs Programs

The lofty network tradition of strictly separating news/public-affairs programs from entertainment began to erode as competition for audience attention became ever more demanding in the 1970s and 1980s. The networks reacted by trying to get more value from their heavy investment in their news divisions—more frequent news programs and more syndication of network news product to affiliate and foreign organizations.

Another reaction, deplored by critics, was to comprise the barrier separating news from entertainment. The show-biz culture invaded news, critics claim, making news increasingly superficial.

recurrent theme: show-biz vs. news

Broadcast News   Back in 1963 CBS and NBC expanded their prime-time news programs from 15 minutes to a half-hour (actually only about 22 minutes, after time for commercials and openings and closings is subtracted). The text of an entire half-hour network newscast fills less than a single page of a full-size newspaper. Nevertheless, moving to the half-hour format played a role in elevating network television to the status of the country's most widely accepted news source.

A CBS movement to expand the evening news to a full hour was defeated in 1975. CBS affiliates voted overwhelmingly against the expansion. They wanted to retain both the evening lead-off slot for their own highly profitable local newscasts and the 7:30 to 8:00 P.M. access half-hour for revenue-producing syndicated fare. CBS, unwilling to invade network prime time with news at the expense of entertainment programs, gave up the plan.

affiliates stymie hour-long commercial-network news

However, all three networks began scheduling morning news or news-magazine programs, as well as short news summaries throughout the day. In 1976 they began inserting one-minute news capsules in breaks between prime-time entertainment programs, usually consisting of about 40 seconds of news, a 10- or 15-second commercial, and 5 to 10 seconds of announcements. Their adjacency to high-rated entertainment gives news capsules and summaries on the major networks the largest audiences of any regularly scheduled news reports.

capsules capture biggest news audience

In 1979 ABC started an experimental late-night network news program, *Nightline,* featuring Ted Koppel. The experiment became a permanent half-hour at 11:30 P.M. Each evening Koppel concentrates on one or two current news stories.

In contrast to the commercial networks, PBS found its affiliates receptive to long-format news. *The MacNeil/Lehrer News Hour* has been acclaimed as one of television's best in-depth informational programs. Hosts Jim Lehrer, in Washington, and Robert MacNeil, in New York City, interview representatives of opposing views at length on significant current topics. PBS began the series as a half-hour program but expanded it to an hour in 1983.

PBS succeeds with long-format news where CBS failed

Despite critical praise, *The MacNeil/Lehrer News Hour* failed to build a large following, even by noncommercial standards. Public-television stations have trouble agreeing on an ideal schedule position for the program, which does best when played against commercial entertainment programs. To accommodate affiliate schedules, PBS relays *MacNeil/Lehrer* every half-hour over a three-hour period, allowing stations to downlink the signal whenever they choose. Individual stations also often juggle the program's start time from day to day, making it difficult for *MacNeil/Lehrer* to build its audience cumulatively over time.

Cable News Networks

Ted Turner launched Cable News Network (CNN) in 1980. With a 24-hour schedule to fill, CNN can supply in-depth reportage as well as continuous coverage of breaking news stories. Between news round-ups, CNN schedules interviews, features on managing money, the stock market, sports news, and public-affairs discussions. Its two-hour *Prime News* counterprograms entertainment on the broadcast networks from 8 to 10 P.M. Over 53 million cable-television subscribers have access to CNN.

Turner's companion news service, CNN Headline News, provides news headlines and frequent updates in continuous half-hour cycles. It resembles all-news radio with pictures. More than half of all cable systems devote an entire channel to Headline News in addition to a channel for CNN.

success of CNN

Some independent broadcast television stations use Headline News in the overnight hours as a syndicated service, carrying a half-hour, two hours, or more. In addition, CNN syndicates news footage and narrated stories to dozens of television stations for inclusion in local newscasts. It also supplies a radio-network service called CNN Radio to hundreds of radio stations.

Public Affairs Programs

News and public-affairs programs tend to overlap, but in its station license forms the FCC made a distinction, defining public affairs as

> local, state, regional, national or international issues or problems, including, but not limited to, talks, commentaries, discussions, speeches, editorials, political programs, documentaries, minidocumentaries, panels, roundtables and vignettes, and extended coverage (whether live or recorded) of public events or proceedings, such as local council meetings, congressional hearings and the like.

The commission stressed public-affairs programs because of the traditional view that broadcasters in a democracy have a special obligation to serve the needs of citizen-voters.

political role of public-affairs programs

The commercial broadcast television networks and most large stations maintain at least one weekly public-affairs discussion series, sometimes also a news documentary series, and often minidocumentaries within newscasts (especially during sweeps periods).

The most striking development in network public-affairs programs during the 1980s was the rise of *60 Minutes,* the weekly CBS magazine-format documentary series. It was one of the top-rated network programs throughout the decade. That success violated all conventional wisdom, which had said that documentaries repelled the mass audience. One reason previous documentaries had low ratings, aside from not being as well done as *60 Minutes,* is that the networks usually scheduled them in unfavorable time slots and denied them the long-term stability they needed to build an audience.

effects of PTAR on scheduling of *60 Minutes*

After years of wandering through the CBS schedule, *60 Minutes* finally achieved stability at a good hour—a by-product of the prime-time access rule, which left the Sunday 7 to 8 P.M. time slot open for nonentertainment network programs. Another factor may have been the CBS counterprogramming strategy of scheduling *60 Minutes* against children's programs and movies. Exhibit 9.3 tells more about its precedent-shattering team.

advantages of magazine format for public-affairs programs

In the 1980s, ABC's *20/20,* a magazine-format show similar to *60 Minutes,* rarely broke into the 25 top-rated programs. Nevertheless, because of its low production cost it could earn a profit with ratings in the 10s. ABC concentrates most of its public-affairs efforts on *Nightline* and its Sunday-morning public-affairs program. NBC failed to develop a successful prime-time news magazine comparable to those of CBS and ABC.

EXHIBIT 9.3   The *60 Minutes* Team

A stellar team of correspondents, originally consisting of Mike Wallace, Harry Reasoner, and Morley Safer, contributed to the *60 Minutes* success story. As a *New York Times* commentator put it

> Their gray or graying hair, their pouched and careworn countenances, the stigmata of countless jet flights, imminent deadlines, and perhaps an occasional relaxing martini, provide a welcome contrast to the Ken and Barbie dolls of television news whose journalistic skills are apt to be exhausted after they have parroted a snippet of wire service copy and asked someone whose home has just been wrecked by an earthquake, How do you feel? (Buckley, 1978)

Later, Dan Rather joined the team and still later, Ed Bradley and (for a time) Diane Sawyer improved its ethnic/gender balance. Rather left the show in the mid-1980s to anchor *CBS Evening News,* the most prestigious news position a network can offer. In 1989 Sawyer left to ABC, which gave her a multi-million-dollar five-year contract.

The *60 Minutes* team, with chief producer Don Hewitt and a staff of some seventy producers, editors, and reporters, develops about 120 segments annually, some serious, some frivolous. The magazine format allows the program to treat a great variety of subjects in segments of varying lengths. The *confrontation formula,* a Mike Wallace specialty, adds drama to investigative reports. Presenting his victims on camera with damning evidence of wrongdoing, Wallace grills them unmercifully. The victims' evasions, lies, and brazen attempts to bluff their way out of their predicaments fascinate some viewers, but others question Wallace's tactics. The tabloid TV programs of the 1980s imitated the Wallace-type confrontation to the point of turning it into a cliché.

Each of the three commercial broadcast networks schedules a public-affairs question-and-answer session with newsworthy figures on Sundays, usually around midday. NBC's *Meet the Press* started in 1947 and is the oldest continuously scheduled program on network television. CBS carries *Face the Nation* and ABC *This Week with David Brinkley*. Every politician of consequence appears on these Sunday public-affairs shows. Their remarks frequently become news on later network newscasts and in Monday newspapers.

Meet the Press: a record in program longevity

Sunday Morning—a relaxed public-affairs program—provides a vehicle for CBS's much-loved Charles Kuralt. It draws only low ratings, but the time slot suits Kuralt's leisurely, reflective, low-key style.

In the late 1980s CBS started a more ratings-conscious public-affairs series, *48 Hours.* It turns cameras on a single topic, such as a hospital, an election, or a school. Shooting over a two-day period, it tries to reveal underlying processes and issues. Its style is documentary, with minimal artistic contrivance and editing. The program typically attracts a 15 to 20 percent audience share.

Public Affairs on Cable   Cable television developed a unique public-affairs vehicle especially to cultivate a positive image for the cable industry—an image marred by frequent technical breakdowns, unanswered calls from subscribers, and charges of monopoly. The cable industry puts its best foot forward with C-SPAN (Cable Satellite Public Affairs Network)—a nonprofit corporation with the mission of originating a full, 24-hour public-affairs service.

By 1989, C-SPAN was available in more than 40 million homes, bringing live coverage of congressional floor sessions, hearings, and other informative programs. When the Senate opened its door to television, C-SPAN II came into being to carry the proceedings of the upper house and other public-affairs material. C-SPAN's two 24-hour services reach the goal that idealists always thought the electronic mass media could uniquely achieve—serious, in-depth reporting of representative government in action.

Radio Network Programs   9.6

Competition from television devastated the original radio networks as full-service program suppliers, but they survived by reducing their role to that of supplements to the radio music formats adopted by their affiliates. In the 1970s, new networks emerged, offering their own music formats. Inexpensive satellite-relay connections made this comeback possible. As of 1990, about 20 national radio networks competed for affiliates in the United States, providing predominantly news, talk, sports, or 24-hour music.

satellite role in radio-network comeback

Network News   In 1968, the ABC radio network responded imaginatively to the needs of its formula-dominated affiliates. Recognizing the central role of audience segmentation in stations' music programming, ABC designed four network services, each for a different type of audience. Each service consisted of five-minute news-and-feature segments styled to suit specific age groups and calculated to fit smoothly into the four most popular radio formats.

The success of this approach to radio networking eventually encouraged ABC to increase its specialized services to seven. For example, ABC's Rock Radio complements the style of hit rock-music stations. It targets 18- to 24-year-olds with one-minute newsbits covering the entertainment world. In contrast, ABC's Information service provides five-minute newscasts on national and international topics to fit the needs of all-news and news/talk formats. ABC gets maximum value from its relay facilities by cycling its short news feeds to its several sets of affiliates throughout each hour, using the remaining time to feed sports and features on a closed-circuit basis for later playback by the stations. Nearly 20 years passed before affiliate pressure persuaded CBS and NBC to copy ABC's innovative multiple networks.

The radio networks that are associated with television networks get the benefit of daily newscasts voiced by well-known television news personalities. Some television journalists anchor radio news bulletins such as morning-drive reports; others prerecord particular news stories for later inclusion in scheduled radio newscasts. Network radio's most popular journalist, however, is a radio veteran Paul Harvey. His radio career goes back to the early 1940s.

Talk Shows and Sports   The Mutual Broadcasting System pioneered all-night talk on network radio with *The Larry King Show*. It remains the most popular program in its genre, though shortened and repeated in the small hours to fill out the night after King's grueling all-night schedule contributed to a heart attack. Night-time talk had previously been regarded as a strictly local format, but King's success led to ABC's *Talkradio* and NBC's *TalkNet*. The all-talk format works best for AM stations in major markets.

The Mutual Broadcasting System has bought radio play-by-play rights for national football for decades. It features college games on Saturdays and professional games on Sundays, supplemented by daily sportscasts and *Wide Weekend of Sports* twice on weekends. The sports component of radio networks is sufficiently important to affiliates for CBS to pay $50 million for radio baseball rights for the early 1990s, nearly doubling the previous contract payment. In addition, the major networks supply sports specials and sports talk for block scheduling with games.

Music Networks   With the advent of inexpensive satellite relays, radio networks featuring 24-hour music formats developed in the 1970s and 1980s. Stations affiliated with them sometimes also affiliate with a second radio network for news.

The largest music networks, such as Westwood One and Satellite Music Network, each have more than a thousand radio affiliates. Perhaps the best-known show on music radio, *Casey's Top 40 with Casey Kasem,* shifted to Westwood One in 1989 after running on ABC for nearly 20 years. Kasem's countdown technique, incorporating brief stories about the artists and their music, has become a radio standard.

Commercial radio networking and syndication are likely to appear indistinguishable to listeners, but each has its own characteristic type of content, delivery means, advertising procedures, and payment practices. The major networks supply news, sports, and specials, or all-talk or all-music, relaying the programs to affiliates by satellite, accompanied by national advertising. Syndicators never supply news, concentrating instead on popular music formats and music-related features on tape. Radio networks often pay compensation to major-market affiliates, but radio syndicators usually charge for their programs.

Syndicated TV Programs 9.7

The mechanics of syndication and how stations and cable television use syndicated programs are discussed in Section 8.4. The present section focuses on the syndicated programs themselves. Most syndicated television product breaks down into three categories: off-network programs, first-run syndication programs, and theatrical films (movies). Some additional syndicated material comes from noncommercial and religious sources.

Off-Network Syndication   After having completed their contractual network runs (usually two showings), network entertainment programs revert to their owners, who then make them available for licensing to broadcast stations or cable networks as off-network syndicated programs.

Sometimes early episodes of long-running network series go into syndication while new episodes are still being produced for the network. Off-network programs are the largest syndicated category. They are highly prized because their previous exposure on networks confers recognizability and a ratings track record. An off-network series in syndication typically earns a rating about 10 points lower than it earned in its initial network appearance. On cable networks, ratings for such programs usually fall still lower.

how a program's network exposure enhances its syndication value

Specialized distributors rather than the networks themselves make off-network programs available for syndication, because the FCC forbids the networks to syndicate self-produced programs in the domestic market. This prohibition is part of the fin/syn rules, discussed in Section 12.15.

Broadcast affiliates not in the top-50 markets (and hence not subject to PTAR) use off-network shows to fill two main time periods: early fringe and access time (these dayparts are defined in Exhibit 8.3). They strip both off-network sitcoms and hour-long adventure shows in late afternoons.

First-Run Syndication   Shows in the second syndication category, first-run programs, are brand new when first sold to stations. They are produced especially for the syndication market, never having been seen on a network. Viewers can hardly distinguish the best first-run syndicated programs from network programs. For example, the daily syndicated magazine show *Entertainment Tonight* is so timely and slickly produced it could easily be taken for a network program before the closing credits appear. Indeed, programs discontinued by the networks sometimes turn up in first-run syndication. ABC canceled *Fame* when its ratings declined, but it came back as a syndicated series that mixed new (first-run) with old (off-network) episodes.

impact of PTAR on syndication

Distributors of first-run syndicated shows target the major-market affiliates, which, because of PTAR, must fill a daily high-audience hour with non-network programs. Most independents found first-run shows too expensive to strip until inexpensive first-run "reality" shows (discussed below) became available. The mass-appeal cable networks use first-run syndicated programs to compete with the broadcast networks in prime time.

Producers of first-run syndicated programs created especially for the access hour usually employ low-budget genres such as quizzes and games, interview programs, and magazine shows. Nevertheless, the reigning king of access programs, *Wheel of Fortune,* typically gets higher ratings than any competition in access time, including off-network shows.

the ongoing conflict of news vs. show-biz

A much-discussed first-run syndicated program genre emerged in the late 1980s to challenge the leading access-time shows, known variously as *reality shows, trash TV,* and *tabloid TV.* These shows have in common a pseudo-journalistic approach to real-life topics, usually items currently or recently in the news. Programs of this genre tend to cater to morbid interest in the sensational and the bizarre and to exploit scandals, sex, and violence. Their blending of entertainment and journalism appeared to be symptomatic of a broad trend toward treating news from an entertainment perspective. *A Current Affair* started the fad in 1988 and was soon followed by *Geraldo, Inside Edition,* and *Unsolved Mysteries.*

Movies   In addition to off-network and first-run programs, television syndicators offer movies, singly or in packages. They release recent hit movies to networks on the basis of "availability windows," as shown in Exhibit 8.4. Stations and cable systems get access to movies through a late window. Distributors often sell "all or none" packages—a questionable practice resembling block booking, a practice legally banned in the motion-picture industry.

block-booking of movie packages

The buyer has to accept second-rate movies in order to get the more desirable films in the group of films sold as a package. Broadcast network affiliates usually strip movies in late-night and Saturday afternoon slots. Independent stations and cable networks are more likely to schedule them in prime time and on Sundays.

Noncommercial Syndication   Syndicated product also comes from educational, government, and industrial sources. Noncommercial syndicators such as the Great Plains National Instructional Television Library in Nebraska (which funds production of classroom series for children) and the Annenberg/CPB Project (which funds prime-time adult learning series) license public-television stations to use their programs. Generally only noncommercial users can obtain the right to use them.

Government, corporate, and other producers furnish program material to commercial broadcasters and cable operators at no charge. The programs consist of training, informational, and promotional programs as well as short pseudo-news segments. Most station news directors use such free video handouts. However, the use of public-relations material in news programs raises ethical problems that are discussed in Section 11.4.

Syndicated Religion

At one time it would have seemed strange to include a section on religious broadcasting in a discussion of syndicated commercial broadcasting and cable programs. But charismatic religious broadcasters contribute materially to the revenue of the commercial electronic mass media.

They do so through a curious variation on commercial syndication practice. Instead of selling programs, televangelists buy time in which to present their own moneymaking programs. Their revenue comes from listeners and viewers. Inspirational messages generously laced with a variety of appeals for money, including the sale of religious artifacts (payments for which are disguised as "love gifts"), bring in millions of dollars.

religious syndicators buy time rather than sell programs

Most stations welcome televangelist time-buyers because they often pay for otherwise unsalable, low-viewership hours. Competitive pressures make them willing to accept the small size of televangelist audiences and the problem of delays in payment—a frequent occurrence because of the thin ice of donated revenue on which televangelists usually skate.

Televangelist syndicators can control production and mailing expenses to some extent, but they cannot shave the relentless bills from the stations from which they buy time. Reaching each donor household costs so much that the televangelists operate under tremendous pressure to maintain a continuously mounting cash flow to keep up with rising time-costs. This need helps account for the fervency of their appeals for money, accompanied by all-too-real threats of going off the air if donations fall short.

The great reach of the electronic mass media, however, enables the most effective televangelist fund raisers to pyramid donations with breathtaking ease. With so many millions of tax-free dollars pouring forth from every mail delivery, successful televangelists tend to take on commercial sidelines such as Jim Bakker's gaudy theme park, Heritage USA. Bakker's fiscal irresponsibility and high-flying lifestyle led to his downfall, as related in Exhibit 9.4. His bankruptcy left many time-sales bills unpaid and put a dent in the entire business of syndicated religion.

Radio Syndication 9.8

recorded music and news as forms of syndication

Radio depends heavily on two types of material not always thought of as syndicated—recorded music and news services. Nevertheless these program

EXHIBIT **9.4**   Trouble in Paradise

As early as 1979, rumblings could be heard from a storm brewing in the earthly paradise of the PTL's 2,300-acre Christian theme park, Heritage USA, from which Jim and Tammy Bakker were broadcasting their fund-raising talk shows. Newspaper allegations that Bakker had misappropriated charitable funds for his personal use led the FCC to question Bakker's eligibility to continue holding a television license. Bakker succeeded in stonewalling the FCC, later exulting over the air at having defeated the Devil and the FCC (he often spent hours on his program refuting "plots" to discredit his ministry).

He embarked on a building frenzy to furnish his theme park with a grandiloquent hotel, campground, mall, huge wave-making swimming pool, water slide, and much else. A master high-pressure salesman, Bakker peddled time-share rights in the park's planned housing units. Showing off model rooms, cajoling prospects with daily warnings that partnerships were almost sold out, he persuaded more than a hundred thousand "life-time partners" to mail in checks for as much as a thousand dollars each in exchange for vacation rights at Heritage USA.

Scandal erupted in mid-1987 when Bakker confessed to a sexual adventure with a woman to whom PTL had paid hush money. But this peccadillo looked insignificant among the avalanche of revelations that followed. Evidence of massive misappropriation of funds to support the Bakkers' self-indulgent lifestyle piled up; building came to a halt; contractors and commercial stations sued for unpaid bills; the Internal Revenue Service and the Justice Department investigated; Bakker resigned; the Assemblies of God church defrocked him.

Another televangelist, Jerry Falwell, tried briefly, amid charges of a takeover, to save the floundering PTL ministry. His stewardship was notable mainly for the bizarre televised scene of the normally dignified Falwell swooshing fully clothed down the Heritage USA water slide.

As the rickety PTL financial structure collapsed, a veritable holy war broke out, with a half-dozen evangelical ministers excoriating one another. Another Assemblies of God televangelist, Jimmy Swaggart, condemned Bakker, only to be tagged himself with sexual indiscretions. A hard core of devoted supporters stoutly defended the self-confessed wrongdoers, but punishment from others came swiftly. Swaggart's revenue fell by 49 percent, Jim Bakker's by 65 percent. Neither saw any inconsistency in continuing their ministries.

In 1989 Bakker, still unrepentant and convinced that a Higher Power had forgiven any mistakes, was convicted of 24 fraud and conspiracy counts, including the sale of $158 million worth of vacation accommodations, that he could not provide—just routine overbooking, like the airlines, Bakker claimed.

Shaken by the debacle, at its 1988 convention the National Religious Broadcasters' (NRB) Association voted 324 to 6 to tighten the financial integrity aspect of its ethical code. Not all the televangelists felt comfortable with rules requiring public disclosure of where the funds went and establishing boards from which their family members were excluded. By the next annual NRB meeting, some 50 members had withdrawn from the association, apparently unwilling to comply, and a large number of ministries still had not agreed to adopt the NRB code of ethics. Meanwhile the Internal Revenue Service had begun auditing a score of television ministries, questioning whether their financial dealings justified continued nontaxable charity status.

Source: Photo from UPI/Bettmann.

materials fit the *syndication* definition—expensive, centrally produced program material whose high costs are justified by distribution to many users.

Format Syndication   Radio stations that produce their own programs would be lost without recorded music and national news services. In most cases, local production is limited to record selection and disc-jockey announcements between the syndicated elements.

Even that limited degree of local input evaporates when stations buy ready-made syndicated formats. Syndicators tailor an entire broadcast day, furnishing not only preselected program material but also a wide range of advisory services. In contrast to most radio networks, which supply only news headlines, brief features, and sportscasts, format syndicators usually supply a full 24-hour schedule of music, interrupted neither by national advertising nor by news. Some beautiful-music stations remain talk-free for hours on end, but typically a local DJ announces music titles.

syndicated music formats

Format syndicators offer choices among rock-music variations, ranging from new wave to hit songs to soft album cuts, calculated to fit the major radio format classifications. Also available are country music, rap, jazz, easy-listening, and beautiful-music formats, and even classical music formats.

Syndicated Radio Features   Radio feature syndicators supply ready-made program items packaged to fit within particular formats. Stations interweave syndicated standalone features, consisting of either series or specials, with a locally or distantly produced music or news/talk format. Syndicated features range from sets of religious sermons to series of domestic budgeting hints to play-by-play sporting events. Feature syndicators also supply telephone interviews with rock and country-music celebrities, divided into one-minute segments for insertion throughout the broadcast day. They go to subscribing stations on tape or by satellite.

Weekly country and rock countdowns of hit songs are among the most popular syndicated features, especially clones of Dick Clark's long-running *Top 40 Countdown* and *Casey's Top 40 with Casey Kasem*. Stations normally schedule syndicated countdowns on weekends, filling many hours without having to pay for a local, live DJ.

Talk-radio stations vary their local sound with syndicated business, health, and other specialized reports voiced by nationally known announcers.

Production Automation   Increasingly, automation takes over former hands-on radio production tasks. The degree of live vs. automated production in music radio varies through three levels:

- In *live* programming, local DJs play the records, talk between songs, conduct contests, promote events, read or cue in commercials, and so on.
- In *live-assist* programming, automatic equipment relays a syndicated music format with breaks for local DJs to add live patter between songs.

levels of automation for syndicated music

- In *automated programming* (also called *satellite radio*), computers handle satellite-delivered music, commercials, and promotional content without the help of live DJs or other local staff.

It is possible for a single, centrally located, on-the-air disc jockey to speak for dozens of stations. The orchestrator plays a single music tape, interspersing it with commercials, weather, and announcements appropriate to each participating station's community. Microprocessors and two-way interconnection enable the orchestrator to cue in prerecorded local advertisements and regional weather at each station. Occasionally the orchestrator feigns the presence of a local DJ by injecting a chatty line or two heard by only one station's audience.

Critics object that this total automation by satellite radio eliminates localism and puts local radio personnel out of work. Its defenders claim that it enhances localism by giving the station staff more time to produce truly local material.

9.9 *Locally Produced TV Programs*

Both broadcasting and cable disappointed the hopes of many who saw them as playing a strong role in giving opportunities for local program making. The economics of program production, however, inevitably favored program centralization—networking and syndication.

Local News Production   The one program category to escape the centralizing tendency is local/regional news. Audience interest in local television newscasts escalated during the 1970s, converting news from a loss leader into a profit center. Multi-million-dollar budgets for local television news departments became commonplace in large markets, enabling stations to invest in high-tech equipment such as customized news vans like the one shown in Exhibit 9.5.

news as high budget product

Major stations developed their own investigative reporting and documentary units. Satellite technology enlarged the reach of local stations even further, minimizing time and distance constraints. By the mid-1980s, large-market stations routinely dispatched local news teams to distant places to get local angles on national news events. They send, or *backhaul,* live stories back to the home base via satellite.

News Origination by Affiliates   Most network affiliates originate an early-evening newscast and a late-fringe newscast. Affiliates' local evening news shows either lead into network news or both precede and follow it to form a "sandwich." In the Eastern and Pacific time zones, network evening news may be scheduled from as early as 5:30 P.M. to as late as 7:00 P.M. but usually starts at 6:30, preceded by local newscasts ranging from a half-hour to two hours in length.

EXHIBIT **9.5** Electronic News-Gathering Equipment

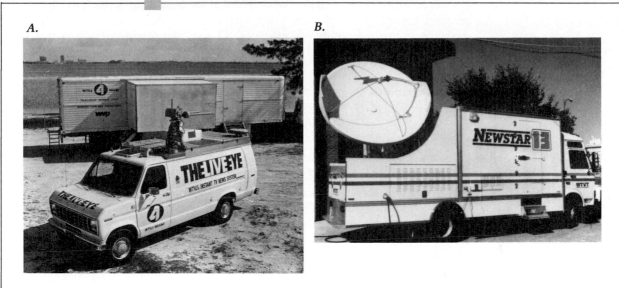

A. The unwieldy remote vehicle in the background contrasts with the compact, lightweight ENG (electronic news-gathering) van in the foreground. The machine-gun-like object atop the van is a microwave relay antenna for relaying pictures back to the studio. Microwave relays must have a line-of-sight view of the studio receiving antenna or an intermediate relay antenna. B. Satellite news gathering (SNG) greatly extends the reporter's range. A mobile Earth station is used to uplink signals to a satellite for relaying to the studio.

Sources: Photo A courtesy WTVJ–TV, Miami, FL: Photo B courtesy WTVT, Tampa, FL.

Many affiliates also schedule a half-hour or hour of noon news. About 80 percent of affiliates originate early-morning half-hour newscasts or magazine/talk shows, preceding the network morning programs. The network shows provide slots into which affiliates can insert local-news segments. The larger the market, the more time stations are likely to devote to local news.

relation between market size and amount of local news

News Origination by Independents Independent stations rarely produce an early evening newscast. They usually schedule their most popular syndicated entertainment shows against local news programs on affiliates, typically counterprogramming the affiliate evening news block with expensive off-network entertainment series to attract the non-news audience.

Many independents produce a late local newscast in the half-hour either before or after the syndicated Independent News Network (INN) 10 P.M. national/international newscast. (INN, the independent stations' equivalent of the affiliated stations' network news service, is discussed in Section 8.5.) The local news show usually follows the INN because the national news program gets bigger audiences. Thus both INN and the independent station steal a march on the network affiliates' 11 P.M. newscasts; attracting news viewers who want to go to bed before 11:30 P.M.

Station-Produced Non-News TV Programs   Aside from news, broadcast stations produce relatively few local programs. Affiliates generally schedule local public-affairs shows on weekday or Sunday mornings. During election years or at times when important local issues arise, they may increase local production, but normally they avoid scheduling local shows in the valuable time periods such as early fringe, access, or prime time. Affiliates that produce regularly scheduled local non-news/public-affairs shows usually choose a magazine/talk program for women, scheduled on weekday mornings. Non-network magazine shows, though actually syndicated, may give the appearance of local productions. In fact syndicated formats sometimes acquire local color by providing for live or recorded inserts by local personalities.

Local Cable Production   Cable television systems rarely produce local newscasts. In fact, only about a quarter of the approximately 10,000 cable systems in the United States originate local programs of any kind. Those that do offer either commercial local-origination channels, programmed by the cable operators themselves, or noncommercial public-access channels, programmed by private citizens and nonprofit institutions such as schools and municipal governments.

difference between cable access and local origination

Local-origination channels number fewer nationally than access channels. However, a trend may be emerging among a few cable systems in large markets to program a local channel full-time in the manner of a cable network or full-service television station. A large MSO-owned system has won special notice for *News 12: Long Island,* a 24-hour news and sports channel. It serves more than 70 villages and towns on Long Island with locally oriented news.

Access channels focus on informational and cultural programs. About half of all cable-access programs consist of public affairs, typically school-board meetings, city and county council sessions, hearings on community issues, and discussion or documentary programs on local political, environmental, and educational matters. Community calendars have been among cable's access-channel successes. They list local events and meetings not usually mentioned by broadcast stations.

9.10   *Local Radio Programs*

Most locally programmed radio stations use modified block scheduling, changing format slightly to suit each daypart. For example, many stations emphasize news and weather/traffic information during drive times, shifting to music at other times.

Local Radio Music Formats Most parsimonious of all broadcast formats, the radio disc-jockey show fully exploits the availability of recorded music, reducing local production costs to the lowest possible level. The format exploits the ability of a DJ to build up a loyal following and to comment on the rapidly changing popular music scene.

the DJ show as a parsimonious format

Formats based on rock music predominate, as Exhibit 9.6 shows. Radio draws more fine distinctions among types of rock than among other musical genres. Rock formats include *adult contemporary* (a broad array of popular music and golden oldies), *contemporary hit radio* (playlists restricted to about a hundred of the most recent hits), *album-oriented rock* (a mixture of the less

EXHIBIT 9.6   Radio-Station Formats by Popularity and Station Type

Format	Popularity in Terms of:		Station Types			
	No. of Stations	% of stations	AMs	FMs	Commercial	Noncommercial
Country/Western	2,421	19%	1,483	938	2,410	11
Adult contemporary	2,325	18	1,043	1,282	2,279	46
Religious/Gospel	1,054	8	643	411	809	245
CHR/Top-40	984	8	188	796	891	93
MOR	729	6	560	169	706	23
Oldies/Classic rock	695	6	473	222	683	12
Diversified	614	5	153	461	192	422
AOR	486	4	56	430	333	153
Talk	408	3	352	56	360	48
Beautiful music	403	3	91	312	372	31
News	384	3	278	106	278	106
Classical	355	3	21	334	59	296
Jazz	296	2	27	269	66	230
Big Band/Nostalgia	259	2	216	43	248	11
Educational	259	2	13	246	7	252
Spanish	237	2	176	61	220	17
Urban contemporary	193	2	86	107	176	17
Black	186	1	126	60	163	23
Agricultural	157	1	115	42	154	3
Progressive	127	1	4	123	14	113
Total Figures	12,572	100%	6,104	6,468	10,420	2,152

The station totals exceed the number on the air because, for this chart, a "format" is defined as a program type scheduled 20 or more hours per week, permitting some stations to carry more than one format.

Source: Based on data in *Broadcasting/Cable Yearbook*, 1989, p. F-120.

popular songs from popular albums and rock classics), *oldies* (hits from the 1950s and 1960s), and *urban contemporary* (a mix of rock and jazz favoring black artists). Among these subformats, adult contemporary has been the most successful.

country music second in radio-format parade

However, in the aggregate, more stations play *country music* than any other single type except rock, if all rock formats are added together. Though Exhibit 9.6 shows country/western as a single format, country music has followed rock's trend of subdividing, splitting into urban, country, country-and-western, country oldies, and other specialties. Most country music is played on commercial AM stations. *Adult contemporary* has been successful on both AM and FM stations. *Religious/gospel* radio, one of the top three formats shown in Exhibit 9.6, shows a steady shift to the AM band, forced out of FM by the more profitable rock music formats.

Easy listening and *beautiful music,* broad-appeal formats using mostly unobtrusive vocal or instrumental music, are broadest in most large radio markets. They saturate waiting rooms, elevators, department stores, and other public spaces. Syndicated easy-listening, commercial-free music services such as Muzak go to subscribers on FM subcarriers. Subscribers need specially adapted sets to receive the signals.

Classical music appears mostly on noncommercial FM stations, but a few commercial FM and AM stations have adopted the format in the largest markets. *Jazz,* though it has a devoted following, has not proved successful commercially. *Urban contemporary,* the major-market variant of rock and jazz, serves black city dwellers, whereas the *black* format mixes music and information to suit smaller, more rural markets. *Progressive,* a catch-all term for secondary cuts on popular albums mixed with avant-garde rock music in loose formats (once called "underground radio"), usually plays on noncommercial FM radio, though a few commercial stations in the largest markets have successfully exploited the format. The latest rock fad, *new wave,* has been adopted by too few stations to appear in Exhibit 9.6.

Information Radio Formats   The radio formats listed in Exhibit 9.6 include four predominantly information types: *talk, news, educational,* and *agricultural.* Collectively, these formats occur on fewer than 10 percent of radio stations. Newly developed AM formats, such as all-business and all-sports, attempt to capture fresh audiences for AM radio, but only about a quarter of radio listeners tune to AM stations. Most under-45 listeners listen to FM.

talk radio found primarily on AM stations

The most popular information format, *talk radio,* occur almost exclusively on commercial AM stations. It combines call-in and interview programs with feature material and local news. Talk content varies between the extremes of sexual innuendo and serious political or social commentary. In major markets, *shock radio* deliberately aims at outraging conservative listeners by violating common taboos and desecrating sacred cows. Shock radio's contempt for adult authority and social tradition tends to attract listeners younger than the usual talk radio audience.

Most talk programs, however, focus on controversial issues, using guest-expert interviews and call-in questions. Authors on book tours, an essential promotional ritual for mass-marketing new books, also provide a constant stream of interviewees. The two-way telephone call-in show attracts an older and generally conservative group of listeners—people who have both time and militant convictions that incline them to engage in discussions with talk-show hosts. Program directors have to be alert lest a small but highly vocal group of repeat callers, often advocates of extremist views, kill advertising interest in telephone-talk shows.

radio talk shows

During the 1980s, talk radio emerged as an important public forum in the black community, even though only a few of the 600 or so black-oriented stations have adopted the format. *Black talk* stations provide a window through which candidates for public office, community organizations, and reporters can obtain a unique perspective on black public opinion. Politicians such as Harold Washington, Chicago's first black mayor, and the Reverend Jesse Jackson, found that black talk radio gave them political input that they could not get through mainstream media.

The *all-news* format costs a lot to run yet gets only low ratings compared with successful music formats. All-news stations count on holding attention for only about 20 minutes at a time, long enough for listeners to arm themselves with the latest headlines, the time of day, weather tips, and advice about driving conditions. To succeed, this revolving-door programming needs a large audience reservoir that only major markets can supply.

Critique: Programs as Consumer Products 9.11

In this and the preceding chapter, broadcast and cable programs have been discussed largely from the industry viewpoint—as vehicles for commercial messages. This concluding section touches briefly on another perspective—that of the consumer.

Issue of Program Diversity A persistent complaint about commercial television, especially prime-time network programming, deplores its lack of diversity—the sameness of its program types, themes, plots, production styles, and sources. Networks risk so much on each program series that they take the safe route of copying successful shows again and again. Spin-offs and clones reduce prime-time entertainment essentially to sitcoms, crime dramas, and movies.

The network's homogenizing influence also affects production styles. Programs from one production company look much like those from another. Yet programmers desperately seek novelty. This seeming paradox comes from wanting to be different but not wanting to take chances.

Cable television, once hailed as the harbinger of greater program diversity, has brought only limited change. The most popular cable networks depend

cable TV: imitator of or alternative to broadcast TV?

on the same mass-appeal programs as the broadcast networks. They follow similar selection and scheduling practices, though on smaller budgets. USA Network, for example, treats dayparts much as do the broadcast networks. It schedules off-network shows such as *Miami Vice* and *Murder, She Wrote* in the evening high-viewing hours.

However, several specialized cable channels expand on subject matter formerly available only in snippets on broadcast networks. The Weather Channel, CNN and CNN Headline News, MTV, C-SPAN, and shopping services, for example, increase viewers' program choices at any hour. Also, cable networks and systems increasingly originate new material, though much is for pay channels, the ones best able to afford original production.

Programs and the Public Interest

Fundamentally, the viewer/listener perspective raises the question of whether commercial motives suffice as primary arbiters of program choice and quality. That question brings up an issue around which debate has swirled ever since broadcasting began, that of commerce vs. culture. How should society balance the sometimes conflicting claims of these two goals?

Is it enough for the industry to treat programs simply as "product"—articles of trade? Those who argue otherwise regard programs as broadly cultural. In this view, programs contribute to the intellectual, artistic, and moral quality of national life. Seen in that perspective, programs should do more than merely entice audiences to expose themselves to commercial messages.

As Chapters 8 and 9 show, programmers seek to attract large numbers of listeners/viewers of the types targeted by advertisers. This goal calls mostly for lightweight entertainment that makes minimum demands on audiences.

programs: commerce or culture?

"Wasteland" vs. "Toaster"

The best-known critique of the industry's program performance in public-interest terms came from an FCC chairperson appointed by the Kennedy administration, Newton Minow (1961–1963). In an address to the National Association of Broadcasters in 1961, Minow challenged station owners and managers to sit down and watch their own programs for a full broadcast day. They would, he assured them, find a "vast wasteland" of violence, repetitive formulas, irritating commercials, and sheer boredom (Minow, 1964: 52). The "vast wasteland" phrase caught on and became a permanent part of broadcasting lore.

Some 20 years later, a Republican-appointed FCC chairperson, Mark Fowler, pointedly refrained from talking to the industry about program quality. In his view, the FCC had no business interfering with the workings of the marketplace. He too coined a memorable descriptive phrase when, in addresses to various broadcast industry groups, he described television as "a toaster with pictures." This dismissive phrase reflected a then-dominant theory in Washington: the economic laws of supply and demand suffice to ensure that commercial television will supply suitable programs; if programs degenerate into a vast wasteland, blame not the industry but the audience.

Newton Minow exaggerated the low state of television in order to challenge the industry to look critically at its own product. Few responsible critics would seriously make such a sweeping judgment as the "vast wasteland" epithet about the entire output of commercial television. Most would concede that television sometimes rises to peaks of excellence—even though between the peaks lie broad valleys (vast wastelands?) of routine programs. How green the valleys are depends on the viewer's personal tastes.

A Question of Taste   A continuously available mass medium such as television cannot satisfy every taste all the time. *Most* of the time it must try to please *most* of the people, but not *all* of the people *all* of the time. No other medium has faced such an extraordinary demand. In meeting it, television made apparent something never before so blatantly exposed: the low common denominator of mass popular taste as contrasted with the more cultivated standards of high taste. As Daniel Boorstin, an authority on American cultural history, put it:

> Much of what we hear complained of as the "vulgarity," the emptiness, the sensationalism, of television is not a peculiar product of television at all. It is simply the translation of the subliterature onto the television screen. . . . Never before were the vulgar tastes so conspicuous and so accessible to the prophets of our high culture. Subculture—which is of course the dominant culture of a democratic society—is now probably no worse, and certainly no better, than it has ever been. But it is emphatically more visible. (Boorstin, 1978: 19)

From the standpoint of the middle ground between the extremes of programs-as-merchandise and programs-as-culture, it is unrealistic to expect programs always to rise above the lowest common denominator. As the most democratic of media, broadcasting necessarily caters to popular tastes. That mission, however, need not preclude serving minority tastes as well. One hallmark of a democracy is that though the majority prevails, minorities still have rights. Public broadcasting exists in part to compensate for the omissions of commercial broadcasting in this regard. But even public broadcasting has had to increase its popular appeal in order to attract program underwriters and to broaden its subscriber base. It has so far lacked the financial support it needs to offer an adequate alternative program service.

Promoters of the marketplace philosophy predicted that liberalizing the rules governing broadcasting and making things easy for new services such as cable television would automatically bring diversity and enhance quality. Deregulation did indeed give viewers more choices, but at an added price. Those who can afford cable or a satellite dish (more than half of homes by the late 1980s) can browse through scores of channels to find programs of interest. Owners of home video recorders (in two-thirds of homes) can browse through tape inventories of video stores and also use time-shifting to escape the tyranny of broadcast/cable schedules.

TV's target: the lowest common denominator of popular taste

deregulation and program quality

So far, however, too many of the new options have turned out to be merely repetitions of the old options. With few exceptions, they have failed to make the "wasteland" bloom. After all, cable and other optional delivery methods respond to the same marketplace imperatives that drive commercial broadcasting. Significantly, the shining exception in the public-affairs field, the program service that opens a window on government in action—C-SPAN—does not operate as a self-supporting commercial venture. The cable industry subsidizes C-SPAN as a public-relations showcase of the good things television can do—when *not* constrained by the need to make money.

C-SPAN realizes a cable ideal but is no commercial venture

Popular Taste vs. Bad Taste   Although commercial broadcasters have always catered to *popular* taste, for most of their history they generally refrained from catering to the appetite for downright *bad* taste in programs. In its now-abandoned Television Code, the National Association of Broadcasters emphasized the role of television as a *family* medium, warning that "great care must be exercised to be sure that treatment and presentation are made in good faith and not for the purpose of sensationalism or to shock or exploit the audience or appeal to prurient interests or morbid curiosity" (NAB, 1978: 2).

TV as a family medium

That kind of sensitivity, along with the Television Code, has fallen victim to changing times. In fact, the code's statement of what not to do accurately describes exactly what succeeded on the air in the late 1980s. "'Raunch' on a Roll," proclaimed a headline in a trade journal over a story about the rise of slobcoms—sitcoms that "stretch the bounds of what's acceptable" (*Broadcasting*, 1988). The Fox network's *Married . . . with Children* occasioned the article. Its plots dealt with such topics as premenstrual syndrome, treated with outrageously vulgar humor. Despite some complaints, such programs drew high ratings. In the absence of any other criterion of evaluation, high ratings assured widespread imitation.

One can speculate on influences that may have had a hand in bringing about this shift in program standards. Among the many possible influences might be these:

themes to explore: influences on program standards

- The FCC's laissez-faire policy during the 1980s, which encouraged broadcasters to test the limits of public tolerance.
- Abandonment of the NAB codes, implying to some that anything goes.
- Heightened competition, encouraged in part by FCC policies, requiring ever more strenuous efforts to capture audience attention.
- The impact of cable television, which has never been constrained either by legislated public-interest standards or by a tradition of self-restraint.
- Corporate mergers that replaced experienced broadcast and cable executives with cost-conscious corporate managers saddled with huge debts.
- Social changes in the direction of more open and permissive behavior, marked especially by violence, sex, and rebellion against conventional standards.

As the pendulum eventually swings in the opposite direction, reversing some of these trends, observers of broadcasting in America will be interested to find out whether deregulated broadcasters and cable operators regain their ability to satisfy popular taste without also pandering to bad taste.

Program Ratings

Ratings research is often dismissed by people who say, "*I've* never been asked *my* opinion by a rating company"—as though rating firms should consult every potential listener/viewer and reflect each person's unique opinion.

The fact is, well-established, scientifically authentic sampling techniques make it unnecessary to poll every one of the over 240 million potential respondents. The chances are good that an individual listener/viewer could spend a lifetime without ever being chosen as part of a sample. And ratings make no pretense of plumbing personal opinions. They simply estimate what percentage of a population sample tuned in to which of the relatively few mass-appeal programs available at any one time (many specialized cable channels attract too few viewers to be measurable by means of sampling).

10.1 *Rule by Ratings*

Many subjects discussed in previous chapters—dayparts, audience flow, program-scheduling strategies, station and network economics, advertising rates—presume knowledge of audience size, composition, and habits. This chapter discusses how the industry obtains such essential information, on which so many key decisions depend.

Researchers collect many types of information about programs and their audiences, but by far the most influential datum is the **program rating.** This all-important number is an estimate of the number of households (sometimes people) that tuned to a program. Ratings reports—called **books** in the trade—contain a vast amount of data in addition to the ratings numbers, but in the final analysis ratings count most. So heavily do they count that an average change of a single point in the rating of a prime-time network series can be worth millions of dollars a year in lost or gained revenue. In the electronic mass media family, ratings rule the roost.

Guaranteed Audiences Broadcast networks rely so completely on ratings that they often supplement advertising sales with ratings guarantees. If commercials fail to reach the numbers and types of people promised, as reflected in ratings reports, the advertiser gets a rebate in the form of enough free commercials **(make-goods)** to compensate for the shortfall. ABC caused some consternation in the industry in 1990 when it confessed insufficient confidence in current people-meter ratings to make such promises. ABC proposed to base future guarantees on PUT (persons using television) ratings averaged over a three-year period.

trend toward PUT
guarantees

Measuring Difficulty Newspaper publishers can count the number of issues sold, and theater owners can count the number of tickets bought. Broadcasting, however, produces no tangible objects that can be readily counted to measure audience size. Programs are "published" in a continuous flow. Audiences do not sit in a specific, ticketed seat but come and go at will. The intangibility of listening/viewing makes audience research both especially vital and especially difficult.

The nearest approach to counting newspaper sales or box-office receipts is to count **tuning behavior**—the acts of turning on a receiving set, selecting a particular channel or program, switching to other channels, and turning off the set at the close of the listening/watching session. The ambiguities inherent in this way of measuring program consumption are obvious, but researchers have not been able to come up with a better method for large-scale, continuous audience measurement.

The Ratings Business 10.2

No one would have much confidence in audience research conducted directly by the media themselves. The conflict of interest would be too obvious. Therefore, broadcasting and cable interests hire firms that make a business of market research. The task is not easy.

Ratings Firms The Arbitron Company and A. C. Nielsen dominate the ratings business. The Nielsen name has become so emblematic of national television-audience measurement that people speak of "the Nielsens," meaning "the ratings." The two companies have been locked in methodological debate and commercial competition for decades. Both issue reports on television ratings, but only Arbitron covers both television and radio. Some 130 other firms offer more specialized research services. A notable example is Birch Radio, a major source of radio-audience measurements.

Nielsen and Arbitron

Arbitron and Nielsen get their revenues mainly from subscriptions bought by stations, networks, advertising agencies, and others. Nearly all television stations subscribe to at least one of these two firms' reports. Many radio stations and advertisers depend on Birch reports. Major advertising agencies are believed to spend upward of a million dollars a year on ratings-book subscriptions.

Types of Ratings Ratings fall into types according to coverage (local vs. national), and medium (radio vs. television). Television ratings can be further subdivided according to method of delivery (over-the-air broadcast vs. cable).

Local ratings measure the audiences of individual stations (and to a limited extent cable systems) in each of the nation's 200-plus local markets (the *market* concept is defined in Section 10.6 later in this chapter). Local ratings reflect the relative position of each radio and television station within its own market. These reports form the chief selling tool used by station sales staffs, as described in Section 6.9.

National ratings, the ones most often quoted in the newspapers, estimate the audiences for programs on the major networks. Reports are also issued on audiences for nationally syndicated programs.

Radio-rating methods differ considerably from television-rating methods, primarily because television can pay more than radio and there are 7 times as many radio stations and 4 times as many national radio networks as there are television stations and networks. Division of the radio audience into so many small segments complicates the problem for researchers. One result of these differences is that television reports come out more frequently than radio reports.

why TV and radio ratings methods differ

Procedures   It would cost far too much to collect data for ratings in local markets continuously, day after day. Instead, researchers gather data only during **ratings periods**—short spurts of measurement activity lasting a few weeks at a time. The number of ratings periods for any particular market depends on its size—the larger the market, the more frequent are the ratings periods.

However, during the few special ratings periods called **sweeps,** the ratings firms survey *all* local markets at the same time. Radio sweeps occur twice yearly, television sweeps four times. These comprehensive surveys allow detailed comparisons on a national scale—essential for networks, national syndicators, and major advertisers. Arbitron and Nielsen issue daily rough-estimate television-network ratings based on viewing in only a few cities (the *overnights,* discussed later in this section).

Radio Ratings   Arbitron and Birch Radio provide market-by-market radio ratings reports.

how often ratings companies survey markets

Arbitron covers 260 radio markets in a 12-week spring sweep. In the fall it remeasures 130 of them, and in summer and winter it remeasures the 79 largest cities. Thus Arbitron surveys the largest radio markets four times a year, the smallest only once. Exhibit 10.1 shows an excerpt from one of Arbitron's four annual radio reports.

Birch Radio has successfully challenged Arbitron as the main source of radio-station ratings. It covers 250 radio markets, varying the frequency of its rating periods according to market size. Birch issues quarterly and monthly reports on the 109 largest markets.

RADAR: only network radio rater

In addition, RADAR (Radio's All-Dimension Audience Research), a cooperative run by the radio networks, obtains the only national radio-network ratings. RADAR contracts with Statistical Research Inc. to make twice yearly reports on network radio audiences.

Television Ratings   Both Arbitron and Nielsen produce local-market television ratings. Arbitron sweeps 209 television markets four times a year and surveys the larger markets more frequently. Nielson does the same for 219 markets to produce its Nielsen Station Index (NSI).

NSI and NTI "books" report TV ratings

Television networks demand more frequent reports on national audiences. Nielsen issues the only television-network ratings (which accounts for the substitution of the world *Nielsen's* for *ratings* mentioned previously). The Nielsen Television Index (NTI) comes out every two weeks. It is based on a sample of about 4,000 households strategically chosen to represent the various regions of the United States. An excerpt from an NTI report is shown in Exhibit 10.2.

Even faster results are obtained from **overnights**—reports based on data collected in a few major markets. Sophisticated computerized systems report in the morning how the previous evening's prime-time network shows rated in those cities. The overnights give only a rough-and-ready estimate because

EXHIBIT 10.1   Local-Market Radio Ratings Report

Specific Audience
MONDAY-FRIDAY   6AM-10AM

			Persons 12+	Persons 18+	Men 18+	Men 18-24	Men 25-34	Men 35-44	Men 45-54	Men 55-64	Women 18+	Women 18-24	Women 25-34	Women 35-44	Women 45-54	Women 55-64	Teens 12-17
WAQI																	
MET	AQH	PERSONS	477	475	166	3	8	33	26	48	309	6	6	57	86	64	2
MET	AQH	RATING	1.8	2.0	1.5	.2	.3	1.5	1.7	3.5	2.4	.4	.2	2.5	5.1	3.7	.1
MET	AQH	SHARE	6.8	7.1	5.3	1.0	1.2	4.6	5.5	12.7	8.6	1.8	.9	8.5	16.2	12.9	.8
MET	CUME	PERSONS	1392	1384	556	8	27	145	68	150	828	19	33	181	199	199	8
MET	CUME	RATING	5.3	5.7	4.9	.6	1.2	6.7	4.4	10.9	6.3	1.4	1.4	7.9	11.8	11.4	.4
TSA	AQH	PERSONS	479	477	168	3	8	33	26	49	309	6	6	57	86	64	2
TSA	CUME	PERSONS	1418	1410	577	8	27	145	68	157	833	19	33	181	204	199	8
+WAQI-FM																	
WTHM-FM																	
MET	AQH	PERSONS	23	23	13	4		5		1	10	3		2	3	2	
MET	AQH	RATING	.1	.1	.1	.3		.2		.1	.1	.2		.1	.2	.1	
MET	AQH	SHARE	.3	.3	.4	1.3		.7		.3	.3	.9		.3	.6	.4	
MET	CUME	PERSONS	120	120	60	8		34		9	60	13		27	10	10	
MET	CUME	RATING	.5	.5	.5	.6		1.6		.7	.5	1.0		1.2	.6	.6	
TSA	AQH	PERSONS	23	23	13	4		5		1	10	3		2	3	2	
TSA	CUME	PERSONS	120	120	60	8		34		9	60	13		27	10	10	
WAXY																	
MET	AQH	PERSONS	206	204	83	4	30	43	4		121	16	42	14	31	9	2
MET	AQH	RATING	.8	.8	.7	.3	1.3	2.0	.3	.1	.9	1.2	1.7	.6	1.8	.5	.1
MET	AQH	SHARE	3.0	3.0	2.7	1.3	4.4	6.0	.8	.3	3.4	4.8	6.1	2.1	5.8	1.8	.8
MET	CUME	PERSONS	1213	1176	468	66	156	170	31	18	708	125	293	152	80	19	37
MET	CUME	RATING	4.6	4.8	4.2	5.0	6.7	7.8	2.0	1.3	5.4	9.3	12.1	6.6	4.7	1.1	1.8
TSA	AQH	PERSONS	235	232	95	4	40	44	5	1	137	17	43	20	39	9	3
TSA	CUME	PERSONS	1509	1433	618	66	285	185	37	18	815	137	321	195	90	19	76
WHQT																	
MET	AQH	PERSONS	265	217	85	37	26	11	2	7	132	49	58	14	11		48
MET	AQH	RATING	1.0	.9	.8	2.8	1.1	.5	.1	.5	1.0	3.6	2.4	.6	.7		2.3
MET	AQH	SHARE	3.8	3.2	2.7	12.1	3.8	1.5	.4	1.8	3.7	14.8	8.4	2.1	2.1		18.8
MET	CUME	PERSONS	1864	1355	629	196	240	105	28	32	726	355	204	101	55		509
MET	CUME	RATING	7.0	5.6	5.6	14.8	10.3	4.8	1.8	2.3	5.5	26.4	8.4	4.4	3.3		24.2
TSA	AQH	PERSONS	310	248	96	43	27	11	6	7	152	57	60	23	11	1	62
TSA	CUME	PERSONS	2212	1593	709	244	261	105	33	32	884	403	239	144	75	12	619

Footnote Symbols: * Audience estimates adjusted for actual broadcast schedule. + Station(s) changed call letters since the prior survey - see Page 5B.
Both of the previous footnotes apply.

ARBITRON RATINGS
MIAMI-FT. LAUDERDALE-HOLLYWOOD   166   FALL 1988

Part of a page in an Arbitron local-market radio report covering the early-morning drive time.

MET AQH = Metropolitan average quarter-hour.
MET CUME = Cumulative listening in metro area (see Exhibit 10.6).
TSA AQH = Total survey area average quarter-hour.

Source: Copyright © 1989 The Arbitron Company. Used by permission.

they use only small samples in a limited number of markets. However, Nielsen planned to expand its local-market measurements to cover 22 major cities. It issues daily on-line overnight reports and weekly printed summaries, as shown in Exhibit 10.4.

Rating syndicated television programs poses special research problems. Although aired nationally, syndicated shows are seen in various markets at various times. Nevertheless, program providers, advertisers, their agencies, and stations all need comparative data on a national scale. Using data from their local-market ratings reports, both Arbitron and Nielsen derive regular

how syndicated programs are rated

EXHIBIT **10.2** National TV Ratings Report

A-6 *Nielsen* NATIONAL TV AUDIENCE ESTIMATES

EVE.WED. JAN.4, 1989

TIME	7:00	7:15	7:30	7:45	8:00	8:15	8:30	8:45	9:00	9:15	9:30	9:45	10:00	10:15	10:30	10:45		
HUT	63.5	64.3	64.1	64.9	65.4	66.4	66.2	66.8	66.7	67.1	65.7	64.9	62.7	60.7	58.7	55.9		

ABC TV

← GROWING PAINS → ← HEAD OF THE CLASS → ← WONDER YEARS (R) → ← HOOPERMAN (R)(PAE) → ←────CHINA BEACH────→

AVERAGE AUDIENCE (Hhlds (000) & %) {	18,440 20.4		17,360 19.2		13,110 14.5		12,020 13.3		12,570 13.9 *	13.9 *		13.8 *				
SHARE AUDIENCE %	31		29		22		20		23	23 *		24 *				
AVG. AUD. BY 1/4 HR %	19.5	21.4	19.2	19.3	14.8	14.2	13.0	13.6	13.9	14.0	13.9	13.7			

CBS TV

←────────TV 101────────→

┌─────────────────────────────┐
│ CBS SPECIAL MOVIE PRSNT   │
│ AGATHA CHRISTIE'S 'THE   │
│ MAN IN THE BROWN SUIT'   │
│ (PAE)   │
└─────────────────────────────┘

AVERAGE AUDIENCE (Hhlds (000) & %) {	6,420 7.1	7.0 *		7.2 *	14,460 16.0	15.0 *		16.5 *		16.6 *		15.9 *			
SHARE AUDIENCE %	11	11 *		11 *	25	22 *		25 *		27 *		28 *			
AVG. AUD. BY 1/4 HR %	7.4	6.6	6.7	7.7	14.4	15.6	16.6	16.3	16.7	16.5	16.2	15.6			

NBC TV

←────UNSOLVED MYSTERIES (R)────→ ← NIGHT COURT (R) → ← BABY BOOM (R) → ←────TATTINGER'S────→

AVERAGE AUDIENCE (Hhlds (000) & %) {	16,720 18.5	17.3 *			14,370 19.6 *	15.9		9,670 10.7		6,870 7.6	7.8 *		7.3 *		
SHARE AUDIENCE %	28	26 *			29 *	24		16		13	13 *		13 *		
AVG. AUD. BY 1/4 HR %	16.8	17.9	20.0	19.3	15.9	16.0	11.0	10.4	8.2	7.4	7.4	7.2			

INDEPENDENTS (INCL. SUPERSTATIONS)

| AVERAGE AUDIENCE | 17.4 | | 14.3 | | 12.0 | | 11.5 | | 11.6 | | 12.2 | | 12.8 | | 10.9 | | | |
| SHARE AUDIENCE % | 27 | | 22 | | 18 | | 17 | | 17 | | 19 | | 21 | | 19 | | | |

SUPERSTATIONS

| AVERAGE AUDIENCE | 5.6 | | 4.8 | | 3.9 | | 3.9 | | 3.7 | | 4.1 | | 4.2 | | 3.1 | | | |
| SHARE AUDIENCE % | 9 | | 7 | | 6 | | 6 | | 6 | | 6 | | 7 | | 5 | | | |

PBS

| AVERAGE AUDIENCE | 2.0 | | 2.4 | | 2.9 | | 3.1 | | 3.5 | | 4.0 | | 3.0 | | 2.7 | | | |
| SHARE AUDIENCE % | 3 | | 4 | | 4 | | 5 | | 5 | | 6 | | 5 | | 5 | | | |

CABLE ORIG.

| AVERAGE AUDIENCE | 7.5 | | 7.7 | | 7.7 | | 7.9 | | 8.7 | | 10.3 | | 9.0 | | 8.1 | | | |
| SHARE AUDIENCE % | 12 | | 12 | | 12 | | 12 | | 13 | | 16 | | 15 | | 14 | | | |

PAY SERVICES

| AVERAGE AUDIENCE | 2.9 | | 3.4 | | 3.7 | | 3.3 | | 3.9 | | 3.5 | | 4.3 | | 3.9 | | | |
| SHARE AUDIENCE % | 5 | | 5 | | 6 | | 5 | | 6 | | 5 | | 7 | | 7 | | | |

U.S. TV HOUSEHOLDS: 90,400,000

For explanation of symbols, See page 8.

The report gives the average audience by quarter-hour only for broadcast networks. Data for independent stations, superstations, the PBS network, and cable origination (meaning basic cable networks) combine ratings for the *time periods* mentioned, not for specific programs.

Source: Nielsen Media Research, *Nielsen Television Index National TV Ratings, 2–8 January 1989.* Used with permission.

reports on the relative rankings of nationally syndicated programs. Both firms provide detailed audience demographic information for first-run as well as off-network syndicated programs.

Collecting Set-Use Data

Ratings are based on receiver-use data. These data are collected by means of audience diaries, meters that record set-use, and telephone calls. Several other measurement methods are used in various combinations for special studies.

Set-Use Criterion   Each ratings company has adopted an arbitrary span of time that a set must be turned on to count as being actually *in use*. The minimum time span is usually six minutes per quarter-hour, though Arbitron plans to reduce its standard to one minute. This simple set-use test of audience membership tells nothing about whether listeners liked a program, whether they understood what they heard or saw, whether they chose the program after considering alternatives or merely passively accepted it because it came on a channel already tuned in, whether they paid attention to it or did something else while the set was on, and so on.

how much does set-use data reveal?

Diaries   Arbitron and Nielsen researchers use diaries kept by listeners/viewers for gathering most of their local-market ratings data.

For radio data, Arbitron sends a separate diary to each person over 12 years of age in each sample household. It asks radio diary keepers to write down their listening times and the stations they tune to daily for one week, keeping track of away-from-home as well as in-home listening. Arbitron also uses diaries for most television markets.

Similarly, Nielsen uses diaries in most cities to prepare its Nielsen Station Index (NSI), which gives market-by-market television ratings. Nielsen asks one person in each diary household to take charge of reporting the viewing of all persons present. Exhibit 10.3 shows sample pages from radio and television diaries.

Diaries suffer a major drawback: respondents can easily enter inaccurate information. They may want to show they have good taste in programs, for example; or they may fill in diaries in "catch up" style at the end of the week rather than daily, as listening or viewing takes place.

drawbacks of diaries

"Passive" Meters   Nielsen first sought to eliminate the uncertainty of diaries back in 1950 by attaching metering devices to receivers in sample houses. Called by Nielsen Audimeters, these devices automatically made a record showing when the set went on and off and to which channels it was tuned. Originally Nielsen representatives called at sample households to pick up the tuning records, but the modern version automatically sends the tuning data to a Nielsen processing center by telephone line.

EXHIBIT *10.3* Viewing/Listening Diary Formats

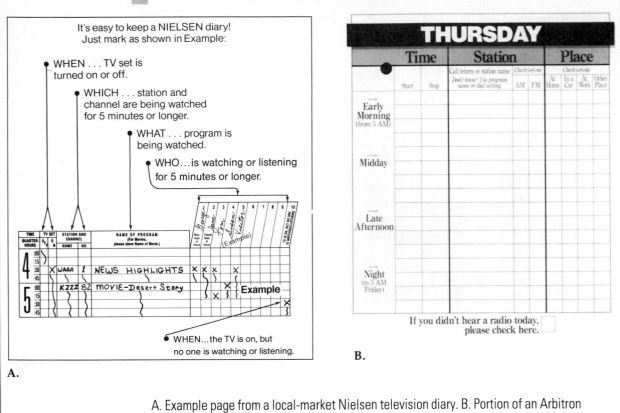

A. Example page from a local-market Nielsen television diary. B. Portion of an Arbitron local-market radio diary.

Source: (A) Nielsen Media Research and (B) © 1989 The Arbitron Company. Used with permission.

This type of meter is called *passive* because it merely records set-tuning, making no demands on viewers to interact with the meter system. A passive meter cannot record who, if anyone, watched when the set was on. Nielsen compensates for this limitation by supplementing its passive-meter homes with another sample of diary homes in 22 markets, using the diaries to obtain information on actual viewing along with demographic data about the viewers. The Nielsen ratings combine information from the two samples, passive meter and diary.

how raters compensate for meter passivity

Arbitron derived its name from its own version of the Audimeter, which it called the Arbitron. Arbitron combines diaries with passive meters in 14 markets. Both research companies began to phase out passive meters for network ratings in 1987, when a new device, the people meter, became available. However, passive meters remained in use for individual market ratings into the 1990s.

People Meters   The interactive people meter eliminates the awkwardness of combining diary and metered data, which is done in order to satisfy advertisers' demands for demographic information on individual audience members. Like passive meters, people meters keep a record of receiver usage. In addition, however, the people meter does the job formerly done by the diaries that were placed in a supplementary household sample. People meters *simultaneously* collect viewing *and* demographic data in the same sample households.

This double-duty meter comes equipped with a hand-held pad with buttons for each viewer in a people-meter household. Each viewer "checks in" and "checks out" whenever watching television.

Viewer response makes the people meters interactive, in contrast to the passive meter. Exhibit 10.4 shows the key-pad and the unit that receives the check-in and check-out signals from viewers. Extra buttons on the pad allow visitors in the household to join with family members in checking in and out. Data on both receiver use and viewer identity go by telephone line to a central computer, where each individual's viewing is linked to that individual's demographic data already stored in the computer. Exhibit 10.4 outlines the entire process of people-meter data gathering, processing, and reporting.

how people meters interact with audience

Nielsen began its people-meter national television ratings service in September 1987. In 1990, the company planned to begin individual market ratings reports with people meters in New York and Los Angeles. Controversy over lower audience ratings from people meters led to lack of industry support, and Nielsen dropped local people meter plans.

At the same time, Arbitron again postponed plans to introduce an enhanced version of the people meter in the early 1990s, calling its new system ScanAmerica. Arbitron planned to use this new system to compete for the first time against Nielsen in the national television ratings field. It also planned local-market people-meter ratings in selected cities.

Arbitron touted ScanAmerica as a three-pronged single-source system—producing set-tuning data, demographic data, and product-purchasing data based on the same sample. ScanAmerica would keep track of purchases made by householders in its sample by means of a hand scanner that reads the Universal Product Codes (UPCs) on labels. Some member of the sample household is expected to scan the UPCs after each shopping trip. Industry observers in mid-1990 expressed doubts about ScanAmerica ever reaching the implementation stage.

Arbitron plan for monitoring both buying and viewing

Telephone Methods   Researchers generally consider the **coincidental telephone** method as the most accurate for obtaining audience-size and listening/viewing information. The term "coincidental" comes from the fact that researchers ask respondents what they are listening to or watching at the time of (that is, coincidental with) the call. The researcher asks whether the respondent has a set turned on at that moment, and if so, to what program, station, or channel. The researcher then adds a few demographic questions about the number, sex, and age of those watching or listening. Putting questions in the present tense eliminates the memory factor and reduces the probability of faked answers.

However, the coincidental method provides only momentary data from each respondent ("What are you listening to or watching *now*?"). To obtain full ratings information for an entire broadcast day would require a very large number of calls, spaced out to cover each period of the day. A properly conducted coincidental telephone survey uses batteries of well-trained callers under close supervision, and new groups of respondents are usually selected each day. All this can become expensive. Moreover, telephoners cannot call late at night. They usually cease calling between 10:30 P.M. and 8:30 A.M. and ask respondents to recall set-use during those hours the next morning.

Those morning calls represent a second telephone method, telephone recall. It is less reliable than the coincidental method but costs less because each call can cover several hours of listening/watching. RADAR, the only source of radio-network ratings, uses telephone recall, collecting data daily (by prearrangement) over a period of seven days from the same sample of 6,000 individual listeners. This unusual daily polling of the same respondents minimizes memory errors while attaining an entire week's coverage.

Interview Method   The use of door-to-door personal interviews based on residential sampling has declined because knocking on strange doors in strange streets can be hazardous to the researcher's health.

EXHIBIT 10.4   Reporting People-Meter TV Ratings

A.

(A) The Nielsen people meter includes the hand-held unit on which each viewing member of the family and guests can "check in" and the base unit atop the television receiver that stores home viewing information.

Source: Photo courtesy Nielsen Media Research.

EXHIBIT *10.4*   Continued

B.

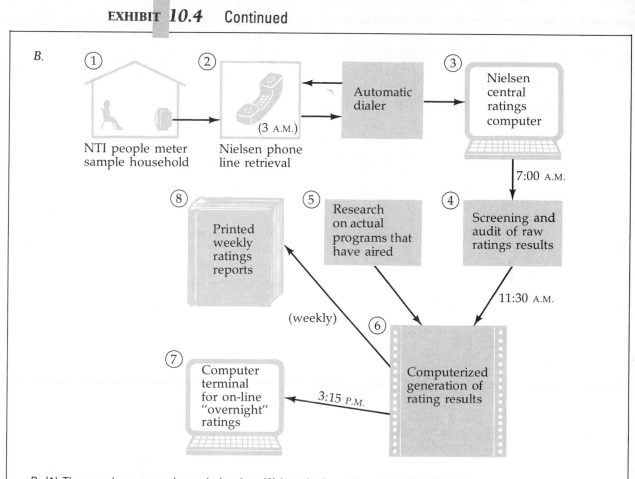

B. (1) The people meter unit sends its data (2) by telephone line, leased by Nielsen, at 3:00 A.M. local time each morning, to (3) the Nielsen central ratings computers, which transmit the raw data to (4) the screening and audit process, where all ratings materials are assembled and (5) matched with constantly updated program information. Viewing and program data go to (6), where computers generate overnight ratings data. By 3:15 the next afternoon the overnights go to (7) client (agencies, stations, networks) computer terminals for processing as (8) weekly printed ratings reports. A similar process is used to compile market reports from the combined data of Nielsen diaries plus passive meters.

However, researchers often use personal interviews for studies other than ratings research, selecting *convenience* (also called *purposive*) samples drawn haphazardly from people in public settings. Typically, interviewers question people on the street or in shopping malls. To study car-radio listening, they sometimes question automobile drivers in the street at stoplights. Data gathered from convenience samples cannot be reliably projected to the general population because it does not use true random sampling to select interviewees. Nevertheless, it can be useful for gaining insights into behavior, attitudes and opinions.

10.4 *Sampling—in Theory*

No matter which method researchers use, they cannot possibly monitor around-the-clock private listening/viewing by millions of people tuning to thousands of stations and cable channels located in more than 200 markets. The task becomes possible only by resorting to drastic simplification of the data and to sampling.

Data Simplification   It has already been pointed out that responses to programs can vary over an endless range of observable human behaviors. Researchers concluded years ago that the only practicable way to quantify listening/viewing behavior was to reduce it to the simple acts of turning on a receiver, selecting a station, and later turning off the set.

A second simplification used in ratings research takes advantage of the repetitive cycles of broadcast and cable programming. Audiences remain fairly constant for the daily soap operas and the weekly situation comedies. For most measuring purposes, dipping into the continuous program stream at intervals of a few weeks or months suffices. Daily measurements occur in only a few major cities and on only prime-time programs.

The most controversial ratings simplification arises from people sampling—using the tuning behavior of people in a few hundred, or at best a few thousand, homes to assess the behavior of more than 240 million people in some 90 million households. Arbitron radio-market ratings depend on surveys using samples of 50 to 3,500 households per market, depending on the market size. Nielsen bases its television-network ratings on about 4,000 people-meter households scattered throughout the country. The RADAR national radio-network ratings use telephone samples of 6,000 persons.

Random Selection   The fact is, small samples *can* give reasonably accurate estimates. The laws of chance, or probability, predict that a *randomly selected* small sample from a large population will be representative of the entire population. Random selection requires that *every* member of the entire population to be surveyed has an *equal* chance of being selected. Under those conditions, major characteristics of the population as a whole will appear in the sample in about the same proportion as their distribution throughout the entire population.

Lotteries involve drawing numbers by chance (at random) from a barrel containing the names of all the lottery players. This procedure meets the requirements of pure probability sampling. *Every* member of the population (lottery-ticket holders) is represented in the barrel, and *each* has an equal chance of being selected.

Picture a gigantic barrel containing the names of all the millions of people who watched television last Tuesday night. Each name is attached to a list of programs the person watched that night. Upon drawing a sample of 500 names at random from the barrel and adding up the number that watched each program, a researcher would get a fairly accurate record of the relative popularity of each program—at least insofar as the relative number of people watching a program is an indicator of its popularity.

Random sampling is indispensable in many situations where complete censuses would be impossible. The efficacy and safety of new drugs are tested on randomly selected samples of patients; the outputs of production lines are randomly selected for quality tests.

Sampling—in Practice 10.5

Random sampling in the real world is not easy to do. Paradoxically, random choices can be made only after systematic planning.

randomness must be planned

Sample Frames The names of all listeners/viewers cannot be written down and put in a barrel. Drawing a sample randomly from a large human population requires some other way of identifying members of the population by name, number, location, or some other unique label.

In practice, sample members are selected from such sources as name-lists (telephone book, automobile registrations) and place-lists (maps of housing-unit locations). Such population listings are called *sample frames*. Ratings companies usually employ either updated telephone directories or census tracts (maps showing the location of dwellings) as frames. Nielsen draws its national sample of metered television households from U.S. census maps by a method known as *multistage area probability sampling*. "Multistage" refers to step-by-step random selection by area, starting with counties and ending with individual housing units, as shown in Exhibit 10.5.

For its market-by-market ratings of stations, however, Nielsen uses special updated telephone directors, as do Arbitron and most other firms engaged in ratings research. The fact that nearly all U.S. households have telephones makes telephone directories the most readily available sampling frames.

However, in a given city, as many as 40 percent of the telephone subscribers have unlisted numbers. Moreover, many listed numbers represent businesses rather than households. Random digit dialing, a computer method of generating telephone numbers without reference to a directory, can reach unlisted and newly installed telephones, but at the cost of wasted effort on unassigned numbers and calls to business addresses. RADAR, the sole source of radio-network ratings, uses random digit dialing.

random digit dialing corrects phonebook faults

EXHIBIT 10.5   Multistage Sampling Method

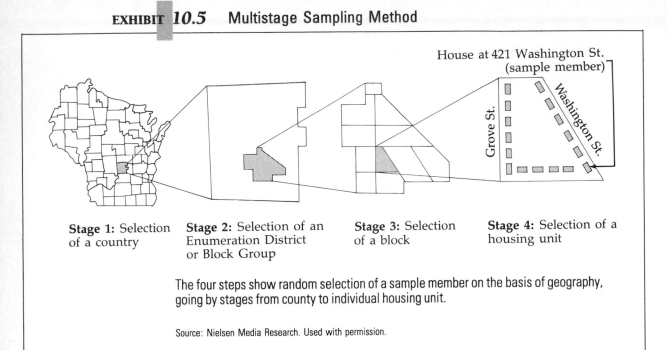

Stage 1: Selection of a country

Stage 2: Selection of an Enumeration District or Block Group

Stage 3: Selection of a block

Stage 4: Selection of a housing unit

House at 421 Washington St. (sample member)

Grove St.

Washington St.

The four steps show random selection of a sample member on the basis of geography, going by stages from county to individual housing unit.

Source: Nielsen Media Research. Used with permission.

Sample Correction   There are ways of improving a sample's representativeness during and after selection. For example, in practice researchers often used **stratified sampling.** Probability sampling might result, for instance, in a sample in which 55 percent of those chosen are female. However, it might already be known from U.S. census data that the actual female percentage is only 51 percent. In this case the researcher randomly discards enough of the female sample members to reduce their proportion in the sample to 51 percent. Thus the female stratum in the sample population matches that of the actual population. Ratings companies routinely use stratified sampling.

A similar corrective matches the sample to a known population characteristic by **weighting** the results. If a given subgroup turns out to be underrepresented in terms of its known proportion in the population, its weight in the sample can be artificially increased. Thus if the U.S. census shows that 20 percent of a city's population consists of blacks and a sample shows only 10 percent as black, the results from black sample members would be doubled to give them their correct weight. Such weighting is another common practice in ratings research.

Reuse of Sample Members   Ideally, each time a company made a survey it would draw a brand-new sample. However, it costs so much to negotiate the placement of meters in sample households that ratings firms cannot afford to discard each sample after only one use. Nielsen tries to retain each people-meter household in its national sample for no more than two years but allows

high costs of selecting sample households

local-market diary families to stay in samples for up to five. The companies stagger contracts with householders, replacing part of the total each year.

Sample Size

Having chosen a sampling method and obtained a sampling frame, the researcher must next decide on sample size. Common sense suggests that a sample's level of reliability (its degree of accuracy) should increase with size—the larger the sample, the more accurate it should be. This is generally true, but not in direct proportion. For example, doubling sample size does not double reliability. Reliability increases as the *square* of sample size. To double the reliability level of a sample of 500 would require squaring that number, increasing the sample to 250,000. Put another way, as sample size increases, the degree of reliability improvement gets smaller and smaller until further gains no longer justify the cost. In ratings research sample sizes large enough to warrant predicting a 95% level of confidence (95 chances out of a hundred that the result will be correct within specified limits) are usually considered acceptable.

why small samples must suffice

The relatively small samples used by ratings firms, as noted earlier (Nielsen's goal of about 4,000 people-meter households for national ratings, for example) represent practical tradeoffs. Greatly increasing the size of such samples would be prohibitively expensive. The small samples yield reasonably reliable results, though always subject to a stipulated margin of error.

Sampling Error

All measurements based on samples are at best only estimates because of inevitable *sampling error*—the term refers not to mistakes made in gathering data but to the laws of probability. These statistical laws state that any given sample-based measurement will be equally correct if the measurement is increased or decreased by a known amount. Measurements based on repeated sample-taking from the same population will vary among themselves, but the chances are that most will be near the real amount. The *probable* amount of statistical uncertainty in ratings (that is, the amount of sampling error to be expected) can be calculated in advance. News writers have become somewhat sensitized to the concept of sampling error. They usually qualify a sample-based number by adding that it is correct within plus or minus so many points.

sampling in the news

Nonsampling Error

Avoidable mistakes are known as *nonsampling errors*. Researchers may be consciously or unconsciously prejudiced. Failures to fulfill sampling designs may occur, some avoidable, some not. The wording of questionnaires may be misleading. Mistakes can occur in recording data and calculating results. Given all these pitfalls, some degree of bias occurs whenever researchers draw samples from large numbers of people.

sources of bias in data gathering

One common nonsampling error comes from failure to reach each and every designated sample member. Ideally, of course, the **response rate** should be 100 percent. Anything less lowers reliability. Ratings companies make special efforts to encourage preselected sample members to participate and to ensure that those who agree to participate actually carry out their assigned tasks. Arbitron, for example, first writes a letter to prospective diary keepers, follows up with a telephone call before and again during the sample week, and offers a small cash payment to encourage sample members to mail in completed diaries.

Despite such efforts, nonresponse (along with incomplete or inadequate response) remains a problem. The coincidental telephone method gets the best response rate, on the order of 75 percent of the people called. Diary and passive-meter methods yield a usable response rate of about 40 percent. Reportedly the special input that people meters require from viewers lowers the response rate.

can ratings be trusted?

The foregoing litany of problems and uncertainties might well justify asking whether sampling is worth the trouble. Can real-world sampling yield reliable data on anything so difficult to assess as program preferences? Certainly it involves compromises and short cuts. The results can be no more reliable than the methods used to obtain them. But sampling, even in its imperfect form, gives more reliable results than mere guesswork or wishful thinking.

10.6 *Calculating Ratings and Shares*

Before ratings can be calculated, some base representing 100 percent has to be established. An ABC television network program rating of 20 represents approximately 20 percent of the 93 million television households in the entire country. But what is the basis of a rating of 12 for a local program on station KWQC in Davenport, Iowa? A decision has to be made about the size of the market served by KWQC before a rating for the station can be calculated.

Market Definition In the previous sections reference has been repeatedly made to the local *markets* about which ratings companies issue reports. The market concept is essential not only for calculating ratings but for many aspects of broadcasting and cable television operations. Stations, networks, syndicators, advertisers, advertising agencies, and even regulators need a universally recognized national system of clearly defined, nonoverlapping markets.

Arbitron's **Area of Dominant Influence (ADI),** first developed in 1965, has become the most widely accepted system for delineating the nation's television markets. Though Nielsen has its own version, the ADI has been accepted as the standard. Even the FCC uses it. The prime-time access rule, for example, applies only to the top-50 markets, as defined by Arbitron's ADIs.

Arbitron assigns each of the more than 3,000 counties in the 50 states to a specific ADI. It updates the assignments annually, but conditions change only slightly from one year to the next. An ADI consists of the counties within which the centrally located (*home market*) television stations account for the preponderance of viewing. ADIs range in size from No. 1 (centered on New

range in size of ADIs

York City, with about 7 million television households) to No. 209 (Alpena, Michigan, with under 16 thousand). Exhibit 10.6 illustrates the ADI and other Arbitron market concepts.

KWQC–Davenport, mentioned above, belongs to a composite market consisting of Burlington, Davenport, Moline, and Rock Island—the Quad Cities. Ratings of programs on any television station in those cities are based on the 400,000 ADI households composing their four-city market.

Listening/Viewing Unit   Ratings researchers need an agreed-upon unit that will count as "one" when they add up audience membership. Television viewing has traditionally been a family activity, making the *household* the logical unit of measurement. The entire household counts as "one" in the ratings data. Nevertheless, researchers go to great lengths, as indicated in Section 10.3, to obtain individual demographic information as well.

Radio researchers prefer to count *persons* rather than households because radio listening usually occurs as an individual activity, and because so much radio listening takes place outside the home. Notice that the page from a local-market ratings report in Exhibit 10.1 refers only to persons, but the national television ratings report shown in Exhibit 10.2 refers to households.

What a Rating Is   After an audience sample has been designed, its listening/viewing behavior recorded, and the results summarized, the researcher finally has the data for calculating ratings.

A **rating** estimates the percentage of all the households or persons equipped with receivers and able to receive programs that were actually in the audience of a specified program for a specified period. A rating of 20 means that 20 percent of the sample of households actually tuned in to the rated program for a minimum length of time (usually only one to six minutes). To the extent that the sample households were randomly selected, that 20 percent is *projectable*—meaning that the sample 20 percent represents 20 percent of the total households that have receivers in the market. Exhibit 10.7 shows how the calculation is made.

what does a rating of "20" mean?

Of course, no program attracts everybody. Moreover, some people who might otherwise watch are not at home, are asleep, or are not using their receivers. Therefore a rating never even approaches 100, in fact rarely reaches 50. The rating of prime-time broadcast television programs averages 17; day-time programs average about 6.

why is a rating of "90" never achieved?

The following examples give an idea of the range of program ratings:

- The most successful nonsports entertainment program of all time, the final episode of *M*A*S*H* in 1983, had a Nielsen rating of 60.2.
- The Super Bowl of 1983 achieved a rating of 48.6.
- HBO averages a prime-time rating of about 2, but only in terms of all cable television households, not all television households.
- Radio stations often earn ratings of less than 1 and rarely more than 2 or 3. Such low ratings make no meaningful distinctions among stations; radio

EXHIBIT **10.6** TV Market Definition Concepts

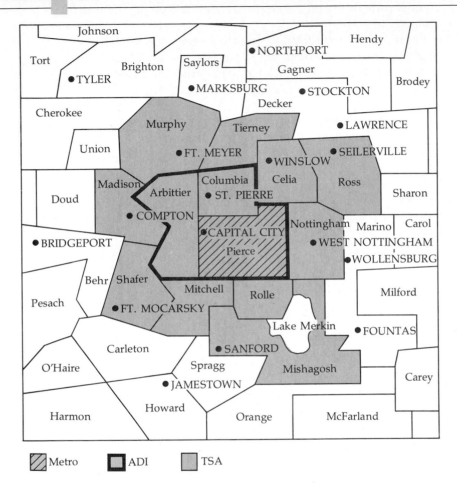

Metro   ADI   TSA

In this hypothetical TV market, the *Area of Dominant Influence* of stations located in or near Capital City extends to three counties—Capital City's own county and two adjacent counties. Arbitron uses the term "dominant" because it assigns every county in the country to a *single* ADI. In practice, viewers often receive programs from stations in two or more markets. In those cases, Arbitron has to decide which stations dominate—that is, which are viewed most frequently by people in the market area being defined. For example, in the illustration, when viewers in Columbia County receive signals from stations in both Capital City and Northport (the large city to the north), Arbitron has determined that most of the Columbia County viewers tune to the Capital City stations. The TSA (Total Service Area) accounts for nearly all (in practice about 98 percent) of the audience of the stations in the Capital City market, including counties beyond their area of dominant influence.

EXHIBIT **10.7** Calculating Ratings and Shares

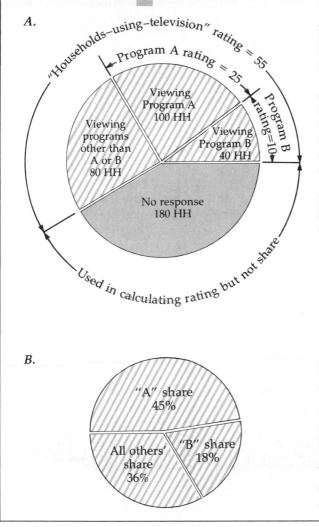

A.

"Households–using–television" rating = 55

Program A rating = 25

Viewing Program A 100 HH

Viewing programs other than A or B 80 HH

Viewing Program B 40 HH

Program B rating = 10

No response 180 HH

Used in calculating rating but not share

A. The pie shows television set-use information gathered from a sample of 400 households, representing a hypothetical market of 100,000 households.

Note that program ratings are percentages based on the entire sample (including the "no response" households). Thus Program A, with 100 households, represents a quarter (25 percent) of the total sample of 400. The formula is 100 ÷ 400 = .25; the decimal is dropped when expressing the number as a rating.

Projected to the entire population, this rating of 25 would mean an estimated audience of 25,000 households. The formula is .25 (the rating with the decimal restored) × 100,000 = 25,000.

B.

"A" share 45%

"B" share 18%

All others' share 36%

B. The smaller pie, 55 percent as large as the pie in A, represents only the households using television, in this case 80 + 100 + 40 households, or a total of 220 (expressed as a households-using-television or HUT rating of 55, as shown in A). Shares are computed by treating the total number of households using television, in this case 220, as 100 percent. Thus program A's 100 households divided by 220 equals about .445, expressed in rounded numbers as a share of 45.

therefore relies more on *cumulative* audience measurements, discussed later in this section.

What a Share Is A program's rating estimates its percentage of the *total possible* households, in contrast to a program's **share**—a percentage based on only the **households using television (HUT)** at the time. HUT measurements refer to viewing in the market as a whole, not to any individual station or program receivable in that market.

A HUT of 50 means that half of the households in the market in question are tuned in to *some* program. It tells nothing about specific programs. HUTs vary with daypart, averaging nationally about 25 for daytime hours and about 60 for prime-time hours. Radio research measurements based on *persons* rather than households yield a **persons using radio (PUR)** measurement rather than a HUT measurement.

why is a program's share always larger than its rating?

Shares derive from HUT or PUR data, as illustrated in Exhibit 10.7B. A station always has a larger share for a given time period than its rating for that time period. For example, top network prime-time programs usually average ratings of just over 20, but their corresponding shares amount to about 30. The share of the record prime-time entertainment program just mentioned was 77, as against its rating of 60.2.

Cumes   A radio program reaches a relatively small number of people in any given quarter-hour. *Cumulatively,* however, over a period of many hours, or during the same hour over a number of days, it will reach a large number of listeners. A **cume rating** gives an estimate of the (cumulative) number of *unduplicated* persons tuning to a station over a period of time.

"Unduplicated" means that during the two or four weeks that typically make up a ratings period, a person who listened to a particular station on seven different days would count as only *one* person. A person tuning in just once to that station during that week would also be counted as one person, because a cume is based on the number of *different* people tuned to the station during a given period of time. The terms *reach* and *circulation* usually refer to cumulative audience measurements.

Demographics   Ratings reports include data on audience composition in terms of gender and age. These **demographic breakouts,** or simply **demographics,** divide the overall ratings into subgroup ratings for men, women, teens (ages to 12 to 17), and children. Adult audience age-group categories typically consist of decade units (such as men 35 to 44) for radio and larger units for television (for example, women 18 to 34 or 25 to 49), although the "adults 12 +" category also occurs. Exhibit 10.1, showing part of a single-market ratio report, breaks down the audience into 15 different demographic subgroups. It reports on ratings, shares, and number of persons in each subgroup.

Exhibit 10.8 shows how demographic differences influence audience set-use behavior. The data in the exhibit enable making generalizations such as the following:

- More viewing in cable households than in over-the-air TV households.
- Among adults, viewing increases with age.
- Younger children view more than older children.
- Large families view more than small families.
- Women view more than men.

how demographics influence radio formats

Radio affords an example of how demographics influence programming. Age strongly affects radio-format preferences. Contemporary music formats

EXHIBIT **10.8**   Influence of Demographics on Time Spent Viewing

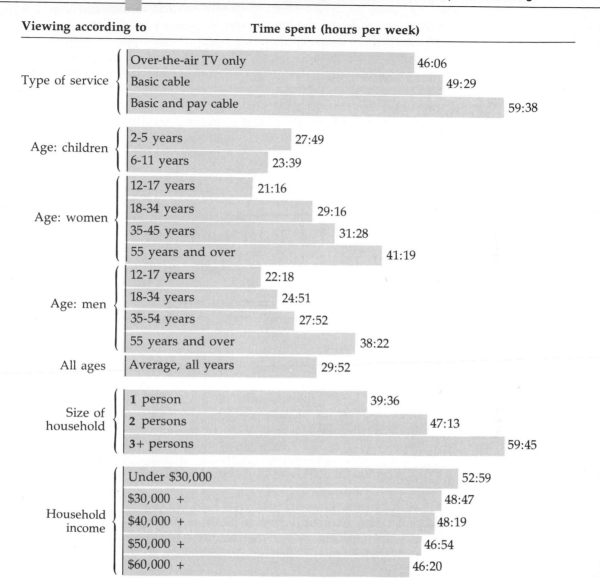

Viewing according to   **Time spent (hours per week)**

Type of service	Over-the-air TV only	46:06
	Basic cable	49:29
	Basic and pay cable	59:38
Age: children	2-5 years	27:49
	6-11 years	23:39
Age: women	12-17 years	21:16
	18-34 years	29:16
	35-45 years	31:28
	55 years and over	41:19
Age: men	12-17 years	22:18
	18-34 years	24:51
	35-54 years	27:52
	55 years and over	38:22
All ages	Average, all years	29:52
Size of household	1 person	39:36
	2 persons	47:13
	3+ persons	59:45
Household income	Under $30,000	52:59
	$30,000 +	48:47
	$40,000 +	48:19
	$50,000 +	46:54
	$60,000 +	46:20

Data are for November 1989, based on early people-meter reports.

Source: Based on A. C. Nielsen Media Research, *1990 Report on Television*, A. C. Nielsen, Northbrook, IL.

appeal mostly to people in their late teens and twenties; classical, country, and middle-of-the-road formats to people in their thirties and forties; and old-time music, news, and talk formats to people in their fifties and older.

In advertising's stereotyped world, most products appeal primarily to specific demographic groups—horror movies to teens, beer to men, denture products to the elderly, and so on. Therefore advertising agencies usually "buy" demographic subgroups rather than generalized audiences. The more precisely an advertiser defines desired target-audience demographics, the higher is the per viewer cost of reaching that audience. Nevertheless, most advertisers would rather have a moderate-size audience with the right demographics for their product than a huge audience many of whose members would not be likely customers.

10.7 *What Ratings Tell About Audiences*

Penetration   The most fundamental statistic about radio and television audiences is **set penetration,** or **saturation**—the percentage of all homes in a market that have broadcast receivers. This statistic provides the base for calculating ratings.

In the United States as a whole, broadcasting penetration has long since peaked at about 99 percent, as shown in Exhibit 10.9. Indeed, most homes have several radios and more than one television set. In short, for practical purposes the entire U.S. population of over 90 million households constitutes the broadcast audience potential.

Cable television introduced a new penetration concept: **homes passed.** Just because a cable runs down a street does not mean that every home subscribes to the service. Exhibit 10.9 shows that though cable passes nearly 90 percent of all households, only 57 percent actually subscribe.

Usage Levels   Not all households have their sets turned on at the same time, a fact reflected in HUT levels. Television HUT figures climb throughout the day. In winter, when television use is heaviest, HUT levels range from about 12 percent at 7:00 A.M. to a high of about 70 in the top prime-time hour of 9:00 P.M. to 10:00 P.M. The advent of cable has not altered these proportions. However, VCR use interrupts both broadcast and cable viewing, making audience measurement more difficult. Radio listening has a flatter profile than television viewing, with the highest peak in the morning drive-time hours.

how radio and TV listening/viewing profiles differ

Television HUT levels change predictably with the seasons. Viewing peaks in January–February and bottoms out in June, reflecting the influence of weather on audience availability.

Medium or Message? Long-term trends aside, in any particular season of the year people tend to turn on their television sets day after day in the same overall numbers, with no apparent regard for the particular programs that may be scheduled. In terms made famous by media theorist Marshall McLuhan, the *medium* matters more than the *message*.

Paul Klein, a television network programming expert, proposed a similar theory, that of the **least objectionable program,** or **LOP** (Klein, 1971). Half jokingly, he theorized that people stay with the same channel until they are driven to another channel by an objectionable program. But even if they find *all* programs objectionable, according to LOP theory, they will stay tuned in to the *least objectionable* one rather than turning off the set entirely.

According to Klein, this behavior accounted for the steady 90 percent of the prime-time audience gathered in by the three broadcast television networks in the 1970s. It also explained why seemingly excellent programs sometimes failed (because of being scheduled against even better programs) and why seemingly mediocre programs sometimes succeeded (because they opposed even more objectionable mediocrities).

how LOP theory explains success of mediocre programs

Whatever the reasons, ratings data confirm that audience size remains stable, varying mostly because of changing dayparts and seasons. This constancy of the audience pool forces each network and station to focus its programming efforts on prying audiences loose from its competitors through counterprogramming. Rarely does a program forge ahead by enlarging the total sets-in-use figure; it usually does so by diverting existing audience members from competing channels.

In the 1980s, however, this static scene began to change. Competition from independent stations, cable channels, and VCR viewing stimulated complex and volatile audience behavior. These changes created problems for programmers and audience researchers, especially in prime time. The broadcast networks could no longer count on sharing 90 percent of the audience (the rate and extent of decline are depicted in Exhibit 3.6). Nevertheless, the three main broadcast networks still have the most massive audiences of any medium and still constitute the most coveted national advertising vehicle.

Time Spent Another frequently cited audience statistic is the amount of time people spend with the media. Exhibit 10.8 indicates that in the average family the television set stays on about 7 hours a day. The figure is less for broadcast-only homes, more for basic cable homes, still more for basic-plus-pay-cable homes. This amazing statistic worries many people concerned about media effects.

Of course, these totals represent the sum of viewing by all members of households. As a group, women spend the most time viewing, followed by children ages 2 to 11. Teenagers and college students view the least. Exhibit 10.8 gives detailed time-spent statistics.

10.8   *Researching Cable TV and VCR Audiences*

cable subscription
records tell audience
size—but for which
channels?

Cable TV Audience   Unlike broadcasting, cable television *does* have objective numerical information on its potential audience—its subscription records. As Exhibit 10.9 shows, by 1989 cable penetration had reached 57 percent of all television households. However, the number of subscribers tells nothing about actual cable use. **Addressability** (the ability to control and record access of each subscribing household to specific programs) solves this problem with respect to pay channels, but they are few in number and have lower subscription levels than basic cable.

The problems of rating individual cable systems on a market-by-market basis using conventional rating methods remain unsolved for several reasons:

difficulties in rating
cable-system audiences

- A cable system's total audience is divided into thirty or so groups watching its different channels. An impossibly large sample would be needed to track the viewing of so many small groups.

EXHIBIT *10.9*   Electronic Mass Media Penetration

Population Base		
U.S. population		246,000,000
U.S. households		93,000,000
Equipment Penetration[a]		
Radio receivers (one or more)		99%
TV receivers (one or more)		98
Color TV receivers	96%	
Remote controls (for TV or VCR)	76	
Two or more receivers	63	
Stereo-equipped TV receivers	19	
Cable TV basic subscriptions		57
Households passed by trunk cable	89[b]	
Pay-cable subscriptions	46	
Addressable cable household (for PPV)	18	
VCRs		68
Home computers		23
CD players		19
Camcorders		10
TVROs		3

[a]Penetration expressed as a percentage of all U.S. households except for cable television penetration, expressed as percentage of TV households.
[b]To reach homes "passed" by trunk cables would require intermediate cabling before drop-off cables to subscriber homes could be installed.

Source: Population and basic receiver penetration data from *U.S. Statistical Abstract* (1988 data). Equipment data from Electronic Industries Association (January 1990 data), National Cable Television Association (November 1989 data), National Association of Broadcasters (1989–1990 data), and *Channels* (November 1989).

- Even in terms of the aggregate audience of all their channels, most cable systems have relatively small audiences. The political boundaries that define cable franchise areas often compose only a single county or even just part of one. Broadcast signals, however, ignore political boundaries, creating larger, multicounty market areas, as can be seen in Exhibit 10.6).
- Most cable systems attract insufficient advertiser interest to justify support of expensive audience research.

Nielsen and Arbitron report on local cable viewing only in markets where the average audiences for specific cable networks meet the rating companies' minimum reporting levels. That usually means a *share* percentage of at least 3. Even this relatively low criterion keeps cable data out of about half of the Nielsen and Arbitron local-market reports.

On the national level, however, cable television audiences are more fully reported. Nielsen began audience reports for major cable networks in 1979, introducing the Nielsen HomeVideo Index (NHI) in 1983. It issues *Pay Cable Report* four times a year.

Since the inception of ratings based on people meters in 1987, Nielsen's national broadcast television audience estimates have also included data on superstations, basic cable networks, and pay-cable services. Exhibit 10.2 gives an example of such a report.

VCR Audience Penetration by videocassette recorders reached 60 percent by 1989, surpassing that of cable. The VCR presents novel problems for media research. Time-shifting enables VCR owners to escape the confines of program schedules. But researchers depend on predictably scheduled programs. VCR viewers further complicate the job of measuring their viewing by changing channels frequently as they zip and zap their way through schedules to avoid commercials, as described in Section 8.7.

Nielsen has studied VCR use generally, however. It has found that users devote two-thirds of their VCR taping to the recording of network programs. During half of that time the receiver is not being used for program viewing (Nielsen Company, 1989). The study thus indicates that VCR owners use their machines primarily to time-shift network programs.

VCRs used most often to tape broadcast programs

Critique: The Credibility of Ratings 10.9

Ratings have always been the subject of much skepticism and debate, both inside and outside the industry. Complaints against rating practices peaked in the early 1960s, when the FCC, the FTC, and Congress all investigated the major companies.

Ratings Council A 1962 FTC cease and desist order forced reform. The companies had to give a true account of the accuracy of their results, to report on noncooperation in sampling, to refrain from mixing data from incompatible sources, and to cease making arbitrary, often undisclosed, "adjustments" of research findings.

The industry responded to the barrage of criticism by founding the Broadcasting (later Electronic Media) Rating Council (EMRC), an independent auditing agency. It accredits ratings services that meet specified standards and submit to annual audits. However, only the major firms spend the time and money needed to meet EMRC requirements. In today's leaner, meaner age of enhanced competition, researchers again tend increasingly to cut corners and to misuse research methods (Couzens, 1989).

rating the raters

Nevertheless, the major companies now take pains to disclose their methods and the limitations of results based on sampling. This information can be found in ratings "books" appendixes.

People-Meter Flap   Introduction of the new people-meter data-gathering method in 1987 created renewed controversy. Its first results differed markedly from results obtained by the older method. The broadcast television-network audiences fell, and cable network audiences rose.

are people-meter buttons a turn-off?

The networks claimed that people meters undercounted viewers who might be intimidated by, or too impatient with, the computer-like button-pushing demanded by the interactive device. These reactions could result in underestimating both older and younger audience segments. Others argued that, on the contrary, the people meters simply gave more precise measurements of actual viewing behavior than had been possible with the previous passive-meter-plus-diary method. The controversy over data-gathering methods seemed likely to persist for a long time.

To quell doubts about the workability of the people meter's reviewer-response system, Nielsen and the David Sarnoff Research Center in Princeton began working on eliminating the need for it. In 1989, they proposed a seeming paradox—a **passive people meter.** It would use an image-recognition device to identify and record the presence of each family member and guests, automatically and individually. Viewers would no longer have to push buttons to signal their presence. They would once more become *passive* with respect to the data-gathering operation. The developers spoke of introducing the passive people meter in the mid-1990s.

Science—or Superstition?   If, as Sylvester Weaver, one-time NBC president, once remarked, the ratings business is "just one step from the entrails of a chicken," even one step away from superstition is worth taking. Ratings based on scientific sampling methods, such as those used by the companies discussed in this chapter, give reasonably reliable results. However, their limitations should be kept in mind:

ratings are reasonably reliable but . . .

- Real-world compromises undermine random selection of sample members and therefore reduce reliability. Previous sections of this chapter pointed out some of these compromises, such as the low response level of sample members.

- Ratings, like all conclusions based on samples, are only estimates. The media often make much of tiny differences between ratings that have no statistical significance.
- Audience samples are likely to underrepresent the very rich, the very poor, ethnic minorities, and rural dwellers. They have less chance to be solicited by, and less inclination to cooperate with, ratings services than do people in the middle range. Recognizing the underrepresentation of minorities, both Arbitron and Nielsen make special efforts to persuade minority respondents in their samples to participate fully.
- Television's use of the household as the unit of measurement leaves out residents of group quarters such as college dormitories, much to the distress of stations in college towns.
- Ratings measure only set-use, revealing nothing about audience satisfaction, appreciation, and understanding.

Social Effects

11 The previous chapter dealt with one particular set of effects as revealed by ratings—audience tuning behavior. This chapter focuses on less easily measured yet more important consequences of radio and television—their social effects. Not only do the electronic mass media entertain, inform, and persuade—they also influence political processes, unite a nation with the common bonds of shared experiences, and play a role in shaping the way audiences perceive reality. We experience most of the world's doings not directly, but vicariously through the eyes and ears of cameras and microphones and of the people who control them.

11.1 ## *Uses of Effects Research*

When Congress wrote the Radio Act of 1927 and the Federal Radio Commission first began making rules to put the act into effect, neither the legislature nor the commission had the benefit of social and economic research on the effects of radio. They relied on legal-historical precedents and guesswork.

Today, however, major policy decisions concerning broadcasting usually rely on social research to support their assumptions, to justify their goals, and to predict probable outcomes. During the 1970s the FCC's decision making about the future of the media it controls came increasingly under the influence of economic theorists. Research on the economics of broadcasting and cable television, along with predictions of their future interrelationships, became a growth industry.

recent regulatory decisions dominated by economic theory

When Congress holds hearings on proposed new legislation or the FCC considers new rules, representatives of the affected industries buttress their arguments with surveys of prior research on the topic, frequently adding specially commissioned research of their own. Consumer organizations, too, have learned that they need more than good intentions and moral fervor. They need to support their claims with the kind of hard evidence that research alone can supply. As typical examples of privately sponsored research, critics of broadcast news regularly conduct or cite content-analysis studies to support allegations of news bias; Action for Children's Television does content-analysis research to support its petitions for improvements in children's programming.

11.2 ## *Communication Research Concepts*

Communication involves a chain of events that can best be regarded as a process. The model in Exhibit 11.1—one of many such diagrams that theorists have constructed to explain the way communication works—represents the communication process. The diagram in the exhibit is especially relevant to the electronic media because it grows out of an engineer's view of the process.

Topics of Study   In studying communications, researchers ask questions about five different stages of the process, either singly or in combination.

- Who are the *originators* of messages—the writers, producers, entertainers, propagandists, salespersons, proselytizers? What are their goals, intentions, agendas?

EXHIBIT 11.1   Communication: The Information Theory Model

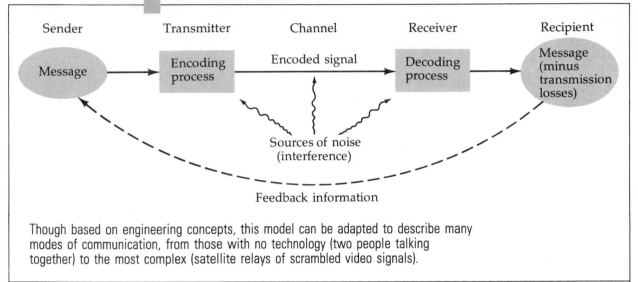

Though based on engineering concepts, this model can be adapted to describe many modes of communication, from those with no technology (two people talking together) to the most complex (satellite relays of scrambled video signals).

- What are the *contents* of messages—their facts, ideas, and moods, their language and style, their implied assumptions?
- Through what *channels* do messages flow—the printed page, the radio or television program, the recording? How does the channel influence the message?
- What about the *audiences* that receive messages—their size, their distribution, their demographic characteristics?
- What *effects* do messages have—subjective reactions in terms of mood, attitude, or opinion; objective reactions such as smiling or frowning or laughing, buying or selling, voting or abstaining, moving or staying put?

A pioneer communications researcher, Harold Lasswell, summarized these stages by posing the following question (adapted from Smith et al., 1946: 121):

"*Who* says *what* through which *channel* to *whom* with what *effect*?"

The "Who" Factor   Congress included the sponsor identification requirement in the Communications Act to make sure audiences would know who was responsible for program content.

The "who" of communications often act as gatekeepers. Government regulation, industry codes, network clearance, and editing processes all have gatekeeping functions. Studies of gatekeeping seek to answer questions about where the gates in the flow of information occur, who opens and closes them, how the controls operate, and what effects they have on the content by the time it finally reaches its destination.

gatekeepers screen communication content

Another way in which gatekeeping research assists in policy decisions is by evaluating the effects of cross-media and group ownership on programming decisions, the influence of advertisers on program content, the roles of professional criticism and of industry self-regulation, and the impact of government regulation on programs.

The "What" Factor

content analysis: research that assesses what's said

Researchers use content analysis to measure and interpret that "what" factor. The classification of programs into various genres is a simple form of content analysis. On a more sophisticated level, content analysts categorize and enumerate the occurrence of specified units of content. Researchers have analyzed such materials as advertising copy, censors' comments, cross-national program differences, television specials, news programs, violent acts in programs, and the portrayal of minorities in television dramas.

The "Which Channel" Factor

Research shows that each channel of communication—newspapers, radio, television, and so on—has its own kind of impact. People form specific attitudes toward and expectations of each medium. Audiences interpret the content of each medium accordingly.

A public-opinion survey company, the Roper Organization, conducted annual image surveys for the broadcast industry over a period of three decades (1959–1989). Roper asked a national sample of respondents their opinions about how well various social institutions performed their jobs. Year by year, respondents consistently reported increasing confidence in television—rising from 59 percent who said television was doing an "excellent" or "good" job in 1959 to 74 percent with that opinion in 1984. Rankings of other media, schools, and government activity, already lower than television in 1959, either stayed the same or declined in respondents' esteem during the 30 years that Roper repeated the question (Roper Organization, 1984: 14).

credibility of TV in cases of conflicting reports

Another key question in the Roper series dealt with media credibility. Surveyors asked respondents which of several media they would believe in case of conflicting news reports. Since 1961, respondents consistently chose television over other media by a wide margin. In 1988, 49 percent chose television, 26 percent newspapers, and 7 percent radio as the most credible medium (Roper Organization, 1989: 15).

The "To Whom" Factor

The ratings business discussed in the previous chapter focuses on the "to whom" factor in Lasswell's paradigm. Ratings tell how many people of various kinds pay attention to various kinds of programs. Scholars go beyond the ratings and their limited data, using more detailed personal and social-group indicators to study the composition of electronic mass media audiences. In particular, the child audience has been extensively analyzed on the basis of such variables as race, intelligence, social class, home environment, and personality type. Researchers ask questions such as these: What types of children will be most likely to believe what they see on television? What types will be likely to imitate what they see?

The "Effects" Factor Lasswell's culminating question, "with what effects?," involves all the previous questions—those about communicators, content, channels, and audiences. All help to determine the ultimate outcome of communicating. In an influential pioneer study, *The Effects of Mass Communication,* Joseph Klapper, a Columbia University specialist in public-opinion studies, summarized the status of effects theories as of 1960. He analyzed more than a thousand media-effects research reports. Klapper reached the tentative conclusion that "mass communication *ordinarily* does not serve as a necessary and sufficient cause of audience effects, but rather functions among and through a nexus of mediating factors and influences" (Klapper, 1960: 8). In plain language, communication effects are usually not simple, direct, one-for-one responses to media but depend on the circumstances surrounding the person affected as well as the media messages.

Klapper concluded that the media *reinforce* existing perceptions and beliefs. They might persuade people to buy a product, but not to change a political allegiance or to adopt a new religion. The broadcasting industry welcomed this conservative conclusion, known as the **law of minimal effects,** because it gave apparent scientific sanction to the industry's rejection of the contention that programs could be blamed for causing antisocial behavior.

During the 1970s, however, opinion began to shift away from the minimal-effects concept, because of intensive research on the effects of violence (discussed in Section 11.8). Many researchers now prefer to avoid talking about effects as such. The very word *effects* implies an oversimplification of what is now understood to be an extremely complex process.

> media influence: not a simple cause-and-effect sequence

Without denying that some specific media content might under specific conditions have specific effects on some specific people, researchers prefer to speak in terms of the *association* of certain inputs with certain outputs. They avoid going so far as to imply a simple, straight-line cause-and-effect relationship. Exhibit 11.2 summarizes the stages of research development, from the simplistic cause-and-effect concept of the early studies to the contemporary goal of looking more deeply into the antecedent processes.

Effects of Advertising 11.3

No aspect of broadcasting and cable has been more measured and manipulated than advertising. Business interests spare no effort in attempting to assure desired media effects on sales and image formation. In this chapter, the focus is not so much on market research, however, as on the broader social consequence of advertising.

Consumers and Advertising Advertising's long-range effects include influencing the content of programs and reducing the direct costs of media to the public. But does advertising also penalize consumers by generating desires

EXHIBIT 11.2   Evolution of Research on Media Effects

Time Period	Prevailing viewpoint	Empirical basis
1 (1920s–1930s)	Mass media have strong effects	Observation of apparent success of propaganda campaigns Experiments demonstrating immediate attitude change after exposure to messages Evidence of selective perception—persons ignore messages contrary to existing predispositions
2 (1940s–1950s)	Mass media largely reinforce existing predispositions, and thus outcomes are likely to be the same in their absence	Evidence of personal influence—persons are more influenced by others than the mass media Evidence of negligible influence on voting No relationship observed between exposure to mass-media violence and delinquent behavior among the young
3 (1950s–1960s)	Mass media have effects independent of other influences, which would not occur in the absence of the particular mass-media stimuli under scrutiny	Evidence that selective perception is only partially operative Evidence that media influence by setting the context and identifying the persons, events, and issues toward which existing predispositions affect attitudes and behavior Evidence that television violence increases aggressiveness among the young
4 (1970s–1980s)	Processes behind effects so far studied may be more general, suggesting new areas for research	New research is finding that under some circumstances television may influence behavior and attitudes other than those related to aggressiveness

Source: Data from George Comstock et al., "Evolution of Research on Effects of Mass Media," from *Television and Human Behavior* (Santa Monica, CA: RAND Corporation, 1978), p. 392. Used by permission.

for unnecessary purchases—what economist John Kenneth Galbraith termed the *synthesizing of wants*? It is generally believed that electronic mass media advertising can stimulate widespread demand for goods and services for which consumers had no prior need. Overnight it can build markets for virtually useless products or "new and improved" versions of old products. The standard rebuttal from advertising interests is that their activity plays an essential role in the mass marketing of consumer goods that enables lowering prices and enhancing variety.

Critics often conclude from its successes that advertising can overcome almost any defense a consumer can muster. Advertising practitioners find themselves wishing that were so. The failure of a high proportion of heavily advertised new products each year hardly supports the assumption that advertising is all-powerful. Not only do many products fail to catch on, but leading products often give way to competitors despite intensive advertising support. Marketers recognize this transfer of brand loyalty as an ever-present threat.

Effects on Children The possible effects of commercials in children's programs raise special issues of fairness and equity. Children start watching television early and find commercials just as fascinating as programs. Action for Children's Television (ACT) and other consumer organizations believe that commercials often take unfair advantage of young children who are not yet able to differentiate between advertising and programs.

During the 1970s, academic researchers, the industry, and government agencies conducted extensive research on the impact of children's television— both programs and advertising. Industry lobbying fended off effective Federal Trade Commission and Federal Communications Commission action. The FCC adopted rather ineffectual guidelines but refused to impose hard-and-fast rules. Deregulation in the 1980s further watered down the FCC's guidance.

FCC chooses guidelines, not rules, for children's programs

Action for Children's Television contested the FCC's failure to adopt rules, both in hearings before the commission and in the courts. A series of court decisions brought the proposal to limit advertising in children's programs back before the commission for reconsideration at the end of the 1980s. Under pressure from ACT and others, Congress passed a bill limiting the amount of advertising in children's programs. President Ronald Reagan vetoed the bill in 1988, but its proponents seemed likely to revive the issue in future sessions.

Impact of News 11.4

Research indicates that most people in the United States depend primarily on television for news (Roper Organization, 1984: 4). It therefore seems safe to assume that television journalism has important effects. Presumably, most of us perceive the world beyond our neighborhoods pretty much the way the media—especially the video media—present it to us.

Gatekeeping Only a tiny fraction of the events that occur in the world on any given day end up on our plate as "the news of the day." On its way to becoming the neatly packaged tidbits of the evening news, the raw reportage of events passes through the hands of many gatekeepers. Some gatekeepers decide which news events to cover and how stories should be written, edited, and positioned in the news presentation. Some gatekeepers are institutional— network organizations, for example. Individual allegiances to political, social, economic, or religious beliefs affect gatekeeping. Thus the media themselves profoundly influence their own content.

effects of TV's visual bias

Some gatekeeping occurs because of television's visual bias. Stories about combat, riot, mayhem, and vehicle crashes make better pictures than stories about less easily pictured but nevertheless important matters such as the economy, political issues, science, education, and the environment. Images tend to win out over substance in both factual and fictional television, opening the gate widely for exciting, dramatic happenings that make good pictures— hence the popularity of the action-news format and dramatic car-chase sequences in dramas.

Agenda Setting Gatekeeping focuses attention on selected events, persons, and issues that temporarily dominate the news. The list changes frequently as old items drop out and new ones claim attention. Researchers term this selection and ranking process *agenda setting,* one of the primary ways in which media affect our perception of the world.

In 1984–1985 television focused world attention on starvation in parts of Africa. The drought-induced disaster had been building for two years before a BBC film team's report appeared on *NBC Nightly News* in November 1984. The grim scenes of Ethiopian refugee camps, soon repeated on other television news programs, created a public outcry that vastly increased assistance to the victims. The 1990 Persian Gulf crisis brought the reality of wartime conditions in the desert to millions of homes through television coverage of the military build-up and fate of thousands of hostages held in Iraq.

A related effect, *prestige conferral,* arises from the very fact that an event appears on the current news agenda. Anything in the news acquires an aura of importance. Well-known anchors and correspondents lend glamour and significance to the events and persons they cover. If a story were not important, would Dan Rather, Tom Brokaw, and Peter Jennings bother to cover it? Conversely, can an event really matter if the networks choose to ignore it?

News Staging Television's need for images creates an ever-present temptation to beef up the pictorial impact of news stories artificially.

As a practical matter, a certain amount of artifice is accepted in news coverage. In televised interviews, for example, the camera usually focuses on the interviewee the entire time. "Reverse angle" shots of the interviewer can be taken afterward and spliced into the interview to provide visual give-and-take. This tactic allows single-camera interview coverage.

Outright staging of events by the subjects of news occurs when press agents and public-relations counselors seek to plant information in the media or to create happenings designed to attract media coverage. Daniel Boorstin (1964) coined the term *pseudo-events* to describe these contrived happenings. He analyzed such pseudo-event formats as press conferences, the trial balloon, the photo opportunity, the leaking of confidential information, and the background briefings "not for attribution."

personal experiment: look for news that reflects an influence by those being covered

Self-serving video handouts tempt stations that are hard pressed for photographic news material. The commercial and government purveyors of these handouts, which are known as *video news releases* (*VNRs*), bury their real message unobtrusively in pictorial material. In a rare instance of media self-criticism of such material, Dan Rather and others "decried as a whitewash" an Exxon VNR that exaggerated the oil company's role in cleaning up the 1989 *Valdez* oil spill in Alaska (Robins, 1990). Despite the obvious commercial or propaganda purpose of VNRs, few stations identify their sources.

Publicity Crimes   News staging for self-publicity took a vicious turn when terrorist organizations realized that their crimes gained enormous television news coverage. With increasing frequency in the 1980s, small and desperate political or religious groups sought world attention with airport bombings, hijackings, and kidnappings. These *publicity crimes* posed difficult ethical dilemmas for the news media. In a sense, the very act of reporting a publicity crime transforms the media into accomplices. The avidity with which audiences await the latest news about the crime makes members of the public accomplices as well.

Cameras in the Courts   Because of its glamour and influence, television itself tends to become an actor in the scenes it covers. At times news crews have been accused of deliberately intervening in news events—for example, encouraging mob action for the sake of enhancing the visual impact of a story. But even when video journalists remain scrupulously objective, the very presence of cameras tends to escalate or sensationalize ongoing action.

The problem of the effect of the medium on its subjects of coverage has long been debated in connection with courtroom trials. The assumption that the presence of cameras would influence defendants, witnesses, juries, and attorneys to the detriment of justice led legal authorities to ban live coverage in virtually all courtrooms. Judges took it for granted that radio and television coverage would endanger the right of fair trial. Yet one of the elements of a fair trial is that it be conducted in public.

long-time ban on court coverage

In time, news crews learned to downplay their presence. At the same time, improved equipment made their cameras and lights less conspicuous. Once the novelty of being photographed wears off, people become less self-conscious. They begin to accept the media paraphernalia as a normal part of the court environment. Changing coverage rules and other issues arising from cameras in courtrooms are discussed in Section 13.5.

Government as regulator of electronic mass media, the media as conduits of political information, advertising as a major factor in electing government officials—all these roles make the political effects of the media especially significant.

Election Campaigns   Almost from its beginning, broadcasting influenced political campaigning. Radio speeches by Calvin Coolidge, whose low-key delivery suited the microphone, may have been a factor in his 1924 reelection. President Franklin Roosevelt used radio masterfully in his four presidential campaigns, starting in 1932. Radio became especially important to Democratic candidates because it gave them a chance to appeal directly to voters, going over the heads of the newspapers, which were mostly controlled by Republicans.

how political spot-advertising began

Television brought hard-sell advertising techniques to the presidential campaign of 1952, when a leading advertising agency executive, Rosser Reeves, designed political spots for candidate Dwight Eisenhower. By the time Richard Nixon won the presidential election in 1968, television had become a key factor in political campaigning.

Since 1968, national party conventions have been staged to make them effective as television programs. Timing events to the second, convention managers allot a certain number of minutes for "spontaneous" demonstrations. By 1988, network officials said that conventions had become so predictable that viewer interest had dropped off, making it doubtful that future performances of the quadrennial political-party ritual would receive as extensive coverage as before, outside the normal news programs.

presidential candidate debates

Presidential candidate debates featuring the two leading opponents began to steal the spotlight from the conventions. The debate tradition began in 1960 with the confrontation between candidates Kennedy and Nixon. A special act of Congress suspended the Communication Act's mandate that *all* candidates must be given equal opportunities. The unusual confrontation stimulated a flurry of research. An exhaustive evaluation of the studies suggested that the "Great Debates" (as they were called) may have decided the close Kennedy-Nixon race (Rubin, 1967).

In the two 1988 televised debates between Vice President George Bush and Democratic nominee Michael Dukakis, Bush came across as "lean and mean." In contrast, Dukakis seemed wooden and cold. The debates appeared merely to confirm the cleverly orchestrated negativism of relentless Bush campaign advertising.

If political advertising is so powerful, it might seem a foregone conclusion that candidates with the most money and the best media consultants would win elections. Experience does not always bear out this conclusion. One reason may be that viewers have other sources of information: bona fide news and public-affairs programs about candidates continue side by side with the 30-second spots and contrived candidate appearances.

Moreover, candidates by no means rely entirely on broadcasting. A study commissioned by the National Association of Broadcasters analyzed official reports of 1986 campaign expenditures by federal Senate and House candidates. The study confirmed that broadcasting claimed the single biggest slice of the aggregate $400 million campaign budgets, but it accounted for only a quarter of the total. Direct mail came in as the second most costly medium (NAB, 1988).

On-air predictions of the outcomes even as the votes come in on national election days are especially controversial. Critics claim that early reports on voting trends based on incomplete returns in the eastern states cause lower turnout at voting booths in the West. Voters there sometimes conclude from television reports that their ballots cannot affect the outcome. In 1985, the networks responded to this complaint by promising to refrain from predicting the outcome of any state's voting until after the polls in that state had closed. By and large they adhered to that promise in reporting results of the 1986 and 1988 federal elections.

predicting outcomes
before polls are closed

Presidential Television   After the campaign is over, an elected American president enjoys almost insurmountable advantages over political opponents in exploiting the media. Other branches of government and members of opposing parties can do little to counterbalance the pervasive influence of presidential television. Presidents have endless opportunities to manufacture pseudo-events to support their policies or to divert attention from their failures. No matter how blatant the exploitation by presidents and their staffs may seem, news departments dare not entirely ignore presidential events. Virtually everything the head of state says or does has inherent news value.

the power of
presidential TV

As their single most potent weapon, chief executives can call on the broadcast and cable news networks to provide simultaneous national coverage of a presidential address. The national electronic forum gives the president a gigantic captive television audience—virtual monopoly access to some 70 percent of the potential viewers. Moreover, according to opinion surveys, such exposure usually pays off in increased acceptance of presidential policies. Exhibit 11.3 summarizes how presidents have varied in their use of television.

No law requires networks to grant presidential time requests. Indeed, not until President Lyndon Johnson's administration (1963–1969) did such requests become customary. The Nixon administration's attempts to control news and the loss of face caused by the Watergate scandal emboldened network news divisions to evaluate such requests more critically. The networks turned down time requests by Presidents Nixon, Ford, Carter, and Reagan at least once.

Ronald Reagan's use of broadcasting was more effective than any president's since Franklin Roosevelt's radio addresses in the 1930s. A one-time radio sports announcer, an experienced movie actor, and a veteran political speaker, Reagan was a consummate broadcaster. His commanding presidential physical presence made him extremely effective on television, but he also revived the

EXHIBIT **11.3**   Presidential TV

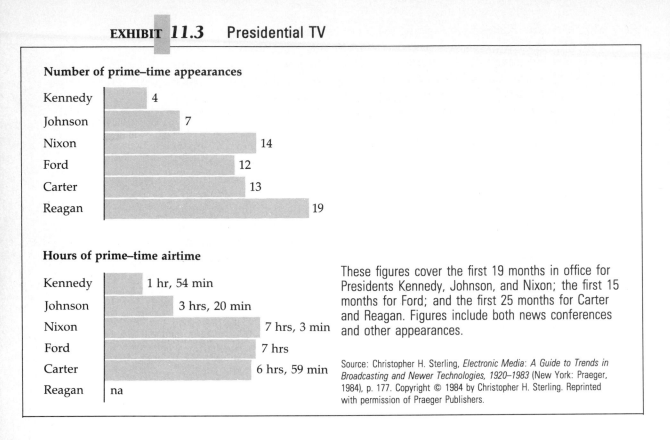

Number of prime–time appearances

Kennedy   4
Johnson   7
Nixon   14
Ford   12
Carter   13
Reagan   19

Hours of prime–time airtime

Kennedy   1 hr, 54 min
Johnson   3 hrs, 20 min
Nixon   7 hrs, 3 min
Ford   7 hrs
Carter   6 hrs, 59 min
Reagan   na

These figures cover the first 19 months in office for Presidents Kennedy, Johnson, and Nixon; the first 15 months for Ford; and the first 25 months for Carter and Reagan. Figures include both news conferences and other appearances.

Source: Christopher H. Sterling, *Electronic Media: A Guide to Trends in Broadcasting and Newer Technologies, 1920–1983* (New York: Praeger, 1984), p. 177. Copyright © 1984 by Christopher H. Sterling. Reprinted with permission of Praeger Publishers.

use of radio as a political weapon. His weekly recorded radio addresses, aired Saturdays throughout his two terms, were often quoted by other media.

However, Reagan's show-business discipline and uncanny ability to "hit his mark" (stop at the spot marked as just right for photography) gave him no help in unscripted situations. Because of blunders in the give-and-take of press conferences, Reagan's staff kept him even more isolated from reporters than previous chief executives of the television era had been. White House correspondents, frustrated by their lack of access, resorted to shouting questions at the president as he crossed the White House lawn to and from the presidential helicopter—an undignified practice, useful to the administration as a way of making reporters appear uncouth.

Congressional Television   The Senate, but not the House, began allowing television coverage of its committee hearings (subject to committee-chair approval) as early as the 1950s, leading to some notable television public-affairs coverage that had repercussions on the careers of participants. The names of Senators Estes Kefauver, Sam Ervin, and Joseph McCarthy became household words largely because of their roles in televised hearings. The first

committee hearings coverage precedes broadcasts of Congressional settings televised House committee deliberations came in 1974, when the Judiciary Committee debated the Nixon impeachment resolution.

However, for decades both houses resisted demands for the broadcasting of actual legislative sessions—in retrospect a strange reluctance on the part of democratically elected bodies. Finally, the House agreed to radio and television coverage in 1979—though it insisted on using House employees to handle the television pickup. The great liberty to carry the signal, live or recorded, at will. Unenthusiastic about coverage they themselves do not control, commercial broadcasters use only occasional excerpts of House debates. Cable subscribers, however, see gavel-to-gavel coverage on C-SPAN, the cable industry's noncommercial public-affairs network.

The favorable outcome of House television encouraged the Senate, which finally approved television coverage of its floor sessions in 1986. C-SPAN added a second channel, C-SPAN II, enabling live coverage of both legislative bodies in formal session. Congress had at last achieved a degree of video parity with the White House. Each can make the public aware of its activities and present its point of view on a daily basis via controlled television and radio facilities.

video parity: President vs. Congress

Furthermore, by the 1980s, the administration and Congress had developed sophisticated facilities for personal television appearances by individual officials. The House and Senate maintain fully equipped studios for members' use, and the White House can originate and feed interviews on short notice from its own studios.

TV and War 11.6

In World War II, radio broadcasting played a highly supportive role, helping to build both civilian and military morale. Television's first experience of war came with the Vietnam conflict (the Korean War of 1950–1953 occurred during the formative years of television news, before live coverage from remote places became possible).

Living-Room War Television made Vietnam a "living-room war," in the memorable phrase coined by Michael Arlen, television critic of *The New Yorker* (Arlen, 1969). In total, this longest war in American history played in the nation's living rooms for 15 years. CBS sent its first combat news team to Vietnam in 1961 and photographed the U.S. evacuation of Saigon in 1975. In the final shots, U.S. personnel beat back pro-American Vietnamese desperately trying to board the helicopters that picked up U.S. civilian employees at the last minute on the landing pad atop the U.S. Embassy.

Military censorship was minimal in this undeclared war, but White House officials and the generals in the field went to great lengths to steer reporters toward the kind of optimistic coverage expected by the administration.

During the early years of the Vietnam conflict, therefore, television coverage stressed U.S. efficiency and military might, playing down the gore and suffering of actual combat. But a new, more violent phase of news coverage followed the North Vietnamese 1968 Tet Offensive, which brought fighting to the very doors of the Saigon hotels where correspondents stayed. Thereafter, broadcast news teams began focusing more on combat realities. Vietnam became a real war in American living rooms, not the sanitized war of military public relations.

switch from PR to covering the real Vietnam War

Each network maintained its own news bureau in the field, and each bureau sent back two or three photographic stories and eight or ten radio tapes daily. In addition, many individual stations assigned reporters to the scene.

Following the communist Tet Offensive, several memorable televised events played a role in turning U.S. opinion against the war. The leading television journalist, CBS's Walter Cronkite, came back from a visit to Vietnam with a strongly negative report. Loss of Cronkite's support for the war is said to have confirmed President Lyndon Johnson in his surprise decision not to run for reelection. As historian David Halberstam put it, for the first time a war had been declared over by a news anchor. At about the same time, especially vivid photographic images from the battlefields such as those shown in Exhibit 11.4 became icons of American disillusionment with the Vietnam intervention.

influence of TV news on ending Vietnam involvement

Post-Vietnam Military TV   The role of broadcast news reporting in the Vietnam conflict raised troubling questions about future war reporting. Some commentators questioned whether it would be possible for the nation to wage war if television were allowed to reveal the brutal facts of combat night after night in the evening newscasts.

Illustrative of this problem was the reaction to the 1983 loss of American marines in Beirut. Vivid television aftermath coverage of a terrorist bombing that killed some 240 Americans in the Beirut U.S. Marine Barracks undermined public support for the "peacekeeping" role of U.S. forces in Lebanon. Public reaction seemingly made the venture politically untenable. In any event, despite prior assurances to the contrary, President Reagan pulled U.S. troops out of the area shortly after the bombing.

Military Censorship   Could the American public be trusted to support blindly a war whose real impact was kept invisible, at least temporarily, by rigid military censorship? Doubt on this point as well as obsessive concern with military security may have accounted for a White House order to bar press access to the initial American-led assault on the tiny Caribbean island of Grenada in 1984. For the first 48 hours, the world learned about events in Grenada mainly from military handouts.

military censorship denies coverage of Grenada landing

Subsequently, journalists disclosed military bumbling in conducting the invasion and apparent official misrepresentation of the circumstances leading

EXHIBIT 11.4   Televised War

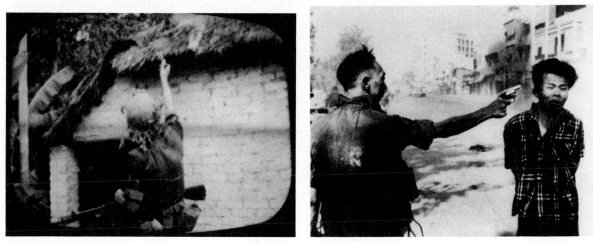

A.   B.

Two famous visual images of the war still have impact years later. Both came from televised stories carried on evening network newscasts. (*A*) In a report sent by correspondent Morley Safer, a marine touches the roof thatch of a South Vietnamese hut with his lighter to burn potential enemy hiding places. (*B*) The chief of the South Vietnamese police kills a Viet Cong suspect during the 1968 Tet Offensive.

Source: (A) Courtesy CBS; (B) AP/Wide World Photos.

up to it. These revelations came too late to dispel entirely the aura of success and righteousness surrounding "rescue" of American civilians allegedly endangered by the volatile political situation on the island. The public apparently supported the news blackout in Grenada, applauding the administration's actions. Nevertheless, the Grenada incident represented an abrupt departure from the usual practice. For example, journalists landed in France with the first assault waves on D-Day in World War II, an infinitely more sensitive security risk than the landing on Grenada.

The Pentagon eventually tacitly admitted that it had gone too far in banning coverage of the Grenada landing. It agreed to set up news pools to cover future military actions from the outset. But the Pentagon failed to follow through, blacking out the first few hours of the U.S. military assault on Panama in 1990. Not only the press but the Department of Defense itself blamed "obsessive secrecy" for this needless censorship (*Broadcasting*, 1990).

Effects of Entertainment

Any big news story that captures the headlines will soon become subject-matter for non-news television programs. In blending fact with fiction, **docudramas** add still more distortions to the already simplified version of reality presented in the news itself. Dramatic and comedy genres reflect news events less explicitly but nevertheless rely on them for much of their content.

Stereotypes Fiction influences audience perceptions by reinforcing **stereotypes**—stock characters deliberately oversimplified to fit in with pre-conceived images. Stereotypes usually convey detrimental images of the classes of people they portray—most often minorities and women. Among the character stereotypes familiar in popular drama are the Italian gangster, the in-scrutable Asian, the mad scientist, and the bespectacled female librarian.

why fiction cannot avoid stereotypes

A government-financed study examined how and why minorities and women are depicted the way they are in television. It explained that stereotypical character portrayal in television plays is virtually unavoidable:

> Television dramas have little time to develop situations or characters, necessi-tating the use of widely accepted notions of good and evil. Since the emphasis is on resolving the conflict or the problem at hand, there is little time to project the complexities of a character's thoughts or feelings or for dialogues which explore human relationships. To move the action along rapidly, the characters must be portrayed in ways which quickly identify them. Thus the character's physical appearance, environment, and behavior conform to widely accepted notions of the types of people they represent. (USCC, 1977: 27)

In short, stereotypes act as a kind of universally understood shorthand, re-ducing the need to spell out (or even *think* out) cast members' characters in detail.

The World of Fiction Often researchers doing content analyses take cen-suses of fictional characters. The demographic profiles of fictional populations invariably differ markedly from those of real-world populations.

For example, compared with real life, the world of fiction has far more men than women. The population consists mostly of young adults, with few very young or elderly persons. Many leading characters have no visible means of support, but those who do work have interesting, exciting, action-filled jobs. Fiction therefore contains an unrealistically high proportion of detec-tives, criminals, doctors, scientists, business executives, and adventurers com-pared with the real world, where unglamorous, dull, and repetitive jobs dominate. Most people in the real world solve their personal problems un-dramatically, even anticlimactically or incompletely, using socially approved methods. Fictional characters tend to solve their problems with decisive, highly visible acts, often entailing violence.

Of course, none of this should surprise us. Fact may be stranger than fiction, but fact does not occur in neatly packaged half-hour episodes with periodic commercial interruptions. Fiction necessarily involves creative artifice. Despite complaints from pressure groups that their members are inaccurately portrayed, fiction has no inherent obligation to reflect the literal facts of "real" life.

Socialization   The make-believe world of radio and television offers a persuasive model of reality for countless people. It especially influences children at the very time when they are eagerly reaching out to learn about the world. Viewers and listeners identify with heroes, participating vicariously in their adventures and therefore perhaps unconsciously absorbing their ways of thinking and doing.

The electronic mass media have become major agents of socialization—that all-important process that turns a squalling infant into a functioning member of society. Socialization, though a lifelong process, occurs intensively during the first few years of life, the time when children begin to learn the language, the meticulously detailed rules of behavior, and the value system of their culture.

In the past, socialization was always the jealously guarded prerogative of family and religion. It is formalized by education and reinforced by peer-group experiences. The intrusion of the electronic mass media as new, external agents of socialization represents a profound change. Most programs come from beyond the immediate circle of the family and its community-linked supports. Though part of the national culture, they import ideas, language, images, and practices that may be alien to the local culture. That was what the Supreme Court had in mind when it said obscenity should be defined in terms of local standards.

media as new, external agent of socialization

Significance of Time Spent   Whatever its content, entertainment that takes up so much of people's time presumably must have profound effects. At the very least, time spent watching or listening could have been spent in some other way—perhaps devoted to some useful, constructive activity. Some critics take it for granted that *anything* active would be more beneficial than the passive absorption of the couch potato. Somehow it seems *wrong* for people to waste their time staring like zombies at the television tube.

But it has not been proved that listening and watching necessarily displace more useful and active forms of recreation. In the absence of radio and television, people would do other things with their time, of course, but these would not necessarily be better or more beneficial things.

"Glow and Flow" Principle   Spending so much time listening and watching seems to imply uncritical acceptance of programs without regard to their content. Early in the television era, a commentator observed that it is "the watching experience that entertains. Viewers seem to be entertained by the *glow and the flow*" (Meyersohn, 1957: 347, italics added).

A landmark study of television-audience attitudes found that most of the people surveyed said they felt more satisfied with television as a medium than

TV as medium satisfies more than do individual programs

with specific programs. The researcher noted that "A large number of respondents were ready to say television is both relaxing and a waste of time" (Steiner, 1963: 411). Similar studies of attitudes made in the 1970s and 1980s indicated that this ambivalence persisted (Bower, 1973, 1985).

The glow-and-flow principle comes sharply to the fore in situations where electronic mass media become the only companions people have. Upon asking respondents to describe the satisfactions they derived from watching television, the researcher sometimes received moving testimonials such as this:

> I'm an old man and all alone, and the TV brings people and talk into my life. Maybe without TV, I would be ready to die; but this TV gives me life. It gives me what to look forward to—that tomorrow, if I live, I'll watch this and that program. (Steiner, 1963: 26)

TV as therapy

At extreme levels of deprivation, in hospitals and similar institutions, television has a recognized therapeutic function as the most valuable nonchemical sedative available.

Such findings suggest that perhaps a legitimate role of the electronic media may be that of simply killing time painlessly, providing a way to fill an otherwise unendurable void. The media give people a way of "performing leisure." But social critics worry that while we relax watching television with our guard down, some of its contents may have destructive antisocial effects. One such type of possibly detrimental content is violence.

11.8 *Theories About Televised Violence*

Research on media violence antedates television, going back to the 1930s, when a foundation underwrote a series of studies on the social effects of feature films (Jowett, 1976: 220). Concern about the potential effects of violence in fiction shifted to radio and comic books in the 1950s and later to television and rock videos. Along the way, emphasis progressed from merely measuring violent content and deploring its presumed effects toward buttressing conclusions about effects with explanatory theories.

Direct Imitation   Reports occasionally surface of real-life violence apparently modeled on actions seen in films or television programs. A particularly repellent example of apparent direct imitation led to an unprecedented lawsuit. In 1974 NBC broadcast a made-for-television movie called *Born Innocent,* in which inmates of a detention home for young delinquents "raped" a young girl with a mop handle. Four days after the telecast, older children subjected a 9-year-old California girl to a similar ordeal, using a soft-drink bottle. Parents of the child sued NBC, asking $11 million in damages for negligence in showing the rape scene, which, they alleged, had directly incited the attack on their daughter (Cal., 1981).

NBC's attorneys successfully argued that the suit raised a First Amendment issue, not a negligence issue. Did NBC, by broadcasting the program in question, deliberately incite the children to attack their victim? Finding that such incitement could not be proved, the court dismissed the suit.

responsibility of networks for programs that incite violence

A less traumatic incident of alleged imitation happened in 1990, when a pair of young men riding a motorcycle snatched a Miami woman's purse. The thieves later claimed that one of Karl Malden's "don't leave home without it" credit-card commercials had inspired their action.

Generalized Violence Effects Public concern about televised violence focuses more on pervasive, generalized effects than on such isolated instances of imitation, unfortunate though they are.

Another much-publicized court case in 1977 illustrates the generalized-effects theory. The state of Florida charged a 16-year-old boy, Ronnie Zamora, with using a gun, found in the victim's house, to murder an elderly neighbor during an attempted robbery. The boy's attorney tried to build a defense on the argument that Zamora could not be held legally responsible for the crime because the boy was a television addict. As such, he had become intoxicated by the thousands of murders he had seen enacted on the screen. Though he had never held a gun before the shooting, television had so conditioned him that he used it without thinking. The intoxication defense failed to convince the jury. Zamora received a 25-year mandatory jail sentence.

TV "intoxication" as a cause of crime

The Zamora case won worldwide attention and its repercussions continue to this day. Following the 1989 publication of a book by Zamora's attorney, he and the psychiatrist who testified in the case publicly blamed each other for the failure of the television intoxication defense (Rubin, 1989). Whether or not Zamora's attorney botched his defense, as alleged by some Miami lawyers, the argument gained strength from research accumulated during the 1960s and 1970s.

As long ago as 1972, the U.S. surgeon general, reporting to Congress on a large group of scientific effects studies, warned,

> the unanimous Scientific Advisory Committee's report indicates that televised violence, indeed, does have an adverse effect on certain members of our society. . . . The causal relationship between televised violence and antisocial behavior is sufficient to warrant appropriate and immediate remedial action. (Senate CC, 1972: 26)

The comprehensive analysis of the research literature commissioned by the surgeon general's committee established that, of all the types of television effects that had been studied, television's linkage to violent aggression had been the most intensively analyzed. Every research method available had been employed in the study of televised violence, making the cumulative evidence of its effects especially persuasive. The researchers later summarized their findings by saying,

violence: most-studied aspect of TV content

The evidence is that television may increase aggression by teaching viewers previously unfamiliar hostile acts, by generally encouraging in various ways the use of aggression, and by triggering aggressive behavior both imitative and different in kind from what has been viewed. (Comstock et al., 1978: 13)

Despite these findings and even further confirmation in subsequent studies, the First Amendment continues to stand in the way of the "appropriate and immediate remedial action" recommended by the surgeon general.

Desensitization One effects theory holds that repeated viewing of fictional violence reduces its impact by making it seem routine. This **desensitization hypothesis** speculates that constant exposure to television violence makes people indifferent to real-life violence. Reports of the many instances of passers-by ignoring calls for help in episodes of urban violence lend color to this hypothesis.

A related notion, the **sanitization hypothesis,** holds that self-imposed program codes cause television to depict violence unrealistically because graphic literalness would encounter viewer backlash. Even news reports have to be sanitized to some extent in conformity with public expectations. As a result, the televised consequences of fictional violence seem so neat and clean that viewers remain indifferent. They never see or hear the revolting, bloody aftermath of real-life violence.

In Defense of Violence Can anything be said in justification of violence in fiction? Despite the range and depth of research evidence that antisocial effects result from televised violence, not only the First Amendment but also the needs of program creators stand in the way of change. Writers would face a difficult challenge if they had to meet television's relentless appetite for drama without resorting to violent clashes between opposing forces. Writers point out that violence occurs in all forms of literature. Bodies litter the stage when the curtain falls on some of Shakespeare's tragedies. Even the classic fairy tales for children contain many scary episodes of violence.

When researchers studied the attitudes and opinions of writers, producers, network executives, and program-standards chiefs, these professionals said they simply could not create enough interesting entertainment programs without recourse to violence (Baldwin and Lewis, 1972).

why TV drama writers resort to violent conflicts

For example, a successful television playwright pointed out that scriptwriters rely on four basic types of conflicts around which to build dramatic plots:

- *Man against nature*: "This is usually too expensive for television."
- *Man against God*: "Too intellectual for television."
- *Man against himself*: "Too psychological, and doesn't leave enough room for action."
- *Man against man*: "This is what you usually end up with."

In short, the one type of dramatic conflict that best suits the exigencies of television happens to be the one most likely to involve personal violence.

Another justification cites the ancient Greek dramatic theory propounded by Aristotle, that of catharsis—violence in stage tragedy arouses pity and fear, relieving tension and purging the emotions. According to the analogous modern argument, fictional violence defuses television viewers' aggressive feelings by diverting them into harmless fantasies. Most experimental studies, however, suggest that seeing fictional violence arouses viewers' aggressive feelings rather than purging them (Comstock et al., 1978: 237). catharsis theory

To summarize the conflicting viewpoints on the violence issue: research indicates that televised violence *can* cause adverse social effects; that conclusion calls for the imposition of restraints. Any restraints other than voluntary ones, however, encounter resistance from writers, producers, media managers, and ultimately from the courts in terms of First Amendment rights. Such collisions between the goal of speech freedom and other desirable social goals occur in other contexts as well. Some of the dilemmas caused by this conflict of goals are discussed further in Chapter 13.

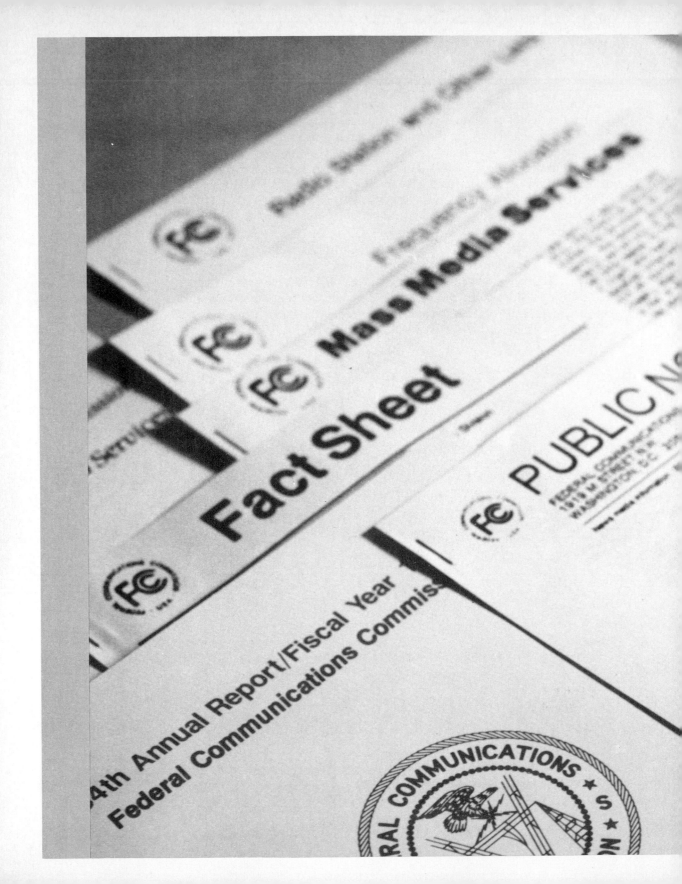

Regulation: Laws, Agencies, and Pressure Groups

12

The previous chapter surveyed the pervasive social effects of the electronic mass media—some real, some probably only imagined. As long as people believe that effects actually take place, they want to have some control over them. They want to maximize beneficial effects (from wholesome entertainment and useful information, for example) while at the same time minimizing possible harmful effects (from pornography and misleading propaganda, for example).

Social control comes primarily from government licensing, which determines who is allowed to operate stations, cable television systems, and other program outlets. Licensing not only selects operators but also enables monitoring and regulating their performance. In addition to these formal controls imposed by government in the name of the people generally, individuals and advocacy groups also exert more specific influences. They make their wishes known to legislators, regulators, and courts, and they bring pressures to bear on station and cable-system operators, networks, advertisers, and production companies.

12.1 *Federal Jurisdiction*

The commerce clause in Article I of the Constitution gives Congress the power "to regulate commerce with foreign nations, and among the several states." This constitutional power has been vital to U.S. economic development. It has prevented the individual states from erecting internal trade barriers that could undermine economic efficiency and national unity.

Communicating by mail and wire had long been accepted as forms of "commerce" under the Constitution. This precedent justified passing laws to govern radio communication. The current statute, the Communications Act of 1934, forms a link in the chain of responsibility extending from the Constitution to the people, as shown in Exhibit 12.1

The commerce clause gives Congress jurisdiction over *interstate* and *foreign* commerce but not over commerce within individual states. The law regards radio communications, including all kinds of broadcasting, as *interstate by definition*. Radio transmissions, even if low in power and designed to cover a limited area within a state, do not simply stop at state boundaries. Wire communication, in contrast, can be cut off precisely at the state line, justifying *state* regulation of services such as telephony as long as they remain *intrastate* in scope.

Congress established the Federal Radio Commission in 1927 and its successor, the Federal Communications Commission (FCC), in 1934 to act on its behalf. The legislative body assigns day-to-day regulatory authority to the FCC. House and Senate committees constantly monitor the FCC, which must come back to Congress annually for budget appropriations.

Congress gives the FCC power to adopt, modify, and repeal regulations, concerning interstate electronic media. These regulations, derived from the Communications Act, carry the force of federal law. Any FCC regulation not fully justified by the act can be nullified by a successful appeal to the courts. Thus an understanding of the Communications Act is vital to an understanding of the FCC's day-to-day regulatory role.

12.2 *Communications Act Basics*

Definitions The act defines the term **broadcasting** as "the dissemination of radio communications intended to be received by the public directly or

EXHIBIT **12.1**   Broadcasting Regulation: The Chain of Legal Authority

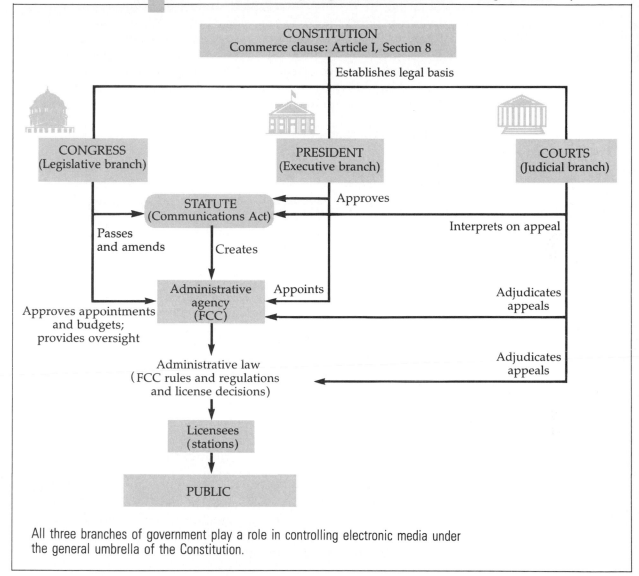

All three branches of government play a role in controlling electronic media under the general umbrella of the Constitution.

by intermediary or relay stations." The phrase "intended to be received by the public" excludes from the definition of *broadcasting* private radio communications aimed at individuals or specific groups of individuals. It is illegal for the public to intercept *non*broadcast signals such as pay television without permission. Nor may people use broadcasting to send private messages— sports figures who wave and say "Hi, Mom" technically violate the law. And the unauthorized-publication clause in the Communications Act (Section

705a) forbids disclosure of nonbroadcast messages to people for whom they were not intended.

law includes TV as "transmission by radio"

Finally, the act gives the term *radio* wide meaning. Radio communication means "transmission by radio of writing, signs, signals, pictures, and sounds of all kinds, including all instrumentalities, facilities, apparatus, and services . . . incidental to such transmission" (Section 3). Thus the FCC was able to extend its regulations to television without asking for an amendment to an act originally written to cover only AM radio.

Federal Communications Commission   Congress wrote the law that established the Federal Communications Commission, but the president appoints the five commissioners, with the advice and consent of the Senate. The act gives the commission broad powers to "perform any and all acts, make such rules and regulations, and issue such orders . . . as may be necessary in the execution of its functions."

In only a few instances did Congress tie the commission's hands with hard-and-fast requirements. For example, the act limits the term of broadcasting licenses and restricts ownership of broadcast stations to U.S. citizens.

Public-Interest Standard   Congress used a highly flexible but legally recognized standard to limit the commission's discretion—*public interest, convenience, or* (sometimes *and*) *necessity.* This phrase occurs in key sections of the broadcasting parts of the act. For example, Section 303 begins: "Except as otherwise provided in this Act, the Commission from time to time, as *public convenience, interest, or necessity* requires shall . . . " (italics added). That section goes on to list 19 functions, ranging from the power to classify radio stations to the power to make whatever rules and regulations are necessary to carry out the provisions of the law. The crucial acts of granting, renewing, and transferring broadcast licenses must also serve the *public interest* (the shorthand phrase that usually stands in for "public convenience, interest, or necessity").

"public-interest" standard not extended to cable TV

Congress chose the public-interest standard to give the FCC maximum flexibility in meeting unforeseeable situations. In contrast, the 1984 Cable Act (added as an amendment to the Communications Act) nowhere uses the *public-interest* phrase. This omission means that the FCC has far less latitude in regulating cable than broadcasting.

Communications Act Amendments   The Communications Act of 1934 has been continually updated since its passage. However, its basic principles have changed little, despite modifications to meet the modern needs of a much larger and more complicated electronic media industry.

One of the longest and most far-reaching amendments was the Cable Communications Policy Act of 1984 (here referred to simply as the Cable Act). For decades the legal status of cable television under the Communications Act remained uncertain. Cable systems usually cover limited *intra*state areas, technically falling outside FCC jurisdiction over *inter*state wire communication. In some ways cable operators play nonbroadcast roles, acting more like common carriers, as when they designate channels for commercial leasing and for local access. But they act like broadcasters when they retain editorial control over the content of other channels.

hybrid character of cable TV

The Cable Act finally clarified the long-standing question of definition, identifying cable television as *neither* a common carrier *nor* a broadcasting service. It gives the all-important licensing power (called *franchising* in this case) to the local communities in which cable systems operate. The franchising process is discussed later, in Section 12.10.

FCC Basics   12.3

Functions   Under the federal separation-of-powers doctrine, separate branches of government normally carry out administrative, legislative, and judicial tasks. But the FCC and other federal independent regulatory agencies combine the three functions. As a "creature of Congress" the FCC enacts federal regulations, taking on a quasi-legislative role. It also functions as an executive agency by putting the will of Congress into effect. And when the FCC interprets the Communications Act, conducts hearings, and decides disputes, it takes on a judicial role.

Budget and Staff   For fiscal year 1990, Congress appropriated just over $100 million for the FCC. This budget level makes the commission a small federal agency, employing about 1,800 persons. Exhibit 12.2 depicts its organizational structure. The unit of most interest here, the Mass Media Bureau, has four divisions—Audio Services, Video Services, Policy and Rules, and Enforcement.

The five commissioners (seven prior to 1983) serve five-year terms and may be reappointed. Commissioners must be citizens, may not have a financial interest in any type of communications business, and must devote full time to the job. They meet several times each month in formal sessions open to the public. An incoming president can have immediate impact on the commission by designating one of the existing members as chair.

statutory requirements for appointment to FCC

Staff Role in Decision Making   References to "the commission" usually signify not only the five commissioners but also the senior staff members. The FCC staff handles most applications, inquiries, and complaints, few of which need to come to the commissioners' personal attention. Except for top administrators, whom the chairperson appoints, the staff consists of permanent federal civil service employees.

EXHIBIT **12.2**   FCC Organization

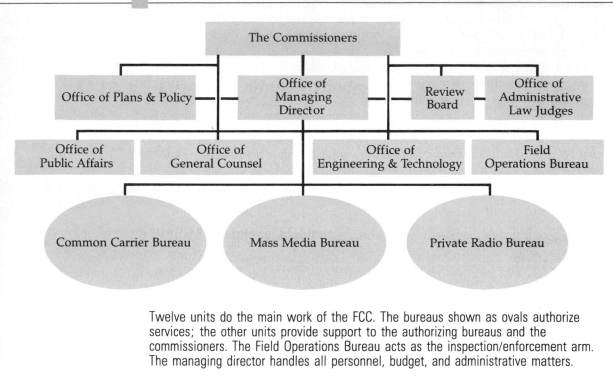

Twelve units do the main work of the FCC. The bureaus shown as ovals authorize services; the other units provide support to the authorizing bureaus and the commissioners. The Field Operations Bureau acts as the inspection/enforcement arm. The managing director handles all personnel, budget, and administrative matters.

To be entitled to make decisions on its own, the staff needs formally delegated authority from the commissioners and guidance by *processing rules.* These rules spell out which decisions may be settled at the staff level and which need to be considered by the commissioners themselves.

Rule Making   A major part of the FCC's work consists in making "rules and regulations" (a formal term—rules do not differ from regulations). Collectively, they form a large body of *administrative law.* Commission proposals or petitioners' requests for a new rule or a change in an old one can take several routes, as outlined in Exhibit 12.3. On rare occasions, proposed rule changes of special significance or of a controversial nature may be scheduled for *oral argument* on "The Eighth Floor," meaning the public hearing room in the FCC's Washington headquarters building.

In some situations, rule making would be too cumbersome, too restrictive, or simply too difficult to defend. In such cases, the FCC may resort to the less formal, less definitive action of *policy making.* Policy statements summarize past actions and lay down general guidelines for the future, but they do not make hard-and-fast rules.

EXHIBIT 12.3 FCC Rule Making Process

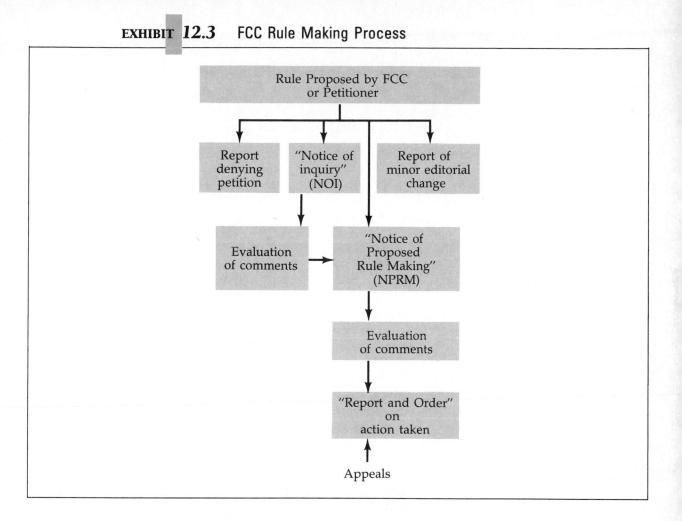

Adjudication A second major part of the FCC's job consists of *adjudication*—the settling of specific disputes. Disputes occur between outside parties (such as rival applicants for a television channel) or between the FCC and an outside party (the Mass Media Bureau versus a station owner who protests the imposition of a fine, for example).

The staff settles simpler disputes summarily in accordance with the guidelines previously mentioned, but many become the subjects of formal *hearings*. Broadcasters normally try to avoid hearings, which resemble court-room proceedings. They nearly always take place in Washington, require expensive legal representation, and can take a long time.

Informal FCC Regulation In addition to making formal rules and adjudicating disputes, the FCC can influence licensee conduct informally. Station owners pay close attention to FCC members' public statements in meetings, speeches, and articles. A commissioner's "raised eyebrow" can give licensees a hint, a warning, or a threat.

Carried a step further, such informal regulation sometimes takes the more explicit form of *jawboning*—persuasion of a rather heavy-handed, intimidating quality. In a notorious jawboning case in the 1970s, the FCC attempted to deflect congressional heat aroused by the commission's failure to deal with alleged indecent broadcasts. The commission persuaded the industry itself to take action against objectionable broadcasts by amending the voluntary Television Code that was then in effect. However, a court overturned the action, saying that the FCC had used indirect censorship, in violation of the First Amendment. The case is discussed at more length in Section 12.14.

Critique of FCC   Over the years, the FCC has been among the most frequently dissected and analyzed of the federal regulatory agencies. It has not fared well in these analyses. Official investigations and private studies have reached scathing conclusions with monotonous regularity. Following are examples of the recurrent points of criticism:

political requirements for appointment to FCC

- Presidents use commission appointments to pay off political debts—minor ones in the case of FCC members because their jobs rank low in the hierarchy of Washington positions that an incoming administration can fill.
- As political appointees, commissioners tend to lack the expertise and sometimes the dedication implied by the Communications Act. Experts in communication engineering, the media, common carriers, and the relevant academic specialties have rarely been appointed. Instead appointees have usually been lawyers or bureaucrats.
- Few commissioners stay in office long enough to attain great expertise, sometimes resigning even before the end of their five-year terms. They move on to higher-paying positions, usually in private law practices dealing with the very industries they have previously been regulating.

However, it is somewhat misleading to speak of *the* FCC. As its membership (along with the administration in Washington) changes, the commission takes on varying complexions—sometimes reform minded, sometimes more interested in the welfare of the businesses it regulates than in the public interest. The Reagan commission of the 1980s under Mark Fowler pushed deregulation with such unrelenting zeal that it frequently clashed with Congress. Its successor of the 1990s under Al Sikes also followed conservative policies but seemed ready to restore some of the public-interest safeguards abandoned by the Fowler commission.

12.4 *Station Licensing*

The *authorizing* of services—licensing of broadcasting stations and franchising of cable television systems—is the single most important regulatory function.

Most other regulation derives from the basic act of authorization. Licensing a broadcast station does not confer ownership of a channel. No one can literally "own" any part of the electromagnetic spectrum. Therefore licenses are always subject to renewal and even to withdrawal.

no one can "own" a channel

Construction Permit   Before applying for a license, a would-be station operator must first apply for a construction permit (CP). The permit allows the applicant to construct a new station or to make changes in an existing station, such as relocating the transmitter or main studio. A CP gives its holder a limited time (usually 24 months for television and 18 for radio) to construct and test the station. After showing satisfactory proof of performance as planned, the CP holder applies for a full license. While awaiting formal license approval, a permittee may request permission to begin on-air program testing.

Licensee Qualifications   The Communications Act allows the FCC to grant licenses only to applicants who qualify as to U.S. citizenship, character, financial resources, and technical ability. Congress left the FCC wide discretion in implementing and interpreting these basic ownership requirements.

Citizenship   An alien may not control a broadcast license, though foreign investors may own up to 20 percent of a license-holding corporation's shares.

aliens may not have broadcast licenses

Character   Applicants must have personal and business histories free of evidence suggesting defects in character that would cast doubt on their ability to operate in the public interest. "Character" in this context can refer to evidence of questionable corporate financial practices as well as to personal defects. In 1990 the commission said it would broaden the scope of the character test to include *nonbroadcast* misconduct. In the recent past, the commission had disregarded evidence of character defects of applicants and licensees if the defects did not bear directly on broadcasting.

Financial resources   Applicants certify that they have "sufficient" money. The FCC has varied the definition of "sufficient," but currently it means ability to construct and operate the proposed facilities for the first 90 days of broadcasting without reliance on revenues from advertising.

Technical ability   Most applicants hire engineering consultants who specialize in showing how a proposed station can maximize the coverage area of its signal without causing objectionable interference to existing stations. Plans must also show expertise in meeting FCC engineering standards.

Comparative Hearings   When more than one applicant seeks the same channel, they all usually meet the minimum statutory qualifications outlined above. These *mutually exclusive* applicants then become subject to a *comparative hearing*. In comparative hearings, the FCC exercises its right under the

Communications Act to specify "other qualifications," such as the degree of local ownership and the role of minorities and women in management of the proposed station.

Not all mutually exclusive applications warrant the expense and effort of formal comparative hearings. When an embarrassingly large build-up of low-power television (LPTV) construction applications occurred in the early 1980s, the FCC asked Congress to authorize it to choose among mutually exclusive applicants by lot instead of going through hearings.

Congress amended the Communications Act in 1982 accordingly for new (*not* renewal) applicants. The amendment also covers MMDS, cellular telephone, and radio paging applications. By the end of the 1980's, LPTV and MMDS lotteries had been held for all markets, virtually ending the application backlog.

Minority Preferences One of the goals of issuing LPTV licenses is to diversify station ownership (and hence, indirectly, programming). Congress therefore included in the lottery amendment a provision giving a two-to-one *minority preference* to firms controlled more than 50 percent by minorities and a two-to-one *diversity preference* to applicants with no ownership interests in other media.

Minority and diversity preferences can be combined. For example, the chances of a minority-controlled firm with no other media interests being selected in a lottery would be four times as great as the chances of firms not having those preferential characteristics. The firm's name would appear on four tokens in the lottery barrel instead of only one. The first LPTV lottery, held in September 1983, resulted in 23 grants, 8 to minority applicants. The constitutionality of minority preferences was challenged, but in 1990 the Supreme Court upheld them.

Nonlicensed Services The FCC requires virtually all spectrum-using electronic mass media and common carriers to obtain licenses in order to operate. The few exceptions include

- Radio-station auxiliary services transmitted on subcarriers and neither related to broadcasting nor decoded by regular radio receivers.
- Teletext and closed-caption services broadcast by television stations.
- Carrier-current radio stations such as those used on college campuses.

12.5 *Licensees and Networks*

The Communications Act focuses attention on *stations,* making no explicit provision for regulating networks. Congress apparently failed to foresee that, as a natural outgrowth of the medium's economics and technology, networks would become the dominant force in broadcasting.

preferences given women, minorities, and local owners

choosing applicants by lottery

minority preferences upheld by Supreme Court

Chain Broadcasting Regulations   When the FCC became concerned about the extent to which radio-network affiliates were losing their autonomy as independent stations serving their own local communities, it resorted to indirect regulation based on rules governing affiliation agreements. The first network-affiliation rules came into force in 1943, when the Supreme Court upheld the FCC's **chain broadcasting regulations.** Among other things, they forbade radio (and later, television) affiliates from

network regulation through rules on affiliation contracts

- Giving a network exclusive access to its time.
- Preventing another station in an affiliate's market from taking network programs that the affiliate turns down.
- Making affiliation agreements for longer than two years at a time.
- Surrendering the right to reject network programs.

Fin/Syn Rules   In 1972–1973 the FCC adopted further rules aimed directly at networks—the *financial interest* and the *network syndication* rules, known collectively as "fin/syn." **Fin/syn regulations** forbid networks from having a financial interest in programs produced for them by outside companies (the networks may pay only **license fees**—the amount producers charge for initial network showings of such programs). Nor may networks act as program syndicators within the United States (they may syndicate programs abroad). Similar rules limit network in-house entertainment productions to no more than ten half-hour series per network in prime time. The slowly expanding Fox network was exempted from these rules. That gave the other networks added reason to pressure the FCC to drop its fin/syn rules. They argue that the increased competition they face nowadays removes any need for such restrictions.

pressure to drop fin/syn rules

Monitoring Station Operations   12.6

Ideally, the FCC should monitor station operations constantly to ensure operation in the public interest, as required by the Communications Act. However, it is just not feasible for the commission to keep watch over all the programs of some 12,000 stations.

FCC Inspections   In the course of normal operations, broadcasters experience little official supervision. Inspectors from the FCC's Field Operations Bureau check on technical aspects of station operations, but only occasionally and in random fashion. The FCC relies on complaints from the general public, from competitors, and from would-be competitors to call attention to most transgressions.

the public's complaints get FCC attention

EXHIBIT 12.4   EEO Mandates and Staff Size

Number of full-time employees	EEO requirements
1 to 4*	Need not file an EEO plan.
5 to 10	Station EEO programs will be reviewed by the FCC unless the percentage of minority and women employees equals half of their representation in the local labor force. In other words, if a market's labor force, as defined by the Census Bureau, is half black, at least one-quarter of a licensee's employees in that market should be from that minority group. In the top job categories (officers and managers, professionals, technicians, and salespersons), a station should have a minority-employee ratio of at least one-quarter of that minority's representation in the local labor force. If half of the local labor force is black, at least one-eighth of the top-4 station jobs should be held by blacks.
11 or more	Should employ at least half as many minorities and women as are represented in the local labor force overall *and* in the top-4 job categories (officers and managers, professionals, technicians, and salespersons).
50 or more†	Same as for stations with 11 or more employees; but in addition, EEO programs are regularly reviewed.

*This category consists mainly of radio stations.
†Most of these are television operations.

Employment Practices   However, Congress explicitly directed the FCC to monitor employment practices. Each station employing more than five people full-time must set up a "positive, continuing program of practices assuring equal employment opportunities." These equal employment opportunity (EEO) requirements refer to women in all cases and to minority ethnic groups in cases where they form 5 percent or more of the workforce in a station's or cable system's service area.

Both stations and cable systems must submit annual employment reports to the FCC. These reports must also be kept in the station's or cable system's public file, discussed below. The FCC may review licensees' recent EEO records when considering applications for license renewal. Exhibit 12.4 shows how EEO reporting requirements differ according to unit size.

another clash between FCC and Congress

In the early 1980s, conservatives in the Reagan administration and at the FCC who opposed quotas in employment objected to the EEO guidelines. Nevertheless, Congress extended the broadcast EEO requirements to cable systems in the 1984 Cable Act. The FCC persisted in questioning the role of quotas until Congress ruled in an FCC budget bill that all EEO requirements must remain in place. A Supreme Court test of the legality of the EEO procedures is pending.

Station Public File   The station's *public file,* in which EEO employment reports must be placed, consists of a packet of documents that each licensee must assemble and keep ready to show, during business hours, to any member of the public on request. Cable systems have to maintain a public file consisting only of employment-related documents. The more inclusive broadcast public file includes

- The latest construction permits or license applications, including any for major changes.
- The last two license-renewal applications.
- Ownership and annual employment reports.
- A pamphlet entitled "The Public and Broadcasting—A Procedural Manual" issued by the FCC in 1974, now much out of date.
- A record of political candidates' requests for broadcast time during the past two years.
- A quarterly listing of programs, broadcast by the licensee, dealing with significant community issues.
- Letters received from members of the public (to be kept for three years) and a copy of any agreement a station may have made with citizens' groups (stations sometimes formally agree to concessions demanded by organized audience groups in order to forestall citizen opposition to license renewal).

Deregulation reduced the size of the public file, but broadcasters and other supporters of deregulation still regard keeping it as a waste of time. Members of the public rarely ask to see it. The public file has become so meaningless that when college broadcasting students are sent on field-trip assignments to examine the files, they often get blank stares or flat refusals from station personnel, who apparently either know nothing about the rule or believe the FCC will not come down on them for violating it. Which reason prevails might be an interesting parting question for the student investigator to ask!

personal experiment: examine a station's public file

Complaints to FCC   Although members of the public rarely consult a station's public file, they frequently complain directly to the FCC about program and commercial practices. The Mass Media Bureau's Enforcement Division receives more public comments than any other federal agency, aside from those dealing with environmental protection and consumer product safety.

Few complainants seem to understand the FCC's legal limitations. Most ask the commission to violate the First Amendment by censoring material that the writers personally dislike. The leading topics vary only slightly from year to year, influenced by program trends and organized letter-writing campaigns.

1st Amendment blocks FCC action on most complaints

One notorious organized letter-writing campaign began in 1975 and still goes on. A maverick critic petitioned the FCC to impose a freeze on the licensing of noncommercial educational stations to government and religious groups. The petitioner wanted the FCC to investigate the extent to which these groups complied with the fairness doctrine (then still in effect) and whether they fulfilled the educational purposes of the noncommercial allocations. The FCC rejected the petition less than a year after it was submitted. Nevertheless, the Mass Media Bureau received millions of complaints about this short-lived threat to religious broadcasters. Complaints still pour in, 15 years after the matter was closed.

12.7 *Station License Renewal*

length of broadcast license periods

The Communications Act says that licenses may be awarded for only "limited periods of time." A television licensee must apply for renewal before the end of the five-year license period (seven years for radio stations). The temporary nature of licenses greatly enhances the power implicit in the FCC's licensing authority. Although the FCC renews more than 98 percent of all licenses without asking any searching questions, licensees always feel the possibility of nonrenewal lurking in the background.

License-Renewal Routes Challenges to renewal applications can come from other would-be licensees and from dissatisfied citizens in the licensee's community. Incumbents win most such contests, but defending renewal challenges can be both expensive and time consuming.

The Communications Act stipulates that licenses shall be renewed "if the public interest, convenience, and necessity would be served" by renewal. Before deregulation simplified the process, a renewal application required

EXHIBIT 12.5   Renewal Paperwork: Before and After Deregulation

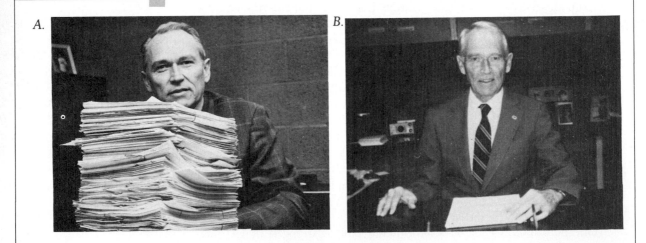

A.   B.

A. In 1971, before deregulation, it took more than 16 pounds of paperwork to file for renewal of four Nebraska stations. B. In 1983, this small stack of papers along with (C) a double-sided renewal postcard did the same job.

EXHIBIT **12.5** *Continued*

C.

Federal Communications Commission
Washington, D.C. 20554

**APPLICATION FOR RENEWAL OF LICENSE FOR
COMMERCIAL AND NONCOMMERCIAL AM, FM OR TV BROADCAST STATION**

Approved by OMB
3060-0110
Expires 5/31/91

For Commission Fee Use Only	For Applicant Fee Use Only
FEE NO:	Is a fee submitted with this application? ☐ Yes ☐ No
FEE TYPE:	If No, indicate reason therefor (check one box): ☐ Nonfeeable application
FEE AMT:	Fee Exempt (See 47 C.F.R. Section 1.1112)
ID SEQ:	☐ Noncommercial educational licensee
For Commission Use Only: File No.	☐ Governmental entity

1. Name of Applicant

Mailing Address

City	State	ZIP Code

2. This application is for: ☐ AM   ☐ FM   ☐ TV

(a) Call Letters:	(b) Principal Community: City State

3. Attach as Exhibit No. _____ an identification of any FM booster or TV booster station for which renewal of license is also requested.

4. Have the following reports been filed with the Commission:

(a) The Broadcast Station Annual Employment Reports (FCC Form 395-B) as required by 47 C.F.R. Section 73.3612?   ☐ Yes ☐ No

If No, attach as Exhibit No. _____ an explanation.

(b) The applicant's Ownership Report (FCC Form 323 or 323-E) as required by 47 C.F.R. Section 73.3615?   ☐ Yes ☐ No

If No, give the following information:
Date last ownership report was filed _____
Call letters of station for which it was filed _____

FCC 303-S
May 1988

---

5. Is the applicant in compliance with the provisions of Section 310 of the Communications Act of 1934, as amended, relating to interests of aliens and foreign governments?   ☐ Yes ☐ No

If No, attach as Exhibit No. _____ an explanation.

6. Since the filing of the applicant's last renewal application for this station or other major application, has an adverse finding been made or final action been taken by any court or administrative body with respect to the applicant or parties to the application in a civil or criminal proceeding, brought under the provisions of any law relating to the following: any felony; broadcast related antitrust or unfair competition; criminal fraud or fraud before another governmental unit; or discrimination?   ☐ Yes ☐ No

If Yes, attach as Exhibit No. _____ a full description of the persons and matters involved, including an identification of the court or administrative body and the proceeding (by dates and file numbers) and the disposition of the litigation.

7. Would a Commission grant of this application come within 47 C.F.R. Section 1.1307, such that it may have a significant environmental impact?   ☐ Yes ☐ No

If Yes, attach as Exhibit No. _____ an Environmental Assessment required by 47 C.F.R. Section 1.1311.

If No, explain briefly why not.

8. Has the applicant placed in its station's public inspection file at the appropriate times the documentation required by 47 C.F.R. Sections 73.3526 or 73.3527?   ☐ Yes ☐ No

If No, attach as Exhibit No. _____ a complete statement of explanation.

The APPLICANT hereby waives any claim to the use of any particular frequency or of the electromagnetic spectrum as against the regulatory power of the United States because of the previous use of the same, whether by license or otherwise, and requests an authorization in accordance with this application. (See Section 304 of the Communications Act of 1934, as amended.)

The APPLICANT acknowledges that all the statements made in this application and attached exhibits are considered material representations and that all the exhibits are a material part hereof and are incorporated herein as set out in full in the application.

CERTIFICATION: I certify that the statements in this application are true, complete, and correct to the best of my knowledge and belief, and are made in good faith.

Name	Signature
Title	Date

WILLFUL FALSE STATEMENTS MADE ON THIS FORM ARE PUNISHABLE BY FINE AND IMPRISONMENT. U.S. CODE, TITLE 18, SECTION 1001.

SOURCE: Photos from *Broadcasting* magazine; postcard from FCC.

mounds of documents attempting to prove that the licensee had in fact served the public interest. In 1981, the FCC began to cut the red tape by phasing in a simple, postcard-size renewal form that station licensees submit four months before the expiration of the current license. Exhibit 12.5 vividly contrasts pre- and post-deregulation paperwork.

Exhibit 12.6 shows that renewal applications can take one of three basic paths: the uncontested route, the petition-to-deny route, or the mutually exclusive application route.

Some 98 percent of all renewal applications fall in the *uncontested* category. The FCC staff uses its delegated authority to renew those licenses almost

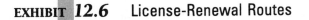

EXHIBIT 12.6 License-Renewal Routes

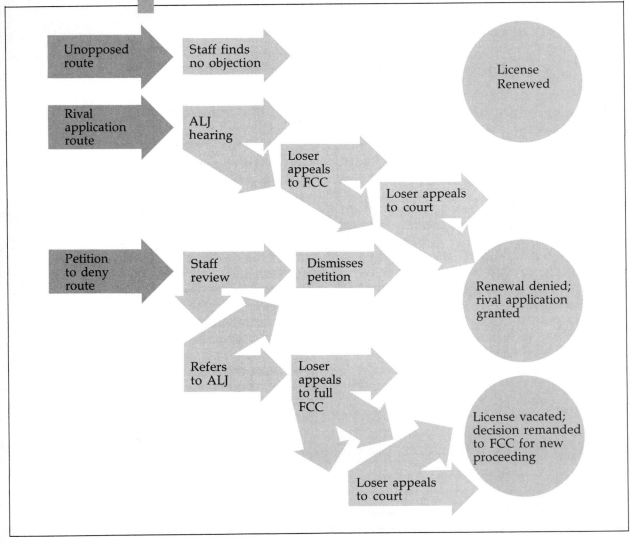

automatically. In fact, consumer advocates complain that the Mass Media Bureau merely rubber-stamps uncontested applications, no matter how mediocre a station's performance in the public interest may have been.

staff renews most licenses routinely

The rare *petition-to-deny* route must be taken when citizen groups or other parties oppose an incumbent licensee without wanting to take over the license. Such groups claim that incumbents do not merit renewal because they have failed to meet their public-interest obligations. Citizens won the right to participate in renewal proceedings with the WLBT case, a marathon campaign to dislodge a licensee by audience members outraged by the station's blatant failure to serve their interests. Exhibit 12.8 later in the chapter gives details of this landmark case.

Renewal Expectation Rights   *Mutually exclusive* applications occur when would-be licensees try to displace incumbents, claiming they can do a better job in serving the public interest. This type of application presents the FCC with a conflict of incompatible goals: that of giving an incumbent licensee a *legitimate renewal expectation* versus that of subjecting the incumbent to a *competitive spur* to improve service to the public.

Without a strong expectation of renewal at the end of a license period, no prudent investor, commercial or noncommercial, would be willing to build a station. However, assurance that a license will be renewed, no matter how poor the incumbent's program performance, invites licensees to take the low road, wringing maximum profit out of their stations and giving no serious consideration to the public interest. Assured renewal would in effect give existing licensees a monopoly on their channels, freezing out worthy competitors.

how much assurance of renewal security should incumbent licensees have?

Comparative Renewal Criteria   When faced with the need to make a comparative renewal decision, the commission falls back on a list of criteria issued a quarter-century ago as guidelines for deciding the comparative merits of mutually exclusive applicants for new licenses (FCCR, 1965: 393). The criteria include

- Technical questions. For example: Which proposed antenna location would serve the most listeners/viewers?
- Ownership and management questions. For example, which applicant would add to the diversification of media ownership? Which would be more local? Which promises active participation in management? Which includes women or members of minority groups in ownership and management roles?
- The past record of broadcasting in the public interest by the incumbent and, if applicable, by the opposing applicant.
- Program proposals (especially the amount and type of nonentertainment programming).

Exhibit 12.7 describes an otherwise inconsequential comparative renewal case that illustrates the difficulty of applying some of these criteria.

EXHIBIT *12.7*   David vs. Goliath: The Simon Geller Renewal Case

Simon Geller, the eccentric owner and sole staff member of classical music station WVCA–FM in Gloucester, MA, a fishing and resort community north of Boston, was a folk hero to his loyal listeners. Geller, who put his station on the air in 1964, adopted a wall-to-wall classical music format that ran 15 hours daily, interrupted only with barely enough advertising to keep the station solvent. In fact, many of his 90,000 appreciative listeners sent in donations to keep the station afloat. Geller did not let news or public-affairs programs interrupt the music; he felt that the Boston stations that put signals over the Gloucester area took care of those needs.

Grandbanke Corporation, a group owner of radio stations in Massachusetts, became interested in the potential of the Gloucester market. As no other FM channels were allotted to the small town, Grandbanke tried to buy Geller's station, offering to keep him on the payroll. Geller, for whom the station was a way of life, turned down the offer. Grandbanke thereupon filed a competing application for the facility when Geller's license came up for renewal. The corporation assembled a textbook set of management and program promises closely paralleling the FCC's 1965 comparative renewal criteria. It promised to devote nearly 29 percent of the station's overall schedule to news and public

affairs, while retaining the classical music format the rest of the time. The management would work closely with Gloucester groups to air community issues.

The FCC administrative law judge who heard the case initially approved Geller's renewal. However, the commission, concerned about Geller's total lack of news and public-affairs programs, set the case for an oral argument before making a final decision. Geller, who was unable to pay for an attorney, came to Washington and gave the FCC an emotional personal defense of his stewardship, noting that the station had to go off the air while he appeared before the FCC because there was no one else to run it. Unmoved, the FCC found Grandbanke's several attorneys persuasive in proving that their client could better fulfill the public interest as defined by the FCC's 1965 statement.

Geller appealed the case, meanwhile keeping his station on the air. In 1985, the court of appeals returned the case to the FCC, telling the commission that it had been inconsistent in applying its own 1965 statement of comparative criteria to this case. Specifically, Geller should be awarded a preference for his absolute integration of ownership and management and for localism (the station was in Geller's two-room apartment). Finally, late in 1985, the FCC reversed itself and renewed Geller's license (FCCR, 1985: 1443). David had faced Goliath in unequal combat and won. In 1988, Geller had the last laugh: he sold his station for a cool million dollars—and not to Grandbanke—and retired to the movie theaters and delicatessens of the Upper East Side of Manhattan. The new owner promised to keep the classical format—and to hire 10 people to run the station 24 hours a day.

SOURCE: Photo from Rick Friedman/New York *Times* pictures.

The FCC can impose a variety of penalties on licensees for infractions of its rules. They range from simple letters of admonition, through fines (up to $250,000 per infraction) to short-term license renewal or—the ultimate penalty—no renewal at all. When a licensee proves incorrigible, the FCC can either refuse to renew the license or revoke it outright. The FCC prefers the nonrenewal route because it puts the burden of proof on the licensee, whereas revocation puts the burden of proof on the FCC.

why FCC prefers punishment by nonrenewal over revocation

License Deletions   From the FCC's creation in 1934 through 1987, only 141 stations lost their licenses. The average rate of *involuntary deletions,* the term for both nonrenewals and revocations, was a mere three stations per year. FCC records show no revocations and only ten nonrenewals in the 1980s. In short, loss of license, though an ever-present background threat, hardly ever becomes a reality.

Deleted stations have usually been obscure radio outlets whose licensees have accumulated long lists of willful misdemeanors. Transgressions accumulate because the FCC usually treats them leniently as long as the guilty licensee candidly admits error and contritely promises to reform. Eventually, however, a straw may break the camel's back and some specific transgression results in deletion.

Examples of Deletions   Here are examples of infractions cited by the FCC (or, in one case, by a court) as the basis for deleting licenses in specific cases.

Fraudulent billing   In 1978 the FCC denied renewal to a Berlin, New Hampshire, AM radio station because of double billing that resulted in more than $22,000 in overcharges to national advertisers. Claiming that the two other stations and the newspaper in the market did the same thing, the owner pleaded "business necessity"—a candid acknowledgment that market forces do not always operate in the public interest. Despite its earlier zeal to prevent double-billing, in 1986 the FCC deleted the rules against it. It said that competing stations should keep one another in line. If that failed, the Federal Trade Commission and the courts—not the FCC—are the appropriate forums for action against fraudulent practices.

Staging of news   The FCC denied the renewal of a Tucson, AM station in 1980 because of an irresponsible promotional stunt. When a recently employed DJ temporarily left town on personal business, station management concocted a story that he had been kidnapped. The station broadcast "news" of the kidnapping over a period of five days, even faking a police interview. Listeners flooded the Tucson police lines with calls. A local television station finally exposed the hoax.

Equal employment and contest violations   In 1989 the FCC refused to renew the license of a Fredonia, New York, AM station, citing deliberate misrepresentation by the licensee to the commission about an equal employment opportunity decision and a station contest prize that was promised but not given.

Failure to serve local community   During the consumerism heyday of the 1960s, a case began that 25 years later resulted in a new licensee taking over a major television station. Audience members charged the deleted station with discrimination and gross failure to serve the public interest. A direct order from an appeals court was needed to force a reluctant FCC to delete the license after a long-drawn-out series of hearings and court battles. Exhibit 12.8 gives the details.

EXHIBIT 12.8   Citizen Involvement in License Renewal: The WLBT Case

Until the late 1960s, a broadcast station's audience members had no right to take part in regulatory proceedings concerning that station. That situation changed as a result of a court case that began in 1955 when a group of citizens made the first of a series of complaints to the FCC about the conduct of WLBT, a VHF television station in Jackson, MS. The group accused the station of blatant discrimination against blacks, who formed 45 percent of its audience. The FCC dismissed the citizens' complaints, saying that they had no legal right to participate in a licensing decision. When WLBT's license again came up for renewal in 1964, local groups obtained legal assistance from the Office of Communications of the United Church of Christ (UCC) in New York.

The UCC petitioned the FCC on behalf of the local groups for permission to intervene in the WLBT renewal application proceeding, but the FCC again rejected the petition, saying that citizens had no *legal standing* to intervene. At that time the commission recognized only signal interference or economic injury (to another broadcaster) as reasons to give parties the right to participate in renewal hearings. Thus only other broadcasters had standing to challenge existing licensees.

The UCC went to the Court of Appeals, claiming that the FCC had no right to bar representatives of the viewing public from intervening in renewals, or to award a renewal without a hearing in the face of

substantial public opposition. The court agreed, directing the FCC to hold hearings on WLBT's renewal and to give standing to representatives of the public (F, 1966). The FCC held a hearing and grudgingly permitted UCC to participate as ordered. However, it once again renewed WLBT's license.

The UCC returned to court and in 1969 an exasperated appeals court reconsidered the case—14 years after the first complaints had been recorded. In the last opinion written by Warren Burger before he became Chief Justice of the Supreme Court, the court rebuked the FCC for "scandalous delay." It ordered the FCC to cancel WLBT's license and to appoint an interim operator pending selection of a new licensee (F, 1969). But ten *more* years passed before the FCC finally selected a new permanent licensee. Altogether, the case dragged on for more than a quarter of a century.

As the FCC had feared, the WLBT case triggered many petitions to deny renewal of other licenses. However, this "reign of terror," as a trade magazine put it, resulted in few actual hearings and still fewer denials. Of the 342 challenges filed in 1971–1973, only 16 resulted in denials of license renewal. An exacting standard of evidence established by the FCC and approved by the court ensured this high rate of petition failure. Only after an opponent presented overwhelming evidence would the FCC schedule a license-renewal hearing (F, 1972).

The FCC may not impose penalties arbitrarily. The constitution's due-process clause prevents the government from depriving any citizen of "life, liberty, or property without due process of law." Parties adversely affected by decisions of government officials or agencies have the right to appeal for rehearing and for review by authorities other than the ones that made the initial decisions.

constitution's due-process clause ensures right of appeal

FCC Hearings   When an issue arises that calls for formal argumentation, the FCC may hold a hearing to settle the dispute. One of several senior FCC staff attorneys who serve as administrative law judges (ALJs) presides over initial FCC hearings. ALJs conduct hearings in the manner of courtroom trials. Witnesses are sworn in, legal counsels represent each side, testimony is taken, and so on.

role of ALJs in hearing process

However, ALJs differ from court judges in acting as both judge and jury. The FCC's Review Board looks over ALJ initial decisions. They then go to the commissioners themselves for final review.

Procedural rules head off frivolous interventions and intentional delays by defining the circumstances that justify hearings and the qualifications of parties entitled to *standing* (the legal right to participate in a formal proceeding). For example, the commission must tell unsuccessful license applicants why it rejected their applications. The applicant may reply, and if the commission still decides against the applicant, the FCC must then set the matter for a formal hearing in Washington, "specifying the particular matter and things at issue" (47 USC 309e). However, if the commission grants a license application without a hearing, for the ensuing 30 days after publication of the decision the grant can be contested by "any party in interest."

Appeals to the Courts   Even after all the safeguards of FCC hearings and rehearings have been exhausted, the Communications Act gives people adversely affected by FCC actions a chance to appeal to a U.S. Court of Appeals. For appeals concerning licenses, the District of Columbia Circuit, in Washington, is the designated appeals court.

why DC court hears most appeals from FCC license decisions

The Court of Appeals may confirm or overturn commission actions, in part or in whole. It may also *remand* a case, sending it back to the FCC for further consideration in keeping with the court's interpretation of the Communications Act and other laws.

From the federal circuit courts, final appeals in broadcasting matters may be taken to the Supreme Court of the United States. The Supreme Court may or may not accept a case for review; if it does not, the appeal process can go no further. Refusal to hear a case does not necessarily mean that the Supreme Court entirely agrees with the lower court, but the lower court's decision becomes final. Obviously, when the opposing sides exploit all the possibilities for reviews and appeals, years can go by before final decisions are reached.

Cable Franchising

The 1984 Cable Act, incorporated as Title VI of the Communications Act, established only a loose FCC regulatory authority over cable television. The actual licensing of cable systems is delegated to local municipal authorities. Municipalities issue franchises entitling cable systems to string their cables along streets and other public property that is subject to municipal jurisdiction.

cable TV operators get franchises instead of licenses

Cable Act Provisions   Key provisions of the Cable Act include the following:

- Cable television is defined as a *one-way video programming service*. The act does not cover two-way services.
- Local franchising authorities may require public, educational, and governmental (PEG) *access channels* over which the cable operator has no editorial control.
- Cable systems with more than 36 channels must set aside 10 to 15 percent of those channels for *leased access* to parties other than the cable-system owner. The cable owner sets rates for leasing the channels but has no editorial control over programs on those channels.
- Local franchising authorities may charge *franchise fees* of no more than 5 percent of gross cable-system revenues.
- Federal or state authorities may not regulate cable service *subscriber rates*.
- Local authorities may require the upgrading of cable facilities and channel capacity when granting franchise renewals.

Franchising Procedure   When a local franchising authority (city, town, or county) decides it wants cable service, it first develops a *cable ordinance*. The ordinance prescribes the conditions under which a cable system will be allowed to operate. Drawn up in many cases with the advice of outside experts, such ordinances typically stipulate

- The period of the franchise (usually 10 to 15 years).
- The quality of service that must be maintained.
- Technical standards, such as the minimum of channels and requirements for interconnection with other systems.
- The franchise fee.
- PEG channel requirements, if any.

cable franchises award *de facto* monopolies

Bidders for cable-system franchises base their offers on the design and timetable, as outlined in the franchise authority's *request for proposals (RFP)*. Franchising authorities usually grant a franchise to only one bidder, giving the winner a monopoly within its coverage area. Some cable operators have argued in court that cities should grant multiple franchises so long as space for additional systems remains available on telephone poles or in underground conduits. Opponents say that overlapping cable systems would be uneconomical, causing demands for unreasonably high subscription fees. In 1990 the monopoly issue remained unresolved.

Franchise Renewals   Upon the expiration of a franchise, the local franchising authority is not required to ascertain that renewal would serve the public interest (as does the FCC with reference to broadcast renewals). The authority may simply renew a franchise without ceremony.

If, however, the local authority wants to deny renewal, the Cable Act requires it to hold a hearing. Such a hearing would raise public-interest issues. The authority would have to decide whether the incumbent operator has provided a quality of service that is "reasonable in light of the community needs" and has prepared a renewal proposal that is "reasonable to meet the future cable-related community needs and interests." The act makes no mention of considering proposals from competing would-be franchisees during the course of renewal grants or renewal hearings.

Deregulation   12.11

In the preceding discussion of licensing and franchising, it has frequently been necessary to refer to the softening or deletion of FCC rules as a result of deregulation. The radical surgery performed on government regulations during the 1980s—not just on FCC regulations but on government oversight of economic activities in general—has such profound implications for national life that it deserves detailed consideration.

deregulation not confined to electronic mass media

Levels of Deregulation   On the least controversial level, deregulation simply meant discarding outdated rules, simplifying unnecessarily complex rules, reducing paperwork, ensuring that the remaining rules can actually achieve their goals, lightening the FCC's administrative load, and reducing the cost of regulation. Deregulation based on these motives began in the 1970s, supported by both Democratic and Republican administrations.

On a more controversial level, the impulse to deregulate also stems from ideological motives, representing a specific vision of the government's proper role in national life. This vision sees little need for government intervention, relying instead on the marketplace to control private economic behavior. Deregulation of this type emerged as a major item on the national agenda when the Republican administration came to power with President Ronald Reagan in 1980.

ideological motives behind deregulation

Deregulatory Theory   In brief, deregulatory theory asserts that competition and consumer choice impose more sensitive, efficient controls over economic activities than can government agencies. Private economic forces can stimulate production of better, more varied, and cheaper consumer goods and services without official guidance from above. Insofar as government

cost-benefit formula
used to test need for
regulations

regulation may be necessary, it should be tested by a cost/benefit formula to make sure that the losses arising from such regulation do not outweigh the gains.

The FCC did not go so far as to advocate abandoning all regulation. It divided rules into two categories, behavioral and structural. *Behavioral regulation,* which deregulators seek to discard or at least to minimize, controls what licensees may or may not do in conducting their businesses. Rules requiring a licensee to carry a certain percentage of children's programs or to limit the amount of time devoted to commercials would be examples of behavioral regulation.

Structural regulation controls the overall shape of the businesses in which licensees engage and the terms on which would-be competitors can enter the marketplace. Rules preventing a licensee from owning another, related communications business or from owning more than 12 stations of the same type are examples of structural regulations. Deregulatory theory generally supports structural regulation because it increases competition by making marketplace entry easier.

Deregulatory theory admits that market failure can occur. Sometimes competition fails to produce the expected favorable results. For example, antitrust laws are justified by the fact that uncontrolled growth may eventually result in monopolies that suppress competition and raise prices. Some "public goods" may fall outside the domain of marketplace economics; therefore, competition to produce them may fail to materialize. If, for example, one agrees that public broadcasting provides a valuable public good but costs too much to produce profitably on a commercial basis, it may be necessary to by-pass the market by ensuring other means of support such as private contributions or government subsidy.

Deregulation in Practice   In the mid-1970s, early deregulation did away with many incidental bureaucratic rules. During the 1980s a more zealously deregulatory FCC began dismantling or softening more basic rules, first in commercial radio (1981), then in educational broadcasting (1984), then in commercial television (1985). Exhibit 12.9 summarizes some of these changes.

Television networks underwent yet another FCC special inquiry in 1979–1980, this time from a deregulatory perspective. That meant looking toward less network regulation instead of more. A special staff reported that prior network regulation (outlined in Section 12.5.) had utterly failed to bring about its stated goal of fostering increased program diversity. Instead, network rules had stifled competition, often by protecting the networks from the inroads of such new technologies as cable. The study recommended that the commission undo most of its existing network rules (FCC, 1980: 491).

When the commission tried to follow these network deregulation recommendations, however, industry lobbyists brought the effort to a standstill. Program syndicators urged retention of the prime-time access rule (PTAR) even though it does little to curb network domination of evening television time, as originally intended. Opposition to lifting rules limiting network

EXHIBIT 12.9 Before and After: Examples of Deregulation

Before 1980	Changes Since 1980
A. Licensing	
License lasts three years for both radio and TV stations	License lasts 5 years for television, 7 for radio (action by Congress, 1981)
Comparative hearings required for choosing among competing applications	Applicants for newer services chosen by lot (LPTV, MMDS, etc.; action by Congress, 1982)
B. Ownership	
Ownership limit of 7-7-7 (AM-FM-TV) stations	Limit raised to 12-12-12 (action by Congress, 1985)
Trafficking rule: Must hold a station at least three years	May sell at any time (action by FCC, 1982)
C. Programs and Advertising	
FCC application processing guidelines to staff call for minimum amounts of nonentertainment programming	No quantitative program guidelines (action by FCC: radio-1982, television-1985)
Specific rules for ascertaining local program needs (ascertainment)	No rules remain, just generalized requirement to "know" community of license (action by FCC: radio-1982, television-1985)
Guidelines (not rules) on maximum amounts of advertising per hour	No guidelines or rules on amount of advertising carried (action by FCC: 1982-radio, 1985-TV)
Controversial issues must be aired and opposing sides treated fairly (fairness doctrine)	Fairness doctrine dropped (action by FCC, 1987)
D. Cable Carriage	
Cable systems must carry all local TV stations	Must-carry rules dropped (action by U.S. Appeals Court, 1985, 1987)
Syndicated exclusivity rules allow stations to enforce contract provisions on syndicated programs	Rules dropped (action by FCC, 1980) but then reinstated (action by FCC, 1988, effective 1990)
E. Technical Rules	
Specific technical standards mandated for each new service (color TV, FM stereo, etc.)	Starting with AM stereo decision, standards left to marketplace forces (action by FCC, 1982)
Engineers ranked by class and specific ranks required for certain jobs.	Engineers no longer ranked by class (action by FCC, 1981)
Rules on maintaining signal quality and avoiding interference.	Stations use own methods (actions at various times by FCC)

The FCC modified or eliminated many other broadcasting and cable rules during the deregulation drive of the 1980s. Unchanged, however, are rules on equal employment opportunity and political broadcast access, among others.

financial interest in production and program-syndication activities (fin/syn rules) proved even stronger. The FCC was forced to abandon plans to delete the rules, as described in Section 12.14.

Deregulation of Cable TV   The FCC had more success in streamlining procedures and requirements for newer delivery services. As the first major nonbroadcast mass electronic medium to develop, cable television took the brunt of the FCC's original policy of protecting the status quo in broadcasting. However, a series of court reversals caused the FCC to drop most of its cable regulations by 1980. The 1984 Cable Act completed the process by taking the minimal-regulation approach. Exhibit 12.10 traces the rise and fall of cable regulation over the years.

Until 1985, only the controversial **must-carry rule** remained in place. It required each cable system to carry the signals of all "significantly viewed" television stations within that system's coverage area, as determined by the stations' audience shares. The FCC adopted the must-carry rule to protect broadcasters from discriminatory treatment by cable operators, who could help or harm stations by either carrying or not carrying them. The FCC also wanted to help stations with weak signals—usually non-network UHF and public stations—by equalizing the reach of all stations' signals within cabled areas. (When operating properly, a cable system delivers all signals at the same level, regardless of the varying strength of the stations they come from.)

The must-carry rule put an unfair burden on cable systems with only small channel capacity. Must-carry television signals filled so many of their available channels they had insufficient "shelf space" for cable-specific programs. Systems whose service areas straddled two or more broadcast markets sometimes had to carry duplicate programs from several affiliates of the same network.

impact of abolishing must-carry rule

In 1985 an appeals court agreed that the must-carry rule, as written, violated the Constitution. The FCC tried rewriting the rule, but in 1987 the same appeals court once more found it unconstitutional. At that the FCC gave up and withdrew the rule (F, 1987).

After the must-carry repeal, a few television stations went so far as to pay cable systems to continue carrying their channels. However, most cable systems continued carrying most stations because stations represent the cheapest source of popular programs with which to fill the hungry cable channels. In fact, broadcasters started a countermove—**if carry, must pay.** This slogan stands for the notion that cable systems should no longer be allowed to retransmit over-the-air broadcast signals without recompensing the broadcasters in addition to the mandatory retransmission copyright fee they already pay (described in Section 12.12).

Deregulation and Technical Standards   In the past the FCC assumed the responsibility for setting technical standards for a new technology when it was made available commercially. Universally mandated standards protect the public from investing in new products that might later prove incompatible with existing products or prove to be of less than optimum quality. The

EXHIBIT **12.10**   Cable Regulation Comes Full Circle

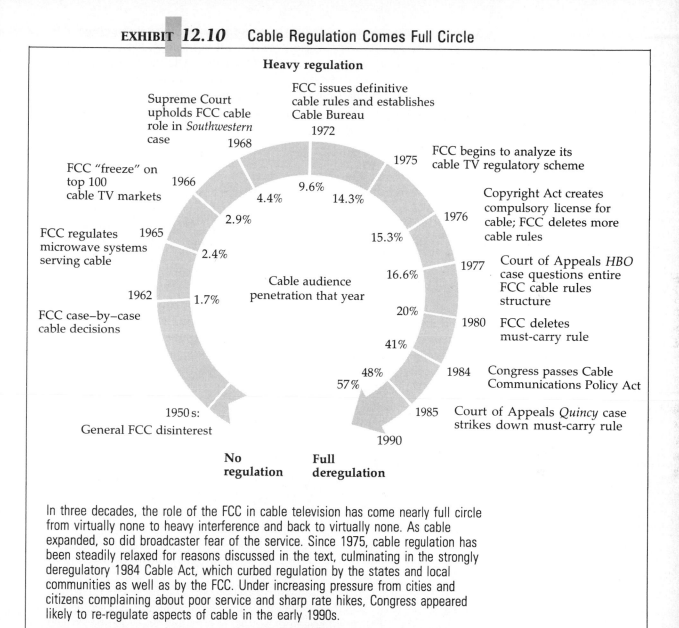

Heavy regulation

FCC issues definitive cable rules and establishes Cable Bureau
1972

Supreme Court upholds FCC cable role in *Southwestern* case
1968

FCC begins to analyze its cable TV regulatory scheme
1975

FCC "freeze" on top 100 cable TV markets
1966

Copyright Act creates compulsory license for cable; FCC deletes more cable rules
1976

FCC regulates microwave systems serving cable
1965

Court of Appeals *HBO* case questions entire FCC cable rules structure
1977

FCC case–by–case cable decisions
1962

FCC deletes must-carry rule
1980

Congress passes Cable Communications Policy Act
1984

Court of Appeals *Quincy* case strikes down must-carry rule
1985

1950s: General FCC disinterest

9.6%
14.3%
4.4%
2.9%
15.3%
2.4%
16.6%
1.7%
20%
41%
48%
57%

Cable audience penetration that year

1990

No regulation   **Full deregulation**

In three decades, the role of the FCC in cable television has come nearly full circle from virtually none to heavy interference and back to virtually none. As cable expanded, so did broadcaster fear of the service. Since 1975, cable regulation has been steadily relaxed for reasons discussed in the text, culminating in the strongly deregulatory 1984 Cable Act, which curbed regulation by the states and local communities as well as by the FCC. Under increasing pressure from cities and citizens complaining about poor service and sharp rate hikes, Congress appeared likely to re-regulate aspects of cable in the early 1990s.

deregulatory approach, however, tends to reject official standard-setting, leaving the choice of standards to the marketplace.

This new approach emerged in connection with the choice of an AM radio stereo system. FM began using a stereo transmission method standardized by the FCC in 1961. The success of FM stereo made the owners of AM radio stations desperate to achieve AM stereophony.

impact of standards
deregulation on adoption
of AM stereo

After some unsatisfactory attempts at choosing among five competing AM-stereo systems, none of which would work with the others, the commission abandoned the effort to adopt a single standard. It left the choice to marketplace competition. In this case station owners, operators, and equipment manufacturers, rather than consumers, constituted "the marketplace." But industry members could not legally get together to agree on a common standard. Such an agreement might seem logical, but it would violate antitrust restraint-of-trade laws that forbid companies to make agreements that limit competition.

With no enforced standardization, few AM-station owners wanted to risk choosing a stereo system that might prove only temporary. Nor would manufacturers tool up for mass production of stereo receivers that might soon become outmoded by a different stereo technology. By the end of the 1980s, only about 700 of the nearly 5,000 AM stations had begun stereo broadcasting. Similar FCC nondecisions on standards for DBS, teletext, and television stereo followed. Economists had superseded engineers in commission policy making, even in largely technical matters.

Industry debate over the FCC's hands-off approach to technical standards rose to a fever pitch over high-definition television (HDTV). In 1986, the FCC set up a committee to consider the many competing HDTV proposals, test them, and make recommendations for commission action. Late in 1988, the FCC made its first HDTV standards decision: any system adopted in the United States must be compatible with existing receivers and must fit into the existing 6-megahertz television channels, using the currently allocated spectrum positions. HDTV loomed as a major standards issue for the 1990s, with billions of dollars riding on the outcome.

Deregulation Critique: How Far to Go?   On balance, what have been the benefits and costs of deregulation? On the plus side, deregulation has eliminated FCC decisional delays in many areas. It has weeded out obsolete rules, encouraged the development of new technologies, and given audiences more program choices. As an example, the open-skies policies that in 1972 allowed satellite companies to compete freely and in 1979 permitted anyone to set up a TVRO antenna to downlink satellite signals brought benefits to stations, cable systems, networks, and consumers.

Not all outcomes have been so positive in the eyes of critics. The chairman of the House of Representatives subcommittee responsible for overseeing the FCC accused the 1980s commission of zealously pursuing deregulation "solely on the basis of ideology instead of reason and fact" (Markey, 1988). The congressman had just read a study showing that the FCC suffered court reversals on a quarter of the appeals from its 1986–1988 decisions—an embarrassingly high rate of judicial rebuffs.

Other deregulation criticisms, some of which have been previously mentioned:

Programs as trade goods.   The FCC's vision of all human activity reduced to simplistic economic terms ("the marketplace") treats programs as the equivalent of manufactured goods (as suggested by FCC Chairperson Mark Fowler's reference to television as a "toaster with pictures"). This view of programs leaves the FCC with no responsibility for ensuring program diversity, quality, and cultural content.

Decline of record-keeping. The money-saving tactic of abandoning many types of record keeping left huge blanks in the official records of the broadcasting services. For example, discontinuation of annual financial reports in 1980 deprives the regulators of official knowledge about the financial health of the industry. Canceling the requirement for keeping program logs wiped out a record of station performance, once useful in evaluating the merits of renewal applications.

License qualifications. Applicants for construction permits and licenses no longer have to include significant information that was once considered relevant to their qualifications to hold licenses.

End of fairness doctrine. FCC abandonment of the fairness doctrine over the opposition of Congress (discussed in Section 13.6) poisoned relations between Congress and the commission for years, causing delays in FCC appointments and other important actions requiring congressional cooperation.

Failure to protect children. With its acceptance of program-length commercials aimed at children, the FCC now considers allegations of harm to children only upon a specific showing of provable damage. It regards the lack of positive benefit in such programs as irrelevant.

Deletion of anti-trafficking rule. The abandonment of the antitrafficking rule that required licensees to hold on to stations for at least three years before selling them encouraged rapid ownership turnover for the sake of overnight profits. Fast-buck sales ignore the public interest and, because they often involve borrowing large sums, often force cutbacks in personnel and public-service programs.

Cable subscription fees. The 1984 Cable Act curbed the right of cities to control cable-television subscription fees. Cable systems acquired a monopoly status that enabled them to raise rates at will. Some of the research on cable suggests that as prices have increased, quality of service has declined. In 1990, Congress was moving to reinstate some rate regulation.

Copyright Law 12.12

The Communications Act and the FCC are not the only sources of legal control over broadcasting and cable. Among federal laws that directly affect these media, the Copyright Act of 1976 probably ranks as most important. When broadcasting began, authors and composers had to rely on the Copyright Law of 1909, which dealt primarily with print and live performance. Despite amendments, it never caught up with all the novel copyright problems created by new technology. After long study, Congress passed a new law in 1976, effective for works published in 1978 and later.

Copyright Act of 1976   The Copyright Office, a Library of Congress subsidiary unit, administers the Copyright Act of 1976. Some of its salient provisions follow.

Purpose   Copyright holders are entitled to profit from their products and may license others to use them in exchange for royalty payments. "Use" consists of making public by publishing, performing, displaying, and the like.

What is copyrightable   In addition to traditionally copyrightable works such as books, plays, musical compositions, and motion pictures, works such as broadcast programs, sculptures, choreographic notations, and computer programs may be copyrighted. Things *not* copyrightable include ideas, slogans, brand names, and titles (though brand names, logos, and slogans can be protected under trademark law). News stories can be copyrighted, but not the facts on which they are based.

what is not copyrightable

Length of copyright   In general, a copyright lasts for the life of the work's creator plus 50 or more years. After that, a work enters the *public domain* and can be used without securing permission or paying royalties.

Compulsory licensing   Owners of copyrighted material who license television stations to use their works must also grant *retransmission rights* to cable systems that lawfully pick up such programs off the air and deliver them to subscribers. Cable systems, in turn, must pay a stipulated small proportion of their revenue for these uses. Compulsory licensing means that copyright owners of programs imported by cable systems from distant stations receive two payments: one for the license to the originating station, a second for the compulsory license to the cable owner who retransmits the program to subscribers.

Fair use   The new act retains the traditional concept of *fair use,* which permits limited uses of copyrighted works for educational, critical, and creative purposes without payment or permission. Fair use may include, for example, a student's photocopying of a magazine article for study purposes, a scholar's quoting from other writers, or a critic's citing examples of an author's writing in a review.

Role of Copyright Royalty Tribunal   The Copyright Act established the Copyright Royalty Tribunal (CRT). The CRT has three major tasks connected with cable television:

- Setting the rates cable systems must pay to retransmit imported, distant, television broadcast signals.

- Collecting and pooling the resulting revenue.
- Dividing the pooled royalty money among the copyright holders.

The process of apportioning payments of the pooled copyright revenue has been snarled in legal wrangles from the day the CRT began work. Copyright holders and broadcasters complained about extremely low levels of payment. In the late 1980s cable systems had to pay just under 1 percent of their gross revenues to the CRT every six months. The total amount paid by a cable system depends on the number and type of stations it carries (independent stations cost more than affiliates).

Signal Piracy   The new technologies have created fertile grounds for copyright violations. Pirating program materials, both in the form of signals en route to consumers and in the form of recordings, costs the entertainment industries billions of dollars a year worldwide. Piracy includes illicit hookups to cable-television feeder lines, illegal "black boxes" (decoders) for reception of pay-program signals (which are scrambled to prevent piracy), and the unauthorized copying and sale of videotaped and filmed programs.

Program copying became the subject of a major court case in 1976, when a group of program producers sued Sony, the pioneer manufacturer of home videorecorders. The suit alleged *indirect* copyright infringement ("indirect" because Sony provided the VCRs, which are the *means* of infringement, but did not do the copying). The Supreme Court confirmed a lower court decision favoring Sony by a five-to-four vote (US, 1984). The high court cited audience research showing that people record broadcast signals primarily for time-shifting purposes, which it regarded as coming under the fair-use clause.

home videorecorders and the copyright law

The Sony decision covered only the recording of over-the-air (so-called free) broadcast material for use within the home. The legality of showing a taped copy of a copyrighted film or program to a group outside the home remained in question, a problem intensified by the growth of video rentals. Hollywood producers pressured Congress to modify the copyright act once again, this time to impose indirect royalty payments from those who do home recording. Such payments could take the form of surcharges on recorders or on blank tapes at the time of purchase or rental fees paid by customers to video rental stores.

In the meantime another source of concern about piracy had emerged: digital audio tape (DAT) recorders with built-in facilities for making perfect copies. Copyright holders delayed sales of the machines in the United States until safeguards were developed to prevent unauthorized use of DAT recorders to make multiple copies of copyrighted material.

sale of DAT recorders delayed by recording industry

Other Laws Affecting Electronic Mass Media   12.13

Many other federal laws, as well as state and municipal statutes, affect the electronic mass media. The following sections briefly survey some of the most relevant.

Treaties The tendency of radio signals to ignore political boundaries necessitates international treaties to prevent interference. Regional treaties between the United States and neighboring countries govern aspects of AM radio, FM radio, and television broadcasting. AM agreements cover the widest territory because long-distance sky-wave propagation affects reception in the scattered islands of the Caribbean as well as in the two common-border nations, Canada and Mexico. Agreements on FM and television have long been in place with Canada and Mexico.

As a member of the International Telecommunication Union (ITU), the United States participates in worldwide regulation of both wire and radio communication, including satellite use. The FCC is the designated U.S. agency that coordinates with the ITU, whose activities are described in Section 14.4.

Fraudulent Advertising The FCC itself has no authority to punish licensees directly for unfair advertising. All it can do is cite fraudulent advertising as evidence that an applicant or licensee lacks the requisite character qualification to be a licensee and refer cases of deceptive advertising to a sister agency, the Federal Trade Commission (FTC).

The FTC settles most cases of alleged advertising deception by *stipulation,* an informal (and hence time-saving) way of getting advertisers to drop objectionable practices voluntarily. If a formal complaint becomes necessary, the FTC can seek a *consent order,* another nonpunitive measure under which the advertiser agrees to stop the offending practice without admitting guilt. Actual guilt has to be proved before the FTC can obtain a *cease and desist order* forcing compliance with the law. Such orders can be appealed to the courts. The appeal process can mean long delay in bringing the objectionable advertising to an end if the advertiser chooses to use it.

Even this clumsy machinery ground to a halt in the 1980s when the FTC chairperson declared that market forces rather than government regulations should protect consumers from exploitation. However, as the 1990s dawned, the FTC showed signs of renewed vigor. For example, in mid-1990 the FTC Bureau of Consumer Protection obtained its first consent order canceling allegedly fraudulent program-length commercials. The offending company, which sold "cures" for baldness, impotency, and obesity, agreed to pay refunds to consumers and to identify future program-length commercials as paid advertisements.

The only legal product officially banned from broadcast and cable advertising is cigarettes and related tobacco products. A federal statute adopted in 1971 imposed the ban. Many broadcasters claim that they were unfairly singled out because cigarette ads continue to appear in other media.

Lotteries The advertising of illegal lotteries can subject a licensee to a fine of $1,000 and a year's imprisonment for each day's offense, according to a provision of the U.S. Criminal Code (18 USC 1304). This statute concerns broadcasters because they frequently use contests in advertising and promotional campaigns. They must take care not to let an innocent promotional gimmick turn into an illegal lottery—defined as a *chance* to win a *prize* for a *price*.

A contest becomes a lottery if it requires participants to pay any kind of fee or go out of their way (*price or consideration*), chooses the winner by lot (*chance*), and awards the winner something of value (*prize*). Contests involving these elements can get a station into serious trouble. The advertising of legal state lotteries is exempted from the antilottery statute.

how to tell when a contest becomes an illegal lottery

Constitutional Issues

Laws in several areas critically important to the media impinge on the First Amendment's guarantees of speech, press, and religious freedom. These laws deal with such matters as libel, obscenity and indecency, fair trial, freedom of access to information, and the right of privacy. Discussion of these laws is reserved for the next chapter, which focuses on constitutional issues.

Nonstatutory Controls 12.14

Statutes, ordinances, and regulations are not the only sources of control over the electronic mass media. The regulatory agencies themselves are subject to informal pressures, as are station and cable-system owners, networks, and producers. Influence comes from government officials, private individuals, and organized pressure groups.

Congressional and Executive-Branch Influence

Congress, by virtue of giving the FCC both its statutory authority and its annual budget, exerts a great deal of influence on the regulatory agency. It tends to micromanage the commission—second-guessing it on virtually every major regulatory issue.

The executive branch is inclined to take advantage of the fact that commissioners owe political allegiance to the president who appointed them. For example, in the mid-1980s, the Reagan White House played a role in short-circuiting an FCC plan to drop rules that curb the networks' control over program production (the financial interest rules discussed in Section 12.5). The Hollywood producers, who stood to lose business if the change went through, lobbied President Ronald Reagan (no stranger to Hollywood) to intervene. He called in the FCC chair for an "informational" talk—an unusual impinging upon the commission's neutrality. Congress, too, felt the heat from Hollywood lobbyists, adding its pressure on the commission. The FCC promptly shelved its plan to deregulate the restrictions on network program making.

lobbyists help to uphold financial interest rule

Consumer Activism

The prominence and impact of prime-time programs make them favorite targets of organized advocacy groups. A study analyzing the impact of such influence commented on elaborate campaigns that advocacy groups had waged against such series as *Amos 'n' Andy* and *Beulah Land* (racial stereotyping), *Maude* and *Cagney and Lacey* (abortion), *The Day After* (nuclear armaments), and *That Certain Summer* (homosexuality). The author of the study concluded that the "aggregate impact of advocacy groups on prime time has been substantial" (Montgomery, 1989: 218).

Religious groups routinely attacked alleged immorality on network television in the early 1980s. A coalition of such groups set up a national panel of monitors to evaluate levels of sex, profanity, and violence in television programs, threatening to boycott advertisers who failed to withdraw ads from programs that the coalition found objectionable. Assessing the significance of the research was impossible because the coalition kept its monitors' identity secret and released no data on the validity of its research methods.

advertisers sensitive to
pressures from moral
crusaders

The networks and others denounced the coalition's goal of forcing its standards on the rest of the public, but the advertising community proved less militant. Many of the major television advertisers withdrew their spots from program episodes labeled morally objectionable.

Despite advertiser capitulation, such boycott threats appear to have little long-term effect. As the decade wore on, television seemed if anything to become even more obsessed with sex and violence. In a pluralistic society, boycotters have difficulty achieving the consensus and discipline needed to achieve serious long-term economic impact.

PBS also subject to
pressure-group tactics

Even noncommercial broadcasting, supposedly free of advertiser influence and therefore better able to tolerate varied viewpoints, is not immune from group pressures. In 1984, PBS aired *Vietnam: A Television History,* a highly acclaimed 13-part series on the Vietnam War. Though a decade had passed since the war ended, the U.S. role and hence the series' depiction of that role remained controversial. A conservative media watchdog group, Accuracy in Media (AIM), produced a 50-minute documentary "reply" to the PBS series, attacking both specific details and the overall tone of the program. PBS aired the AIM response in mid-1985, following it with a 45-minute discussion between producers and researchers of both programs. This attempt at defusing the controversy brought new complaints against PBS, charging it with having "given in" to its right-wing critics.

Children's Lobby   Action for Children's Television (ACT) has been a persistent lobby for reform of children's programs and advertising. ACT presented a well-researched petition for rule making to the FCC in the 1970s, but the commission made only a policy statement calling for voluntary standards on children's commercials. The FCC recommended limits on the amount of commercial time in children's programs, clear separation of commercials from program materials, and avoidance of product tie-ins and selling by program hosts.

In 1983 the FCC watered down the broadcasters' obligation to carry children's programming but left the advertising standards for children's programs intact. The next year's deregulation package eliminated all commercial time guidelines, including those applicable to children's programs, but left the other children's guidelines in place.

ACT attempts to invoke
FCC intervention in
children's TV

ACT complained to the FCC in 1984 that sponsors designed programs such as *He-Man* and *G.I. Joe* more to sell dolls and accessories than to entertain children. ACT also objected to program syndication deals, such as that used with *Thunder Cats,* in which stations carrying the program shared profits from the sale of Thunder Cat products. In 1985 the FCC, noting the absence of any evidence that these practices in fact produced any specific harm, rejected ACT's complaints.

In 1987, an appellate court, acting on an appeal brought by ACT and others, ordered the FCC to reconsider its guidelines for children's advertising. While the commission reconsidered, Congress passed a bill that would have limited children's ads and required stations to serve the "educational and informational needs" of children in their overall programming. President Reagan vetoed the bill, saying that such a law "simply cannot be reconciled with the freedom of expression secured by our Constitution." Peggy Charren, president of ACT, responded by calling Reagan's action "ideological child abuse." Supporters of the bill planned to reintroduce it.

president vetoes bill to improve children's TV

Self-Regulation   Industries that impinge on the public welfare usually adopt codes for self-regulation—voluntary rules for conducting business. Such codes cultivate favorable public relations. They also forestall abuses that might otherwise bring on government regulation. But industries cannot enforce self-regulatory codes. Enforcement runs afoul of the antitrust laws, which forbid industries to take any joint action that restrains freedom of trade.

The National Association of Broadcasters (NAB) began developing codes for radio program and advertising practices as early as the late 1920s. It extended them to television in 1952. The codes used broad generalizations and a lot of "shoulds" and "should nots," leaving most decisions to the discretion of station management. Nonetheless, the codes reinforced generally observed standards, especially as to the amount of time broadcasters should devote to advertising.

NAB radio and TV codes

Despite NAB precautions to avoid any hint of coercion, the Department of Justice brought suit against the codes in 1979. The suit alleged that the advertising time standards in the codes "artificially curtailed" advertising, repressing price competition and depriving advertisers of "the benefits of free and open competition." Late in 1982, a federal district court approved a consent decree by which the NAB disbanded its code-making activities, to the regret not only of some broadcasters but of many advertisers as well.

Self-regulation is one of the complex of forces by which society indirectly seeks to bring the electronic mass media into line with public policy and the desires of private individuals and groups. But self-regulatory forces risk violation of anti-trust laws, and when the government backs such efforts at control it risks colliding with the Constitution. The First Amendment explicitly forbids government to make laws abridging freedom of speech and press. Yet the Communications Act is such a law. The next chapter addresses the issues arising from this conflict between ideal freedom and social reality.

Constitutional Issues

13

The First Amendment to the constitution prohibits federal regulation of speech, yet the Communications Act imposes federal regulations on those who own or speak on broadcasting stations. This fundamental contradiction has been a frequent cause of litigation.

The courts have struck down many specific FCC regulations because they encroached too far on First Amendment rights. Nevertheless, the Supreme Court has repeatedly endorsed the basic proposition that the federal government has the right to regulate the electronic mass media. Here, as in many other situations, the welfare of society calls for striking a balance between ideal freedom and the practical need to limit speech that might be harmful. The essence of the constitutional issues discussed in this chapter lies in defining the point of compromise between these contradictory goals.

13.1   *First Amendment Basics*

Although freedom of expression occupies only part of only one of the ten amendments that make up the Bill of Rights, it plays a pivotal role in the American political system. In the words of late Supreme Court Justice William O. Douglas, the First Amendment "has been the safeguard of every religious, political, philosophical, economic and racial group amongst us" (US, 1951: 584).

The Marketplace of Ideas   The freedom of speech guaranteed by the First Amendment (see Exhibit 13.1 for its actual wording) enables a robust, wide-open marketplace of ideas. First Amendment theory holds that concepts

EXHIBIT *13.1*   "Congress Shall Make No Law ...": The First Amendment

The First Amendment protects four fundamental rights of citizens that governments throughout history have had the most reason to fear and the greatest inclination to violate—freedom to *believe,* to *speak,* to *gather together,* and to ask rulers to *correct injustices.* The amendment conveys all this in only

45 words, of which just 14 guarantee freedom of expression:

> Congress shall make no law respecting an establishment of religion, or prohibiting the free excercise thereof, or abridging the freedom of speech, or of the press; or the right of the people peaceably to assemble, and to petition the Government for a redress of grievances.

These words limit not only Congress but also state and local governments, thanks to the Fourteenth Amendment, passed in 1868, which says, "No state shall make or enforce any law which shall abridge the privileges or immunities of citizens of the United States...." Section 326 of the Communications Act of 1934 explicitly extends the First Amendment's protection to broadcasting:

> Nothing in this Act shall be understood or construed to give the Commission the power of censorship over the radio communications or signals transmitted by any radio station, and no regulation or condition shall be promulgated or fixed by the Commission which shall interfere with the right of free speech by means of radio communication.

Source: Kerwin B. Roache/FPG.

and opinions from all possible sources should compete for acceptance in that arena. As the Supreme Court noted in a major broadcasting decision, "it is the purpose of the First Amendment to preserve an uninhibited marketplace of ideas in which truth will ultimately prevail, rather than to countenance monopolization of the market" (US, 1969: 390).

The First Amendment actually *encourages* disagreement. "A function of free speech under our system of government is to invite dispute," wrote Justice Douglas. "It may indeed best serve its highest purpose when it induces a condition of unrest, creates dissatisfaction with conditions as they are, or even stirs people to anger" (US, 1949: 4).

Just such a condition arose in the 1980s in a town made famous in cowboy pictures, Dodge City, Kansas. Radio station KTTL–FM broadcast daily hour-long sermons by two fundamentalist ministers attacking Jews, blacks, and other groups. They urged listeners to ignore police officers and attack such groups at will. The invective poured out in such abundance that several local groups protested renewal of KTTL's license.

A huge media uproar resulted. A congressional subcommittee held hearings, and the press gave extensive coverage to the station owner's extremist conservative views favoring local armed vigilantes. In mid-1985, the FCC designated the license for a comparative hearing with another applicant for the same frequency.

The comparative hearing led to a controversial decision: the FCC renewed KTTL's license on the understanding that the licensee would sell the station (it could not be sold while its license was in question). The First Amendment, said the commission, protected KTTL's broadcasts from government suppression, offensive though they might be to many listeners (RR, 1985). The commission found that because the material presented no "clear and present danger" to the public (a test long since established by the U.S. Supreme Court), it qualified as protected speech. Such incitement to take illegal or dangerous actions did not, as the FCC had said in an earlier case, "rise far above public inconvenience, annoyance, or unrest" (FCCR, 1972c: 637).

In Kansas City, Missouri, the Ku Klux Klan announced in 1988 that it planned to produce a weekly series on an access cable channel. Such channels are supposed to be open to all and not subject to editorial control by the cable system. A deluge of citizen complaints poured in on the cable operator and the city council (because the council was the franchising authority that stipulated the access channel). Barred by the Communications Act from ordering the cable company to censor anything on the access channel, the city council voted to delete the channel entirely. This indirect censorship raised what one commentator called "an exquisitely vexing" First Amendment issue (Kaplan, 1988). Pointing out that the First Amendment protects even the KKK's right to speak, a civil rights group threatened to sue the city council. The council backed off, and eventually the Klan had its say without causing any serious public disorder; and only two cable customers cancelled their subscriptions (Quinn, 1990).

1st Amendment protects
Ku Klux Klan broadcasts

Government vs. Private Censorship   In the cases just mentioned, the First Amendment protected individuals against *government* censorship. It affords no such shield against censorship by *private* authorities acting on their own. Media editors or managers who edit, cut, bleep, delete, revise, and otherwise mangle programs may be guilty of bad judgment, excessive timidity, and other faults, but they do not violate the First Amendment. Private censorship becomes a violation only when it disguises *state action*.

For example, when the FCC found itself under intense pressure from Congress and public groups to "do something" about increasing amounts of violence and sex in television, fear of violating the First Amendment kept the commission from outright suppression of such material. Instead the FCC jawboned (forcefully persuaded, as explained more fully in Section 12.3) broadcasters into self-suppression. In 1975 it persuaded the broadcasters to adopt a **family viewing-time rule** that advised against scheduling "entertainment programming inappropriate for viewing by a general family audience" before 10:00 P.M., unless the broadcaster warned viewers that family standards might be violated.

When a federal district court heard a challenge to this indirect censorship, the court held that the family viewing hour constituted state action. It violated the First Amendment because the government (that is, the FCC) had coerced the industry into acting on its behalf (F Sup, 1976).

Religion and the First Amendment   Another First Amendment clause of interest to the electronic mass media guarantees religious freedom. In addition to assuring the "free excercise" of religion, the amendment explicitly rules out the designation of any particular creed as the established—that is, state-sponsored—religion. The Supreme Court has used the image of a "wall of separation" erected between government and religion, holding that even the smallest step in the direction of state approval of any particular religious observance violates the First Amendment.

religious broadcasters
make claims to double
1ˢᵗ Amendment
protection

Some religious licensees, feeling doubly protected by the freedom of speech and freedom of religion clauses of the First Amendment, have at times claimed near-immunity from commission investigation into their conduct as licensees. They have, for example, at times defied EEO requirements and FCC orders to disclose their financial status.

13.2   *Concept of First Amendment Parity*

As Exhibit 13.1 shows, the framers of the First Amendment mentioned only "freedom of speech or of the press." They could not, of course, have imagined all the ways of amplifying speech and extending the press that future centuries would bring.

The courts have therefore had to wrestle repeatedly with questions about the scope of the First Amendment words "speech" and "press". Do those terms include speech amplified by public-address systems, speech in shopping malls and airports, speech in the form of flag burning, speech disseminated by motion pictures, broadcasting, and cable? Can all these forms of expression claim equal protection from government interference?

Specifically, should the government-regulated electronic mass media have the same freedom as the newspapers and other unregulated media? Should all media enjoy *First Amendment parity?* Until the 1980s, the answer had generally been no. It was taken for granted that the First Amendment protects some media more completely than others. Broadcasting, the argument ran, has unique attributes that justify imposing certain regulations that would violate the First Amendment if imposed on the newspapers. The three main arguments favoring this assumption of "uniqueness" follow.

unique issues of regulating electronic mass media

Spectrum as a National Resource

Broadcasting uses a limited resource in the public domain, the electromagnetic spectrum. It is not a physical entity and cannot be held or traded like physical property. It exists to serve the entire nation—in fact the entire world—not just the private commercial interests of station operators.

Channel Scarcity

The pivotal argument usually cited in support of government regulation is the shortage of frequencies available for all types of over-the-air communication. The spectrum is finite, and demand for access to it exceeds supply. Scarcity of channels involves the FCC in making choices. Hearings on mutually exclusive applications necessarily end in some applicants being denied the freedom of speech they would have enjoyed as station owners.

Publishers, in contrast, suffer no such problem: they need no spectrum space, only presses, and supplies of ink and paper. As many people as want to and can afford the machinery can publish without limit. They need no license, and they neither cause nor receive electronic interference. The cost need not be high—those who cannot afford presses can use desktop computer publishing and duplicating machines.

Opponents of government regulation claim that channel scarcity is a thing of the past. They cite the twentyfold increase in the number of broadcast stations since Congress wrote the 1927 Radio Act—from about 600 to over 12,000. They argue that even though demand for more channels in densely populated areas continues, cable television makes virtually unlimited numbers of additional channels available.

In rebuttal, opponents point out that numerous applicants scramble to pay astronomical prices for every desirable channel. Would that happen if channels were not scarce? As for cable channels, they reach only about 60 percent of the television households, whereas broadcasting reaches virtually everybody. In any event, cable requires payment of subscription fees every month, whereas broadcasting requires only the purchasing and maintaining of receivers.

does cable TV compensate for spectrum shortage?

Intrusiveness Factor   As a home audio/visual medium clearly distinguishable from print media, broadcasting has an intrusiveness that lays special obligations on it, calling for more government oversight than is warranted for less intrusive media. Broadcasting enters virtually every home, where programs become readily available to all ages and all types of people. Literacy is not required.

This intimate presence within the family stronghold bars the use of some kinds of material that would be commonplace in other media. Few would argue that pornographic magazine content should be just as free to appear in homes via broadcasting as it is to appear on newsstands in print or even in video stores on tape.

These arguments have been repeatedly accepted by the courts as justifying specific instances of FCC intrusion on program matters—regulations of a sort that would not be tolerated in the case of newspapers or magazines.

13.3   *Diversity of Voices*

First Amendment theory stresses the value of maintaining an open marketplace of ideas. Information and opinions from many diverse and antagonistic sources compete in that arena for acceptance.

Changing Conditions in the Marketplace   The writers of the Constitution saw the marketplace in 18th-century terms, as a forum in which small traders in the spoken and printed word competed on relatively equal terms. They expected a leisurely *self-righting* process to occur as citizens heard, read, and digested diverse viewpoints and developed their own, informed conclusions.

example of structural regulation: rules to diversify ownership

Under modern conditions, however, unregulated competition may lead to monopoly control. Government can play a positive First Amendment role by countering the medium's proneness to centralization. Diversification of ownership has therefore always been a major regulatory goal. This type of structural regulation contrasts with the behavioral regulation discussed in Section 12.11. To regulate ownership, FCC rules place limits on the number and kind of stations licensed to any one owner, on **media cross ownership** (stations, systems, newspapers, and other media under common control), and on the concentration of control over program production and distribution.

Multiple-Station Ownership   Every broadcast station monopolizes the channel it occupies—no one else can broadcast on that channel in that market. Each cable system holds a more complete monopoly—viewers usually have no choice but to subscribe to the one and only cable system in the franchise area where they live. Once viewers "go on the cable," installers disconnect antennas so that home owners usually receive broadcast stations *only* by cable. Following deletion of the must-carry rule, the cable operator acquired effective monopoly on the choice of *all* video signals coming into a home, other than rented or purchased videotapes and DBS transmissions.

The FCC limits a single owner to no more than 12 stations in each broadcast service—AM, FM, and television. Additionally, a single owner may not control television stations covering more than a quarter of the country's households. In some cases the FCC raises these maximums. For example, members of a minority group may own 14 stations of each type.

"12-12-12" rule

In any one broadcast market, the **one-to-a-customer rule** prevails: a single owner may have only one television station, one radio station, or one AM/FM combination. Individual exceptions sometimes allow coownership of radio and UHF television stations to help strengthen the UHF service.

When the FCC adopted multiple-station ownership rules, it exempted current owners (except for the one-to-a-customer rule). This exemption, called *grandfathering,* allowed existing owners to exceed the ownership ceilings as long as the same licensee retained ownership. Thus, the restructuring of local ownership is a continuing process. When grandfathered groups are sold, buyers are subject to the one-to-a-customer rule. The FCC exempts noncommercial stations from the multiple-ownership rules and grants waivers in specific cases.

None of this regulatory complexity limits multiple ownership of other electronic media such as cable television systems. Nor is there any limit on the ownership of low-power television stations. Ceilings have been proposed on the number of cable systems a single multiple-system operator (MSO) may own and on the number of subscribers one MSO may serve. So far no such limits have been adopted.

no limit on number of cable systems under single ownership

Media Crossownership   Every instance of media crossownership, such as common control of newspapers and broadcasting stations, automatically reduces diversification. Reduction in the number of media *voices* (the number of *separately owned* outlets, not just the number of outlets) is especially undesirable in small communities. An obvious loss in diversification occurs when the only newspaper in a town owns the only broadcast station or cable system—two outlets but only one voice.

For years the powerful newspaper lobby deterred the FCC from issuing rules banning newspaper/broadcasting crossownership. The FCC adopted such rules in 1975, avoiding a confrontation by grandfathering all but a few existing combinations in small towns where the only paper controlled the only station. Lobbying has frustrated repeated efforts by both the FCC and Congress to limit newspaper/cable crossownership. Exhibit 13.2 gives details on other crossownership rules.

no limit on newspaper/cable cross-ownership

Telco Crossownership   Toward the end of the 1980s, a new crossownership controversy developed, one in which broadcasters and cable owners agreed for once. They both opposed allowing telephone companies (telcos) to own cable systems and broadcast stations within their telephone service areas. Bans against such crossownership kept common-carrier and media

EXHIBIT 13.2 Summary of Electronic Mass Media Crossownership Rules

| | May co-own the following: | | | | | |
| | Broadcast Stations: | | | Broadcast Networks | Cable | |
The owner of a(n):	AM	FM	TV[a]		Systems	Networks
AM radio station[b]	11 more	12	12	No limit	No limit	No limit
FM radio station[b]	12	11 more	12	No limit	No limit	No limit
TV station	12	12	11 more[a]	No limit	No limit if not in same market	No limit
Broadcast network	12	12	12	—	None	No limit
Cable TV system	12	12	12 (but none in same market)	No limit if radio only	No limit	No limit
Cable TV network	12	12	12 (but not in market with co-owned cable system)	No limit	No limit	No limit

[a]For television stations only, the total potential national audience reach of all coowned stations must not exceed 25 percent. Thus the actual limit on the number of television stations licensed to a single owner may be lower, especially if the stations are in top markets.
[b]As many as 14 stations in each category may be licensed by minority groups.

owners on separate tracks, one providing transmission services, the other information services. But telcos increasingly seek a share in the information business, including the electronic mass media.

The Department of Justice has been particularly sensitive to the possibility of telco dominance. Telcos already have access to the national telephone wire/cable/microwave/satellite network that extends to nearly every home in the country. The breakup of the AT&T monopoly, described in Section 3.5 still left powerful regional telephone monopolies. One of their goals, referred to as the **video dial-tone concept,** envisions telephone companies linking facilities for broadcast/cable *transmission* to telephone homes, without necessarily becoming involved in the programming function.

Ownership by Minority-Group Members For years the FCC took no interest in whether or not licensees were members of minority groups. It took the position that the Communications Act is "color blind," but a series of court setbacks eventually sensitized the commission to the issue of minority ownership. To increase rather than to limit ownership by members of minority groups, the commission set up preference machinery to enhance minority ownership.

The award of minority preferences in lotteries to choose among applicants for LPTV and MMDS licenses was described in Section 12.4. The FCC gives minority applicants a two-to-one advantage over other applicants.

Tax certificates encourage sales to minority buyers. Sellers to minorities may defer paying capital gains taxes on their profits.

station owner may not sell out if license is in jeopardy—unless . . .

To encourage sales to minority applicants, the FCC permits owners whose licenses are in serious danger of nonrenewal to recover some, but not all, of the market value of their intangible assets if they sell to minorities. Normally such licensees may not evade punishment by selling their stations at full value. They may sell their stations' physical assets but not the intangible assets represented by the license to broadcast. Such a sale is known as a *distress sale*.

The FCC agreed in 1979 to drop fradulent billing charges against a small AM station in Connecticut when the incumbent offered to sell the property to a minority group for 75 percent of its appraised value. The 25 percent discount became a de facto standard for subsequent distress sales to minorities.

Minority ownership of stations increased from about 50 in 1978 to about 300 a decade later. But to achieve station ownership proportional to the actual size of major minorities in America would require ownership of some 1,250 broadcast stations by blacks and about 450 by Hispanics. The industry has a long way to go before minorities achieve ownership parity.

Despite this record, the FCC briefly suspended the distress-sale option in the late 1980s. Conservatives who opposed giving minorities special breaks regarded the distress-sale advantage as "reverse discrimination." However, pressure from Congress soon forced the commission to reinstate the rules encouraging minority ownership. The Supreme Court cited this evidence of congressional intent when it upheld minority preferences in a 1990 decision.

rules giving minorities preferences upheld

Political Access   13.4

The most explicit program-related provision of the Communications Act deals with how stations should respond to requests for time from candidates for public office. In 1927 Congress correctly foresaw that broadcasting would one day exert a major influence on voters. If the party in power could monopolize broadcasting (as now happens under authoritarian regimes where), candidates of opposing parties would stand little chance of winning elections.

"Equal Opportunities" for Candidates   Section 315 of the Communications Act requires stations to allow *equal opportunities* (often somewhat misleadingly called "equal time") for political candidates. The same requirement was later extended to cable television. Section 315 reads:

> If any licensee shall permit any person who is a legally qualified candidate for any public office to use a broadcasting station, he shall afford equal opportunities to all other such candidates for that office in the use of such broadcasting station; Provided, That such licensee shall have no power of censorship over the material broadcast under the provisions of this section. (47 USC 315)

A 1971 amendment to the Communications Act *mandates* allowing time for *federal* candidates. It did so by adding a new basis for license revocation— the "willful and repeated failure" to allow time to federal candidates for public office (Section 312).

Candidates in the News   What about the presence of candidates in news stories? Do such "users" also trigger Section 315's equal opportunities obligation? At first the FCC said no; later it said yes. Congress thereupon amended Section 315 to exempt news coverage of all candidates:

> Appearance by a legally qualified candidate on any—
> (1) bona fide newscast,
> (2) bona fide news interview,
> (3) bona fide news documentary (if the appearance of the candidate is incidental to the presentation of the subject or subjects covered by the news documentary), or
> (4) on-the-spot news coverage of bona fide news events (including but not limited to political conventions and activities incidental thereto), *shall not be deemed to be use of a broadcasting station within the meaning of this subsection.* (47 USC 315a, italics added)

Equal Opportunities in Practice   Section 315 is rigorously enforced— candidates themselves see to that. Stations keep meticulous records of time requests by candidates and of the "equal opportunities" afforded them. Nevertheless, Section 315 as amended left licensees and the FCC with many knotty problems of interpretation. Political candidates' rights are one of the most frequent subjects of inquiry from stations seeking interpretation of FCC rules. Some examples of the questions raised and the FCC's responses follow.

Which candidates get "equal opportunities"? The rules apply both to candidates for party nomination in a primary election and to nominees in a general election. Equal opportunities can be claimed only by candidates for a specific office for which one candidate has already received time.

When an incumbent president is running for reelection, do presidential news conferences count as bona fide news programs? Yes.

Do presidential candidate debates count as news? After 1975, the FCC held that debates qualified as bona fide news events as long as third parties with no personal interest in the outcome controlled the event. Thus in 1976 and 1980 the League of Women Voters, a nonpartisan group, sponsored the debates. In 1983, however, the FCC ruled (and an appeals court upheld the ruling) that the electronic media could sponsor as well as cover such debates without violating Section 315. The television networks themselves presented the two presidential and one vice-presidential campaign debates in both 1984 and 1988.

Expediency dictated this ruling—demands from off-the-wall minor candidates for debate opportunities would have made it impossible to schedule the presidential candidate debates. But excluding minor-party candidates from the debates weakens the possibility of a third-party candidate ever winning an election—a seemingly clear perversion of congressional intent in adopting Section 315.

Are regularly scheduled interview and talk programs exempt from equal-time requests? Yes, including quasi-public-affairs programs such as *Donahue,* the *Oprah Winfrey Show*, and pseudo-news "reality" programs such as *Hard Copy*. Candidate appearances on *Today* and such news-interview programs as *Meet the Press* have long qualified for exemption.

even pseudo-news shows qualify as news under Section 315

Is a candidate entitled to whatever time of the day he or she wants? No, equal opportunities does mean identical opportunities. The FCC has held that banning *all* political advertising in prime time violates Section 312's requirement of "reasonable access" for federal candidates, but stations may keep political spots out of particular programs. For example, the FCC has allowed stations to bar political advertising on news programs.

If a candidate plans to use obscene material on the air, does the no-censorship clause in Section 315 oblige the station to broadcast it? No. When in 1984 *Hustler* magazine publisher Larry Flynt threatened to use arguably obscene material in a possible campaign for the presidency, the commission held that the U.S. Criminal Code ban on broadcasting obscenity overrode the no-censorship rule.

May electronic mass media endorse political candidates in editorials? Yes, but if they do, they must notify opposing candidates and offer reply time.

Are cable systems held to the same regulations on political candidates as broadcast stations? The regulations apply only to programs that the cable operator *originates*. Cable systems are not responsible for political program decisions made by stations or services whose programs they carry but do not originate.

equal opportunities for candidates on cable TV

While profiting from the sale of time to candidates, the electronic mass media also have a responsibility to inform the electorate about political issues in a nonpartisan way. The tricky combination of enforced cooperation, profit making, and the obligation to journalistic objectivity is a continuing source of problems for the media.

13.5 Free Press vs. Fair Trial

Another news-related constitutional issue arises when radio and television do on-the-spot reports of court trials. The right to cover the news collides with defendents' rights to due process.

Due Process The Sixth Amendment assures defendants the right to a *public* trial. But the due-process clause of the Fifth Amendment assures fair play to persons accused of crimes. Ordinarily, the news media freely report trials. However, on-the-spot coverage can be distracting and in notorious cases can subject defendants to intense publicity. A fair trial can become impossible under such circumstances.

constitutional conflict

In the confrontation between press freedom and a fair trial, the constitutional rights of reporters sometimes have to give way to the constitutional rights of defendants. Electronic mass media become deeply involved in this thorny issue when they attempt to air on-the-spot coverage of highly publicized trials or pretrial proceedings.

Canon 35 For decades virtually no live or recorded radio or television coverage of trials occurred. The American Bar Association (ABA) recommended in 1935 that judges discourage broadcast and photo coverage because it tended "to detract from the essential dignity of the proceedings, degrade the court, and create misconceptions. . . ." Known as *Canon 35,* this rule prevailed for some thirty years.

By the 1970s, however, less intrusive equipment, changing social standards, and more mature broadcast journalism practices persuaded the ABA to recommend giving judges wider latitude in allowing radio/television coverage of trials. The Supreme Court still bans cameras and microphones in its own proceedings. Nevertheless, in 1981 it acknowledged improvements in technology, holding that "the risk of juror prejudice . . . does not warrant an absolute constitutional ban on all broadcast coverage" (US, 1981: 575).

federal courts discontinue ban of live TV and radio

By the end of the 1980s more than 40 states had either allowed cameras in their courtrooms or conducted experiments to that end. Selected federal courts began a three-year experiment using live television and radio coverage for civil (not criminal) trials in 1991, suggesting an end to their long-time ban on such media access.

13.6 Public Access to Media

First Amendment theory calls not only for the chance to listen to diverse voices in the marketplace but also for the chance to add a voice of one's own. The notion of **public access** has reciprocal aspects—access both to what others express and access to the means of expression for oneself or one's social group.

Localism   The FCC encourages localism by licensing stations on a local basis so as to give as many communities as possible their own outlets. Ideally, access to stations affords opportunities for localized expression: public-service agencies can promote their objectives; partisans in local controversies can air their points of view; local governments and political candidates can inform the electorate; local educational and cultural institutions can broaden their community services; local firms can advertise; local talent can have an outlet; and so on. A station or cable system that offers such programs thus serves its area by affording it a means of community self-expression.

Of course, cable systems, too, are franchised to serve specific local areas, and some systems offer community access channels and their own local-origination channels. On the whole, however, cable tends to be more network oriented than broadcasting. Broadcasters therefore regard their potential for local production as an important advantage in competing against cable and direct-to-home satellite services.

broadcasting tends more toward localism than does cable TV

Unfortunately, when marketplace economics dictates where stations will be built, maldistribution inevitably results—too many outlets in rich, populous communities and not enough in underpopulated poor ones. As cable penetration increased, it evened up the choices available in most urban and suburban areas. But cable too underserves rural areas; moreover, the cable portion of the Communications Act does not rest on a public-service mandate as does the broadcasting portion.

Hopes for extensive local production by broadcast stations faded when networks and syndication took over all the desirable time slots. The licensing and renewal policies discussed in Chapter 12 continue to hold localism up as a formal goal. Possibly cable and DBS competition will revive interest in achieving the localism goal as a unique broadcasting asset.

The Fairness Doctrine   Not everyone who wants to express ideas can own a station or cable system, nor can everyone expect to gain access to stations or systems owned by others. The FCC attempted to assure nonowners a voice, at least on significant issues, by mandating access to broadcasting for *ideas* rather than for specific *people*. Of course, stations could not be forced to give time for literally every idea that might be put forward. The FCC mandated access only for ideas about controversial issues of public importance.

Eventually the FCC elaborated this access concept into a formalized set of procedures called the *fairness doctrine*. Although the doctrine was withdrawn in 1987, it still has many supporters and may yet be revived. Reviewing some of its history is therefore worthwhile.

The **fairness doctrine** put stations on notice that the FCC expected them to devote some time, unspecified as to amount, to (a) controversial issues of public importance and (b) opportunities for the expression of opposing views when only one side of such an issue had been aired. Both the FCC and the stations largely ignored (a), focusing attention on (b), the right of reply. In practice, therefore, most fairness-doctrine programs countered points of view that had already been aired, rather than initiating discussions or new issues.

two parts to Fairness Doctrine

Licensees had great latitude in deciding whether or not a subject qualified as both a *controversial issue* and one of *public importance*. They also had leeway in deciding *how much time* should be devoted to replies, *when* replies should be scheduled, and *who* should speak for opposing viewpoints.

The doctrine therefore made no rigid demands. Nevertheless, in order to forestall complaints, stations tended to monitor their programs closely for controversial topics of public importance to make sure time was given for opposing views. In creating this wariness about controversy, critics contended, the fairness doctrine had a chilling effect. As a result, stations gave less airtime instead of more to controversial issues.

broadcasters claim doctrine inhibits controversial programs

In 1969, the Supreme Court upheld the FCC's fairness doctrine and its related personal-attack and political-editorializing rules in a landmark decision—the *Red Lion* case (US, 1969). Exhibit 13.3 gives details of the case, which involved a station's refusal to allow reply time to a personal attack. The Court unanimously affirmed the FCC's right to impose these program requirements, in spite of the First Amendment's prohibition against government censorship. The Court emphasized three key principles:

recurring theme: unique broadcasting attributes

- *Broadcasting has a unique First Amendment status:* "It is idle to posit an unbridgeable First Amendment right to broadcast comparable to the right of every individual to speak, write, or publish."
- *Broadcasters have fiduciary obligations:* "There is nothing in the First Amendment which prevents the Government from requiring a licensee to share his frequency with others and to conduct himself as a proxy or fiduciary."
- *The public interest has priority:* "It is the right of the viewers and listeners, not the right of the broadcasters, which is paramount."

EXHIBIT *13.3*   A Place and a Case Called *Red Lion*

WGCB AM/FM, Red Lion, PA

An unlikely small-town station, formed the setting for one of the leading Supreme Court decisions on the electronic media. During the 1960s, right-wing radio preachers inundated radio with paid syndicated political commentary, backed by ultraconservative supporters such as Texas multimillionaire H. L. Hunt through tax-exempt foundations. Purchased time for these religious/political programs provided much-needed radio income in small markets.

The landmark case got its name from WGCB, a southeastern Pennsylvania AM/FM outlet licensed to a conservative minister under the name Red Lion Broadcasting. In 1964, one of the Reverend Billy James Hargis's syndicated broadcasts, carried by the

EXHIBIT **13.3**   Continued

station, attacked author Fred Cook, who had criticized defeated Republican presidential candidate Barry Goldwater and had written an article on what he termed the "hate clubs of the air," referring to the Hargis series *Christian Crusade,* among others. Hargis attacked Cook on the air, charging him with Communist affiliations and with criticizing the FBI and the CIA—the standard litany of accusations Hargis routinely made against liberals.

Cook then accused the station of violating FCC rules by failing to inform him of a personal attack. When he wrote asking for time to reply, the station responded with a rate card, inviting him to buy time like anyone else. Cook appealed to the FCC, which agreed that he had a right to free air time for a reply. It ordered WGCB to comply.

It would have been easy for the conservative Reverend Mr. Norris to grant Cook a few minutes of time on the Red Lion station, but he refused on First Amendment grounds, appealing the commission decision. The court of appeals upheld the FCC, but Norris took the case to the Supreme Court. Once again the Court upheld the FCC, issuing an opinion strongly defensive of the FCC's right to demand program fairness.

Several years later, Fred Friendly, a former head of CBS news but by then a Columbia University journalism professor, began looking into the background of this well-known case for a book about the fairness doctrine (Friendly, 1976). He discovered

Fred Friendly

that Cook had been a subsidized writer for the Democratic National Committee and that his fairness complaint had been linked to a systematic campaign mounted by the Democrats to discredit right-wing extremists such as Hargis. According to Friendly, the Democrats set out to exploit the fairness doctrine as a means of harassing stations that sold time for the airing of ultraconservative political programs. Cook and the Democratic National Committee claimed that Friendly had misinterpreted their activities, maintaining that Cook acted as a private individual, not as an agent of the Democratic party.

Fred Cook

Billy James Hargis

Source: First three photos from George Tames/New York *Times;* Fred Friendly photo from Neal Buenzi/New York *Times.*

In practice, the fairness doctrine gave listeners/viewers a voice they otherwise lacked. A licensee who persistently and blatantly presented only one side of controversies could be called to account. Listeners/viewers, however, had to work hard to prepare a fairness-doctrine complaint that could trigger FCC action against a station. Complaints had to be based not on just any controversies but on those that had *public importance* in the station's community of license. Complainants had to monitor the offending station to find an overall pattern of one-sidedness. A single one-sided program was not enough to trigger FCC action.

The FCC dismissed most fairness complaints out of hand. Complainants either cited no legally definable controversial issue of public importance or failed to show how the overall programming of accused stations had in fact denied reasonable opportunities for opposing arguments.

Demise of the Fairness Doctrine

In 1985 the FCC, by then dedicated to deregulation, reported, after a lengthy analysis of the fairness doctrine:

> On the basis of the voluminous record compiled in this proceeding, our experience in administering the doctrine and our general expertise in broadcast regulation, we no longer believe that the fairness doctrine, as a matter of policy, serves the public interest. . . . Furthermore, we find that the fairness doctrine, in operation, actually inhibits the presentation of controversial issues of public importance to the detriment of the public and in degradation of the editorial prerogatives of broadcast journalists. (FCCR, 1985: 143)

FCC agrees that fairness doctrine had chilling effect

Unconvinced, Congress directed the FCC to make a further study, exploring alternatives to the doctrine. The FCC stubbornly reiterated its view that an open marketplace of ideas made the fairness doctrine unnecessary. In 1987 it took advantage of a court remand requiring it to reconsider an earlier fairness decision. The FCC settled the case by abolishing the doctrine entirely (FCCR, 1987).

That should have ended the long dispute over the fairness doctrine. But the FCC's defiance in ending a practice that Congress had gone on record as favoring enraged key legislators. They vowed to reinstate the doctrine in the future by way of an amendment to the Communications Act. By 1991, however, no such amendment had resulted, and it appeared unlikely one would.

Congress disagrees with FCC, seeks to reinstate doctrine

Rights of Reply

Two specific fairness requirements, the personal-attack and political-editorializing rules, both adopted in 1967, remained on the books. They continued to concern opponents of FCC interference in program matters.

The **personal-attack rule** requires stations to inform individuals or groups of personal attacks on their "honesty, character, integrity or like personal qualities" that occur in the course of discussions of controversial public issues. Within a week of the offending broadcast, licensees must inform those attacked, telling them of the nature of the attack and how replies can be made. Specifically exempted from this right of reply are on-the-air attacks made against foreigners, those made by political candidates and their spokespersons during campaigns, and those occurring in news interviews, on-the-spot news coverage, and news commentaries (47 CFR 73, 1920).

The **political-editorializing rule** stipulates that a candidate must be given a chance to respond when a licensee endorses any of his or her opponents. A station must inform the opposing candidate(s) within 24 hours of such editorial endorsements. The rule does *not* apply to the use of a station's facilities by opposing candidates, a situation covered by the equal-opportunities rules discussed in Section 13.4.

Access for Advertising and Counteradvertising   Cigarette advertising became the subject of a famous fairness-doctrine complaint. In 1968, the FCC decided that the surgeon general's first report on the dangers of smoking and Congress's 1965 act requiring a health warning on cigarette packages justified treating cigarette advertising as a unique fairness-doctrine issue. It ruled that stations had to carry antismoking spots if they carried cigarette commercials. These countercommercials subsided after Congress banned broadcast advertising of cigarettes in 1971.

Editorial advertising, sometimes called **advertorials,** however, poses a different kind of problem. Traditionally, broadcasters have declined to let advertisers use commercials as vehicles for comment on controversial issues. They argued that serious issues cannot be adequately discussed in short announcements. Alternatively, selling larger blocks of time for editorializing by outsiders would involve illegal surrender of licensees' editorial responsibility. Most stations now accept advertorials on a case-by-case basis, but the networks still resist selling time for them.

arguments against allowing editorial advertising

First Amendment vs. Libel/Privacy Laws   13.7

Among laws *other* than the Communications Act that involve First Amendment issues, *libel* laws have special significance for the electronic mass media.

Relation of Libel Laws to Press Freedom   When a person is unfairly held up to public ridicule or his or her character is defamed, libel laws provide a chance to retaliate and collect damages. But easily won libel cases can also be used by corrupt or incompetent officials to avoid being exposed by the media. The right to publicly criticize those in power affords a significant test of whether a society enjoys true freedom of expression.

key 1st Amendment goal: right to criticize public officials

Democratic societies count on tenacious news reporting to uncover official wrongdoing, sloth, or incompetence, even at the highest political levels. The story of the Watergate burglary that led ultimately to the resignation of President Richard Nixon is a case in point.

But vigorous investigative reporting and hard-hitting documentaries cannot flourish when harsh, easily invoked libel laws threaten journalists with ruinous fines or imprisonment when they dare to criticize public officials. Politicians must therefore be prepared to face harsh, even unfair and ill-founded criticism from the media without being able to retaliate with push-over libel suits.

"Actual Malice" Test

Public figures are especially sensitive to criticism on television because of its wide coverage and its perceived impact. This sensitivity makes broadcasting a frequent target of libel suits. However, the case that gave the media their best protection from such suits happened to involve a newspaper.

The case grew out of a key antisegregation demonstration during the civil rights struggle of the 1960s—the bus boycott by blacks in Montgomery, Alabama. Supporters of the boycott bought space in the *New York Times* for a full-page advertisement criticizing the way Montgomery officials attacked freedom-marchers. Some of the statements in the advertisement turned out to be untrue, although apparently they were not deliberate lies. One of the officials in question, a man named Sullivan, sued for libel. The Supreme Court rejected the award of damages to Sullivan by lower courts, saying that criticism of public officials had broad First Amendment protection. Even though some of the allegations against the unnamed officials were untrue, they did not constitute libel.

Argument over public issues, said the Court, should be "uninhibited, robust, and wide-open." It may include "vehement, caustic, and sometimes unpleasantly sharp attacks on government and public officials." Such free-wheeling debate would be discouraged if, in the heat of controversy, the critic must pause to weigh every unfavorable word. The Constitution, the Court concluded, allows a public official to win libel damages only if the offending statement amounted to " 'actual malice'—that is, with knowledge that it was false or with reckless disregard of whether it was false or not" (US, 1964: 279). Thus for public figures, *actual malice* became the crucial test in proving libel.

libel defense of "actual malice"

Subsequent libel cases broadened the term "public officials" to include anyone whose notoriety projected them into the news as *public figures*. People so classified have little chance of bringing a successful libel suit against the media—even when, as in the *New York Times* case, unintentional falsehood can be proved.

Right of Privacy

Broadcasters also need to understand *privacy* law. The Constitution does not explicitly mention privacy rights but implies them in the Fourth Amendment. That amendment guarantees "the right of the people to be secure in their persons, houses, papers, and effects." This provision has been interpreted to mean that an individual has the right to physical solitude, to protection from intrusion on private property and into the details of personal life, to protection from being presented in a false light (for example, being said to support something one actually opposes), and to protection from unauthorized use of one's name or image for commercial gain.

what is implied by the right of privacy?

Although the courts have held that public officials, performers, and anyone involved in news events have a lesser right to privacy because of legitimate public interest in those persons or events, privacy laws still limit the media's First Amendment rights when they infringe on privacy. As an everyday example, investigative television reporters might want to take pictures of a restaurant kitchen that received adverse publicity because of violating local health codes. Such an intrusion may involve a conflict between the reporters' First Amendment rights and the restaurant owner's right to control access to private property.

Suppressing Obscenity/Indecency 13.8

Another major First Amendment confrontation occurs when government attempts to suppress alleged obscenity or indecency in the media. The First Amendment does not protect obscenity from government suppression. But what is obscenity?

Legal Tests of Obscenity   Current obscenity law goes back to the 1973 *Miller* case, in which the Supreme Court ruled on the constitutionality of a California state obscenity law (US, 1973b). The decision emphasized that there is no single standard for judging obscenity. *Community standards* for the unacceptable vary from place to place: "It is neither realistic nor constitutionally sound to read the First Amendment as requiring that the people of Maine or Mississippi accept public depiction of conduct found tolerable in Las Vegas or New York City" (US, 1973b: 32).

In warning states to avoid overly broad obscenity statutes, the Court gave a definition that has become the standard test: obscenity consists of

> works which, taken as a whole, appeal to the prurient [obsessive and improper] interest in sex, which portray sexual conduct in a patently offensive way, and which, taken as a whole, do not have serious literary, artistic, political, or scientific value. (US, 1973b: 24)

The *Miller* case, along with some later cases that added minor modifications, restricted obscenity censorship to hard-core pornography. Under the community-standards doctrine, the Court left to the states the unenviable job of defining *obscenity,* but it ruled out abuses of power that censors had freely committed in the past. A government censor may not

what government censors no longer may do when alleging obscenity

- Condemn an entire work because of a few isolated obscene words.
- Use outdated standards no longer common to the local community.
- Apply as a standard the opinions of hypersensitive persons not typical of the general public.
- Ignore serious artistic or scientific purpose in judging a work.

For broadcasting, the *Miller* definition poses some problems. Material acceptable in other media might be regarded as obscene, indecent, or profane by members of broadcast and cable audiences, especially because these media are so readily available to children in the home itself. Furthermore, the national reach of broadcast and cable network services means that they confront a great variety of community standards.

"Seven Dirty Words" Case

The tolerant social climate of the 1960s affected broadcasting belatedly. The FCC issued a few minor punishments for alleged obscenity, hoping some station would precipitate a test case by charging the FCC with censorship.

The FCC finally got its test in 1973. In the course of a discussion of social attitudes about language, a noncommercial station, WBAI–FM in New York, played the recording of a George Carlin nightclub monolog called "Filthy Words". The monolog satirized society's hang-ups about sexually oriented words not considered fit to be heard on the air. This time, though, they were heard—106 times in 12 minutes.

The single complaint came, as it later turned out, not from an average citizen but from a man with an ax to grind—an associate of a group called Morality in Media. He happened to hear the early-afternoon broadcast while driving into the city with his teenage son. The fact that the youth heard Carlin's filthy words became a key element in the case.

how indecency differs from obscenity

On the basis of that lone complaint, the FCC advised the station management that the broadcast contained *indecent* material. (Indecency is obscenity for children, who presumably are not mature enough sexually to respond according to the classic tests mentioned above.) The FCC defined *indecency* as material that in a "potentially offensive fashion, according to contemporary community standards for broadcasting, depicted sexual or excretory activities or organs" when children were likely to be in the audience. The licensee, a nonprofit station group called Pacifica, challenged the ruling as a matter of First Amendment principle.

The FCC won Supreme Court approval of its reasoning. Focusing its argument on the Carlin monolog as indecent rather than obscene, the FCC stressed the fact that the broadcast came at a time when children would normally be in the audience. Children, said the commission, deserve protection from indecency, as defined above.

special consideration given to children

Referring to the Supreme Court–approved "community-standards" test, the commission slipped in a significant qualifier of its own, making that phrase read "community standards *for broadcast media*"—an explicit acknowledgment that it believed broadcasting's First Amendment status differed from that of other media. The Court accepted the FCC's redefinition of *community standards,* adding, "We have long recognized that each medium of expression presents special First Amendment problems. . . . And of all forms of communication, it is broadcasting that has received the most limited First Amendment protection" (US, 1978: 748). Thus the Supreme Court, as constituted

special 1st Amendment status for broadcasting

in the 1970s, rejected the notion of First Amendment parity, treating broadcasting as a special case under the First Amendment.

Instead of confronting the First Amendment directly by flatly banning material such as the Carlin monolog, the FCC said it should be *channeled* to a part of the day when children are least likely to be in the audience. The channeling concept had a precedent in nuisance law, which recognizes that something that is acceptable in one setting could be an illegal nuisance in other settings.

The Supreme Court agreed with the nuisance-law rationale. Recalling that a judge had once said that a nuisance "may be merely a right thing in a wrong place—like a pig in the parlor instead of the barnyard," the Court added that if the FCC "finds a pig has entered the parlor, the exercise of regulatory power does not depend on proof that the pig is obscene" (US, 1978: 750–751).

Failure of the Channeling Concept

Fifteen years later, in 1987, a new flood of complaints about perceived obscenity on the air caused the FCC to issue a policy statement announcing plans to enforce Section 1464 of the Criminal Code, the radio obscenity law (17 USC 1464). The commission reprimanded three radio stations for using overly explicit language at times when children might be in the audience.

Reviving the channeling concept that it used in evading a First Amendment confrontation in the "Seven Dirty Words" case, the FCC opined that marginal program materials (indecent, perhaps, but not obscene) should be scheduled during the midnight to 6:00 A.M. period, when children would be least likely to see or hear them. Previously the informal guidelines had allowed such material to begin as early as 10:00 P.M. The narrower definition of allowable time for marginally "adult" material led to a court appeal.

A number of broadcasters joined in challenging the FCC, winning a court reversal in 1988 on the grounds that limiting indecent language to the midnight-to-6:00 A.M. hours violated the First Amendment. The Court remanded to the FCC the question of how best to "promote parental—as distinguished from government—control" of children's listening (F, 1988: 1332).

Thereupon Congress entered the arena. In approving the FCC budget for the 1989 fiscal year, the legislators added a rider ordering the FCC to ban indecent material *at all hours* of the broadcast day. The FCC complied, triggering an appeal that was pending at the Supreme Court in 1990.

Congress clashes again with FCC

Obscenity on Cable

The 1984 Cable Act authorizes a $10,000 fine or up to two years of imprisonment for anyone who "transmits over any cable system any matter which is obscene or otherwise unprotected by the Constitution" (47 USC 639). How this rule squares with the limits imposed on broadcasting and with First Amendment protections remains to be fully tested at the federal level.

Individual states, however, have tried to apply the Supreme Court's *Miller* and *Pacifica* reasoning to questionable cable-television content. Four court decisions in the mid-1980s, three of them initiated the Utah courts, all ruled that state laws banning cable obscenity/indecency violated the First Amendment. These courts threw out indecency statutes, finding them too broad in scope. The courts reasoned that cable is not as *uniquely intrusive* as broadcasting or as available to children. By paying cable subscription fees, subscribers make deliberate, conscious, frequently renewed choices. In 1986, the Supreme Court ruled unanimously that cable television *does* have First Amendment protection—but in a case involving franchising rights, not obscenity/indecency (US, 1986).

<aside>cable not as intrusive as broadcasting</aside>

Obscenity/indecency laws keep evolving as society's standards evolve. After three decades of increasing liberalization, during which many taboos fell and audiences grew more tolerant of explicit language and scenes, the time may have come for a swing toward family values. The country's trend toward political conservatism in the 1980s inclined in that direction. Another indicator may be the increasing willingness of advertisers to give in to pressure groups by cancelling ads on programs containing material that such groups find objectionable. ABC Television, for example, reported that prime-time advertiser cancellations cost it $14 million in 1989 (*Broadcasting*, 30 July 1990).

13.9 *Changing Constitutional Perspectives*

As the 20th century winds down, broadcasting in America faces a hostile climate. At one time it enjoyed special status as a uniquely democratic medium, worth preserving because it played an especially important informational role and made its services available equally to all at minimum cost. It received protection from the competition of cable television, a less democratic medium in the sense of costing more and being far less universal than broadcasting.

<aside>broadcasting as most democratic of media</aside>

In the new predatory, competitive environment, numerous media and media outlets stridently call for attention and scramble ruthlessly for consumer dollars. Technological convergence and deregulation have forced a rethinking of the traditional First Amendment concept of the marketplace. Instantaneous corporate communicators blanket the entire nation. They cut down on the diversity of competing voices and narrow the window of opportunity for the self-righting process to occur.

Diametrically opposed courses of action are proposed. One side envisions the communication marketplace in literal economic terms; the other regards the marketplace as a metaphor, seeing mass communication more in cultural terms. On one side stands the *deregulator,* confident that the marketplace will regulate itself if only maximum competition and unconstrained consumer choice prevail. On the other side stands the *re-regulator,* demanding that the

<aside>arguments for and against regulation</aside>

government intervene once more to oppose monopolistic tendencies and to protect the public interest from the effects of unrestrained commercial competition.

The deregulator wants all media to compete on an even playing field, all equally protected from government interference. The re-regulator wants a flexible interpretation of the First Amendment, one that takes into account the fact that different media differ in their impact, reach, and accessibility.

This fundamental clash of views has been discussed in this and earlier chapters, where questions such as the following were raised:

continuing questions on 1st Amendment parameters

- Should obscenity in broadcasting and cable have the same First Amendment protection that it has on the newsstand and in the movie theater?
- Does violence as depicted in the electronic mass media have such damaging social effects as to justify tilting the regulatory playing field against it?
- Should electronic mass media have special responsibilities for ensuring fairness in the airing of controversial issues of social importance?
- Does the socializing role of these media warrant special regulations for children's programs?

As detailed in the final chapter, such questions are also being asked in other countries. There, the primacy of culture over commerce in broadcasting has generally been taken for granted in the past. But there, too, deregulation and the increased competition that it brings are causing changes whose ultimate effects cannot yet be predicted.

Global View

14

The study of broadcasting in America would be incomplete without some reference to broadcasting elsewhere. The ability of radio waves to ignore national boundaries (especially now that satellites can cover 40 percent of the globe from a single point in space) makes broadcasting a truly international medium. Numerous international regulatory, trade, academic, and legal organizations facilitate global exchange of equipment, concepts, programs, techniques, and training.

14.1　*Broadcasting and National Character*

Each country starts with identical potentials for broadcasting yet adopts a system uniquely adapted to serve the nation's particular needs and ambitions. Three attributes of broadcasting, already discussed in the U.S. context, promote a mirror-like relationship between a nation's character and its broadcasting system:

- Broadcasting invites *government regulation* because it uses the electromagnetic spectrum, which governments view as public property. Each government interprets its responsibility to control spectrum use in accordance with its own political philosophy. A country's history, geography, economics, and culture also influence broadcasting, but always with political overtones.
- Radio-frequency transmissions cause *interference,* making essential both international and national regulation of the physical aspects of transmission. Again, political philosophy affects how, and how much, a country chooses to regulate signal transmission.
- Broadcasting has *political and social power* because it can communicate instantly with an entire nation and can penetrate the borders of other nations. It can by-pass the official superstructure, going directly to the people, both at home and abroad. Whatever its politics, no nation can afford to leave so persuasive a means of public communication unregulated.

14.2　*Broadcasting and Political Philosophies*

The amount and kinds of controls a nation imposes on broadcasting give a clue to the attitude the country's leadership takes toward its people. Ruling attitudes fall broadly into three orientations: permissive, paternalistic, and authoritarian.

Permissive Orientation　Broadcasting in America is the major exemplar of a predominantly permissive system. The Constitution makes freedom of communication a central article of faith and encourages free enterprise. The resulting all-out commercialism achieves more lively, popular, and expertly produced programs than can be found elsewhere in the world.

Generally speaking, countries within the traditional U.S. sphere of influence, such as Central America and the Philippines, have adopted similar permissive, profit-driven systems. Many other countries deplore America's rampant commercialism because it focuses almost exclusively on what people want rather than on what critics, experts, and government leaders think they need.

Paternalism　Most countries, lacking the avowed melting pot character of the United States, want broadcasting to play a positive role in preserving and enhancing national culture. They take a paternalistic approach, putting special emphasis on preserving the national language and on ensuring a "balanced" program diet—meaning not too much light entertainment at the expense of information and culture. And they take special care to regulate children's programs to ensure that they set positive and culturally relevant examples.

The British Broadcasting Corporation (BBC) offers the classic example of the paternalistic viewpoint. It started in 1926 with the conscious goal of avoiding America's "mistakes" such as commercializing the medium. The BBC's funds come primarily from license fees imposed by the government on television receivers, relieving the BBC of any dependence on advertising.

BBC as paternalistic model

A well-articulated ideal of **public-service broadcasting** emerged from the BBC experience. Adopted by many democracies, public-service broadcasting subscribes in general to principles of

- Balanced programming, representing all the main genres.
- Control by a public body, independent of both political and commercial controls.
- Relative financial autonomy, usually secured by partial or complete dependence on receiver license fees.
- Program services that can be received by, and that hold interest for, the entire population, including rural dwellers and minorities.
- Strict impartiality in political broadcasts.
- Respect for the artistic integrity of program makers.

goals of public-service broadcasting

This public-service philosophy of broadcasting, adapted to varying national circumstances, spread worldwide. Thousands of practitioners from scores of countries have visited the famous Broadcasting House in London, shown in Exhibit 14.1. Many stayed on to take training courses, which the BBC has long offered in all aspects of production, engineering, and management. Other major national services modeled with varying degrees of fidelity on the BBC tradition include Australia's ABC, Canada's CBC, and Japan's NHK.

The BBC is generally acknowledged as the most influential and widely imitated broadcasting service. Yet other countries never came even close to replicating it. Too much of its special character arose from the special character of the British nation—evidence of the fact that every broadcasting system is uniquely adapted to its own national setting.

BBC as most widely imitated system

Authoritarianism   Traditionally, Communist and many Third World countries take an authoritarian approach to broadcasting. The state itself finances and operates the system, along with other telecommunication services. Governments own and operate the great majority of the world's broadcasting systems, though the number of privately owned services began to increase during the 1980s.

Because Communist ideology stresses the importance of the media in mass political education, the Soviets embraced broadcasting early, embarking on a vigorous "radiofication" program. The Russian masses, however, failed to invest in home receivers as eagerly as did Western audiences, no doubt

EXHIBIT *14.1*   Broadcasting House, London

In pre-television days, broadcasters from all over the world journeyed to this famous art deco building in the heart of London as a kind of broadcaster's mecca. The Eric Gill sculpture above the entrance represents Prospero, the wise magician of Shakespeare's *The Tempest,* with Ariel, a sprite whose lightning speed symbolized radio. The BBC moved here from its original quarters on the Thames bank in 1932. Though Broadcasting House tripled the corporation's previous space, the new building proved too small for the BBC's activities even before its completion. The giant BBC television center is located in a London suburb—and BBC radio and television own or lease many other buildings around the city.

Source: Photo from BBC.

because of low purchasing power but probably also because government programs gave them little incentive to buy.

The authoritarian outlook pays little heed to popular taste. Programs have a propaganda, or at best an educational, goal. Broadcasting officials pay scant attention to the marketing techniques that permissive and even paternalistic broadcasters employ to ensure attractive, palatable, cost-effective programs. In fact, authoritarians look on broadcasting as a one-way medium—all give and no take. They do not understand its essentially democratic nature, as a medium that depends on free-will cooperation from audiences.

democratic nature of broadcasting

Third World Authoritarianism

In the Third World, woeful lack of purchasing power limits set penetration. Absence of electrical power in rural areas and of relay facilities for networking further restricts television growth. Neither receiver license fees nor advertising, alone or in combination, can bring in enough revenue to support broadcasting. Therefore in most Third World countries, broadcasting systems are government owned and operated. In any event, the authoritarian leaders of often shaky regimes in Africa and the Far East dare not allow broadcasters free rein to interact with the illiterate masses. Prudence more than ideology dictates authoritarian control.

Pluralistic Trend

None of the three prototype regulatory regimes—permissive, paternalistic, and authoritarian—exists anywhere in its pure form. Compromises eventually lead toward mixtures of the three orientations.

Role of Competition

Three-quarters of a century's experience has proved that pluralistic broadcasting systems work best. In this context, *pluralism* means more than simply competition among rival services. If the same motives drive all services, they tend merely to imitate one another, dragging each other down to meet the lowest levels of expectation.

Pluralism means putting more than one motive to work, each on an approximately equal footing—in practice, usually a mix of commercial and public-service motives. Healthy competition between differently motivated broadcasting organizations stimulates creativity, encourages innovation, and ensures variety. The result is a wider range of genuine program choices than a system with a single motive can produce.

British Pluralism

The British developed a widely admired pluralistic system based on control by two noncommercial public authorities: the BBC and the Independent Broadcasting Authority (IBA). Britain's "comfortable duopoly"—a benign, paternalistic monopoly of two, ended in 1990, as detailed later. Nevertheless, it is worth looking at for its historic achievements.

BBC and IBA form "comfortable duopoly"

The IBA, a nonprofit, government-chartered corporation, selected and supervised regional commercial television companies known as Independent Television (ITV), as well as specialized national television networks (Channel Four and AM–tv) and local radio stations.

Like the BBC, the IBA owned and operated its own transmitters, so commercial motives could not distort geographical coverage by concentrating outlets in high-population areas. Unlike the BBC, however, the IBA had no programming function. Instead, the privately owned commercial companies did the programming and sold the advertising.

Pluralism calls for national network competition on a more or less equal footing. The IBA therefore allowed the regional program companies to join forces for most of the broadcast day to form a cooperative national network, known as ITV. A commonly owned nonprofit subsidiary, Independent

Television News (ITN), supplied the ITV network with national and international news programs. The five most lucrative companies furnished most of the network entertainment programs. American viewers know the names of the ITV companies from the billboards of such well-known imported series as *The Benny Hill Show* (Thames Television) and *The Jewel in the Crown* (Granada Television).

Channel 4: an alternative type of TV network

The fourth British network (after BBC-1, BBC-2, and ITV), appropriately called Channel Four, began operations in 1982. IBA again supplied the transmitter facilities. Channel Four acts as an "electronic publisher": it originates no programs of its own but buys or commissions programs from others. It repeats a number of ITV programs, buys productions from independent producers, and obtains others from international syndicators. One of Channel Four's innovations was the successful introduction of American professional football to audiences previously dedicated to soccer. The IBA required the ITV companies to subsidize Channel Four, but the companies recovered at least part of the subsidy through commercials they were allowed to schedule on the network.

Although British viewers until recently had only four terrestrial domestic broadcast television choices, all four could be received throughout the United Kingdom. Moreover, at any one time each usually offered a distinctly different program, assuring genuine choice. British viewers lacked local television, however, although both the BBC and the ITV companies supplied regional programs, especially news.

The two competing national television services, those of the BBC and the IBA, achieved approximate ratings equality. Nevertheless, the BBC still offered alternatives to commercial programs and still served cultural and intellectual minorities. The BBC-1 mass-appeal network confronted the ITV competition, whereas BBC-2 aimed at smaller, more specialized audiences, as does the semicommercial network, Channel Four.

In radio, the BBC retained its monopoly on national and regional services, operating four national networks plus regional services in Northern Ireland, Scotland, and Wales. Its networks feature pop music (Radio 1), middle-of-the-road programs (Radio 2), serious music/talk (Radio 3), and news/current affairs (Radio 4). Some 40 BBC local radio stations compete with the IBA-supervised local commercial radio stations.

A new broadcasting law ended the "comfortable" British duopoly in 1990, as described in the next section.

14.4 Deregulation

During the 1980s, U.S.-inspired deregulatory theory swept the telecommunications world. American influence was not the sole cause of the deregulatory trend, which reflects a worldwide evolutionary process. Nevertheless, foreign governments and industrialists studied the U.S. broadcasting model intensively, and U.S. government officials and industrialists zealously promoted deregulation and private ownership abroad.

Impact on Public-Service Broadcasting   With deregulation, traditional, centralized, public-service broadcasting organizations faced unaccustomed competition. Cable television, satellite-distributed programs for both cable and direct-to-home viewing, VCR rentals, and new privately owned terrestrial broadcasting services fight them for audiences, advertisers, and programs. Observers fear that excessive competition may force public-service broadcasters to lower program standards as they struggle to survive.

will deregulation lower public-service program standards?

U.S. deregulators found an especially enthusiastic proponent in Britain's Conservative government under Prime Minister Margaret Thatcher. Conservatives do not look kindly on public-service broadcasting, and the BBC's political neutrality (seen as leftist tendencies by the Conservatives) was a thorn in the government's side. A government-appointed committee suggested that BBC television should be deprived of its income from receiver license fees and become a subscription service. Only those willing to pay for BBC programs directly would receive them (Great Britain, 1986).

Parliament did not accept that specific suggestion, but a new British broadcasting law passed by Parliament in 1990 reflected the report's deregulatory approach. Major features of the law provide that

- The BBC will continue as the "cornerstone of public-service broadcasting," still deriving revenue from receiver license fees, at least for the time being. The fees are pegged to the rate of inflation, ensuring automatic increases annually.
- The ITV network becomes Channel 3 (with the BBC-1 and BBC-2 networks renamed Channels 1 and 2).
- Channel Four retains its character as an "electronic publisher" but sells its own commercials. The ITV/Channel 3 companies will still be responsible for making up any financial shortfall.
- A commercial Channel 5, able to reach about 70 percent of the population, is to be created.
- The IBA and the Cable Authority combine into a new "light touch" regulatory authority called Independent Television Commission (ITC).
- The new ITC will auction regional franchises for ITV/Channel 3 and the new Channel 5 to the highest bidders, subject to the bidders' meeting program-quality requirements.
- The ITC will also franchise local MDS and SMATV operations.
- A new Radio Authority will auction 200 to 300 new local commercial radio-station franchises.
- A Broadcasting Standards Council will have statutory authority to set up a program code controlling sex and violence in programs.

changes wrought by the new British law

The new law reflects changes that are taking place with varying degrees of speed and completeness worldwide—increases in competition, in local services, in privatization, and in commercialism. Also involved in this equation are DBS services and cable television, discussed in Sections 14.10 and 14.11.

Privatization   The conversion of state-owned broadcasting facilities to private ownership and the legalizing of new privately operated facilities is known as *privatization*. This kind of deregulation moved especially rapidly in France. The French government once operated all the country's broadcasting stations and networks. In 1984, a French socialist government began licensing private stations and·networks. Two years later, the conservatives won control of the government and took the unprecedented steps of selling off France's leading public-service television broadcasting network, TF1, and of authorizing competition from several other privately owned television networks. Similar, though usually less drastic, deregulatory measures have been taken in other European countries, as well as in Australia, Canada, Japan, and New Zealand.

Privatization came earlier in Italy and by a different route. In the 1970s, the official Italian broadcasting monopoly, RAI, went to court to suppress unauthorized cable television operations. The Italian Constitutional Court ruled in 1975 that RAI's legal monopoly covered only *national network* broadcasting. RAI could prevent neither cable nor broadcast *local* operations by private owners. This ruling opened the floodgates to thousands of private stations. Fifteen years later, these stations still operated without benefit of formal regulation because the Italian parliament, though always about to pass a new law, could not agree on the form it should take.

Impact on USSR and Its Client States   In the Soviet Union, and to an even greater degree among its East European client states, democratization has brought parallel liberalizing moves in different political settings. In 1985, the new Soviet leader, Mikhail Gorbachev, announced a radical policy change, called *glasnost*—roughly, "candor" or "openness." It may well be that the infiltration of electronic mass media—spillover signals from neighboring countries, insistent penetration by official external services such as the Voice of America (described in Section 14.9), satellite-borne programs from Western Europe, and videocassettes—played a major role in preparing the Communist societies for change. Certainly broadcasting had an active part in the actual changeover.

Mismanagement by Soviet media of news about the 1986 Chernobyl atomic-plant disaster hastened drastic reforms. The accident devastated not only the surrounding countryside but also the credibility of the Soviet media, which simply failed to cover the disaster, one of the biggest international news stories of the decade, if not the century. The Soviet government finally released a statement after Sweden publicly demanded an explanation of why nuclear contamination, drifting over its territory from the USSR, had reached a dangerous level.

Encouraged by the *glasnost* policy and embarrassed by their Chernobyl failure, Soviet broadcasters, along with journalists in other media, began profound changes. They started covering hitherto banned subjects—other

a first: privatization of a major public-service network

Italian court decision authorizes private ownership

impact of Chernobyl news suppression on USSR broadcasting

domestic disasters, the Afghan war, runaway environmental pollution, public criticism of government officials.

In the late 1980s, United States–USSR broadcast "bridges" frequently enabled Soviet and U.S. citizens to exchange uncensored views by satellite. Soviet broadcasters scheduled more live shows, spontaneous interviews (in place of the obviously rehearsed recitals formerly used), and telephone call-in programs. They extended schedules into the early-morning and late-night dayparts. For the first time in the Soviet Union, broadcasting—the most democratic of media—began to fulfill its mission of pleasing and informing the public instead of lecturing and hectoring it. Even more dramatic changes took place in USSR-supported regimes as they toppled domino-like in the wake of Gorbachev's reforms.

The 1989 revolt against Romania's dictator, Nicolae Ceausescu, affords an extreme example. Ceausescu had exploited the Romanian state television apparatus relentlessly for years as a means of personal glorification. At the time of the revolution, his opponents turned the television cameras around, using them to document his crimes and his execution as a genocidal traitor. A U.S. State Department committee that studied communication conditions in Eastern Europe in the spring of 1990 described broadcasting's role:

liberated TV depicts defeat and death of Romanian leader

> Romanian TV was in many respects the central nervous system during the bloody December [1989] revolution. . . . In the months following the revolution, television consolidated its role by broadcasting the trials of those accused of genocide, and also offering hours every day of public access commentary and political campaigning to all political parties. (USDOS, 1990: 39)

Nothing in broadcasting history has matched the startling suddenness with which the entire structure of rigid Communist control crumbled—literally overnight in country after country.

International Regulation   International regulation, too, underwent revision during the 1980s. Most nations belong to the International Telecommunication Union (ITU), an affiliate of the United Nations, headquartered in Geneva, Switzerland. As sovereign nations, its members cannot be forced to obey the regulations adopted by the ITU. Nevertheless, nations usually find it in their own best interest to obey ITU rules for both wire and wireless communication and to adopt ITU standardized terminology and procedures for international exchange of telecommunications.

For example, ITU members agree to allocate specific frequency bands to specific services. Thus throughout the world, AM radio, FM radio, television, and broadcast satellite service each has its own spectrum allocations. The ITU allots initial letters for station-identification call signs—hence the "K" or "W" that starts all U.S. broadcast stations' call signs. The ITU also plays a leading role in helping developing nations improve their telecommunication facilities.

ITU role in setting world standards

At one time the agency dealt strictly with technical matters, apportioning frequencies to countries on a first-come, first-served basis. With the emergence of the Third World, however, ITU conferences became politicized. Dissatisfaction surfaced as early as a 1971 Space Conference, when newly independent countries complained that the ITU had been neglecting their needs. The same complaint arises at each international conference.

Third World countries argue that spectrum and orbital allocations should be planned for the long term. They want reserved channels and slots for their future use, even though decades may pass before the less developed countries can activate them. The United States, however, wants immediate use of these resources to meet current needs and to foster technological development. Clash of wills on this still-unsettled issue occurs at each ITU meeting.

Competing National Standards

Although ITU standardization encourages internationalism, national chauvinism tends to impede it. Thanks to uniform spectrum allocations by the ITU, a traveler taking a portable radio receiver abroad can pick up stations almost anywhere. However, despite the fact that television has approximately the same channel allocations throughout the world, national television standards are not uniform. Fourteen different monochrome technical standards and three main color standards make it necessary in most cases to use converters to interchange programs or to use one country's television equipment in another country.

The three basic color-television systems—NTSC, PAL, and SECAM—reflect American, German, and French government decisions. Each of the three countries lobbied frantically to persuade other governments to adopt its version. Adoptions meant not only national prestige but also tremendous profits from international sales by manufacturers of equipment using the favored system. The French stole a march on competing systems when they persuaded the USSR to adopt a version of SECAM, but France, the USSR, and their dependencies and client states remained virtually the only SECAM users.

The new beginnings made possible by both direct-broadcast satellites (DBS) and high-definition television (HDTV) opened the way to a fresh start. Universal, ITU-approved television-signal processing standards could be adopted. Certainly, satellite-to-cable and DBS services designed to cover several countries simultaneously cry out for such standardization. Nevertheless, in the early 1990s the leading contenders (Europe, Japan, and the United States) each had different, incompatible HDTV standards on the drawing boards.

PTT Deregulation

In the common-carrier realm, deregulation has also had widespread effect, loosening the grip of highly centralized national monopolies of post, telephone, and telegraph known as **PTTs.** PTTs often hold the exclusive right to install and operate broadcast transmitters and to lay the cables for cable television. Thus in many countries the transmission function and the programming function fall under separate government authorities.

In the development of cable television, marketing and promotion play key roles: consumers need a persuasive explanation of how this strange new service will benefit them. Their lack of experience in facing competition, however, generally deprives the PTT monopolies of expertise in marketing. Progress in cable installations therefore tends to languish under PTT leadership.

Access to the Air

The potential of broadcasting to inform (or disinform), to persuade, and to cultivate values has always made access to it a jealously guarded prerogative. Traditionally, access was limited to professional broadcasters, experts on subjects of public interest, people currently in the news, and politicians.

Political Access   Democratic political ideology requires preserving fairness in political uses of broadcasting without at the same time crippling its role as a means of informing voters.

In keeping with the permissive orientation of the U.S. broadcasting system, the weakest American parties and candidates have the same access rights as the strongest—provided they can raise the money to buy advertising time. No other industrialized democracy permits such broad political access for candidates and such commercialization of elections.

Great Britain, for example, severely limits election broadcasts, for which no charges are made. Campaign broadcasts focus on parties rather than on individual candidates (in keeping with the parliamentary system, in which party membership plays a more important role than it does in U.S. elections). In recent years, only parties offering 50 or more parliamentary candidates received television time. Each party had from one to five free broadcasts, each of five to ten minutes' duration, the number depending on each party's strength in the previous election.

Britain gives politicians free, but limited, access

These restrictions, plus the fact that British national election campaigns last only 30 days, mean that British voters are spared the interminable merchandising of candidates. Nor do candidates have to beg for donations and accept money from lobbyists to pay for expensive broadcast advertising. In other European countries, despite strict fairness regulations on paper, the ruling political parties often evade the rules by controlling appointments to the state broadcasting services and the regulatory agencies.

Citizen Access   During the restless 1960s, people in many countries began to ask why ordinary citizens had no access to the airwaves. They argued that if the electromagnetic spectrum really does function like a national park or other natural resources, then everybody should get a chance to use it. This access movement reflected a widespread rise in ethnic and regional awareness. Broadcasting is still adapting to access demands that began in the 1960s.

The access movement, though certainly evident in the United States, had less urgency there because of the American policy of licensing stations to serve specific local communities. In addition, FCC licensing policies give weight to localism in the choice of licensees. These policies generally ensure a certain amount of local access. Elsewhere, broadcasting tends to be more centralized, affording little or no chance for local access. Those seeking access could hardly expect national or regional networks to open their studios to them if they had nothing to say of national or regional significance. Access seekers tried instead to persuade the authorities to create new classes of small local and (even smaller) community stations, exempt from the formal regulation that governs the large stations and network services.

Most democracies responded in the 1970s and 1980s by authorizing such stations. France, for example, legitimized more than a thousand small, privately owned FM radio stations following passage of a new broadcasting law in 1982. Many had started as pirate stations, which had previously been rigorously suppressed by the French government. The new British broadcasting law opts for "light touch" regulation of up to 300 new local radio stations. In Scandinavia, governments finance low-power FM *när radio* (neighborhood stations), inviting local groups to cooperate in programming them, free of virtually all regulation.

Group Access   Another way of dealing with demands for access is to shift the emphasis from the individual to the group to which the individual belongs. The now-deleted FCC fairness doctrine attempted to use this strategy, as detailed in Section 13.6.

The uniquely structured access system of the Netherlands has gone the farthest in ensuring groups their own programs on nationally owned broadcasting facilities. The government turns over most of the program time on the government networks to citizen broadcasting associations. Some represent religious faiths; some are nonsectarian in outlook. Even very small constituencies, such as immigrant workers or people from Dutch colonies, can regularly obtain airtime.

innovative group-access
system in the
Netherlands

An umbrella organization, NOS, coordinates time-sharing and produces certain programs of broad national interest, such as national and international news and major sporting events. Another central organization handles the sale of advertising time. Advertising revenue goes to the central program fund. The program associations have hitherto not been allowed to insert advertisements in their programs (though they apparently have done so surreptitiously). In 1988, however, the Dutch adopted a new media law that allowed some of the broadcasting associations to operate commercially.

14.6   *Economics*

Economics comes second only to politics in determining the shape of a country's electronic mass media system. National systems vary widely as to facilities, revenue sources, and the ability to produce homegrown programs.

Economic constraints account for these differences, though political and cultural factors also play an important role.

Traditional Facilities   Some 200 countries and dependencies have their own radio broadcasting systems. In 1989, only 37 of them (mostly small islands) lacked television stations. Receiver penetration varies widely. As of 1989, the United States led the major countries in television-set penetration, with 797 sets per thousand population, followed by Canada, with 600 (international set-penetration comparisons use sets-per-thousand population figures rather than family-based statistics). High penetration levels depend only partly on economics. Also important are such factors as strong motivation for set purchasing, aroused by highly attractive mass-appeal programming, and a national policy of licensing numerous localized stations.

comparative levels of set penetration

In the former and present Communist countries, governments invested heavily in transmitters, relays, and production facilities. Nevertheless, set penetration remained disproportionately low. The USSR, for example, had 314 sets per thousand population in 1989. China did not start television until 1958. Twenty years later it still had pitifully few receivers for a nation of over a billion population. Television penetration reached only 117 sets per thousand population by 1989.

In the tropical Third World countries, a high percentage of radio sets do not work because of battery shortages and humidity. Government investment in transmitters and production facilities can therefore be extremely uneconomic. It costs just as much in program and transmission expenses to reach a few scattered individuals as to reach the total population within a transmitter's coverage area.

Lack of communications infrastructure, such as electric power, telephones, and relay facilities for networks, further impedes Third World broadcasting growth. However, a few of the oil-rich Middle East states have achieved high set penetration—for example, 580 per thousand population in Oman and 414 in Kuwait (set counts in this subsection come from TV/RAI, 1989).

Revenue Sources   The three main sources of broadcast funding are budgeting by the central government, advertising, and receiver license fees. Most countries depend on government, in whole or in part.

In industrialized democracies, however, most funding depends on receiver license fees. This source insulates the broadcasting organization from the inevitable biases caused by dependence on direct government funding and advertising. But the protection is only partial. Governments have a hand in the laws requiring payment of fees and in setting fee levels. And most fee-supported systems gain part of their revenue from advertising, though theoretically advertising contributes too small a part to give advertisers any influence over programs.

how receiver license fees work as revenue source

Western Europe's 1990 color-television-set licenses ran from the equivalent of about $100 a year (Ireland) per household to as much as $190 (Sweden).

Britain's fee, on which the BBC depends, was $130. In most countries licensing of radio sets has been either dropped or combined with the television fee.

Color television brought increased production costs, causing serious financial problems for systems that rely heavily on receiver fees. As set penetration reached the saturation point, the license-fee revenue curve leveled off but operational costs kept rising. Moreover, the politicians, who control fee levels, always delay the unpopular task of authorizing increases as long as possible.

Though Marxist doctrine frowns on advertising as a capitalistic device for exploiting the workers, in practice Communist countries found broadcast commercials useful for moving consumer goods that sometimes piled up because of central-planning errors. In a sharp change of policy, China began introducing Western-style advertising in 1979, in collaboration with U.S. companies such as CBS Television.

In the late 1980s, the USSR, under the liberalizing influence of its own version of deregulation, also became more tolerant of advertising. For example, in 1990 one of the USSR state television networks contracted with CNN to supply news services on a commercially supported basis, agreeing to split the revenue 50/50 with CNN.

Program Economics Television consumes expensive program materials at such a rate that even highly advanced countries with strong economies cannot afford to program several different television networks exclusively with homegrown productions. Britain is unusual in having as many as four full-scale terrestrial broadcast television networks (with another planned), but it needs to import some entertainment programs. Broadcasters impose a voluntary ceiling of 14 percent of their airtime on such imports.

in Europe, small countries lead in cable TV development

Most countries have fewer national broadcasting television networks than Britain, and even those few operate on limited schedules and depend on imports more than Britain does. In the smaller European countries, the dearth of programs from domestic sources stimulated the growth of cable television even before satellite-to-cable program networks came into being. Community antennas in small countries such as Holland can pick up a half-dozen services from neighboring countries.

The bulk of imported programs come from the United States (as discussed further in Section 14.12), and a relatively large number come from Britain. However, Communist and Third World countries increasingly display their wares at international program fairs.

alternative forms of program financing

No simple solution to shortages of television programs, other than international syndication, has emerged, although strategems for alternative forms of cost and talent sharing have been developed. For example, the European Broadcasting Union (EBU), an association of official broadcasting services in Europe and nearby countries, shares programs through Eurovision. It arranges regular exchanges among its members, mainly of sports and news materials. Similar associations exist in Asia, Eastern Europe, the Middle East, and the Caribbean, though they are not as active as the EBU in program exchanges.

Coproduction has been increasingly used as a way of dealing with high program costs. Producers from two or more countries combine financial and other resources to coproduce television series or movies. They divide the capital outlay and benefit from the assured distribution of the product in two or more participating countries.

Geography 14.7

A nation's size, shape, population distribution, nearness to neighbors, and historical development all affect the kind of broadcasting system that evolves. Geography plays an especially prominent role.

Coverage Problems   Cost-effective coverage of a country depends on its shape as well as its size. The continental United States has the advantage of a roughly rectangular land mass insulated on two sides from spillover programs by large bodies of water. Alaska, Hawaii, and offshore territories had to await satellites to enjoy coverage simultaneously with the mainland.

In contrast, Japan consists of an archipelago of mountainous islands extending across nearly 2,000 miles of ocean. The Indonesian archipelago's 6,000 or so widely scattered inhabited islands with diverse populations speaking many different languages present even more formidable coverage problems. The USSR's territory extends so far east and west that its schedules have to be adapted to serve 11 different time zones (contrasted with the 4 zones of the continental United States). Their program-distribution difficulties motivated such countries to become the first to use domestic satellites.

Spillover   Geography insulates most American listeners and viewers from spillover programs originating in foreign countries. But spillover from the United States has strongly influenced not only broadcasting but also satellite and cable development in neighboring Canada. Most Canadians live near the United States border and are easily able to pick up American radio and television signals. In addition, Canadian cable television companies deliver American programs to their subscribers. As a result, Canada became the first heavily cabled country in the world.

demand for U.S. programs in Canada stimulates cable TV

To prevent its own culture from being overwhelmed by American programs and to ensure work for its own creative community, Canada imposes quotas limiting the amount of syndicated programming that Canadian broadcasters and cable operators may import. To help fill the gap, it also subsidizes indigenous productions.

Programs and Schedules 14.8

The interchangeability of programs reflects the fact that the inherent technical, economic, and social characteristics of broadcasting caused the same basic program formats to emerge and flourish throughout the world. News, commentary, public affairs, music, drama, variety, studio games, sports events—such program genres appeal everywhere. National differences show up in the way these genres are treated.

News and Public Affairs   The prime-time daily news presentation is a universally popular program, but its content and style differ from one country to another. Parochialism, chauvinism, and ideological biases affect the choice of news stories, their treatment, and their timing. Each country stresses its own national happenings, few of which hold interest for the rest of the world. In highly authoritarian societies, news tends to focus on the doings of the national leader, to the exclusion of all else. Some broadcasting systems devote their external pickup facilities entirely to following the head of state around, reporting on his every public move.

Program Balance   Audiences everywhere prefer light entertainment to more serious content. Accordingly, wherever popular demand controls programs, entertainment dominates. Most industrialized democracies other than the United States try to strike a balance between light entertainment and the news/information/culture/education program genres.

Third World nations cannot afford many homegrown productions with popular appeal. They can rent foreign syndicated entertainment that attracts audiences for a fraction of what it would cost to produce programs locally. But imports throw schedules out of balance by overemphasizing light entertainment and playing up alien cultures.

Schedules   Broadcast days of 18 to 24 hours, commonplace in the United States, rarely occurred in other countries until recently. Traditionally, the less well-heeled radio services went on the air for a short morning segment, took a midmorning break before a midday segment, then took another break in midafternoon before the evening programs, closing down for the night relatively early. Even in such a highly developed system as Britain's, the BBC did not begin 24-hour radio until 1979, when Radio 2 filled in the previously blank hours of 2:00 to 5:00 A.M.

many countries have only part-time TV services

Television in many parts of the world commences late in the afternoon, going off the air by about 11:00 P.M. Extending programming into previously unused early-morning and late-night hours became one of the signs of change in the 1980s as new networks, stations, and cable systems heightened competition. A report of European broadcasters' first international conference on "breakfast television" in 1987 was headed "Morning Has Broken: An Idea Whose Time Has Come" (EBUR, 1987).

14.9   *Transborder Broadcasting*

The ability to use radio waves to surmount political boundaries introduced a potent new factor into relations among nations. Never before had it been possible to talk directly to masses of foreigners, crossing even the most heavily defended national borders. More than 80 countries operate official external services—government broadcasts aimed at foreign countries.

Official External Broadcasting   Colonial commitments abroad first prompted nations to broadcast external services. The Dutch and Germans started theirs in 1929, the French in 1931. After experimenting for several years, Britain's BBC formally launched external broadcasting (then called the Empire Service) in 1932. At first it broadcast only in English, primarily seeking to maintain home-country ties with expatriates in the colonies and with residents in the dominions (independent former colonies such as Canada and Australia).

On the eve of World War II, the Italians began radio propaganda in Arabic aimed at the Middle East. The BBC countered with its own Arabic programs, and soon the Allies and the Axis powers were locked in a deadly war of words using many languages.

During World War II, foreign listeners came to regard the BBC as having the highest credibility among external broadcasters. It has retained that reputation ever since. Throughout the world, listeners automatically tune to the BBC World Service when they are doubtful about the authenticity of other sources.

BBC's independence gives its external service high credibility

The World Service has over a million American radio listeners, some listening via short wave, some via American Public Radio. It can also be heard as a direct-to-home satellite service in Europe. The corporation expects to start distributing a television version via satellite to subscribers in 1991.

Radio Moscow   When broadcasting began, the Soviets had no overseas colonial empire but used early radio to explain their revolution to sympathizers in Western Europe. From the outset, the Soviets recognized the importance of broadcasting in foreign languages as a means of gaining and influencing friends abroad. Radio Moscow began regular external services in 1929.

Voice of America   The United States added its voice to the battle of words during the World War II early in 1942. Wary of creating a federal propaganda agency that the party in power might exploit to its own political advantage, Congress forbids the VOA to release its programs in the United States. Anyone with a short-wave radio can pick up VOA programs aimed at overseas listeners, but to this day only scholars, journalists, and government agencies can gain access to VOA scripts and recordings. In Britain, by contrast, the BBC external service comes from a nongovernmental source. It welcomes domestic listeners, who can readily pick up the 24-hour World Service on regular AM radio sets.

In 1990, the VOA used 42 languages in addition to English, broadcasting 1,132 hours a week. VOA programs originate in Washington, going overseas via leased satellite channels and 114 VOA short-wave transmitters located in

Greenville, North Carolina, and several secondary U.S. sites. The VOA also leases sites in a dozen foreign countries, where it maintains transmitters for rebroadcasting programs to listeners in nearby areas. Protests from environmentalists are currently holding up completion of a new U.S. rebroadcast site in Israel. They claim that the extremely high-power signals planned for the U.S. installation could produce dangerous radiations in the vicinity.

VOA news and public-affairs programs reflect official U.S. policies. News commentaries are explicitly labeled as coming from the U.S. government. For the sake of credibility, however, the VOA tries to observe the spirit of its original 1942 manifesto: "Daily at this time we shall speak to you about America. . . . The news may be good or bad. We shall tell you the truth." Truth telling continues to be VOA policy, despite occasional lapses when partisan officials appointed by the party in power bend the facts to suit momentary political objectives.

Worldnet   The short range of broadcast television makes it unusable for external services aimed at distant targets in the manner of short-wave radio. The United States Information Agency (USIA), VOA's parent agency, used to rely entirely on persuading foreign broadcasters to carry American television programs on their own domestic television services.

During the 1980s, the USIA created Worldnet, a daily television service distributed abroad by satellite. To entice foreign broadcasters into using its material, Worldnet stages interactive teleconferences that feature important U.S. officials responding to live questions from foreign news personnel. The American interviewees speak from Washington, the questioners from their own countries. Participation by a recipient country's own broadcasters make the American presence more acceptable on that country's television service.

Worldnet fills out the rest of its schedule with "passive" programs—news and general information minus the interactive feature. U.S. diplomatic posts throughout the world pick up Worldnet on their own TVROs, as do some foreign cable systems and broadcast stations. In 1990, Worldnet reached 150 U.S. owned-and-operated TVROs erected at U.S. diplomatic posts. Worldnet is available via INTELSAT (discussed in Section 14.10) to any foreign broadcasting or cable television operation that wishes to use it.

U.S. Surrogate Services   In addition to conventional external broadcasting, the United States also engages in special types of programming known as *surrogate domestic services*. These broadcasts simulate domestic networks within target countries, by-passing the censored domestic media in authoritarian regimes.

Radio Liberty (RL) aims at Soviet audiences, and Radio Free Europe (RFE) aims at the East European states that were formerly within the Soviet sphere of influence. RFE and RL have studios and transmitters in Munich, West Germany. It has additional transmitters situated in Portugal, Spain, and Israel (prospectively in 1994), at sites favorable for sky-wave transmission to the target countries in Eastern Europe. Broadcasting by radio, entirely in the languages of the target countries, RFE and RL choose domestic and foreign news from the listeners' perspective. The VOA broadcasts to the same target areas, but from the U.S. perspective. The United States spends more on operating these surrogate services than on the VOA itself.

Radio/TV Martí   In 1985 the United States introduced a new surrogate service, Radio Martí, aimed at giving the people of Cuba news and information free of Castro-regime bias. Radio Martí started in May 1985. Supporters claim that it has had a powerful effect, heightening dissatisfaction with the Castro regime by revealing facts that it conceals from its own people. The expatriate Cuban community in south Florida, which has strong Republican political ties in Washington, sets great store by the operation.

Congress authorized funds in 1988 to start experiments with a television version of Radio Martí, using a transmitter hung from a balloon tethered 10,000 feet above Cudjoe Key in Florida. This height enabled sending line-of-sight signals 110 miles to reach Havana. Tests conducted in 1990 incited Cuba to jam the Television Martí transmissions and to interfere with American AM radio stations. The Cuban government appealed to the International Telecommunication Union, claiming that Television Martí violated ITU allocation rules that designate television channels for domestic use only. Many American broadcasters also objected to the scheme, which was characterized by an editorial in a leading trade magazine as a "huge, disastrous silliness" (*Broadcasting,* 1990).

TV transmitter suspended from a balloon to reach Cuba

Impact of Communist Liberalization   Early in 1990 Congress and the White House began an inquiry into the future of U.S. external services. In the light of the new political realities of a Communist bloc no longer entirely Communist and no longer a bloc, it seemed to some inexcusably wasteful to continue spending several hundred million dollars annually to combat communism over the airwaves. Surrogate services in particular appear to have become an anachronism. Domestic services in RFE/RL target countries now carry uncensored news and criticize the party in power, making surrogate services seem pointless.

liberalization of Communist regimes casts doubt on value of surrogate services

Religious Broadcasting   A different ideological motivation led to transborder religious broadcasting. International radio gave evangelical proselytizers their first opportunity to deliver their messages directly to potential converts in closed societies dominated by state religions. Official hostility—by some Muslim countries toward Evangelical Christians, for example—can prevent the setting up of on-site missions but cannot easily bar radio messages. Religious broadcasters have so saturated the short-wave bands that listeners can pick them up almost anywhere in the world, 24 hours a day.

Peripheral Services   Commercial motives account for transborder broadcasters known as *peripherals*. Several European ministates on the periphery of large countries have long operated such stations. They capitalized on unfilled demand for broadcast advertising and the appetite for alternative programs. Both audiences and advertisers, frustrated by severely regulated domestic services, welcomed these alternatives.

Peripherals beam commercial radio services in the appropriate languages to neighboring countries. They specialize in popular music formats, sometimes supplemented by objective news programs, which are welcome in countries where the ruling political parties dominate broadcast news.

The Grand Duchy of Luxembourg, ideally located for peripheral transmitters at the intersection of Belgium, France, and Germany, gets much of its national income from international commercial television as well as radio broadcasting. Exhibit 14.2 gives further details. Other notable transborder commercial radio stations operate in the German Saar (Europe No. 1), Monaco (Radio Monte Carlo), Cyprus (Radio Monte Carlo East), Morocco (Radio Mediterranean International), Yugoslavia (Studio Koper/Radio Capodistria), and Gabon (Africa No. 1).

Pirate Stations   Peripherals tend to be rather staid operations, tolerated by their target countries, some of which have even invested in them. They still leave some commercial and program demands unsatisfied, creating a vacuum filled by pirate radio outlets.

The first offshore pirates began broadcasting from a ship anchored between Denmark and Sweden in 1958. They were often financed by the United States and were always frankly imitative of American pop-music formats, advertising techniques, and promotional gimmicks. The pirates captured large and devoted youthful audiences. Their very illegality added spice to their attractiveness.

Some pirates made a lot of money, but at considerable risk. They suffered from storms, from raids by rival pirates, and from stringent laws that penalized land-based firms for supplying them or doing any other business with them. In spite of suppressive legislation, offshore pirates occasionally still crop up.

The appetite for pop music whetted by the pirates forced national systems to take notice of hitherto ignored musical tastes. The BBC, as one example, reorganized its national radio-network offerings, adding a pop-music network (Radio 1) imitative of the pirates. Some of the offshore DJs ended up working for the BBC and other established broadcasters.

Controversy over pirate broadcasting caused the fall of a Dutch government, and the Netherlands reorganized its broadcasting system as a result. It permitted two former pirate organizations to come ashore and develop into leading legitimate broadcasters.

Recently, commercial services began to cross national borders in the form of satellite-to-cable networks and direct-to-home (DBS) broadcasting. These developments are discussed in the next section.

pirates use American formats and techniques

pirates bring about changes in broadcast programming

EXHIBIT 14.2   Luxembourg: Home of Peripherals

The tiny Grand Duchy of Luxembourg granted a broadcasting monopoly to a hybrid government/private corporation, now known as RTL (Radio-Télé-Luxembourg), in 1930. In 1931, it began operating as what the French called a *radio périphérique* (peripheral radio). In those days, when official European radio services tended to be rather highbrow and stuffy, listeners far and wide avidly tuned in to its pop-music programs. Legend has it that Radio Luxembourg, received in Liverpool, England, gave the Beatles their first taste of pop music.

Today, RTL has high-power long-wave (2,000 kw), medium-wave (1,200 kw), and short-wave (500 kw) radio transmitters radiating across the borders carrying programs in English, Dutch, French, and German. It broadcasts television in both the PAL and SECAM systems in order to reach both French and German viewers. RTL holds shares in a number of European privately owned broadcasting services and owns extensive production facilities in Luxembourg.

Television's short range made it impossible for the Grand Duchy of Luxembourg to repeat its radio coverage with the newer medium, but it overcame this problem in part by setting up jointly owned broadcasting services in neighboring countries, notably RTL Plus in Germany (both a broadcast and a satellite-to-cable service), TVi (French-speaking Belgium's first commercial broadcast channel), and RTL-Veronique (Holland's first privately owned commercial broadcasting channel).

The ITU's 1977 allocation of DBS orbital slots to European countries offered Luxembourg a chance to extend its television coverage to the whole of Europe. SES (Societé Européenne des Satellites), founded in 1985, launched ASTRA in 1988—the first privately owned European communication satellite. The numbers on the map below indicate the width of the home television antennas needed to receive ASTRA in the zones defined by the contour lines.

ASTRA contracted with a variety of direct-to-home and satellite-to-cable services to occupy its 16 channels, including Disney and MTV–Europe. It also downlinks the first British DBS services, Sky Television.

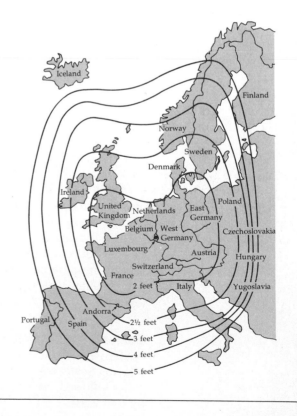

14.10　*World Satellite Developments*

International Satellites　The United States made an operational leap into international space communication in 1964 when it led in the founding of the International Telecommunications Satellite Organizations (INTELSAT). With relay satellites stationed above the Atlantic, Indian, and Pacific oceans, INTELSAT eventually made possible instant worldwide distribution not only of television programs but also of telephone conversations, new-agency services, and business data.

Over a hundred countries share ownership of INTELSAT, but the United States originated it, owns the largest block of its shares (about 25 percent), houses its headquarters (in Washington, DC), and initially operated it under contract on behalf of the rest of the consortium. The Communications Satellite Corporation (Comsat) held the contract until 1979, when INTELSAT itself took over. Exhibit 14.3 gives more details on INTELSAT and its recently emerged competition.

INTELSAT gives Third World short-cut to domsat services

Though primarily an international carrier, INTELSAT also leases satellite access at reasonable rates to Third World countries for *domestic* use. Thus INTELSAT enables many Third World nations to vault directly into the satellite era, avoiding the need to install costly microwave and coaxial-cable circuits throughout their territories.

Satellite Launching　Originally NASA, the U.S. government space agency, monopolized the West's capacity to launch communication satellites. In 1984, however, a consortium of European countries began to challenge NASA's monopoly with their own launch facility, Arianespace, named for Ariane, the rocket that launches the satellites. Ariane rockets take off from a site in French Guiana on the northern coast of South America, near the equator. That location gives Arianespace better conditions for attaining equatorial orbit than does NASA's Cape Canaveral, Florida location.

other nations competing with U.S. as launcher

After the *Challenger* shuttle exploded on takeoff in 1986, the U.S. government decided to confine NASA launches to government projects. This decision opened the launch market to private U.S. rocket makers. Also, China and the USSR made their government launch facilities available to foreign commercial users. China's first customer for the use of its Long March rocket was a Singapore consortium. It launched AsiaSat in 1990, using one of the two satellites that had been rescued by U.S. shuttles after being stranded in low orbit.

Domsats　The USSR took the lead in domestic satellite (domsat) development. In 1965 it began launching the Molniya satellite series, which enabled relaying Soviet television throughout its vast territory. Canada's Anik domsat series followed, starting in 1972. Anik preceded the first U.S. domsat, Westar, by two years.

EXHIBIT **14.3**   INTELSAT and "Separate Systems"

American satellite firms, strongly backed by the U.S. government, argue that INTELSAT's monopoly is inefficient, that its rates do not reflect actual costs, and that its sheer size makes it inflexible. Competition from smaller, nimbler satellite firms, they contend, would lower prices for all, enhance services, and encourage innovation. The first private U.S. "separate system" to launch a satellite, Pan American Satellite Corporation (PAS), offers both domestic and international satellite services. It links the United States and countries of the Hispanic world—Central and South America and the Caribbean—with Europe and serves Hispanic domestic needs as well.

Peru became the first PAS customer, followed by the Dominican Republic and Costa Rica on this side of the Atlantic, and by Britain, Ireland, Luxembourg, Sweden, and West Germany on the other, with more yet to come. CNN and other U.S. satellite-to-cable networks contracted with PAS to relay their programs to countries to the south.

The globe shows an example of INTELSAT coverage. INTELSAT V (F-15) is located above the Atlantic Ocean and is beaming to both the east and the west. The west hemispheric beam (unbroken line) covers all of Africa and Western Europe.

Source: Satellite footprints courtesy INTELSAT and Pan American Satellite.

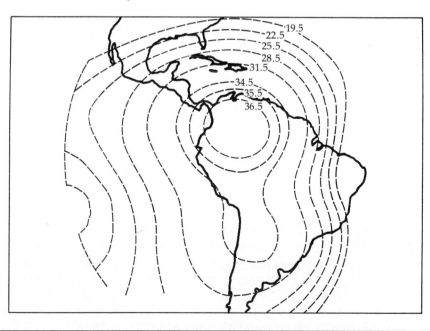

The 1970s also saw the launching of domestic and regional satellite services in several other countries: Indonesia's Palapa, the first Third World satellite; Europe's Eutelsat forerunner, the first of a regional satellite series; and Japan's first satellite. France, first among the European countries with its own domsat, launched its Télécom in 1985, in part to enable relays to French overseas territories.

DBS Satellites   The United States proved inhospitable initially to direct-broadcast satellite operations. The first American DBS service failed in 1985. It lacked a specialized, high-power satellite, essential for easy home reception, and could offer only a few program channels.

deep cable penetration
discourages DBS

DBS services had more immediate promise in countries where they did not have to compete with deep penetration by cable television, such as Australia and Japan. Japan forestalled cable by early concentration on DBS experiments. It led the world with the first full-time DBS service in 1987. Australia's AUSSAT, though a general-purpose satellite rather than a specialized DBS vehicle, transformed Australian broadcasting in the late 1980s. It brought television for the first time to the remotest areas—regions too thinly populated to support either terrestrial relay or cable television systems.

ASTRA: First European Private Satellite   In 1989, a Luxembourg corporation launched ASTRA, Europe's first privately owned satellite. ASTRA, a medium-power vehicle suitable for DBS services, is described in Exhibit 14.2. It is used by Sky Television, the first British direct-to-home satellite venture. Rupert Murdoch bought out Britain's pioneer satellite-to-cable network, Sky Channel, prior to launching the ambitious Sky Television services in 1989. A second British DBS service, British Satellite Broadcasting (BSB), launched a true high-power, Ku-band DBS satellite in 1990.

These immensely costly gambles represented a dramatic clash of business titans. It seemed doubtful that the two British DBS services could long coexist, especially as much of their programming overlaps. In 1990, Sky Television, the first to go on the air, was costing Murdoch $3.2 million a week while attempting to build subscribership. Exhibit 14.4 summarizes some of the characteristics of the two contenders for direct-to-home broadcast leadership in Britain.

Radio by Satellite   One tends to think of DBS services exclusively in television terms, but in Europe some 60 *radio* services can be received from satellites. In addition to the major public-service broadcasters such as the BBC, a number of colorfully named private radio stations can be received by satellite—Kiss FM, Radio Radio, Fun FM, and Skyrock, for example. Europeans receive satellite radio services directly by means of home TVROs or indirectly via cable systems and FM radio stations.

DBS radio in Europe

EXHIBIT **14.4**   DBS Showdown in the UK: BSB vs. Sky Television

	BSB (British Satellite Broadcasting)	Sky Television
Owner	International Consortium	Rupert Murdoch (News International)
Startup date	Mid-1990	Early 1989
Channels	1. Movie Channel (mostly U.S.) 2. Now (mainly for women, consumer oriented) 3. Sports Channel 4. Power Station (popular music) 5. Galaxy (children daytimes, drama nights)	1. Sky Movies (mostly U.S.) 2. Sky One (entertainment) 3. Eurosport (with E.B.U.) 4. Sky News (includes U.S. nets)
Satellite	BSB (UK, high power)	ASTRA (Luxembourg, medium power)
Revenue sources	Mainly subscription, some advertising	Mainly subscription, some advertising

BSB touts itself as representing the best British tradition. For example, it paid $5 million for a package of BBC classics—the first such sale by the BBC. By implication, Sky Television comes off as tainted by American program tastes, though in fact both firms buy large numbers of U.S. syndicated programs.

Cable TV and Other New Media   14.11

Europe had primitive cable television in the limited form of CATV (community antenna television) for many years before modern cable existed. However, these early systems merely extended domestic broadcast-station coverage, sometimes adding a few channels for the purpose of carrying neighboring foreign broadcast networks. Most operated noncommercially, often owned by municipalities. They had few channels, no local origination, and no pay television.

Modern Cable-TV Systems   Modern cable has developed most extensively in Canada, the United States, and well-developed small countries such as Belgium (around 93 percent cable penetration by 1990) and the Netherlands (around 80 percent). The larger European countries have only low

low cable TV
penetration in large
European countries

penetration. In 1990 Britain and France still had only between 2 and 3 percent cable penetration. West Germany, whose government gave cable strong support, had 24 percent (C&SE, 1990).

Although cable penetration continues to deepen, public demand in the larger countries remains sluggish. Apparently, if basic cable systems cannot offer a wide variety of high-interest programs, subscribership remains low. High-interest cable services began in the United States with satellite-to-cable networks, starting in the mid-1970s. Satellite networks did not begin in Europe until 1982 with the launch of Sky Channel, a London-based English-language service. After that, satellite networks grew rapidly. More than 50 served European cable systems by 1990. Some targeted only a single country, some several countries that had a common language. Attempts to launch a pan-European, multilingual service did not succeed. Exhibit 14.5 gives data on the major multinational satellite networks.

VCRs   As an alternative as well as a supplement to cable and DBS, VCRs proved a boon to viewers in countries where broadcast services failed to satisfy demand. They furnished a relatively inexpensive short cut to programs banned from, or just not available on, national broadcast or cable channels.

In some cases heavy censorship encourages VCR growth—for example, in Saudi Arabia, where puritanical Muslim standards severely limit movies and broadcast television. In formerly Communist countries, rigid political censorship created appetites that VCRs could help satisfy. Clandestine VCR tapes hastened the decline of repressive regimes. VCRs also abound in Britain, not primarily because of frustration with available programs but in order to time-shift desired programs to more convenient viewing hours.

In the Third World, VCRs help make up for the often inadequate television schedules and poor program quality of national broadcast television services. Few individuals in such countries can afford to buy a VCR outright, but rentals, club purchases, and group viewing in bars and on buses solve the cost problem. A worldwide underground market in VCRs and tapes defeats government attempts to limit sales and rentals. It also undermines the profitability of video sales. In Europe, by 1990 VCR penetration had stabilized at an average of 42 percent per country. Britain (66 percent), Luxembourg (54 percent), and West Germany (52 percent) were in the lead (C&SE, 1990).

Teletext and Videotex   The BBC and the IBA invented teletext. Though not a runaway success, it has nevertheless found greater acceptance in Britain and Europe generally than in the United States.

France leads the world in videotex development. Its Minitel system is available in 18 percent of French households. The government telecommunications monopoly promotes the Minitel, offering the hardware free to consumers. Telephone subscribers forgo the printed telephone directory in exchange, paying about six cents a minute for Minitel's many services, which include, in addition to the telephone directory and assistance, hundreds of

EXHIBIT 14.5 Major European Multinational Satellite Program Channels

Channel Name (Place, Start Date)	Satellite(s)	Potential Households (Millions)	Comment
Super Channel (UK, 1986)	Eutelsat	18	English programs drawn from BBC and ITV (commercial companies) networks
TV-5 (France, 1984)	Eutelsat	13	Programs in French from France, Belgium, Switzerland, and Canada; culturally oriented
MTV Europe (UK, 1987)	ASTRA	11	Modeled on U.S. videoclip network, owned in part by the owner of MTV-U.S., Viacom.
3Sat (W. Germany, 1984)	Eutelsat; Kopernikus	8	German-language co-venture by Austria, Switzerland, and West Germany; cultural orientation
Sat1 (W. Germany, 1985)	Eutelsat; ASTRA; Kopernikus	8	German publishers' channel; commercial
RTL-Plus (W. Germany, 1984)	INTELSAT; ASTRA	8	Started in Luxembourg; later primarily German-owned and headquartered in Germany
CNN (USA, 1985)	INTELSAT	3	A U.S. export, Ted Turner's Cable News Network, at first seen mostly in hotels, embassies, government offices, etc.
Screensport (UK, 1984)	ASTRA	5	Owned by UK's top newsagent and bookseller, WH Smith
Lifestyle (UK, 1985)	ASTRA	4	Women's programs drawn from British and U.S. sources

This list comes from a roster of over 50 European satellite services, selected on the basis of their ability to reach more than 3 million homes in more than one country. Eutelsat is operated by a consortium of European countries, INTELSAT by a world consortium, ASTRA by a private company headquartered in Luxembourg (described in Exhibit 14.2), Kopernikus by West Germany. Cable television accounts for most reception, but some direct-to-home reception also occurs.

Note: Data as of early 1989, listed by potential audience size.

Source: Data from "Quarterly Connections" and "Datafile Channel Guide," *Cable and Satellite Europe*, February 1990, pp. 81 ff.

electronic services such as transportation schedules, banking, and personal "chat lines."

Subscription TV STV (subscription television, an over-the-air pay service) failed in the United States but succeeded brilliantly in France. The French STV service, Canal Plus, features recent movies (many from the United States),

CBS news (dubbed in French), and major sports events. It has succeeded so well that it has been able to participate in launching clones in Belgium, West Germany, and Spain.

14.12 *Free Flow vs. Balanced Flow*

International Program Syndication   U.S. programs, always dominant in the world syndication market, came to new prominence in the age of satellite-distributed cable networks, direct-broadcast satellite channels, and VCRs. These services vacuum up programs from whatever sources they can find.

Enhanced demand for American feature films and television series intensified fears of American cultural domination. Most countries try to limit foreign imports, but they still use U.S. syndicated offerings. The low cost of American programs (because the original investments have already been recouped in the domestic U.S. market) and their almost sure-fire mass appeal keep them in demand. Exhibit 14.6 shows typical prices paid overseas for syndicated American programs.

EXHIBIT *14.6*   Program Bargains from U.S. Syndicators

| Purchasing Country | Cost per Program (U.S. Dollars) | |
	Half Hour	Theatrical Movie
Iceland	$250–300	$500–1,000
Israel	550–650	1,200–4,000
Yugoslavia	500–750	2,500
Argentina	750–850	3,000–6,000
Turkey	800–900	3,000
Brazil	2,000–3,000	15,000–30,000
Japan	4,000–6,000	60,000–200,000
Italy	4,500–10,000	20,000–750,000
Great Britain	8,000–16,000	50,000–500,000
France	10,000–20,000	30,000–150,000
Australia	12,000–18,000	75,000–500,000

Prices for U.S. syndicated material vary widely according to potential audience and ability to pay. As an extreme example, note that a British outlet can pay up to a thousand times as much for a feature film as an outlet in Iceland.

Source: Based on data in "Global Programming Prices," *Variety*, 19–25 April 1989, p. 79. Reprinted with permission from Variety, Inc. *Variety* is a registered trademark of Variety, Inc.

Cultural Imperialism
In the Third World, U.S. dominance in the international syndication market has led to charges of cultural imperialism. Critics assert that the images and values depicted in imported television undermine pre-industrial cultures. Such shows encourage excessive consumption, materialism, and disregard for indigenous traditions. Moreover, every program purchased from abroad denies indigenous artists and craftspersons opportunities to develop their own talents and skills. Thus imported programs perpetuate dependence on foreigners.

Nor do such complaints come only from the Third World. Even highly developed nations with their own flourishing production resources put ceilings on the amount of entertainment their national systems may import. Program-import restrictions proposed for the 12-nation European Community (representing a market larger than that of the United States, though less unified) were defeated by only a narrow margin.

ceilings on imported TV programs are universal

Free-Flow Doctrine
The United States resists any attempts by other countries to limit program imports. Long before the deregulation frenzy of the 1980s, the United States advocated a free-flow international communication policy. When the United Nations was established in 1945, its members accepted this policy without question as a corollary of the U.S. Constitution's guarantee of free speech and press.

However, both the world and its means of communication have changed drastically since the United Nations was founded. More than 70 new nations, most of them extremely conscious of their prior histories as colonial territories of the Western powers, have since joined the organization. These nations see neocolonialism as threatening to drag emergent countries back into dependent status. What value does free flow have for us, ask Third World leaders, when it runs almost entirely in one direction—*from* the United States and a few other industrialized countries *to* the Third World?

We need balanced flow, not free flow, they say. We need news reporting that treats us fairly and in proportion to our numerical significance. And we need our own access to the means of international communication. Third World leaders put forth these claims vigorously at meetings of international agencies such as the United Nations, the United Nations Educational, Scientific and Cultural Organization (UNESCO), and the International Telecommunication Union.

Third World argues for balanced flow rather than free flow

NWICO
Under the leadership of a wily Senegalese director general, UNESCO took the lead in demanding a new world information and communication order (NWICO). American media leaders and politicians saw the NWICO as an attack on journalistic independence and free-enterprise advertising. Claiming that UNESCO wasted its resources (a quarter of its budget came from the United States) and had become hopelessly politicized, the U.S. government took the drastic step of withdrawing from UNESCO in 1984.

Undoubtedly the Third World has legitimate grievances. As a result of NWICO claims, Western news agencies have become more sensitized to Third

World feelings, and Western governments have increased their aid to Third World communications. The ITU elevated its Third World aid program to a top-level department (over U.S. protests).

In the matter of program exports, however, a look at the experience of Europe's small but well-financed media systems suggests that it is not realistic to expect television program autonomy in countries of limited size. Those that lack both the infrastructure (production facilities, for example) and the cultural resources (trained talent and a theatrical tradition, for example) to support television production operate under a double disadvantage. If such countries want to have viable television services, they will always need to import a substantial amount of program material.

Conclusion Meanwhile, a different "new world information and communication order" began emerging from the global political changes that occurred during the 1980s and on into the 1990s—democratization of the media in former authoritarian and communist regimes and deregulation of the media in democratic countries.

The American electronic mass media played a role in these changes. Ironically, however, liberalization abroad has not cleared the way for unconstrained marketing of American media products and for the wholesale acceptance of American investments in overseas media. In the formerly communist countries, new-found freedoms have enhanced ethnic and regional awareness and stimulated indigenous productivity. These developments make the new regimes wary of cultural domination from the West, mirroring concerns expressed by the Third World in its NWICO campaign.

By the 1990s, American international syndication firms began experiencing a slowdown in the growth-rate of sales abroad. Numerous American firms negotiated overseas media investments, but these ventures encountered legal and cultural opposition to rapid adoption of American notions of cost-effective operating methods. Nor could investors count on easy profits from newly introduced, advertising-supported, privately owned media services. The rundown economies of the formerly communist dependencies needed cash for the most basic economic necessities, leaving the mass audience with little money for discretionary purchasing of media-advertised goods.

The democratic countries of western Europe have had second thoughts about continuing the wholesale privatization of facilities and the junking of traditional public-service broadcasting ideals. Even in the United States, re-regulation has begun to emerge as a corrective to some of the abuses and excesses permitted by overzealous deregulation.

A new world information and communication order is indeed taking shape. But it has taken on a life of its own, driven by forces larger and more inclusive than the concerns of any one particular group of nations.

favorable cultural and infrastructural climate needed for home-grown TV

Citations

References within the text alluding to court cases, FCC decisions, and certain other official documents use a format based on the standard legal bibliographic convention. Such citations consist of a number referring to the volume in the reporter series in which the item occurs, the title of the series, and the page number on which the item begins or a quoted passage occurs. For example, "464 US 417" refers to the 464th volume of *United States Reports* (the reporter series containing Supreme Court decisions), page 417. The list below discloses that this citation refers to *Universal Studios versus Sony* (a Supreme Court decision denying the claim that home tape recording violates copyright law).

The following describes the series most often cited:

- CFR *(Code of Federal Regulations)* is a compilation of all regulations issued by federal agencies such as the FCC and the FTC. FCC regulations fall under Chapter 47 of the code.
- FCC (Federal Communications Commission) refers to publications issued individually by the commission as distinguished from items collected in FCCR.
- FCCR refers to both *FCC Reports* and its successor series, *FCC Record,* in which are found most FCC decisions and orders.
- F *(Federal Reporter),* refers to the official record of all decisions of the federal Circuit Courts of Appeal, the courts in which most electronic mass media cases originate.

- US (*United States Reports*) is the official record of decisions and accompanying opinions of the Supreme Court of the United States.
- USC (*United States Code*) is the official compilation of all federal laws. Those pertaining to electronic mass media are found in Chapter 47.

All can be found in any law library and in most large public and university libraries. Page numbers given with citations in the text refer to the locations of specific topics or quotations; page numbers in the list of references below show the page on which topics or cases actually begin.

See also source citations for tables, diagrams, and the exhibit text (which are not separately listed here) throughout text.

List of References

Arlen, Michael J. 1969. *Living-Room War*. Viking, New York.

Baldwin, Thomas F., and Lewis, Colby. 1972. "Violence in Television: The Industry Looks at Itself." In *Television and Social Behavior: Media Content and Control,* vol. 1, edited by George Comstock and E. Rubinstein, 290–365. Government Printing Office, Washington, DC.

Banning, William P. 1946. *Commercial Broadcasting Pioneer: The WEAF Experiment. 1922–1926*. Harvard U. Press, Cambridge, MA.

Barnouw, Erik. 1978. *The Sponsor: Notes on a Modern Potentate*. Oxford U. Press, New York.

Baudino, Joseph E., and Kittross, John M. 1977. "Broadcasting's Oldest Station: An Examination of Four Claimants." *Journal of Broadcasting* 21 (Winter): 61–83.

Blanchard, Robert O. 1988. "Put the Roper Survey on the Shelf—We Have Our Own Agenda." *Feedback* (Summer).

Boorstin, Daniel J. 1964. *The Image: A Guide to Pseudo-Events in America*. Harper and Row, New York.

———— . 1978. "The Significance of Broadcasting in Human History." In Hoso-Bunka Foundation, *Symposium on the Cultural Role of Broadcasting, October 3-5. 1978* (Summary Report, 9–23). Hoso-Bunka Foundation, Tokyo.

Bower, Robert T. 1973. *Television and the Public*. Holt, Rinehart and Winston, New York. ———— . 1985. *The Changing Television Audience*. Columbia U. Press, New York.

Briggs, Asa. 1961. *The History of British Broadcasting*. Vol. 1, *The Birth of Broadcasting*. Oxford U. Press, London.

Broadcasting. 1987. "Hill Concerned over CBS News Cuts." (16 March): 39. ———— . 1988. " 'Raunch' on a Roll." (21 November): 27. ———— . 1990. "DOD Criticizes U.S. Handling of Panama Coverage." (26 March): 100.

———— . 1990. "Iger Chastises Sponsors for Leaping Before Looking." (30 July): 53.

———— . 1990. "Up, Up and Away" (editorial). (9 April): 98.

Brown, Les. 1971. *Televi$ion: The Business Behind the Box.* Harcourt Brace Jovanovich, New York.

Buckley, Tom. 1978. "Game Shows—TV's Glittering Gold." *New York Times Magazine* (18 November): 49.

C&SE *(Cable and Satellite Europe).* 1990. "Looking Like a Million." (February): 64.

Cal. *(California Reporter).* 1981. *Olivia N. v. National Broadcasting Co.* 178 Cal. Rptr. 888 (California Court of Appeal, First District).

CCET (Carnegie Commission on Educational Television). 1967. *Public Television: A Program for Action.* Harper and Row, New York.

CCFPB (Carnegie Commission on the Future of Public Broadcasting). 1979. *A Public Trust.* Bantam Books, New York.

CFR (Code of Federal Regulations). Annual. Government Printing Office. Washington, DC. Allotment Table. 47 CFR 73.606. Coverage Zones. 47 CFR 73.609–613.

Personal Attacks. 47 USC 73.1920

Power/Height Limitations. 47 CFR 73. 699. Diversification of Control. 47 CFR 76.5.

Comstock, George, et al. 1978. *Television and Human Behavior.* Columbia U. Press, New York.

Coolidge, Calvin. 1926. *Message to Congress, 68 Congressional Record* 32.

Couzens, Michael. 1989. "An Aging Watchdog." *Channels* (July–August): 12.

Drake–Chenault Enterprises, Inc. 1978. "History of Rock and Roll." Author, Canoga Park, CA.

EBUR *(European Broadcasting Union Review).* 1987. Special issue on breakfast TV. (September): 12–28.

EIA (Electronic Industries Association). Annual. *Consumer Electronics.* Author. Washington, DC.

F *(Federal Reporter,* 2d Series). Government Printing Office, Washington, DC.

1926. *U.S. v. Zenith Radio Corp.,* 12 F 2d 614.

1969. *Office of Communication* v. *FCC,* 425 F 2d 543.

1972. *Stone et al.* v. *FCC,* 478 F 2d 316.

1977. *Home Box Office* v. *FCC,* 567 F 2d 9.

1987. *Century Communications Corp.* v. *FCC,* 835 F 2d 292.

1988 *Action for Children's Television et al.* v. *FCC,* 852 F 2d 1332.

F Sup *(Federal Supplement).* Government Printing Office, Washington, DC.

1976. 1976 *Writers Guild et al.* v. *FCC,* 423, F Sup 1064.

FCC (Federal Communications Commission). Government Printing Office,

Washington, DC. 1980. (Network Inquiry Staff). *New Television Networks: Entry, Jurisdiction, Ownership and Regulations. Final Report,* vol. 1. *Background Reports,* vol. 2.

FCCR *(FCC Reports,* 1st & 2d Series, and *FCC Record).* Government Printing Office, Washington, DC.

> 1952. *Amendment of Sec. 3.606 [adopting new television rules] . . . Sixth Report and Order.* 41 FCC 148.
>
> 1965. *Comparative Broadcast Hearings.* Policy Statement. 1 FCC 2d 393.
>
> 1972a. *Establishment of Domestic Communication Satellite Facilities. . . .*Report and Order. 35 FCC 2d 844.
>
> 1972b. *Cable Television.* Report and Order. 36 FCC 2d 143.
>
> 1972c. *Complaint by Atlanta NAACP.* Letter. 36 FCC 2d 635.
>
> 1985. *Inquiry into. . . .the General Fairness Doctrine Obligations of Broadcast Licensees.* Report. 102 FCC 2d 143.
>
> 1987. *Complaint of Syracuse Peace Council Against Television Station WTVH.* Memorandum Opinion and Order. 2 FCC Rcd 5043.
>
> 1985. *Application of Simon Geller.* Memorandum Opinion and Order. 102 FCC 2d 1443.

Friendly, Fred. 1976. *The Good Guys, the Bad Guys, and the First Amendment: Free Speech vs. Fairness in Broadcasting.* Random House, New York.

Great Britain. Home Office. 1986. *Report of the Committee on Financing the BBC* [Peacock Report]. Cmnd. 9824. HMSO, London.

Halberstam, David. 1979. *The Powers That Be.* Knopf, New York.

Jowett, Garth. 1976. *Film: The Democratic Medium.* Little, Brown, Boston.

Kaltenborn, H.V. 1938. *I Broadcast the Crisis.* Random House, New York.

Kaplan, David A. 1988. "Is the Klan Entitled to Public Access?" *New York Times* (31 July), H26.

Kendrick, Alexander. 1969. *Prime Time: The Life of Edward R. Murrow.* Little, Brown, Boston.

Klapper, Joseph T. 1960. *The Effects of Mass Communication.* Free Press, New York.

Klein, Paul. 1971. "The Men Who Run TV Aren't That Stupid . . . They Know Us Better Than You Think." *New York* (5 January): 20.

Markey, Edward J. 1988. "Statement Accompanying Congressional Research Service Letter to House Subcommittee on Telecommunications and Finance. Cases Involving the Federal Communications Commission That Were Reversed. . . ." Library of Congress, Washington, DC.

Metz, Robert. 1975. *CBS: Reflections in a Bloodshot Eye.* Playboy Press, Chicago.

Meyersohn, Rolf B. 1957. "Social Research in Television." In *Mass Culture: The Popular Arts in America,* edited by Bernard Rosenberg and David Manning White, 345–357. Free Press, Glencoe, IL.

Minow, Newton N. 1964. *Equal Time: The Private Broadcaster and the Public Interest.* Athenaeum, New York.

Montgomery, Kathryn C. 1989. *Target: Prime Time—Advocacy Groups and the Struggle over Entertainment Television.* Oxford U. Press, New York.

NAB (National Association of Broadcasters). 1978. *The Television Code.* Author, Washington, DC.

————. 1988. "Political Broadcast Expenditures." Press Release. Author, Washington, DC.

Nielsen Company, A.C. 1989. *The Television Audience 1989.* Author, Northbrook, IL.

Paley, William S. 1979. *As It Happened: A Memoir.* Doubleday, New York.

Pareles, John. 1989. "After Music Videos, All the World Has Become a Screen," *New York Times* (10 December): E6.

Quinn, John. 1990. "'Klansas City' Bows in K. C. After Fracas Upsets Production." *Variety* (11 April): 46.

Rather, Dan. 1987. "From Murrow to Mediocrity?" *New York Times* (10 March): A27.

Robins, J. Max. 1990. "Ready-Made News." *Channels* (February): 26.

Robins, J. Max. 1990. "Slick Superblurbs Go Upmarket: Infomercials Spawn $500-Million Biz as Firms Battle Sleeze Factor." *Variety* (May 2): 1.

Roper Organization. 1984. *Public Attitudes Toward Television and Other Media in a time of Change.* Author, New York.

————. 1987a. *America's Watching: Public Attitudes Toward Television.* Author, New York.

————. 1987b. *Electronic Media Career Preparation Study: Executive Summary.* Author, New York.

————. 1989. *America's Watching: The 1989 TIO/Roper Report. 16th Report in a Series.* Television Information Office, New York. (Distributed by the National Association of Broadcasters, Washington, DC.)

RR (*Radio Regulation,* Pike & Fischer, Washington, DC). 1985. *Cattle Country Broadcasting [KTTL–FM].* (FCC) Hearing Designation Order and Notice of Apparent Liability. 58 RR 1109.

Rubin, Bernard. 1967. *Political Television.* Wadsworth, Belmont, CA.

Rubin, Ellis. 1989. *Get Me Ellis Rubin: The Life and Times of a Maverick Lawyer.* St. Martin's Press, New York.

Senate CC (U.S. Congress, Senate Committee on Commerce). 1972. *Surgeon General's Report by Scientific Advisory Committee on Television and Social Behavior.* Hearings. 92 Cong., 2d Sess. Government Printing Office, Washington, DC.

Sieber, Robert. 1988. "Industry Views on the People Meter: Cable Networks." *Gannet Center Journal* 2 (Summer): 70–74.

Smith, Bruce L., et al. 1946. *Propaganda, Communication, and Public Opinion.* Princeton U. Press, Princeton, NJ.

Steiner, Gary A. 1963. *The People Look at Television: A Study of Audience Attitudes.* Knopf, New York.

Sterling, Christopher H., and Kittross, John M. 1990. *Stay Tuned: A Concise History of American Broadcasting.* 2d ed. Wadsworth Publishing Co., Belmont, CA.

Sterling, Christopher H. 1984. *Electronic Media: A Guide to Trends in Broadcasting and Newer Technologies, 1920–1983.* Praeger Publishers, New York.

TCAF (Temporary Commission on Alternative Financing for Public Telecommunications). 1983. *Final Report.* Federal Communications Commission, Washington, DC.

TV/RAI *(Television/Radio Age International).* 1989. "Worldwide TV Set Count." (October): 181–183.

U.S. Department of Commerce. 1922. "Minutes of Open Meeting of Department of Commerce on Radio Telephony." Mimeograph.

US *(United States Reports).* Government Printing Office, Washington DC.
  1942. *Marconi Wireless Telegraph Company of America* v. *U.S.* 320 US 1.
  1943. *NBC* v. *U.S.* 319 US 190.
  1949. *Terminiello* v. *Chicago* 337 US 1.
  1968a. *U.S.* v. *Southwestern Cable.* 392 U.S. 157.
  1984. *Universal Studios* v. *Sony.* 464 US 417.

USC *(United States Code).* Government Printing Office, Washington, DC.
  Broadcast Lottery Information 18 USC 1304.
  Action Upon Applications 47 USC 309.

USCC (U.S. Commission on Civil Rights). 1977. *Window Dressing on the Set: Women and Minorities in Television.* 2 vols. Government Printing Office, Washington, DC.

USDOS (U.S. Department of State). Advisory Committee on International Communications and Information Policy. 1990. *Eastern Europe: Please Stand By.* Department of State Washington, DC.

Index

Association (RTNDA), job survey by, 184
Radio war, 44
RAI (Italy), 394
Random digit dialing (in research), 289
Random sampling, 288–289
Rate grid (sales tool), 175
Rather, Dan: on bottom line, 191; and Exxon VNR, 313; on *60 Minutes,* 258
Ratings, program: calculation of, 278–281, 292–298, 295 (graph); critique of, 301–303; local, 279; limitations of, 302–303; national, 279
RCA, Inc.: and cross-licensing, 31–32; origins, 29; as Radio Group member, 41; sale of, to GE, 86
Reagan, Pres. Ronald: and CPB funding, 198 (caption); and presidential TV, 315–316, 316 (chart); radio use by, 315–316; veto by, of bill to limit advertising on children's programs, 311, 359
Real-time factor, 14
Reasoner, Harry (CBS News), 258
Receiver(s): HDTV, 12; solid-state, 145. *See also* License fees, receiver; TVRO
Recording(s): digital, 146–147; radio network ban on, 43; technology of, 120–121. *See also* Videocassette; Videotape
Red Lion case (fairness), 376–377
Red Network (NBC), 35
Refraction, wave (propagation phenomenon), 101
Registration (film synchronization), 108
Regulation(s): behavioral vs. structural, 350; federal jurisdiction over, 328; informal, 333–334; international, 395–396. *See also* Cable Act; Communications Act of 1934; Deregulation; Federal Communications Commission; Federal Radio Commission; Radio Act of 1912; Radio Act of 1927; Re-regulation; Self-regulation
Relay(s): defined, 10; fiber-optic, 154; microwave, 63–64, 123 (diagram), 124; network, 35; satellite, 64, 65, 74, 201. *See also*
Cable, coaxial; Fiber optics; Satellites
Religious broadcasting: and fairness doctrine, 339–340; and First Amendment, 366; on radio, 269 (table), 270; and *Red Lion* case, 376–377; and syndicated TV programs, 263; transborder, 405
Renewal, license. *See* License(s), station, renewal of
Repeater transmitter. *See* Translator
Repetition (schedule strategy), 234
Reps (national sales representatives), 179
Request for proposals (RFP), cable TV, 348
Request Television (PPV), 167 (table)
Re-regulation (as reaction to deregulation), 16, 384–385
Reruns. *See* Off-network programs
Research, audience: and flow, 232–233; and sales, 179. *See also* Effect(s) of and on electronic media; Meters, audience measurement; Ratings, program
Reserved channels for public broadcasting, 194
Resolution, picture: of film, 108; of TV, 48, 49, 111, 114. *See also* High-definition TV
Response rate, sampling, 291–292
Retrace (in TV picture scanning), 111 (diagram), 112. *See also* Vertical blanking interval
Retransmission rights (copyright law), 356
Reuters (news agency), 22, 230
Revenue, of foreign systems, 399–400
"Reverse angle" shots, 312
Revocation, license, 345–346
Rigging. *See* News: staging of
Rights of reply, 378–379
RJR Nabisco, ad strategy of, 172 (table)
Rock music: as dominant radio format, 269–270; and radio revival, 57
Romania, broadcasting in, 395
Roosevelt, Pres. Franklin D., 39–40, 314
Roots (miniseries), 244
Roper Organization, public-opinion survey by, 308
Roseanne (sitcom), 242, 243
RTL (Radio-Télé Luxembourg), 407 (map)
RTL Plus (German network), 413 (table)
RTNDA. *See* Radio-Television News Directors Association
Run-of-schedule (ROS) spots, 175

Safer, Morley (CBS News), 258 (caption)
Sajak, Pat (MC), 247
Salaries in electronic media, 184, 185 (graph)
Sales: of broadcast and cable TV ads, 179–180; jobs in, 179
Sales representatives. *See* National sales representatives
Sampling: in audience research, 288–292; in digital signal processing, 141
Sanitization: of violence, 324; of war, 317
Sarnoff, David (RCA), 30 (photo), 31, 36, 48, 49
Satellite(s), space communication, 132–141, 408–411, 413 (table). *See also* INTELSAT; MATV; SMATV; TVRO
Satellite Music Network (radio), 260
Satellite Orbit (program guide), 239
Sat1 (German satellite network), 413 (table)
Saturation. *See* Penetration
Sawyer, Diane (*60 Minutes*), 258 (exhibit)
ScanAmerica (research service), 285
Scanning, TV: evolution of, 47–48; in pickup tube, 110 (diagram); standards for, 111–112. *See also* Interlace scanning
Scarcity, channel, as factor in regulation, 367
Scatter buying (of ads), 172
Scheduling strategies, 232–237. *See also* Stripping
Scrambling, signal, 9
Screen Actors Guild (SAG), 186
Screensport (UK satellite network), 413 (table)
Sears, Roebuck, ad strategy of, 172 (table)